REPORTING

REPORTING

Second Edition

Mitchell V. Charnley
UNIVERSITY OF MINNESOTA

HOLT, RINEHART AND WINSTON, INC.
New York   Chicago   San Francisco   Toronto   London

Cover: *Newsfoto by Dave McLane.*
City Room, The New York News.

November 1966
Copyright © 1959, 1966 by *Holt, Rinehart and Winston, Inc.*
All Rights Reserved
Library of Congress Catalog Card Number: 66–15556
21378–0216
Printed in the United States of America

About This Book

Reporting is art, and it is craft.

Reporting as a craft is a pragmatic complex of skills, techniques, and designs based on thought and experience; it can be described and it can be taught. The craftsmanship of reporting can be passed along by those who have practiced and studied it and who understand it to others who possess the capacity and the deep-rooted desire to develop it.

The *art* of reporting, though its practitioner may be stimulated or his skill enhanced, can neither be planted nor nurtured in sterile soil. Artistic expression in journalism, as in the communication of musical, plastic, or chromatic ideas, derives from the guidance of craft by native perception, by taste, by intuitive awareness, by an intensely personal impulse that cannot be fully described. A journalist who brings to his work the creative responsiveness that makes him sensitive to the inherent qualities of his materials as well as to their potential impact must support his art by the journalistic crafts; and the extent to which his artistry becomes effective is directly commensurate with his control of them. But he must himself provide the artistic impulse. It cannot be drawn from books, from a voice behind a lectern, or from drill.

A book like *Reporting* offers aid to those who are or hope to become news reporters—reporters for any medium; it is intended to help them understand and use their crafts and apply their artistic endowments in effective gathering and spreading of news materials. Though workmanlike and responsible news reporting may spring from intelligent, balanced use of the crafts with minimum support from artistic impulse, I believe that such impulse is never wholly absent from superior journalistic work. The more fully art and craft form partnership, the more noteworthy the results.

This book essays to describe the principal crafts of reporting so that their natures, uses, and potentialities become clear, and to offer precepts and examples in which their artful as well as their artistic effects are illustrated.

I have been guided both in preparing and in revising *Reporting* by a number of concepts whose statement here may help a user of the book. I claim no priority on them—most have appeared in other approaches to the problems of news communication. Some of the emphases here differ. Briefly, they are these:

News—of any kind—is news, and reporting—through any medium—is reporting. The differences between newspaper reporting, news broadcasts, and news magazines in their news offerings are differences of degree, not of kind. A man who develops competence as a newspaper reporter can move easily and successfully into other news-reporting fields.

Reporting is nothing if it is not self-respecting. The newsman who is prepared to meet his opportunities and responsibilities envisions himself as a great deal more than a news technician. He no longer needs to be told that broad knowledge and informed discrimination—the fruits of sound experience and sound education—are essential. But it is the goal of this book to provide him with some understanding of why news journalism today is what it is—what impulses have gone into establishing news gathering and dissemination as one of the dominant forces of the world, what the social implications and interactions of news practice are. Portions of the book therefore are devoted to historical definition of techniques and principles, others to examination of social as well as practical problems of modern journalism.

A "first" book about news communication should not attempt to be a last book; it should not seek to be all things to all students. It is deeply important that it consider the fundamentals, and just as important that it avoid smothering them in secondaries. The purpose of this book is to examine reportorial problems in their broad applications; this fact explains the absence of chapters on reporting individual kinds of subject matter, specifically, of separate sections on reporting crime, education, city hall, sports, and the like. (This by no means implies that such specifics should be banished from the classroom. But it does suggest my view that the particulars of reportorial work that a man can study, practice, and assimilate on the job should be left largely to the job.)

Nobody can be made a finished reporter in the classroom. He can be informed of and helped to understand the problems and responsibilities of the newsman; he can be introduced to critical examination of news discovery, preparation, and dissemination. He can be given knowledge and awareness that he is unlikely to gain on the job; his period of apprenticeship can be eased and shortened (partly by as much "practical experience" as academic circumstances permit). He can develop pride in news work, confidence in himself, and a view of his own shortcomings. But there's no classroom alchemy to make him a pro.

No textbook is stronger than the student or teacher who uses it. Moreover, no textbook will fully serve the demands of a particular teacher or answer all the needs of any student (rearrangement of the order of chapters in this edition is in part an attempt to meet suggestions of teacher-critics of the first edition. But no arrangement will satisfy everybody, including me.). My hope is that *Reporting* will suggest many questions and answer some of them, and that it will show the way to other answers. I believe it must be used imaginatively, critically, and skeptically, and above all as a springboard rather than a target.

Rearrangement of chapter order may be the most obvious difference between the second and first editions of *Reporting*. Of equal importance, however, are other changes. More than half the news-story examples are new; those retained from the first edition have been kept because of special pertinence as illustrations. The material on news gathering has been expanded; and considerably more attention goes to news writing for radio. Two chapters dealing with human interest and feature news have been combined in one, chapter 15, as have two chapters on social and ethical news problems in chapter 19. A new section draws attention to news dissemination by person-to-person communication. The appendix material on communication theory has been slightly extended.

More change will be noted in the second half of the book, where the news-story examples cluster, than in the first half.

Most of the "projects" or exercises are new or revised. And I believe that the editing that accompanies revision has tightened the prose; it certainly has led to some useful discards.

Reporting emphasizes newspaper practices because the newspaper system of gathering and disseminating news is dominant among all media systems with news outlets of diversified natures and a constantly expanding need for workers. Newspapers deal with more kinds of news, meet more kinds of news situations, and treat news in more detail than the other media do. Americans—beginning students of news included—know more about newspaper practices than about those of broadcasting, magazines, or movies. Because newspapers offer more opportunities of such wide variety, news workers more often begin their careers on newspaper staffs. Newsmen go more commonly from newspapers into other forms of journalism—broadcasting, advertising, public relations, magazines—than in the reverse direction.

The purpose of this book remains, however, to provide a broad background for news work so that, whatever news field its readers enter, their knowledge of general problems and philosophies as well as of common practices will enable them to adjust easily to the requirements of their assignments. There are challenging opportunities in the domains of news, especially for young men and women who have the high attributes of character and the congruent patterns of ability that qualify them for reporting, one of the most demanding of professional occupations. And the need for workers of competence, insight, and devotion will never end.

The writer who knows precisely where to pay his debts, and just how much they come to, is a man I have not yet met. The wellsprings of a book are like those of a northern Minnesota lake—deep and silent, unseen and subtle; they so quickly mingle that their uniqueness may be clouded or lost. A book grows from every experience its begetter has survived; it is the product of work, learning, and counsel, of triumph and blunder. Its germs are as often forgotten or unobserved as remembered.

Some debts are nevertheless keenly apparent and as keenly appreciated. To Ralph D. Casey, a critic both thorough and uncompromising, every page of this book owes a bow. He helped it get started, he went over its script with his inimitable editing stiletto, and he refused firmly to relax his critical standards. To the demanding and patient judgments of another colleague, George S. Hage, the book is similarly indebted.

The second edition demands some new acknowledgements: to instructors who, using it, have found it good or bad and said so, and to students whose sometimes astonishing candor is shockingly helpful. The students are far too many to name; but I would be ungrateful not to report my obligation to my fellow teacher Robert Lindsay, and to the perceptive suggestions of Harold L. Nelson of the University of Wisconsin, William L. Rivers of Stanford University, and John L. Hulteng of the University of Oregon.

But naming names tells only part of the story. *Reporting* could hardly have been brought together without its many exhibits; to the scores of "contributors" who wrote parts of the book merely by doing their jobs I am more grateful than they know. I am happy that so many of them—more than a score—are among my onetime reporting students; I hope they'll be aware, should they learn how I've cribbed from them, that teacher is beholden, and knows it.

I am indebted to authors and publishers whose permission to use copyrighted material has been freely (no loose usage) given. First should be named the Minneapolis Star and Tribune Company, from whose papers I have lifted lavishly —not alone because they are at hand, but because they show things that need to be shown. Permission for use of other materials has come from the St. Paul *Pioneer Press* and *Dispatch*, the New York *Times*, the Chicago *Tribune*, the Washington *Post*, and the Chicago *Daily News*; from the *National Observer*, *Editor & Publisher*, the *Atlantic*, *Time*, and the *Reporter*; from E. P. Dutton & Company. I owe special thanks for material in this edition to Gene Goltz of the Houston *Post*, Drew Middleton of the New York *Times*, and Clark Mollenhoff of the Cowles Publications. The diagrams and some of the concepts in appendix A derive, as anyone can see, from the work of Wilbur Schramm, Malcolm MacLean, and Bruce Westley.

All this can be said. But how can one name, or even know, all his creditors? What about Bill Moxley who, as editor of the Goshen *Daily News-Times* so many years ago, granted me my first 24-point head? What about the city editors in Honolulu and Detroit whose brains I picked—radio and TV news editors with whom I worked? How can I trace my debts to teachers, to colleagues, to friends who have challenged ideas and corrected thinking and often demanded the impossible? And how does one assess truly what his students have given him—students whose questions forced him to understand more of art and craft than mere practice ever demanded?

These questions I cannot answer.

But to all these co-authors I know my obligation, and to all I offer thanks.

Minneapolis, Minnesota   M.V.C.
January 1966

Contents

INTRODUCTION

The Meaning of News

News is tomorrow's history done up in today's neat package. News, said a noted New York *Herald Tribune* city editor, Stanley Walker, is the "inexact measure . . . of the ebb and flow of the tides of human aspiration, the ignominy of mankind, the glory of the human race. It is the best record we have of the incredible meanness and the magnificent courage of man." Without the knowledge of social and technological change that news has carried to the masses of the world, the headlong speed of the twentieth century would have been a crawl. News is the fuel that keeps the wheels of a civilization turning.

News, to define its meaning more precisely, is current information made available to the public about what is going on—information often of vital importance to men and women trying to make up their minds about what to think and how to act. News is the timely, concise, accurate report of an event; it is not the event itself. News isn't the death of a dictator, or the election of a president, or the postponement of a space shot; it's the newsman's record of the death, of the voting, or of the misfire that stopped a countdown at Cape Kennedy.

When the newsman defines news as "report" rather than "event," he is saying, in effect, that until the knowledge of an event is communicated, the event is not news. Let us suppose, for example, that a murder has been accomplished in secret. If no one has missed the victim or discovered the corpse, is the murder news? The question, which sometimes puzzles laymen and reporters alike, is akin to the familiar problem about the tree that falls in a forest out of earshot of any living creature: if no eardrum shivers, is there any sound? An answer to either question must make clear the distinction between the occurrence and the communicated knowledge of the occurrence, between the event and the news of the event. Until the knowledge of the murder is transmitted in one way or another to an audience, the murder is an unreported event, and, therefore, the undiscovered act of murder is not news but merely the stuff of which news might be made.

Extension of this definition reveals three components of news: the event, in which some kind of action occurs; a report, in which the action is described or recorded in comprehensible terms; and an audience to whom the description is presented—in print, on the air, on the television or movie screen, or by word of mouth. The report may provoke its recipients, or some of them, to thought or action, or it may not. Usually it does. Usually an event becomes news because a reporter has decided that a report of it will have kinetic meaning for at least a small group of readers or listeners or viewers—and, often, that the report will sell papers or build audiences. A report may be news, however, whether it succeeds in arousing response or not; to be news, a report need only make current information available to a potential audience.

The term "mass," today used widely (and loosely) in such phrases as "mass media" and "mass communication," deserves more careful treatment. It should not be applied casually to all news media, though it often is, with the implication that all news media seek the same "mass" audience. Quite the reverse is the case. In Boston, for example, the Globe selects for its readers material vastly different from that picked by another Boston newspaper, the Christian Science Monitor *(though both are called "mass media") because their "masses" are almost entirely different. And radio-TV station WBZ, also in Boston, makes still another selection. (Chapters 3 and 4 examine the problems of selecting news for different audiences, and appendix A offers a theoretical approach to mass communication.) Thousands of publications do not seek "mass" audiences. Trade and technical journals, house organs, fraternal magazines, and scores of other specialized periodicals publish important information, news for their own readers, but they rarely provide news that is both timely and of general interest, the type of*

In today's world there are many channels by which news reaches its publics. The growth in the variety of news media is a twentieth-century phenomenon; until the end of World War I there was no serious threat to the newspapers' monopoly of the mass dissemination of news. The year 1920 saw the birth of American broadcasting, and 1923 the first of the modern weekly news magazines. Between the wars motion pictures began superficial reporting of certain kinds of news. At the end of World War II came television. Though news media in other parts of the world did not develop on precisely the same time table, their proliferation in other countries followed a similar pattern.

The new media have had important effects on the life of America and of the world. More people know more about the world they live in, both near home and across seas, than ever before. If the responsibility of the newsman is measured in terms of the number of lives his work affects, he has never before been so heavily burdened.

The responsibilities and the effects of the reporter's work may have been extended by the advent of the new media, but the fundamental concepts of news and the techniques of reporting are less mutable. Reporting, the process of gathering information about events and packaging reports for audiences, is a formalized process, no matter what medium is used. Especially in the news-gathering phases of the process, the techniques for getting the facts with speed, accuracy, and perspective are relatively uniform (ex-

news considered here. Are they truly "mass media"?

• •

Though reportorial methods are the same for all media at any given time in history, they are by no means static. Reporting and news presentation in newspapers, on the air, in the news magazines all differ vastly from their ancestors in the World War II period, and these in turn from those of a generation earlier. As the world grows more involved, as it moves faster, and as it creates new needs and demands for its peoples, news processes have had to change. Discussion of some of the changes and their causes appears in the early chapters of this book.

cept that tools differ), whether the facts are to appear eventually in the black and white of a printed page or emerge from a radio, TV, or movie speaker. The presentation, the shape and size of the news package, differs from one to another, but the reporting task is a constant. Professional performance in all news fields is based on the same ethical and social principles, as well as on the same techniques and skills. The conviction that the basic concepts, purposes, and responsibilities of news reporting are alike in all media, despite different methods of communication or styles of presentation, is a keystone of *Reporting*.

Reporting emphasizes newspaper practices and examples of newspaper usages in its approach to news because the newspaper system of gathering and disseminating news is dominant among media systems. Newspapers deal with more kinds of news, meet more kinds of news situations, and usually treat news with more detail and at greater length than do the other media. Americans know more about newspaper practice than about the operative aspects of broadcasting, magazines, or movies. Because newspapers offer more opportunities of all sorts, news workers more often begin their careers on newspapers. More newsmen go from newspapers into other forms of journalism—broadcasting, advertising, public relations, magazines—than from the other forms of journalism into newspaper work.

The purpose of this book, however, is to provide a broad backdrop for news work, so that, whatever news field its readers eventually enter, their knowledge of the general problems and philosophies as well as the common practices and methods of reporting will enable them to adjust easily to the particular requirements of their assignments. There are challenging opportunities in the field of news, especially for young men and women who have the high attributes of character and the special patterns of ability that will qualify them for reporting, one of the most demanding of professional occupations. And the need for workers of competence, insight, and devotion will never end.

CHAPTER 1

The News Concept and
the Right to Know

In a complex world no man can learn for himself everything he would like to know about his society and his contemporaries' lives. No man can be in a thousand places at once. No man can take the time to gather all the information he would like to have; no man has the breadth of knowledge and background to understand everything that takes place every day.

Let us say that there is a proposal on the ballot to raise the local tax rate. The increased tax income will enable the city to increase teachers' salaries and construct new facilities for the exploding school population. Vigorous forces in the community favor the tax rise; others, equally vigorous, oppose it. The teachers' union says one thing, the taxpayers' group another.

How does the average citizen get the information he wants and needs to help him decide whether to vote yes or no?

There are many sources of information. Word of mouth is one: The men at the office, the girls at the bridge club, friends and acquaintances and neighbors. A civic association issues a nonpartisan analysis; teachers and taxpayers provide frankly biased views. The average citizen is swamped by the flow of material. How is he to know how to evaluate it, to tell the good from the bad?

For the most part, he tends to rely on the news media: the newspaper, radio, television. He finds in these resources and in news magazines a large part of the knowledge he needs in order to come to conclusions about matters he considers important, whether they are taxes, treaties, or tennis titles. These sources of information help him decide whether he wants the Republicans or the Democrats to win the next election. And from them he learns about tonight's movie, the shift of his bowling night from Tuesdays to Thursdays, and the selection of the pretty girl from down the block as Miss Something-or-Other. He finds information on the big and the little, the important and the trifling—information on which he can plan both the routine details of his daily life and its major decisions. In the United States every man has the right to know about matters that concern or interest him.

It would be naïve not to recognize that legally-protected freedom from government restriction or interference by no means protects the press against other kinds of attempted or actual restrictions, political, economic, social, religious. This book will consider restrictions of this kind when it talks about problems of news gathering.

The American news system has come to put its informative function foremost, as through the years it has developed an understanding of the constitutional freedom it enjoys. "Freedom of the press" in the constitutional sense does not mean simply "Government, keep your hands off!" It means "Keep your hands off so that the press and the other news media may serve the people as the democratic system demands." The right of the people to information is the end; freedom of the press is the means. Because the people have the right to full and accurate information, the news media must be free to gather and report the facts. This "right to know" is the principle on which the American news concept is based.

It has not always been this way.

The Growth of the Concept

News grows out of its era and its milieu. There has been some sort of news as long as there has been articulate, purposeful communication among men— what we call "civilization." Before there were newspapers in English, there were newsletters, reports of financial, social, and political currents provided by professional letter writers for friends or subscriber-clients. Newsletters existed in Europe for many years, along with occasional pamphlets and news broadsides. News, to these publications, consisted of reports of public affairs, the activities of government, war, law enforcement, and accounts of common enemies of man such as pestilence and violence. The activities of individuals were not often reported unless crime or accident (or perhaps the accident of royal birth) were involved. Although current information was eagerly sought by some infant American newspapers ("current" meaning the most recent you could get, even if it came to you two months late by sailing ship from England), the news reported by the first professional newsmen was limited in quantity and concept.

Colonial publications, under the English system of government control of printing, were threatened with suppression when they offered fact or comment that displeased authority. In 1671 the British governor of Virginia declared that "learning has brought disobedience and heresy and sects into the world; and printing has divulged them and libels against the government." In a world ruled by personal authority, dissemination of knowledge was a peril to power—a peril the powerful did not intend to face if they could avoid it. One of the early victims of the government's preference for concealing most of its activities from the public was Benjamin Harris, a Boston bookseller who made the first colonial attempt at publication of a newspaper. *Publick Occurrences,* a three-page leaflet published by Harris in 1690 (its fourth page blank), was suppressed before a second issue could appear because, in the governor's opinion, it contained "reflections of a very high nature." The second colonial newspaper, John Campbell's Boston *News-Letter* of 1704, displayed prominently the legend "Published by Authority."

A pioneer newspaper published in New York gave rise, in 1734, to the famous John Peter Zenger trial, in which it was determined that a jury rather than a governor had the right to decide whether or not a publication was libelous. The trial also introduced the then-novel principle that printing the truth was not criminally libelous and that, therefore, truth from any source could be published. These historic decisions helped establish the legal rights of a free press.

Political difficulties were not colonial newspapers' only concern. There were what would seem today appalling technical problems. The lack of swift transportation and communication hampered the news-gathering process. Inadequate mechanical facilities—presses were slow, paper was scarce, and type was set letter by laborious letter—made for snail-paced production, high costs, and limited distribution. The small-paged weeklies and semiweeklies went mostly to subscribers, the few readers who had the money to buy and the education to read, and it was to this elite that the newspapers directed their news.

News in the colonial period was not what we take it to be today. We presume that news has certain innate qualities: that it is fair, current, accurate, concise, balanced, objective. All these attributes are implied when we define news briefly as "full and current information made available to an audience" or as "the accurate report of a recent event." (Chapter 2 discusses these essential qualities.) The news that the early newspapers printed had few of the qualities that characterize twentieth-century news reporting and distinguish it from other forms of prose communication. (A news report from *Publick Occurrences* appears at the beginning of chapter 11.) Although the colonial press strove to win the right to print the news as the editors saw it, it was often less than fair about sharing information with the public. News could be (and was) colored to suit the reporter's bias, and it was easy to omit entirely news unfavorable to the newspaper proprietor's views or wishes. The news that was printed was incomplete, not necessarily accurate or current, and certainly not objective.

Although Benjamin Harris, John Campbell, and many of their successors believed that their papers' principal function was to inform readers about current affairs, news was often selected and written so as to lead its readers to see events as the editors saw them. Especially as the spirit of revolution took root in the colonies, it became common for news presentation to seek not so much to inform as to direct thinking. Many newspapers were "dedicated," party organs or vehicles for the promotion of special interests, and the publisher whose prime concern was the establishment of a political program on the abolition of a tax policy felt slight compulsion to broaden his news coverage beyond the confines of his own purposes.

During the time when the turbulence of a freedom-seeking people was increasing to the point of rebellion, the press, despite its propagandistic tendencies, was an important and stimulating informant. Tories and revolutionaries presented their viewpoints. Both sides had their weekly news organs and their publicists, their James Rivingtons on the Loyalist side and their Sam Adamses demanding independence. Although the newspapers were by no means devoted to ideals of objectivity or factual presentation, and departure from honest news practice was common, their vitality and passion strengthened the development of a free press. Thomas Jefferson and other leaders gave stirring expression to the principlethat a government of the people must allow free expression and that such a government must exercise no suppression or censorship.

More than 150 years after Jefferson, two other American presidents repeated the principle Jefferson expressed. Herbert Hoover and Harry Truman, in a joint statement to support National Library Week in 1958, said: "We Americans know that if freedom means anything, it means the right to think. And the right to think means the right to read—anything, written anywhere, by any man, at any time."

When the nation took form in 1789 there was insistent demand for government guarantee of a free press. Jefferson enthusiastically declared that he would prefer newspapers without government to government without newspapers. This statement, too often quoted without Jefferson's vital qualification: "Every man should receive those papers, and be capable of reading them," may have been an oversimplification, but it gave expression to the views of some of America's most respected thinkers. Jefferson's principle, that a people's government must have a full flow of public information, led to inclusion of a specific provision (italicized in the following excerpt) in the First Amendment to the Constitution:

Congress shall make no law respecting an establishment of religion, or prohibiting the free exercise thereof; *or abridging the freedom of speech, or of the press;* or the right of the people peaceably to assemble, and to petition the Government for a redress of grievances.

Every one of the fifty states includes in its constitution a provision to this effect.

In the early days of the new nation freedom from government control resulted in as much license as liberty. Even Jefferson had to qualify and define his earlier statements because of the scandal-mongering, the scurrilous libel, and the outright falsehood that were used in the name of political liberty during the Washington, Adams, and Jefferson administrations. The obscenities and excesses of this period disappeared; but for many years the press continued primarily as a political instrument or as a special pleader rather than as a medium of general news.

By 1830 the environment was changing. More Americans were becoming readers—the advance of free education was making itself felt. As newspaper advertising revenue began to increase, publishers could envision less dependence on political subsidies and even on sale of papers to readers. Faster presses and general improvement in printing processes meant that in an hour thousands of papers, instead of hundreds, could be produced.

In 1833 a young printer in New York, Benjamin H. Day, took advantage of all these changes and improvements to produce America's first successful penny paper, the New York *Sun.* Ben Day not only published a low-cost daily in quantity, but also developed a new conception of news. He did not ignore entirely the solid news, the news of public affairs, of politics and government; but he cut down the share of space it got. By using unimportant "soft" news, he found a new way of appealing to a new and wider audience. He sent a reporter to New York's police court every day, and the *Sun* regularly gave its readers vignettes of the drunks, the petty thieves, the brawlers who came before the magistrate each morning. The new public to whom Day appealed, a public able to buy the paper because it cost only a penny, quickly became greedy for this new kind of news fare.

Though Ben Day introduced the change, James Gordon Bennett, one of the most talented of American journalists, gets major credit for developing it. Bennett, a Scottish immigrant with a sardonic face and a sharp wit, brought out the New York *Herald* in 1835 to compete with the *Sun*. Within a short time the *Sun* was outstripped in its own field, in circulation and inventiveness, in life, in color, in verve. Bennett had a rich combination of shrewd business sense and high journalistic skill. He saw the "new" public's interest in the news that Day was offering, and he set out full tilt to please it. Indeed, he went beyond Day. When a sensational murder came along in 1836, Bennett himself covered the story, giving it columns of space day after day; to get material, he invented the news technique now known as the interview. Bennett succeeded not only in making all of New York talk about the murder—and the *Herald*—but also in proving that the young blade accused of the crime, who apparently was about to be found guilty, had not committed it.

Bennett had started with Day's idea that the activities of everyday citizens provided acceptable material for news reports. But to this idea he added his own passion as a crusader and his virtuosity as a newsman. For 30 years he balanced his shrewd perception of what the growing public wanted to read against his personal view of what it ought to read, and he stoutly proclaimed his belief that the public must be fully informed. During the Civil War he made the *Herald* a thorn and a goad to President Lincoln and his aides; he also made the *Herald* the most informative paper of its time as well as the most aggressive and the most widely read. The *Herald* was one of the first papers to hold that the causes it disapproved and views it abhorred were nevertheless legitimate basis for news. Bennett thought that news should be offered for its own sake, with the object of giving information rather than of supporting a cause or making converts, and he helped develop the rule of factual reporting required by this new concept of news.

The Development of "Modern" News

The penny-press revolution of the nineteenth century broadened the range of news sources and redirected the American press to some of the ideals of Campbell and other early editors. News came to include not only government, politics, and such subjects as literature and "the science of agriculture," but also the goings-on in the police courts and, increasingly, the progress of business and industry. At first Bennett and Day were considered vulgar and disgusting, panders to decadent taste; they were called everything from heretics to pimps. But gradually their approach to news established a pattern that others found they must follow. They were not long alone, therefore, in their allegiance to the belief in news for its own sake. When the New York *Times* was founded in 1851, one of Henry J. Raymond's aims was to build a newspaper that would avoid the partisan miscoloration of most of the papers of his time. In the 30 years after the Civil War the American press began to change from a political press to a press of information; more and more the purpose of the strong newspapers was to print the facts and let the reader think for himself. Samuel Bowles the younger, for many years the editor of the respected Springfield, Massachusetts, *Republican,* said in 1885 that the prime purpose of the *Republican* was to furnish "the raw material" so that the reader might "compare and weigh and strike a balance for himself." As the nineteenth century waned, the typical newspaper came to be the one whose major efforts went to informing the reader rather than to shaping his opinions.

Fifty years after the *Sun* was founded, a quarter of the daily newspapers in the United States had come to label themselves politically independent, and by the end of the century the political newspaper, with the once-universal habit of printing only the news that would support its own views, had virtually disappeared from American journalism. Today a majority of American daily newspapers call themselves politically "independent," "independent Republican," or "independent Democratic"; but even when they profess clear political affiliation or preference, or strong social or economic views, they seek to report news on all sides of issues (some, it is true, with more success or devotion than others).

This development of the news function seems exactly what Thomas Jefferson would have hoped for. Although Jefferson did not decry the press of opinion, he believed that democracy's success depended on the existence of a responsible press that would inform the people properly, especially of the acts—good and bad— of their government. A press of opinion, even if sincere and competent, might not inform the puzzled reader or give a clear view of the events of the day. A press of information, if sincere and competent, provides at least a minimum number of facts on which the reader can base judgments and decisions. (Later chapters will show, however, that the task of presenting the complexities of modern life in proper context and perspective requires more than the report of facts alone.)

The story of the development of the modern news concept has been told in detail by a number of journalism's historians and critics. Two of the most revealing are in chapter 18 of Herbert Brucker's Freedom of Information *and chapter 11 of Edwin Emery's* The Press and America. The News in America *by Frank Luther Mott also throws light on the topic. (Further readings are suggested at the end of this chapter.)*

As the press developed a sense of obligation toward its readers, it also developed understanding of its constitutional freedom from government control. This freedom, which the American people grant to no industries except those dealing with communications, is necessary because a democratic society cannot function in the dark, but only in the light of full information and knowledge. In other words, the American press is protected from interference in order that it may serve the people.

The intelligence, integrity, and devotion of the news media themselves are the chief guarantees that the freedom of the press will be responsibly used to

What is "license" in news treatment? Usually it means news practices that, though legal and protected by the First Amendment, are not consistent with the responsibility of the press in a free society to keep the people informed of matters of concern to them. License means indulging in news practices that are offensive to public mores, good taste, and good judgment. If its report is accurate and in balance, a news story involving fraud, or prostitution, or use of marijuana, or a sensational homicide is not "yellow journalism." It is license, however, to write or display such a report in a way that overemphasizes sensational aspects or distorts an event by giving it undue significance. It is license to give readers faulty notions of relative values in current events. It is license to sensationalize the news for the purpose of permitting readers to lick their lips over indecency, cruelty, human suffering, or human frailty.

maintain the democratic right to full information. Constant vigilance is necessary not only to detect governmental failures to observe the meaning and purpose of the First Amendment, but also to protect against encroachment by the manifold pressures of a thriving, vigorous, and intensely varied and complex society. A thousand forces, some of which will be referred to later in this book, move in on the press; most of them are innocent of intent to subvert, but nevertheless capable of doing so if they are not recognized and diverted.

The change from service of a goal, political or other, to the ideal of objective news presentation did not occur overnight. Horace Greeley's New York *Tribune* of midcentury was the prototype of the "personal journal" that primarily espoused its proprietor's or editor's personal views, and this kind of journalism has never disappeared completely. Just as there were abuses of the press's freedom during the nation's early history, there were later abuses and excesses in which license replaced liberty. The "yellow journalism" so sharply stimulated in the 1890s by the news war of William Randolph Hearst and Joseph Pulitzer in New York threatened to bury the news responsibility of the press under an avalanche of sensationalism. In their slam-bang fight for circulation leadership, Hearst's *Journal* and Pulitzer's usually careful and humane *World* reached unheard-of circulation figures by resorting to feats of sensationalism that Bennett and his followers had not dreamed of. The two papers made crime, conflict, and outrage their staples; their insistence on war with Spain, though it did not have as much to do with starting the shooting as has sometimes been asserted, yielded new circulation peaks.

The yellow journalism of this period unquestionably influenced American news judgment for the next fifty years. For more than a quarter of a century after the climax of clamor and irresponsibility of the 1890s, the Hearst newspapers were generally characterized by overemphasis on news of crime, lust, and disaster. The circulation fight between New York's sensational "picture papers" in the 1920s, glorifying the same brand of news judgment, lured other papers in other parts of the country into like intemperance.

Few American "scandal sheets" exist today, although most big cities had them in the first third of the century. These cynical newspapers pretended to be interested in cleaning up vice or corruption in their locales, but their real purpose was to build circulation or, in a few cases, to use their disclosures for extortion and blackmail. It is significant, however, that in 1931 the Supreme Court, although recognizing the vicious character of one such publication, nevertheless held that the First Amendment legally forbade its suppression. It is also significant that few such scandal sheets have prospered in recent years; they hold small appeal, it seems, for a sophisticated public able to see their journalistic faults as well as their vicious intent.

The newsmen who relied on yellow journalism were always in a minority, even at the peak of the sensational-news period. Adolph Ochs, in fact, entered the New York City newspaper scene at the time when the Hearst-Pulitzer combat was at its bitterest. Ochs, accepting Henry J. Raymond's platform, took over the New York *Times* with a sober promise to present news impartially and completely, "regardless of party, sect, or interest." the *Times* not only gained circulation quickly and steadily but was described again and again as "the world's greatest newspaper" because of its complete and usually impartial news coverage. In America and other parts of the world the newspapers that are respected and revered—Washington *Post*, Milwaukee *Journal*, New York *Times*, Minneapolis *Tribune*, Manchester *Guardian, Corriere della Sera* of Milan, *Le Monde* of Paris, *Frankfurter Zeitung, Journal de Geneve*—are those that live up to high levels of public service and responsibility. The distortions and cynicisms of yellow journalism, in America, continue to decline. Furthermore, sensational news treatment is much more likely to be an attempt to entertain than an attempt to influence opinion or attitude. Most newspapers today regard furnishing information to the public as their basic function.

The Meaning of News Responsibility

By the middle of the 20th century the American press as a whole had established a practical code of news responsibilities based on the principles of freedom and the right of the public to information. Though such a code can never be fully spelled out, its major tenets are not difficult to suggest:

1) The press recognizes a positive obligation to give its readers the news of genuine significance to their lives as fairly and completely as competent professional practice and judgment permit.

2) The press holds (though it does not always transmute belief into deed) that it must give readers an opportunity to know, understand, and evaluate all facets of important news situations, especially those involving social controversy such as appears in partisan politics. This responsibility has been sharply underlined in a day when more than 90 percent of American dailies have no local newspaper competition. Some publishers of "monopoly" papers say that the very lack of competition obliges such papers to present *all* news and views, including those that might otherwise have been presented by "the opposition."

3) The press must seek to become strong financially, so that it can always maintain position to resist pressures. A strong paper can use its strength to support whatever views and attitudes and groups and parties it believes deserve sup-

port, and it can reject attempts at pressure that it believes arise from selfish or unwise impulses.

4) The press recognizes as valid the principles underlying the restrictive laws that make false or malicious defamation punishable and that forbid offensive and obscene publications.

That the label "independent" as regards partisan politics—a label self-applied in 1964 by hundreds of American daily newspapers—is not entirely an idle boast was demonstrated by the movement of dailies from Republican to Democratic support in the Presidential election. For more than a generation the country's dailies had generally favored Republican candidates (by a high of 67 percent in 1952, a low of 52 percent in 1932). In 1964, however, only 35 percent of dailies made Barry Goldwater their choice.

The fact that these principles are generally accepted does not mean that they are universally observed. It would be unperceptive and unrealistic not to recognize that some news that ought to be published is suppressed; that treatment of political news does not always meet these ideals of fairness; that financial strength can be used against the public interest as well as for it; and that standards of decency and privacy are sometimes violated. Selflessness and high wisdom are possessed by few men. But newspapers performance as well as editorial protestations show that these principles are the guides most responsible journalists seek to follow, whether or not they always succeed.

Although this chapter has referred largely to the newspaper press, the principles of freedom from governmental restraint and of responsibility toward news consumers are the same in other forms of printed journalism and almost the same in news broadcasting. The news purpose of the weekly news magazine is different from that of the daily or weekly newspaper; the news magazines summarize the news, giving the reader general knowledge of current affairs, often with illuminating background, rather than detailed "spot news." But this difference is one of degree and technique, not of fundamental purpose. The basic freedom from governmental interference prior to publication and the basic responsibility to give the reader a full and fair picture of the contemporary scene are present. The news magazines have not gone uncriticized. At times they have emphasized one aspect of a news event at the expense of other aspects; they have played up the trivial; they have expressed editorial points of view in the guise of news or analysis (*Time's* editors, who have been especially criticized, have been quoted as saying that *Time* does not attempt to be objective in all its reporting). But in many areas the news magazines have met their obligations with credit.

The problems of broadcasters are somewhat different from those of workers in other media. In one sense, the radio and television broadcasters are clearly under government control: the Federal Communications Commission is directed under the Federal Communications Act to regulate broadcasting "in the public interest, convenience, or necessity." Broadcasters often complain that the FCC exceeds the intent of Congress in its attempts to secure satisfactory radio and TV programming for the public—by expressing approval of one kind of program and disapproval of another, for instance; but in broad terms the broadcasters have been about as free of governmental tampering as has the press. Although broadcasting quite properly insists on its own right to protection under the First Amendment, it has not always recognized or accepted as thoroughly as it could the obligation to provide the full information to which the public has a right. In fact, since World War II the FCC has urged broadcasters to increase their interest in news broadcasts and in news commentary and interpretation. Radio and TV are not primarily news media, however, and the owners and managers are rarely newsmen.

The advent of new media—news broadcasting, news magazines, news films— has not altered the basic concept of news; but each medium has its own news requirements. Each reports events in a manner appropriate to its peculiar facilities and the special nature of its audiences. What radio selects to report is different in important respects from what the press reports, and both differ in emphasis, style, form, and approach from the news offerings of television and the magazines. Within each medium, moreover, the individual outlets vary widely; *Time* magazine could hardly be confused with the more sober and conservative *U.S. News and World Report,* and the New York *Post* and the New York *Times* are about as dissimilar as two newspapers can be.

The impact of new or improved communication processes in the middle third of the twentieth century has extended the basis of news interest. The new processes have made communications far more rapid both in words and in pictures; they have shrunk the world and made its peoples more sophisticated, more interdependent, and more in need of information about each other. In an age when two world wars and a world depression are crowded into 30 years, when planes cross the Atlantic between breakfast and lunch, when struggles for power are not continental but global and, indeed, universal, when space satellite television lets America see the burial of a great Englishman as it is occurring—in such an age the interests and concerns of men everywhere, in Puyallup, Washington, or Andermatt, Switzerland, or Bangkok, Thailand, are necessarily broader than they were in a simpler era. The character of news audiences and their interests have changed, but the obligation of the newsman is the same: to provide information.

Although the basic concept of news remains unaltered, the middle of the twentieth century has enriched it by bringing new awareness of news responsibility. One new characteristic of news is the stronger emphasis on explanation, as a kind of fourth dimension of news. Today a major news story that stands by itself, without relation to its environment or its genesis, without signposts to help the reader recognize its relevance to other news, is considered only half a story. In this complex era virtually no event is totally isolated; as thoughtful newsmen now fully perceive, reporting that does not show an event's context is unfinished reporting. News must have not only length, breadth, and height, but also depth or orientation. This is not the political or ideological orientation of the nineteenth century; it is "cause-and-effect orientation" rooted in objectivity.

The purpose of such orientation in news reporting is to show relationships that might not otherwise be apparent to many news consumers. It is this kind of orientation, for example, to report an American disarmament proposal in the light of Russian attitudes, past and present; or to show reportorially how the political complexion of the new city council is likely to affect local tax rates. Newsmen usually refer to the fourth dimension of news, orientation, as "interpretation" or "background." They devote many thoughtful hours to discussion of the vital need for interpretation in today's journalism. Almost the entire program of a three-day session of the International Press Institute in London was given to discussion of the subject; few meetings of radio or newspaper newsmen pass without general consideration of it.

Another characteristic of news today is the increased American awareness of the principle of freedom and the right to information. This awareness has been sharpened, at least among newsmen, by efforts that occur in many quarters to conceal information from reporters. The Constitution protects the news media against governmental interference not for the good of the publishers or broadcasters but for the good of the public; the press and the broadcaster are "free" because the public, in the American form of society, has the right and the need to know the truth about current life. The responsible newsman designs his news so that his audience is provided a full and fair presentation of significant facts, insofar as he is able to procure them.

Both the trend to interpretation and the insistence on the right of access to information throw a twentieth-century spotlight on the prime purpose of the news presentation process, which is to make full and accurate information both available and understandable.

Secondary Purposes of News

But the newsman, as he fingers through the day's supply of news copy, deciding what he *might* publish and what he *will* publish, has additional purposes in mind. He would like to entertain his audience. He would also like to attract customers: to sell papers or magazines, or draw listeners to radio sets or viewers to television screens. These purposes are often closely related; for to entertain the consumer as he reads or listens or watches is to attract him to the medium; and to gain his regular attention is to increase the medium's audience and therefore its financial strength. These secondary purposes are easily abused, and their abuse by some media has led to some bitter criticism of American press and broadcasting. But both purposes are deeply imbedded in the pattern of modern news presentation, and both are not only defensible but important to the strength of modern journalism.

Ben Day's "light touch" was not always gentle, as may be seen in this example from the Sun's police court news: "Catharine McBride was brought in for stealing a frock. Catharine said she had just served out six months on Blackwell's Island, and she wouldn't be

Entertaining news was one of Ben Day's goals when he sought new audiences for his *Sun.* He attained his aim by cutting down the customary fare and adding news of "human interest"—news of the petty pains and pleasures of the plain people of New York—and by injecting a light touch into reporting. Today entertainment is added to the news by selecting events that are amusing or exciting or burdened with pathos and by

sent back again for the best glass of punch that ever was made. Her husband, when she last left the penitentiary, took her to a boarding house in Essex Street, but the rascal got mad at her, pulled her hair, pinched her arm, and kicked her out of bed. She was determined not to bear such treatment as this, and so got drunk and stole the frock out of pure spite. Committed."

This kind of "entertainment" is decried by careful newsmen today. The event might well be reported either in print or on the air; but the difference between Ben Day's manners and today's would, it is hoped, change its form.

reporting the events, often of little importance in themselves, so as to emphasize their emotive nature. Much of the most admired journalistic writing grows out of reporting of this type. The sketches Ben Hecht wrote for the Chicago *Daily News,* later collected in *One Thousand and One Afternoons in Chicago,* are classics of news entertainment. So are those in Meyer Berger's *The Eight Million,* written for the New York *Times,* and in Morris Markey's *Manhattan Reporter,* written mostly for the *New Yorker.*

That news can be selected and treated to attract customers needs no proving. Ben Day and Bennett did it, and Hearst and Pulitzer; the gossip, opinion, and speculation offered by Walter Winchell brought to his newspaper column some 25 million readers and to his radio broadcast an audience rating that competed successfully with the leading dramatic and quiz shows. The newspapers of largest circulation in the United States, England, and France are for the most part those that glorify human-interest news. Some of these papers add sensationalized treatment: emphasis on news of crime or sex, details of what happened in the bedroom, merciless dissection of the lives and acts of men and women involved in the news. This kind of reporting often goes beyond the bounds of human sympathy and of good taste.

There are many responsible and dignified methods of selecting news to attract audiences, and these methods are used by most papers in America, and many broadcasters, to gain and hold news consumers. Most media select news because of its importance and relevance for their particular audiences, and most try to present news responsibly. Although separately these media may not be as spectacularly successful in audience attraction as the few representatives of the sensational press, they as a whole reach, and influence, more people.

Some critics of modern journalism, the critics whose zeal exceeds their information or their logic, make the mistake of thinking that it is degrading to seek a large audience. A more supportable view is that it is not only quite proper for a newsman to do so, but that it is also good sense. To fulfill this aim gives him strength because, as has already been suggested, the news medium with broad popular support, the newspaper with a big and assured circulation or the broadcaster with a wide, dependable audience, has financial security. Advertisers, who contribute most of the financial support of the American news media, support most heavily the media with the most "profitable" audiences, the audiences with the greatest buying power; and many advertisers, though not all, consider that the largest audience is the most profitable. The news medium with the greatest financial security has the greatest independence because it is best able to resist any individual advertiser's attempt to control or influence it. Popular legend to the contrary, one advertiser can seldom dominate or dictate to the newspaper or broadcasting station that has a large audience; every newsman knows at first hand many tales of attempted pressures that failed. There is validity in the shoptalk that "the advertiser needs the newspaper more than the newspaper needs the advertiser."

No responsible newsman condones, in his own work or in that of others, distortion, over- or underemphasis, or sensationalizing of news, either to build audiences or for other purpose. But every newsman who respects his profession, his consumers, and himself, works purposefully toward carrying every piece of news he handles to the largest group of readers, listeners, or viewers, to whom it may have significance or interest.

NEWS AS HISTORY   Few newsmen think of themselves as historians. Yet newsmen are historians each time they write a story, for their work is often the only permanent record of the lives and events of their communities. As the first sentence of this book's Introduction says, "News is tomorrow's history . . ." At any future date, from tomorrow to a distant century, the newsman's story may be exhumed for the information it provides about his time and his society. Every newspaper is, therefore, a potential source for the historian, the sociologist, the political scientist; modern research in the social sciences frequently relies heavily on newspaper files for basic information. Most newspapers, it is true, give little thought to news as history, but a few—the New York *Times* is one—consider the historical function of news a fundamental factor in deciding which news, and how much, to print.

Although the historical uses of news broaden the news concept, the requirements of history do not change its meaning or add to the responsible newsman's burden; the main purpose of news is to provide *current* information and the primary responsibility of the reporter is to inform a *contemporary* audience. The reporter who succeeds in meeting today's news demands, however, is inevitably enriching the files of history. When a reporter makes his story accurate and objective and balanced, he has written "current history" that will be as informative and clear on a thousand tomorrows, to thousands of different readers, in thousands of different places, as it is today.

PROJECTS

1. From current issues of the daily paper you read most, select some continuing news story in which the paper is taking editorial interest: a local election, a drive for street improvements, the national tax situation, American foreign policy. After making sure, from editorial-page comment, that you know what the paper's position is, examine all the relevant news you can find to discern whether it is presented with or without prejudice, with or without partiality to the view the paper favors.
2. From three issues of the same paper, make a tabulation of all the local news, all the regional, all the national, and all the international. On the basis of the tabulation, come to a conclusion and write a brief report on your opinion of the news balance (or imbalance) the paper maintains.
3. Recategorize the stories above according to which seem to you to have been chosen

primarily for their informative value, which for their entertainment value, and which for strength in both values. Categorize in the same way all the stories included in three or more radio or TV newscasts, each of 15 minutes or longer. Do you find media differences?

SUGGESTED READINGS

COLLECTIONS OF JOURNALISTIC WRITING

Berger, Meyer, *The Eight Million*. New York: Simon and Schuster, 1942.

Greene, Ward, *Star Reporters and 34 of Their Greatest Stories*. New York: Random House, Inc., 1948.

Hecht, Ben, *One Thousand and One Afternoons in Chicago*. New York: Covici, Friede, Inc., 1935.

Markey, Morris, *Manhattan Reporter*. New York: F. W. Dodge Corporation, 1935.

Rucker, Bryce W., *Twentieth Century Reporting at Its Best*. Ames, Iowa: Iowa State University Press, 1964.

SOCIAL DEVELOPMENT OF THE PRESS

Brucker, Herbert, *Freedom of Information*. New York: Macmillan, 1949.

Emery, Edwin, *The Press and America*. Englewood Cliffs, N.J.: Prentice-Hall, 1963.

Gerald, J. Edward, *The Press and the Constitution*. Minneapolis: University of Minnesota Press, 1948.

———, *The Social Responsibility of the Press*. Minneapolis, Minn.: University of Minnesota Press, 1963.

Mott, Frank Luther, *The News in America*. Cambridge, Mass.: Harvard University Press, 1952.

Schramm, Wilbur, *Responsibility in Mass Communications*. New York: Harper & Row, 1957.

CHAPTER 2

The Qualities of News

Just as cotton can be used in making either baby clothes or high explosives, so the raw materials of news can be used in sociological exposition, propaganda, or even fiction, as well as in reporting. The factual materials from which news stories are made are malleable, delicate, and responsive to a wide variety of pressures. Although woven from raw materials used in all forms of expository writing, news has developed, through the years, a recognizable texture and pattern of its own. A news story today is more than the sum of the facts that compose it; it has characteristic qualities that distinguish it from all other forms of writing.

As chapter 1 noted briefly, modern news is accurate, balanced, fair and objective, clear, concise, and current. Since these are the qualities that give news its distinctive character, a report is not news, though it may be high art or important scholarship, unless it has them. The *Iliad*, for instance, is the report of an event to an audience, but it is not news because it is neither current, concise, nor objective. A chemistry journal gives accurate and objective information to its special audience, but the information is not suitable as news for a general audience because such an audience lacks the special knowledge necessary to make the report clear and balanced.

The distinguishing qualities of news are so firmly accepted as part of the news concept that they not only determine the characteristic texture of news but also serve as standards for judging news presentation. They establish the working principles that condition the newsman's approach to news and guide him in the daily practice of news gathering and reporting.

News Is Accurate

Students at the University of Colorado decided, upon reading and hearing news of demonstrations by University of California students protesting university policies, to hold a supporting rally. Nobody at the Colorado rally had seen or had direct contact with the events at Berkeley; news reports alone underlay the action.

The accuracy of news, that is to say, is commonly taken for granted. Some readers and viewers question this aphorism, especially those who have declared, in moments of irritation, "I never believe what I read in the papers" or "The radio always gets it wrong." But most news consumers accept most of the facts the media offer without question. They know from experience that when a news story says that the ball game is to start at 3:00 P.M., or that the man who was killed failed to stop at a red light, or that the banker's name is Pennyweather Blueskies, or that California students are protesting something at Berkeley, they can rely on the stated facts. Most Americans base their lives and their thinking on their belief in news dependability, whether they admit (or recognize) it or not.

In 1910, soon after retiring as editor of the highly regarded New York World, *Joseph Pulitzer had this, among other things, to say about accuracy:*

"It is not enough to refrain from publishing fake news; it is not enough to avoid the mistakes which arise from the ignorance, the carelessness, the stupidity of one or more of the many men who handle the news before it gets into print; you have got to do more than that; you have got to make everyone connected with the paper— your editors, your reporters, your correspondents, your rewrite men, your proofreaders—believe that accuracy is to a newspaper what virtue is to a woman." (Alleyne Ireland, Adventure with a Genius. *New York: Dutton, 1920.)*

• •

Newsmen write stories, not "articles" or "items." The term news story, *its inventor lost in the legends of a thousand newsrooms, is understood to mean a factual account; it implies no kinship with the "short story" or with any other fiction. Sometimes news workers, characteristically bored by their own jargon, refer among themselves to news "yarns" or "pieces" or*

Almost nobody these days needs to be told of the importance of factual accuracy in news. Almost nobody outside the news profession realizes how enormously difficult it is to achieve. What factual accuracy means is that every statement in a news story, every name and date and age and quotation, every definitive word or expression or sentence must be a precise and unequivocal presentation of verifiable fact. Accuracy means, moreover, not only correctness of specific detail but also correctness of general impression, correctness of the effect achieved by the way the details are put together and by the emphases they are given.

The meaning of accuracy may be easy to understand, but its attainment is not easy to arrive at. A news story with fewer than a dozen facts would be hard to find; many stories have scores of facts. It is difficult for even the most experienced reporter, careful as he tries to be, to make absolutely sure of every detail, especially in view of the haste modern journalism imposes; furthermore, his story may be changed by the copy editor's pencil, by unintentional distortions in the printing process, or by nuances of a news announcer's voice. Any issue of a newspaper or any "edition" of a newscast offers literally hundreds of opportunities for mistakes. (Most of the "possible" errors would necessarily be minor and not misleading— typographical errors, for instance.) Radio and television can't make "typos," but news announcers can "fluff" or misplace emphasis. With the possibility of error so great, the wonder is that the actual number of errors in news presentation is as small as it is.

In spite of this fact, many laymen charge the media with "never getting things right." This is a demonstra-

even, with elaborate irony, "items" or "articles." But these last two terms, except in the mouths of professionals, always suggest unfamiliarity with news work. tion of the human penchant for generalization from insufficient evidence. Most newspaper readers read only a small part of their papers—the stories of interest to them or the sections dealing with subjects about which they have special knowledge. The occasional errors they find in what they read therefore appear disproportionately bulky because of their personal impact. If the paper spells Smyth's name "Smith," if it refers to a yawl as a yacht, if (as one wire service did) it calls President Johnson's new Community Relations Service the "Communist" Relations Service, if it says that a hundred parents attended the PTA meeting when only fifty turned up, the reader who identifies the error loses confidence; he expresses distrust of the paper in general, not limiting his complaints to the specific inaccuracies he can prove. (Should the paper be so careless as to repeat an error, or should it let its standards fall, general criticism may become justified.)

What are the reporter's safeguards? How can he protect himself, and his paper, and his reader against inaccuracy? The best protection is vigilant patience. Every note must be painstakingly written down and checked, particularly such specific details as names, dates, ages, times, addresses, and the like. Nothing may ever be taken for granted: Is the name that sounds like Smith really Smith? or is it Schmidt, or Smeeth, or even Psmythe? When the secretary said the meeting would be on Friday, August 17, was she sure August 17 would fall on a Friday? Is it correct to refer to the minister as "Dr. Brown" (perhaps he has no doctoral degree)?

Vigilant patience needs to be partner to perpetual skepticism, the willingness to double check every fact that can be tested. Skepticism means that the story clipped from the morning paper as a tip for an afternoon treatment must be vouched for by some authoritative source—the story isn't necessarily accurate because it has been printed. Vigilance means constant use of reference sources: city directory, telephone book, dictionary, encyclopedia, *Who's Who*, city, state, and federal government manuals, a score of others. It means telephone calls, visits to the library, and sometimes endless search for the man who really knows the answer.

A wire service story as published by a newspaper opened with a feature lead saying in part that "Orville Wright made history when he flew to a height of 120 feet in 1903." The fact: that Wright had flown a distance of 120 feet, at hardly more than head-high altitude. Whether the error was the wire service writer's or that of the copyreader who edited the story, a few seconds with a newsroom encyclopedia would have averted it. And it also means awareness that sometimes the man who knows the answer won't tell it accurately, either intentionally or through carelessness. It is a hard fact of reportorial life that sources of information are far less reliable than journalists, that they must be checked and checked again.

The experienced reporter knows that even accurate facts do not always add up to a trustworthy story. Accurate facts carelessly or unfairly selected or arranged can be as misleading as outright error; if some facts are given too little or too much emphasis, or if relevant details are omitted or inappropriate details included, the news consumer may be given a false im-

One of the important assignments of the copy desk is to provide a final trap for just such errors. Some news novices ask, "Why shouldn't the reporter get the main lines of the story and leave the addresses and such 'little things' to the desk?" Such use of the copy desk as a crutch would inevitably produce shoddy reporting. Although it's a newsroom stereotype to say that a copyreader is expected to know everything, the copyreader doesn't know everything. It is easier and more efficient for the reporter to get accurate facts as he gathers information than for the copyreader to protect him later.

As for getting the "main lines" of a story and expecting somebody else to fill gaps later, every newsman should read "There Are 00 Trees in Russia," a burning criticism of this very practice by a former newsmagazine editor, Otto Friedrich. (Harper's Magazine, October 1964).

• •

pression of the story's meaning. In several studies of news accuracy in four cities, hundreds of stories from local papers were submitted to individuals intimately enough concerned in the events the stories reported to know whether the facts were reported accurately. The studies found, on the average, fewer than one error per story (the majority of the stories were entirely accurate).

In the most extensive of these studies (reported in "Some Preliminary Notes on Newspaper Accuracy" in *Journalism Quarterly*, December 1936), readers with knowledge of the facts sometimes expressed the view that the stories had not given appropriate emphases, that they gave incomplete, biased, or otherwise faulty impressions about the reported events. It should be noted that such "critics" were not always objective themselves; some clearly (though probably subconsciously) wished that the facts had given impressions slanted to suit their own purposes or preconceptions. But the frequency with which errors in meaning were alleged suggests that many stories probably did mislead readers. In any case, the fact that so many errors in meaning were claimed indicates how difficult it is for reporters to give correct general impressions even with entirely correct specific details. A completely accurate story, one that gives the true meaning of the news, must have balance and objectivity as well as accuracy.

News Is Balanced

If it is no easy task to report every specific fact accurately, it is an even tougher assignment to put all the facts together fairly. To be fair to both its sources and its audience, news must have balance; balance is a matter of emphasis and completeness. As the reader's or listener's representative, the reporter must constantly strive to give each fact its proper proportion, to put it in proper relation to every other fact, and to establish its relative importance to the meaning of the story as a whole. Though a reporter covering a baseball game might make every statement in his story scrupulously accurate, he would give readers a lopsided view of the game if he reported only the action when

A representative of the American Newspaper Guild was one of the participants in a national conference on "The Mass Media in a Liberal Education"; in a story about the conference, the ANG newspaper, the Guild Reporter, reported only the remarks made by the Guild representative. Doing so, it presented to readers an erroneous impression of the meaning and effect of the conference.

the home team was at bat; his story would be neither balanced nor complete. A story about a Rotary Club meeting that reports only the out-of-town visitor's speech and omits the presentation of awards to local citizens for civic accomplishments has the same faults. It would be equally unfair, under most circumstances, to report the speech at length and the awards in a single sentence, especially if the speech were routine and uninspired, and the awards significant to the community or received with cheers.

News is usually considered complete when the reporter has given a competent summary of all relevant portions of the news event. Complete news coverage does not mean reporting every trifling circumstance of the event in painstaking detail; it means selecting and arranging facts so as to give a balanced view of the whole news situation. Although literal completeness is seldom desirable, some stories in modern journalism are close to it: sports stories are frequently in play-by-play form; speeches and court testimony are often printed verbatim; dramatic events such as a president's inauguration or his funeral are sometimes reconstructed with photographic fidelity. For the most part, however, completeness is a matter of balancing facts in order to give the reader a fair understanding of the total event.

The reporter is the agent of the news consumer. He goes to the baseball game or covers the Rotary Club or the city council meeting or collects the facts about next year's school program in order to supply information to thousands of laymen who depend on him. It is the newsman's responsibility to represent those thousands; from his statement of a particular set of facts, his readers or listeners should be enabled to reconstruct the main lines of the news event almost as well as if they had been with the reporter. In order to write a story that will be fair to the thousands who cannot be present at the event, the reporter must make sure that his story is objective, as well as balanced and complete.

News Is Objective

News is the factual report of an event as it occurred. It is not the event as a prejudiced eye might see it, or as the reporter might wish it to be or had thought it would be, or as those concerned in it might like to present it. The facts must be reported impartially, as they occurred; and although the reportorial observers and transcribers are not always as impersonal and disinterested as a man from Mars might be, nor as all-seeing and awesomely wise as would be ideal, there is no excuse in today's news practice for reporting events as they might have been, or should have been, or as somebody wished they had been.

Objectivity in news is one of the dominant principles of modern journalism. Objectivity means that the news comes to the consumer untainted by any personal bias or outside influence that would make it appear anything but what it is. Most news media, not the daily newspaper alone, agree that news should be considered inviolable and that all news, not only political news, should be presented without slanting, shading, or tinting. The reporter should look at events through glasses that are neither rose-colored nor smoked; he must report the news in the white light of impartial and scrupulously honest observation. Only "pure" news can give the consumer confidence that the reports on which he bases his opinions are sound sources of accurate information.

To go back to the years when Day and Bennett were offering their revolutionary penny papers to the New York public, the newspapers they were challenging and hoping to replace were often not newspapers in the modern sense. These papers did not print the facts of current events; they printed the view of the facts that was favored by publisher, editor, or writer. As Elmer Davis put it, these papers printed ". . . 'what helps our side.' No nonsense of fairly reporting what was said on both sides, of giving the other fellow a break. What they printed was what the editor and his political backers wanted." It was when Day and Bennett came along with their broader news coverage and their purpose to give the facts and let the readers think what they would about them that news presentation began to change. As newspaper political adherence became less insistent, the attitude of which political adherence was a symptom faded.

Today objectivity has been accepted as an essential principle of news practice by virtually every American news medium. The American Society of Newspaper Editors recognized the validity of the principle in 1923, when one of its guides to ethical news practice held that partisanship in the news columns must be considered "subversive of a fundamental principle of the profession." In 1943, Paul White, later given a Peabody Award for his superb direction of the Columbia Broadcasting System's news service, expressed his belief that "the fact that objectivity is an ideal difficult to attain . . . does not impair the ideal itself, nor excuse the broadcaster from a constant and vigilant effort to attain it."

Objectivity in political coverage is one of the most trying problems faced by newsmen. In the national election campaign of 1952, for example, Democrats complained that some newspapers favoring Eisenhower had not given Stevenson news its fair share of attention; in 1960 Richard M. Nixon thought the newspapers had been unfair to him. But in every campaign there have been many cases in which "Republican" newspapers (for instance), in their attempts to treat the news impartially, gave more space and more headline emphasis to the Democrat than to his opponent. "We play the news as we think it should be played, whether we like what it says or not," these papers assert.

• •

Though no general news medium would be likely to

In the path of the pursuit of objectivity are obstacles and conflicts. One arises because reporters are humans who, like other humans, can never wholly escape the influence of their own opinions and emotions. Almost any reporter can report with fairness the "straight" news that the Optimists Club will hear a speaker on atomic energy next Thursday; this news makes little demand on a man's emotions and has little effect on his blood pressure. But suppose that on Thursday the speaker uses his subject as a springboard for violent remarks about the administration's policy of keeping secret much of its information about atomic weapons, and further that the reporter happens to believe that the slightest leak in such information may lead to national disaster. His problem of reporting this news fairly, keeping his own leanings out of the story, becomes far more difficult. Presumably a reporter in this case would be aware of his opinion and political orientation. If he is both alert to the difficulties and faithful to his responsibilities, his efforts to remain objective, to keep the story fair and impartial, have at least a good chance of success. But if he doesn't know his own prejudices, his chance of attaining objectivity may be small.

concede it has faltered in fidelity to the principle of objectivity, few newspapers, broadcasting stations, or magazines have lily-white records; and some appear clearly soiled. Critics of the press point out, for instance, that Col. Robert R. McCormick's Chicago Tribune often reported Washington (and other) news in the light of the Colonel's attitudes and the points of view he wanted his readers to hold. The Tribune's notorious edition of November 3, 1948, which announced that Dewey had defeated Truman for the presidency, is an example of a willingness to jump to wished-for conclusions about the news.

Before the death of William Randolph Hearst, every sophisticated reader of the Hearst papers knew that anything they printed about use of animals in medical experimentation was conditioned by the "Old Man's" bitter dislike of vivisection. Hearst's record of dictating his papers' news viewpoints went back to the time, in 1897, when he decided that war with Spain would be good for his New York Journal's circulation.

That objectivity, or its lack, is closely tied to personal attitudes is indicated by the fact that, with the death of Hearst and McCormick, news practices on their papers underwent radical revisions.

Thus objectivity is a lofty goal, not easy to reach. Yet most American newsmen recognize the challenge and accept it. As a rule, the news presented to the American public is reported with a high standard of objectivity; most departures are unintentional. Flagrant instances of intentional distortion, of planned partiality in news, are usually perceived quickly, and their creators are discredited in the long if not in the short run.

A second major problem in arriving at objectivity as a vital principle of reporting arises because objective reporting of the facts "as is" sometimes fails to give the whole picture or a fair understanding of a complex news situation. Objective reporting assumes that the consumer, with his own resources, with no hints from the news story, is able to apply appropriate perspective to whatever facts the story gives him: to separate the genuine from the phony, the pure from the adulterated, the true from the false, the fair from the biased, the complete from the incomplete, the trustworthy and benevolent from the dishonorable and malicious. Even in the nineteenth century it was a rare thing that a news consumer could accomplish this overwhelming feat; today it is more rare. The modern world is so complex that no man can grasp it all, let alone evaluate its parts. No matter how much news he is given, the everyday citizen cannot untangle the mass of facts and forces and frustrations without some form of background or interpretation to guide him. In truth, the very mass of news so overwhelms him that he often gives up hope and escapes to the comics, the movies, or the latest television serial about physicians.

When objectivity collides with complexity, a good reporter should help the consumer to see the objective facts in perspective; he should provide relevant background information to clarify complicated events. It is a fallacy to believe that objective reporting fully discharges the newsman's obligation. Listen again to Elmer Davis, one of the most penetrating and perceptive newsmen this nation has produced:

This striving for objectivity was in its beginning a good thing; but it went a little too far. From holding that newspapers ought to present both sides it went on to the position that it was all right to present only one side, if nobody happened to be talking on the other; and it was not the business of the newspaper to tell the reader if that one argument happened to be a phony.

This is not quite so bad now as it used to be; it reached its peak, I think . . . in the administration of Calvin Coolidge, when it was the opinion of a great many American citizens that things are what they seem. In those days, if the Hon. John P. Hoozis was important enough to be interviewed, you might see half or two-thirds of a column embodying his views on some topic or other, with no indication that what he said was a lie from beginning to end—even if the editor who printed the story happened to know it—and no indication that the Hon. John P. Hoozis might have a powerful personal interest, financial or otherwise, in getting that view over to the public. He had said it; and if it was important enough to be news, it would not have been objective not to print it.

The quotations from Elmer Davis are taken from a lecture, "Must We Mislead the Public?", given by Mr. Davis in the Twin Cities Newspaper Guild Memorial Series at the University of Minnesota School of Journalism. The lecture was the basis for a chapter in Mr. Davis's But We Were Born Free (Indianapolis: Bobbs-Merrill, 1954), a brilliant critique of news handling.

As Davis colorfully points out, objective reporting is admirable in itself, but, in itself, it isn't enough. It is, for instance, admirable to report a speech by a political leader accurately and completely; it is by no means so admirable to report it without mentioning that an authority at least as competent may have previously denied or disproved some of the "facts" in the speech. A fair news story should contain, in addition to the clear facts, whatever related information may be necessary to flesh out the consumer's perspective and orientation. Although objective reporting is the "report of an event as it occurred," a good newsman must frequently report the relevant background as well as the literally observable facts of the event. Unless balanced and complete information is presented in appropriate context, objectivity may only add to the consumer's burden of confusion.

Objectivity based on fairness, as exemplified in the best of American journalism, is a quality much admired and increasingly copied by newsmen of other nations. Indeed, objective reporting has been called America's most significant contribution to the world of journalism.

News Is Concise and Clear

A news story must observe certain conventions of form and manner: it must be unified, concise, clear, and simple. It should not become diffuse, disorganized, or ambiguous. News should be direct, terse, and logically coherent; it should be well paced, and above all it should be written so clearly that the meaning of the story is undebatable.

American news style can be very good or very bad. It is frequently said of one of the most powerful modern short stories, Ernest Hemingway's "The Killers," that much of its strength lies in its journalistic style—that is, in its spare, intense, racing English. On the other hand, writing characterized by trite phrases, careless diction, and banality is also said to be journalistic. A common derogatory word for sloppy writing is "journalese."

A "good" reporting style, like any effective writing style, is not a quality easy to acquire or maintain. A newsman who uses yesterday's cliches instead of seeking fresh and exact terms, and one who uses "secure" for "obtain," "cinema star" for "movie actor," or "statutory crime" or "assault" when he means "rape" is not likely to win prizes for his prose. Nor will the reporter who grows lazy and says, "Let the copyreaders cut it—that's what they're paid for."

Effective reporting is painstakingly precise in word choice, yet full of vigor and movement; colorful, yet without subjective tinting, affectation, or over-writing; brief and pointed, yet balanced and fair. These are qualities realized in most forms of effective writing, not in journalism alone.

News Is Recent

Definitions of news that understate the importance of the time element are incomplete. Emphasis on the time context of a story is necessary because news consumers live in a fast-moving world and are aware of it; events and values are transitory, and readers or listeners demand the most recent information on subjects of concern to them. In the frenetic circumstances of modern life, news developments this morning may outdate or upset completely the "facts" of last night. Because news consumers want fresh news, most news stories are tagged "today" or, at the most distant, "last night" or "yesterday." News media are carefully specific about time, even the time at which news of future events was announced, to show that their news, more than merely "recent," is no less than the last word.

The media have grown expert in handling news fast in order to be able to report events while they are fresh. A prime stimulus to speed is the competition among media for audience attention. The reader is interested in the current and the new, and every newsman hopes to win a clientele by giving it the good or bad tidings or the local tidbits before his rivals do. Every news office in America is organized so that it can gather, write, edit, and publish the news so quickly as to give the consumer the latest word with the least delay.

Even before the telegraph and the cable made the lapse of time between event and report a matter of seconds or minutes or hours rather than days or weeks or months, newspaper rivalry put emphasis on speed. Before 1830 ambitious young Thurlow Weed, instead of sending his story by post took the night boat from Albany to New York to be sure that his paper would have the news ahead of its competitors. The enterprise and fire with which Bennett's *Herald* consistently whipped all competition in speed of news gathering inspired a group of New York papers to band together in order to get the foreign news from the ships entering New York harbor ahead of their rivals; competition thus provided the initial impulse for the cooperative news-gathering organization that years later became the Associated Press.

With the development of telegraph and cable the race to be first became even more intense, and twentieth-century technology has added some final bursts. A man in San Francisco, thanks to television, can see and hear a prize fight in New York in the same second as the man seated at ringside. Space satellite communication has added a new dimension: viewers all over the world can see it too. Even the most distant viewer of the 1952 Republican national convention knew that General Eisenhower had been nominated for the presidency before many of the delegates on the convention floor knew it; the TV camera caught the exact vote that assured the nomination, while confusion in the hall temporarily obscured the decisive act from many of those present.

In the news world the press has permanently lost the race for speed. The palm has passed to radio and television. There is no way in which newspapers can gather, write, print, and distribute news to consumers as rapidly as can broadcasting. As the newspaper's role has changed, newsmen have given a lot of serious thought to the validity of speed as a factor in news selection, particularly speed as it relates to the press. The speed with which news is presented, it is pointed out, does not affect the genuine newsworthiness of most news. Does a man reading the paper really care whether the report on the Governor's Commission on Public Housing is published two hours after it is released rather than two days after? He has a carefully-nurtured taste for "hot" news, and it cannot be stifled overnight; but if a newspaper had two days instead of two hours in which to prepare its news, would it not be likely to turn out more carefully edited, more thorough, and more useful stories?

As Carl Lindstrom, near the end of his distinguished service as editor of the Hartford *Times,* told an audience of newsmen:

> The newsroom clock is the master of us all. We are slaves to its hurrying hands. There's always the deadline; there's never time to do the job as well as we would like to do it. . . . We are rushing through the ripe wheat fields grabbing handfuls of golden grain and leaving the big harvest for the gleaners. The rich aftermath goes to the weekly and monthly periodicals of journalism.

A perceptive and stimulating discussion of the values related to the freshness of news appears in chapter 5 of Frank Luther Mott's The News in America: "Speed: The News as Timely Report" (see chapter 1 of this book). The newspapers seem slowly to be moving toward acceptance of the fact that speed as a dominating characteristic of news handling has to be left to broadcasting. The newspaper extra, for example, has almost disappeared; and voices like Carl Lindstrom's are asking for more penetrating and thorough news treatment by the daily paper. But the time element is here to stay. As long as there is need for currency or recency in news information, a statement of time will be as essential in news stories as accuracy, balance, objectivity, and conciseness.

In some news, timeliness, the appropriateness of the news to the time of year, the date, or the season, is as important as the quality of recency. Timeliness as a factor in news selection is examined in chapter 3.

PROJECTS

1. Select a long news story on an important local event—a major local business development, an important speech, plans for a local holiday celebration—and check every specific fact in it: addresses, dates, times, names, ages, or anything else you find checkable. Use city and telephone directories, census and other government reports, encyclopedias, fact almanacs, and so on. Confer with a reference librarian if necessary.

The checking completed, arrive at a "batting average" for the story—a percentage statement of its accuracy.

2. Now take the story to an "authority" on its facts, somebody involved in the news event in a way that indicates he knows the facts. Ask him to check the story both for factual accuracy and meaning. Compare his comments to your own findings.

3. Make a list of all the style "faults" you find in the news stories on a newspaper's front page, errors in diction, spelling, punctuation, rhetoric, grammar, and the like. Correct the errors to your satisfaction.

CHAPTER 3

The Evaluation and
Selection of News

Not everything that happens becomes news. Most of the things people do and say during the day go unchronicled and unremembered. Most men and women live through weeks, months, and years without taking part in events that are newsworthy. They live their daily lives, they work and eat and sleep and play, without departure from routine of a kind that must be reported to others. Sometimes they adventure into the periphery of news events: they attend baseball games, watch parades, vote in elections that are duly reported by the news media. But they are secondary, not primary, participants in these events.

Once in a while their trifling adventures get into the papers. Let us say that the city hall elevator, which has operated without incident for 27 years, is equipped one morning with brand-new safety doors. On the first day, the safety doors crush the operator's fingers. Neither the elevator nor the operator ever broke into print before, but now a reporter writes a brief story that earns front-page space. Somebody has decided that a minor event should *not* be tossed into limbo, that it should become part of the daily record. It has become news.

Who decides? Why should this event have been turned into news? What makes some events "better" news than others? How are stories selected?

To answer these questions, chapter 3 will examine the theory and the practices that guide the experienced newsman's evaluation and selection of news. Whoever he is, whatever his background, the news expert is no demigod; he works and makes his decisions in an environment dotted with guideposts.

News stories do not develop in a vacuum; on the contrary, as chapter 1 pointed out, they are an integral part of their era and their society. Social customs, history, geography, and economics, for example, may affect the meaning of an event and determine its relative value as a basis for a news story. These conditioning factors are so well established, so well known to news workers, that two, or twenty, or even two hundred, newsmen—given the same group of events from which to select—would make substantially the same decisions. Their decisions would vary in some details because of differing audience requirements and particular medium limitations—some events that become newspaper stories, for example, are not reported on the air—but in the important respects their selections would be alike.

Although there are many guideposts that point toward news decisions, it must be said quickly that there are no precise or codified rules. The newsman does not have a list labeled "Components of News" pasted over his desk; science has not developed a computer that determines which stories ought to be published and which rejected. Nevertheless, even a beginner in news work, with his years of newspaper reading and radio listening, has a fairly good idea of what makes news, and the experienced newsman has his rules of thumb ready to apply instantly and almost automatically.

Some of the many definitions of news:

"News is anything timely that interests a number of persons, and the best news is that which has the greatest interest for the greatest number."—Willard Grosvenor Bleyer

"News is what a well-trained editor decides to put in his paper."—Gerald W. Johnson

"News is usually stimulating information from which the ordinary human being derives satisfaction or stimulation."—Chilton R. Bush

This book's definition: "News is the timely report of facts or opinion that hold interest or importance, or both, for a considerable number of people."

Any professional can describe the requirements of "good" news—news that is worth carrying to an audience. Some of the requisites are sharp and obvious, some so subtle that their description becomes difficult. Although different professionals define news differently, rarely are two definitions the same; they usually agree on two main requirements of "good" news: *significance* and *interest*.

The reporter, as he gathers facts and writes his news stories, and the editors, as they evaluate the stories that cross their desks, continually (and often acting with the patterns of habit) ask themselves two fundamental questions: "Is this event significant—does it hold importance for our particular audience?" and "Will it interest them?" Although reporters or desk men are rarely aware of subjecting a given story to precise "significance-interest analysis," they may go through this mechanical question-and-answer process a thousand times a day. They must do so at top speed, for the news process makes no allowance for time-consuming deliberation. How do they make their rapid-fire decisions?

The news workers who make the decisions know that the news they select must, to repeat, inform or interest their audiences. They know that a news story, if it is to attract and hold audience attention, must be relevant to the lives of their clientele, either because the news it contains is important to a considerable number or because it appeals to individual interests or emotions—or both. A news story, to be either significant or interesting, must *relate* to a particular audience, whether nationwide or limited by geographical, cultural, economic, or other factors. More specifically, a report about the development of a new fertilizer, for instance, is "better" news in an agricultural area of Iowa than in a shoe-manufacturing town in Massachusetts, and a "better" story today, in an age of food-production problems and tired soil, than it would have been in the lush nineteenth century.

The significance and appeal of any story can be evaluated only in its relation to a specific audience. Although no audience is homogeneous—every sizable audience is composed of small groups that have distinct characteristics and needs —the newsman must select news that will satisfy as many as possible of the various interests among such groups. (Chapter 5 discusses audiences and their characteristics.)

Evaluating News for Significance

The newsman must first decide which events and what information are of primary importance to a considerable proportion of the people his medium reaches. During World War II, war news was obviously important to every member of every news audience in the United States; the development of the war had direct and deep-seated relevance for every American. A national election provides nationally important news; a municipal election news that must be reported locally but not often at distant points.

Not all election news is as significant as the choice of a President. Not all war news has the breadth of impact of World War II. In the 1960s, for example, the news editor had often to ask himself, "How much importance has border fighting in India, or in the Near East, for American readers?" And he often made the decision that it was less important than the fighting in Vietnam; moreover, he gave less space and time to all such news than had gone to the Pacific and European wars of the 1940s.

The logic behind these differences in news selection is easy to pin down. Fighting in Tibet, between two groups of Asiatics, had little *direct* or immediate effect on the lives of Americans. The news media reported it as a part of the day's events because of their implicit obligation to inform and because any such international dispute has in it the seeds of developments that could become directly meaningful for America. But they gave greater attention to the war in Vietnam, which had more obvious, more immediate relation to American life. Although physically as distant as the India-China fighting, the undeclared war in Vietnam affected American news consumers personally. Many had some kind of contact with men and women engaged in the conflict; the national economy was affected; national passions were aroused; the national future was clearly involved.

THE GEOGRAPHICAL FACTOR   The relevance of location to news significance may be seen clearly in the evaluation of election news. The election of a senator in Arizona is obviously important news to Arizonans, and Arizona media cover it abundantly. In Pennsylvania the same news has no local significance, but because the election of any senator has effect nationally, Pennsylvania media think it worth a good deal of space. At the same time, the Pennsylvania media may find no national or local significance in news of the election of a new mayor just across the state line in Canton, Ohio; they may choose not to report even his name to their audiences. But the Canton newspaper gives the election banner lines, and papers in nearby Cleveland, Akron, and Columbus report it in some detail.

Geographical factors become important in other ways. Suppose the U.S. Department of the Interior decides to open previously closed areas of a Minnesota national forest to big-game hunters. Newsmen in Indiana, which boasts neither a national forest nor a wild animal larger than a fox, pay little attention. Newsmen in Oregon, which has national forest lands similar to those in Minnesota, give the news space because the same action might be applied to their own forests. Newsmen in Minnesota not only give the news broad prominence but make it the occasion for "local angle" stories, stories that show graphically the impact of the action on Minnesota hunters, the Minnesota resort industry, the conservation of wild life in Minnesota, and so on.

The distance between the news audience and the news event influences news selection in many ways. A tornado that kills citizens and rips off all the roofs in a Nebraska village is reported in a few paragraphs in Los Angeles and Boston; in Omaha, the disaster gets full pages and special newscasts; and in the stricken village itself the next edition of the paper talks of little else. Plans for a new railroad station in Natchitoches, Louisiana, call for columns of space in Natchitoches, and half a column in New Orleans. But the only way the citizens of Great Falls, Montana, hear about it is through a letter from a local boy who moved south. The Great Falls news media wouldn't report it even if the news reached them.

Newsmen recognize that the geographical factor is not a constant, but varies in all media and all areas, and from one decade to the next. Radio stations of different powers have different ranges and, therefore, quite different audience areas—areas measured in states for a 50-kilowatt station, and in counties for a 250-watt station. The speed-up in transportation has widened the newspaper's area; air express and fast trucks make it possible to "lay down" a morning paper at 7:00 A.M. on doorsteps hundreds of miles away from the point of publication. As the area increases and the audience widens, the character and interests of the audience change; and the news selected must reflect these changes.

PERSONAL IMPACT   The relative significance of news may be determined by the number of members of the audience on whose lives a news event impinges directly. Every man in Canton, for example, is somehow affected by the election of a new mayor, and the event is reported locally in intimate detail. But the election of a new chairman for the dramatics group of the Women's Library Club is given only four lines in the paper and no time on the air because relatively few local residents outside the club, perhaps only the new chairman's husband, or her sisters and her cousins and her aunts, would find the event either interesting or significant.

COMPETITION FOR NEWS ATTENTION   The size of the community and the degree of competition for news attention also affect news selection. Newspapers and radio in big cities give no time to the ordinary private affairs of the ordinary citizen, or even to such organized or semipublic activities as the dramatic group's choice of a chairman. In a large city the proportion of lives touched by such an event is very small; events of wider impact claim the always-too-limited news space. In some small towns, however, the weekly paper and the local radio station report cases of chicken pox, shopping trips to the nearby city, and the town druggist's plan to build a third bedroom over his garage. A good many barbs have been aimed at the small-town newspapers that report blessed events in the barnyard and write that "Grocer Sam Bilker has painted his front"; but the barbs ignore the relative significance of the small event in the small world.

The clinical detail with which illnesses at famous addresses have sometimes been reported have drawn critical fire. Nobody denied, when President Eisenhower suffered heart and intestinal ailments, that the news had vast importance; but the intimacy with which the President's troubles were described to the world was thought by many to be in bad taste.

PROMINENCE   Although the run-of-the-mill affairs of the private citizen do not make news in the city, the slightest variation in the routine of the Big Man must be reported. Nobody notices when most of us have colds, but sniffles at 10 Downing Street, or in Palm Springs, are heard around the world. A globe-circling voyage by a textile manufacturer from Lowell, Massachusetts, is worth only a note in the society column; but a modest weekend excursion by a British princess or an American cabinet officer is covered by a corps of newsmen, and the details are reported in daily stories followed by readers and listeners all over the world. What in one case is a private affair, of no general interest, in the other is a matter of concern to millions because a public figure is involved.

BREADTH OF INTEREST   Some relatively unimportant events achieve a kind of significance by virtue of the wide interest they arouse. The World Series each fall can hardly be said to have lasting effect on more than a few hundred Americans, but no annual event gets more news attention. Newsmen argue that an event that for a full October week has 50 million Americans glued for hours before radio and TV sets and devouring thousands of columns of newspaper space—and thus for a brief period alters the pace and texture of the national life—acquires a kind of importance.

SUMMARY   The significance of a piece of news is then, relative. First of all, news becomes significant because of the extent of its influence on the lives of its particular clientele. Some news is important for everybody, everywhere. But much news is important only in limited context, to one group but not to others; and the conditioning factors are proximity, the radius of an event's influence, its power to attract attention and stimulate response, and its relation to a community's size and composition.

Two studies of several Wisconsin dailies, classifying their news according to its "usefulness," showed that they devoted about 40 percent of their news space to "useful" news. But the heart of this analysis lies in the definition of "useful." Useful news was defined by the studies' director as news "of some importance to a share" of a paper's readers: for example, election returns and testimony before a Senate committee (the term "hard news" might have been substituted). Nonuseful news was "merely interesting, curiosity-arousing, or thrilling": for example, a story about a disappearing barn or one about a routine birthday party. The implication that minor news cannot be useful, that its value in helping a reader to know and understand his times or his community is negligible, seems questionable.

News with a strong claim to public attention because of its significance for relatively large numbers of people is often called by newsmen "hard news." "Hard news" is the news of government activity, of politics, of international relations, of education, of religion, of legislatures, courts, and most public and private social agencies—sober news and, to most of the audience, dull news. This kind of news is not always easy to understand, and it often makes difficult reading. The analyses of reader response show clearly that "hard news" draws the smaller audiences, though such news is often of greater importance than the "soft news," human interest stories, news of crime and lust and comedy, that attracts readers more readily and in larger numbers. This presents a problem that is the challenge and the despair of every news worker. Scientific measurements are not needed to demonstrate that most news consumers would rather give their attention to the latest marriage of a millionaire playboy, remote as the event may be from their lives, than to the new federal budget, even though government spending is going to take a painful share out of their income next year.

Evaluating News for Interest

Newsmen have a traditional after-hours game, speculating about the event that would make the "biggest" news story. Their inventions range from the solemn to the absurd, from the irreverent to the catastrophic. During World War I the death of the Kaiser was a favorite "event," and in World War II this event became the deaths of Hitler and Mussolini (when speculation became fantastic fact, the stories appropriately drew enormous headlines). Some men suggest the Second Coming as the biggest story; some the creation of life in a test tube; some the first round trip by man to Saturn. Each such event would be of high significance, but each would also have tremendous popular interest; each would be not only an event of world-wide impact but also news that would make brisk conversation over every breakfast table, every lunch pail, and every cocktail glass. Such an event would rank at the top of the scale of interest—the second major criterion by which newsmen evaluate news events.

An event of great interest may, it is clear, be of little genuine importance. Just as the most important events are sometimes those to which the public is most consistently allergic, so vastly interesting news developments are sometimes those to which nobody but the participants attach any significance. As the newsmen's game shows, however, importance and interest are often coincident. When this is the case, newsmen have the kind of story most satisfying to work with, a story that gives the audience not only something solid but also something entertaining.

In order to select news of interest, the newsman must know what impels attention to news and what leads to preference for one kind of news fare over another. One generalization can safely be offered about all audiences, and all of the millions of men, women, and children in them: they give close attention to news only when they can reasonably expect to "get something out of it." They give eye or ear to news when it promises to fulfill some need or desire, whether one that is recognized or that lies below the horizon of their awareness.

What kinds of news will a man find worth his time and effort when he settles down with his evening paper after supper? Three broad groups of news material can be identified.

1) He wants "important" news, news that will somehow affect his own life and his future. He wants to know the size of the paving assessment that will be added to his local taxes next year. He is concerned about the *coup d'état* in that southeast Asian country—didn't Joe say that it might start another war? He wonders whether the new school building will be completed in time to accommodate his children. He reads stories about these and scores of other subjects because he finds the color and texture of his living bound up with them. But he finds a good many of them hard reading, and he does not linger with them.

2) If he is an "average man," he spends a good share of his total reading time—about forty-five minutes a day—on other types of news, news that entertains him. He enjoys a piece about the zoo keeper locked in a cage by a monkey. Perhaps he likes the baseball news because it satisfies his subconscious desire to be a pitcher; undoubtedly he gets an emotional lift when the home team wins a tight two-hitter. He reads stories that arouse his sympathy, that make him angry, that thrill him with danger or conflict. He spends time on news of movie personalities, of divorce, of crime.

3) He is pleased to find not only news but also nonnews material that will help him to "better himself," to sell more shoes, build a better kitchen shelf, impress the boss, bid better contract bridge. When he reads the recent news about the effects of smoking on health, he congratulates himself for having given it up or wonders whether he shouldn't try again. Perhaps he is intellectually stimulated by the reviews, comments about books and the arts.

When he has exhausted the columns of the paper whose contents affect him personally, he is through with it; he lets it fall with a casual "nothing else here to interest me." In short, he gives his attention primarily to material that has impact on him as an individual, news that will, in one way or another, affect his life, his family, or his neighbors.

RESPONSE TO HARD AND SOFT NEWS   The newsman knows the relative values in the two broad groupings of news: hard news, primarily news of significance, and soft news, primarily news strong in human interest. He bases his process of news selection on an understanding of the reasons that the news consumer reacts more readily, and often more vigorously, to news of human interest than he does to informative or significant news.

News of the new federal budget is important—the news consumer grants that; why then is it difficult for most readers to settle down for a nice relaxed half-hour with a story about the budget? The budget story tells about appropriations and expenditures, it names figures in millions and billions of dollars, it lists congressional committees that will consider various proposals and it reports the approval of some senators and the indignation of others. But all these facts are as far removed from the experience of the average reader as though they came from Tierra del Fuego instead of Capitol Hill. The budget isn't a matter to which he can relate personal experience. It isn't real to him. He has no way of putting himself in the place of a congressman considering the bill. He possesses no picture of the legislative process through which the budget proposal must work its way; sums in billions of dollars might as well be in terms of light-years or feather beds. There is probably nothing in the story to show him how the budget will affect his take-home pay, his plan to start a new house in the spring if he can raise the money, or his hope that he and the wife and kids may be able to swing a couple of weeks at that nice fishing lake in the next state. He finds no real points of contact between his own life and the complex facts the story relates.

The puzzled man, after a brief glance at the budget story, mutters something about an income tax boost next year and turns to the story in the next column. This story is about a local high school girl who yesterday beat all the experts in the week's contest for the largest pan fish taken from the county's lakes. He reads this story thoroughly and with close attention; he looks with a smile of approval at the three-column photograph showing the bathing-suited girl holding her fish out for the judge to weigh. Perhaps he calls out to his wife to tell her about the event or to remark that next week he'd better try to get in on this—he could use one of those outboard motors they're giving out as prizes.

Newsmen constantly use the terms "straight news" and "features." Straight news is news that is presented "straight," that is, in the conventional straight-forward news story form, for informative purpose only. The term "feature" has many meanings (see chapter 15); in contrast to "straight news" it means news whose prime purpose is to entertain or supplement rather than to inform. Straight news may be either hard or soft; the term applies to the form of presentation, not to the type of news.

Why has this story captured him? The obvious reason is that he can relate himself to it. It's a local story; when it mentions lakes in which he might fish himself, it reminds him that he could easily enter next week's contest. He may not know the girl or her family, but her address may mean something to him. And the image of the teen-age girl has a specific meaning for him; it's not something off on another planet, like the federal budget. Moreover, the story includes conflict which stirs the blood—in this case a contest, a winner, and some losers. There's a touch of comedy in the story that a seventeen-year-old girl came out ahead of hundreds of older, more experienced, better equipped men. And the bathing-suit picture, though it is entirely discreet, adds to his interest (as it adds to his wife's—interest in such pictures has been shown to be higher among women than among men).

The contest story is loaded with elements calculated to hold audience attention, elements that make it possible for readers to identify with the tale it tells and with its participants. It is a story about human beings, not one about statistics or abstruse concepts. As professionals say, it is strong in "human interest."

News of Human Interest

A story strong in human interest is one that gives the reader or listener a sense of personal relationship as his prime response to the event it describes. There are often human-interest elements in hard news, elements that provide the sense of personal involvement to the news consumer. But the true human-interest story establishes emotional contact quickly with its audience, and remains primarily an emotional rather than an informative or intellectual experience. When a story horrifies or amuses a reader, excites or depresses him, stimulates his sympathy or his sexual appetites, saddens or angers him, or appeals to his self-interest in any way, he becomes a vicarious participant instead of an outside observer. Since such a story allows the consumer to respond emotionally rather than intellectually, it requires less concentration and effort than hard news demands.

Radio newscasts give a lower percentage of their time to human-interest news than either television or the printed press. A principal reason is that radio has much less time, with its emphasis on newscasts that often last no more than three minutes. Television has been accused of devoting too much time to bathing girls, cats up telephone poles, crumpled fenders, and the like; but as TV newsmen improve in their craft they are reducing the percentage of this kind of material. It remains a fact of TV news life, however, that it is easier to present interesting pictures of a high school girl winning a fishing contest than of a proposal to increase the federal budget.

Human-interest news is published or broadcast, obviously, for purpose of audience entertainment, to fulfill one of the functions described in chapter 1. It is rare that a newspaper goes to press without a seasoning of this kind of content—news of the child who falls into a well, the sports hero crippled by an accident, a gangland murder, a student who breaks out of jail to take his final exam, a movie actress who marries a prince. Everybody knows that such stories are "good" news although they are seldom chosen for their informative value.

ADVENTURE AND CONFLICT   Since most humans respond to tales of adventure and the thrills of contest, newsmen give a degree of priority to such news as that of war, of athletics, of exploration. The extent of newspaper sports pages and the number of sports broadcasts measure the news media's awareness of the pulling power of athletic rivalries and of the hero worship accorded the men who can run faster, punch harder, or throw straighter than anybody else. News of crime and violence, news of conflict, is heavy in emotional impact; news media use of such news has led to sweeping charges that too much of it is published. (Reliable studies show that less than 10 percent of newspaper space goes to crime news.) Newsmen point out, however, that failure to report crime and violence would be failure to report the world as it is. They seem generally aware of the obligation to keep its use in balance; a study of Indiana newspapers' use of the crime news provided them by wire service was in almost exact proportion to their use of the other types of news provided. Readership studies leave no doubt that audiences consume such news eagerly; and some newspapers and some radio stations (few television stations) unquestionably overplay it. The decline of newspaper competition, however, has meant that the newspaper that goes all out to win customers with crime and violence has become more and more rare.

There is some reason to believe that such news gains more emphasis than it might otherwise because of the tradition of headlining or front-paging it. A Texas science editor with general news experience as well as graduate study in psychology, Blair Justice of the Houston *Post*, believes that newsmen pay undue attention to the tradition. In an informal investigation of newsmen's attitudes, he found most of them saying that they give more emphasis to crime news than their personal tastes would dictate. The question he asks: "Is the newsman really so different from all those people outside the building? Might they too have less interest in conflict than they have been given credit for?"

HUMOR   Every editor wants his human-interest news to make his customers chuckle now and then, and the leaven that humor and irony provide is in high demand. Unfortunately it is also in short supply. News with humor, news to make audiences laugh, is not easy to find; the humorous story can rarely be planned in advance. It is usually the result of an unforeseen event, and it has to be caught on the wing—the story of a fire that is delivered to the fire station (see pages 246-247), for instance, or the one about the thugs who cracked a safe and made off with $4000 in stage money. A few papers are blessed with reporters who can turn out humorous features several times a week; but there has never been a "funny" writer who hasn't produced his share of duds. The "brights," brief comic stories with which some radio newscasters like to conclude their offerings, are as often as not notable for their flatness. High level for humorous stories is hard to maintain not only because this kind of writing requires special talent but also because material is scarce.

PATHOS AND BATHOS   In the heyday of yellow journalism, many city newspapers employed "sob sisters" (often cigar-chewing males) who supplied daily tear jerkers; their excesses and their cynical insincerity brought news of human distress into some disrepute. The news media are nonetheless alive to the human-interest appeal of the story about the babies orphaned by an auto accident, or the courageous invalid who died short of reaching his long-sought goal; they use such stories as they come along. But the sob sister is no longer a staff fixture. Any staff member is expected to be able to handle stories about suffering and sorrow. The recent tendency is toward restraint and moderation; the technique of understatement has kept a good many writers on the safe side of bathos.

"THE SEX ANGLE"   Since the end of the Victorian era it has been respectable to acknowledge that men and women respond strongly to the stimulus of sex. The news media did not wait for the decline of Victorian gentility to recognize the human-interest value of sex relationships; from the time of Ben Day, sex crimes and illicit sex relations have been played heavily, often overplayed, in the American press. Emphasis on news with "the sex angle"—divorces among notables, adulterous love, crimes stemming from sexual impulses—came to its peak in the 1920s, during the period of the circulation wars among the New York City tabloids. Since that time, though there have been notable lapses, most media have held their treatment of such news within reasonable bounds. Occasional stories, such as the Charlie Chaplin Mann Act trial of 1943 or the Profumo scandal in London in the mid-60s, have overstepped, with an intemperance that thoughtful newsmen as well as thoughtful readers deplore. Except in a small minority of American newspapers, however, excesses of this kind are uncommon. And most radio and television exercise careful restraint.

"Leg art" and "cheesecake"—bathing suit pictures and the like—seem destined to remain common. It has been said that no French, Swedish, or Italian movie actress can be admitted to the United States until she has posed on a ship's rail with a suitable display of nylon. How the airplane will affect this form of modern art has not been determined.

THE ODD AND THE UNUSUAL   The proper place of the out-of-the-ordinary in news has been much debated. That the atypical provides a useful and often a necessary basis for news selection is evident: that a man goes to his office as usual is not news, but that he leaves home and never gets to the office may be a big story. Only the vital statistics column reports the birth of a single son to a family; but triplets get a paragraph, quadruplets call for big picture space and annual birthday stories, and quintuplets remain news all their lives. The news media are eager to present the odd and the unusual because readers give quick attention to the unusual in contrast to the routine, and because news of this kind brings color into the gray sameness of much of the day's fare. This continues to be true even though news high on the "oddity" scale is often strikingly unimportant. Few lives are affected because a Missouri family names all five of its sons Joe; but the odd fact gets broadcast and print attention on both coasts and everywhere between.

For a year or so the Saturday Review, a thoughtful and responsible journal, published an occasional column under the title "Good News." This was a collection of brief news stories emphasizing "progress and decency in America and elsewhere." The column expressed the editors' belief that such news is custom-

Critics of the news media say that emphasis on the unusual leads to a glorification of the unique, the queer, or the atypical that misrepresents common experience. This is a danger. Yet were the media to exclude all news of "abnormal" events (and who is to decide what is normal?), they would be implying that everything in their communities is on an even keel—no misbehavior, no accidents, no disturbances of the local calm, no departures from routine. Critics who ask that news of odd or unpleasant activity be sup-

arily buried under the weight of news of crime, disaster, and human frailty. "We can't claim to be well informed," said the Review, *"unless we know all the news, and not merely the bad news."*

One may question whether a selection of stories composed entirely of "good news" is more balanced or informative than a selection of the opposite character. It is not likely that the Review *would care to give up warning its readers that some books are bad. Furthermore, the implication that "good news" does not get published or broadcast would take a lot of proving; indeed, many of the specific events the* Review *column reported were reported elsewhere. News events similar to those reported in "Good News" are reported regularly, and usually at greater length than they were in the* Review *column.*

• •

Every newsman is a practicing psychologist whose success depends in some measure on his understanding of human responses and reactions, emotional and intellectual. Part of any reporter's equipment is a sound grasp of the fundamentals of applied psychology. College training and wide and careful reading will supply knowledge, but knowledge becomes understanding only when it is combined with useful experience.

pressed because it is not representative of "normal" life would seem to be creating a worse kind of misrepresentation: the false impression that there is no atypical, abnormal, or evil behavior. Just as society must in self-protection pay attention to the criminal who has put himself into an antisocial minority by robbing or slugging or defrauding, so also must the news media report such activities. Since the first necessity for combating any evil is knowledge of it, the news media have an evident obligation to inform the public of the abnormal as well as of the ordinary.

SELF-INTEREST   One psychological truth that newsmen translate into copy (as has already been made clear) is that a man is more interested in events or concepts that affect his well-being, particularly those that promise to help him toward self-advancement, than in events or ideas that do not appear to touch him one way or the other. Self-interest will make a man read a story from Washington about a new social-security plan with more interest than he would give to one about a new foreign-aid program: the first promises to benefit him directly, the second only indirectly and distantly. He willingly spends time on news of improvements in his own profession, business, or industry; he is eager for stories about medical advances that promise better (or lower-priced) health for himself and his family; he, or she, reads attentively the news about better housing, better clothing, better personal appearance.

PROXIMITY   The factor of physical proximity in the news makes a story more interesting to the consumer, as well as more significant. A man can relate more readily to an automobile smashup, a Fourth of July celebration, a fishing contest, or a political talk if he can picture its scene, if the circumstances involve places and people he knows, or if he can readily imagine himself among the onlookers or participants. He is, therefore, more interested in the event near home than in that at a distance.

News of events, places, people, or facts that a consumer already knows of are of more interest to him than news that is entirely strange. Personal contact is more than a matter of proximity: personal contact is the element in a story that directly relates to the consumer's experiences, and a story gains interest as it increases its personal contact with its consumer. The reader of the story about the girl who won the fishing contest would have been more interested if he had known the young winner, or if he had been a more ardent fisherman, or if he had won the same award himself the previous week. A football fan who has seen a game is in most cases a more enthusiastic and more searching reader of the next day's story about it than the man who didn't attend, unless perhaps the man who didn't attend is a player kept home by a broken leg or the father of the tailback who ran 90 yards for a touchdown.

NAMES   In short, stories that give a reader a sense of direct personal association with the news are pretty sure to interest him. This fact is the basis for the shopworn but valid axiom that "names make news." Small-town papers publish many columns of "personals" using specific names because names provide direct contacts for hundreds of readers.

Almost as interesting as the person, name, or fact that the reader knows by direct personal experience is the name he knows because he has seen it in the news, the name that has prominence. The little event involving the big or well-known or notorious name gets play in the papers because the reader quickly recognizes the name and has an attitude toward it; the familiar name has personal meaning for him, even though he may have had no actual contact with its owner. The small event involving the big name—a sore throat in the White House—may of course have importance as well as interest.

"IMMEDIATE" AND "DELAYED" REWARDS   Newsmen select and use human-interest stories of all these types because they know that most people find emotional news to which they have personal responses more interesting and entertaining than hard news. The typical reporter or editor working against a deadline spends no time on the general question of *why* news consumers respond in this way, but students of reader response, men who compare the consumer's news interests with his psychological needs and desires, have examined the question intensively. Although the descriptions of the fundamental human impulses or drives rarely agree exactly, the lists always include self-preservation, self-advancement, ego-satisfaction, sexual stimulus and gratification, and emotional fulfillment of thwarted desires for adventure and conflict.

A scholarly pattern for describing responses to news comes from Dr. Wilbur Schramm of Stanford University, who has extended Freudian principles into studies of what he calls "immediate rewards" and "delayed rewards." The immediate-reward type of news gives its recipient an instant impulse: as soon as he perceives the news, he laughs, or feels a jolt of sympathy, or tingles with excitement. This type of news delivers its reward the moment the news is received; the reward-response may have evaporated entirely a moment later (though it may also be renewed by a return to the subject). In this category Schramm includes news of "crime and corruption, accidents and disasters, sports and recreation, social events."

Delayed-reward news, news of "public affairs, economic matters, social problems, science, education, weather, and health," is news that does not affect the consumer instantly; its full impact comes at a later time. For example, the forecast of decreasing employment might not depress the consumer, but unemployment when it becomes a reality later hits him hard. Most news consumers find more satisfaction in immediate-reward news, and most give it the greater attention. In most cases, the instantaneous reward is a pleasurable one; the distant "reward" may often impose an unpleasant effect on the consumer's life.

These classifications of news are not hard and fast. Some news dealing with health or weather, for example, may have strong immediate rewards. Schramm points out also that these classifications do not apply to all members of all audiences in just the same ways: "a sociologist may read news of crime as a social problem, rather than for its immediate reward." A student doing a term paper on the United Nations will respond instantly to UN news; his roommate who is studying petroleum engineering couldn't care less. Herbert Kay, in analytic comment on the Schramm definitions, carries the distinction further: the rewards will be different, he says, for two men one of whom is a violent partisan of the UN idea and the other a man emotionally and intellectually uninvolved. He also points out that no reward at all will be obtained by a man who doesn't understand a word of the story.

The Schramm study from which these paragraphs are drawn is reported in "The Nature of News" in Mass Communications *(Urbana: University of Illinois Press, 1949).*

Any thoughtful man, newsman or consumer, may make his own analysis of these terms and ideas to see how they can be applied to his own and others' news interests. Newsmen, of course, are fully aware, though they would express the ideas in different words, that people are more ready to give time and attention to fulfillment of emotional desires and current appetites than to intellectual or distant needs. It is important, however, for the newsman to recognize that these psychological drives are stimuli affecting news consumption and that different kinds of news gratify different impulses. Nobody becomes a news consumer without having some kind of drive for satisfaction. Even the reader or the listener who takes time for news because "there is nothing else to do" is trying to fill a need to increase his enjoyment of life. Although psychologists *talk* about the news consumer's needs and drives, the newsman must *do* something about them. He must not only understand the ideas and be able to translate them into terms of consumer interests; he must also provide the kinds of news stories that satisfy his audience.

The Time Element in News

The time of a news event, when it occurred, when it will occur, is, as chapter 2 pointed out, an essential component of any news story. Time is an element that is always considered in the evaluation and selection of news, either of significance or of human interest. A news editor often chooses one story over another because the time element of the one makes its news more clearly relevant to his audience.

Newsmen have not always valued the currentness of news as highly as they do today. Until a hundred years ago when the telegraph and the cable brought a new emphasis to speed in news communication, news published in the papers was often weeks, and sometimes months, old. The test of news was not its newness but whether it reported events related to its readers' lives, whether it was appropriate to its audience. Letters received by sailing ship from Europe made news although the events they reported might already have been forgotten in the communities where they occurred.

A pragmatic reason for reporting the time of news events is cited by the perceptive assistant managing editor of the New York Times, Theodore M. Bernstein, in his informal "bulletin of second-guessing," Winners & Sinners, put out to help Times writers and editors do their work better: "Readers often like to identify themselves with news stories; thus they are interested not only in the place but also in the time the event occurred. 'Where was I when that boy on the ledge at One Fifth Avenue was pulled to safety?' they are apt to ask. The story [in the Times] merely gave the time element as 'yesterday.' . . . In stories of 'happenings' the hour—even if it is an approximation—should be given."

As wire communication made the time between the event and its reporting a matter of minutes rather than days or weeks, the insistence on speed in news grew stronger. On top of technological advances, however, another influence led to more and more emphasis on the newness of news: competition among newspapers. Primarily, the newsman seeks speed because he hopes to please customers by giving them "the latest" before his rivals do. A second and more defensible reason for speed is that consumers want the most recent facts about subjects that interest them because they know that nothing in life is fixed or immutable and that change is certain and often rapid, especially in the modern world with its breakneck pace. A consequence of the two forces of media competition and consumer demand has been the growth of a partly artificial criterion of newsworthiness: the more recent the event, the "hotter" the news that reports it. Although the consumer is genuinely interested in the latest news, for good reason, his interest is unquestionably heightened synthetically by the press and the broadcasters, with their stress on the superior quality of "hot" news.

Significant or interesting news stories are not invariably concerned with "hot" events, however, and newsworthy stories are not always reported within hours after the events take place. Two related qualities, timeliness and seasonableness, may give news materials validity for their audiences even when the news events are not current.

TIMELINESS   A story is timely if it is appropriate to the audience at the time it is printed or broadcast, whether the events or facts it reports are current or not. The difference between current news and timely news may be seen in the ways a newspaper published in a city celebrating the hundredth anniversary of its founding treats material on the centenary. On the day the celebration is at its height, the paper publishes a special edition. In one section of the paper, the news section, the reader finds all the details of the celebration: where the parade will pass, what the speaker said at last night's rally, what the governor said in his congratulatory message. All this is fresh news about current events, with a clear time element. In a second section, the paper uses historical articles, stories of the city's founding, its pioneers, its early days, and stories about the future of the city, the changes that the next hundred years may bring. None of this information is "recent" in the sense of relation to current spot occurrences; it is not news in the usual sense of the word. Yet its strong element of timeliness gives its publication *at this time* special meaning for its readers. The propriety of a story's timing may lend it news value even though the element of recency is missing.

Not everything that a news medium presents to its audience is news. In addition to timely stories that may not be recent and may not report current events, there is always material that has no time element. Obvious examples are pure entertainment features, comic strips and cartoons, or columns of family, household, and medical advice and comment. Newsmen use the all-inclusive term "feature" to blanket in all such material (see chapter 15).

Some of this material without time element is what newsmen call "time copy," the story or feature that may be published a month from today just as appropriately as today. Time copy—perhaps "anytime copy" would be a better term—is not pegged to a specific time, season, or date. It is material that the editor keeps under his desk blotter to pull out on the day when the flow of news slows up—the feature retelling an old tale in local history, one describing the many suggestions made during the last hundred years for revising or abandoning the Gregorian calendar, the story recounting all the attempts to conquer Mt. Everest.

The advertising content of a publication is not under discussion here. But it should not be forgotten that much advertising is news, recent facts about events of interest to a considerable number of readers.

SEASONABLENESS   Timeliness tied to a period of the year or a season is seasonableness, timeliness of a special kind. Seasonable stories are those that could be used appropriately at the same time of any year. They may be tied to a natural season, spring, the winter-storm period, harvest time, or to a date or period that has traditional and accepted customs and characteristics: Christmas, the Fourth of July, Halloween, Washington's Birthday. A news story about the increase of toy production in the United States is appropriate to the average reader's interests if it is published during the Christmas season; in July it would lack seasonableness (except for toy manufacturers, toy workers, importers whose key season occurs in summer). An article on the protection of tulip bulbs during the winter is seasonable only if it appears in the fall. A story about a well-known mishap to a cherry tree is appropriate on February 22, banal at another time.

Much material worth reporting because of timeliness or seasonableness is not properly news since it has no current or recent time element. Historical articles are not news; nor are stories about the origin of April Fool's Day, or about cherry trees or witches on broomsticks. On the other hand, genuine news may become particularly newsworthy because of timeliness or seasonableness. The story about the increase in toy production is current news made more significant or interesting because it is seasonable. A story in early February reporting that a forgotten set of Abraham Lincoln letters has been unearthed, important news at any time of year, gains added interest because it comes close to February 12.

News That Runs in Streaks

Older American newsmen remember the bleak day when the upside-down stomach became news. When physicians in a Midwestern city discovered that a little girl had a congenital condition that had disarranged some of her internal organs, it was decided to take her to a distant hospital for corrective surgery. A reporter in her city learned of the case, saw the opportunity for a human-interest piece, and coined the phrase "upside-down stomach," a reasonably accurate description, to make the ailment understandable for lay readers. Since the child and her family did not object to appearing in the public eye, the reporter's story was legitimate, and indeed imaginative, news enterprise. The story attracted national interest, the wire services followed it at length, and the upside-down stomach became nationwide table talk.

Then, suddenly, upside-down stomachs became endemic. If one upside-down stomach was news, the news editors seemed to believe, so was every other one. The wire services went along, dutifully reporting each new case. For days the daily news report seemed as dotted with them as a Dalmatian with spots. The newsmen had allowed themselves to become both perpetrators and victims of a news stereotype. They finally tired of the upside-down stomach, but not until after a good many of their customers' stomachs had turned. The reportorial shallowness was apparent to medical men, for, as one commendably curious reporter finally revealed, neither the upside-down stomach nor the corrective surgery was uncommon. They were not worth much more attention than thousands of other illnesses and operations that are daily occurrences.

The news writers and editors who belabored the upside-down stomach story were remembering the important principle of emphasizing news strong in audience interest. Here was a subject rich in human interest. It had oddity, it had pathos, it had suspense. It was soft news, news easy for almost any audience to grasp. What these newsmen were not remembering, however, was that the story became less effective each time it was retold. In its first telling, it had originality, warmth, intrinsic immediate-reward or entertainment value. But as newsmen kept repeating it because "if it was good yesterday, it's good today," it lost its freshness and became progressively more hackneyed and banal.

The upside-down story is a somewhat exaggerated example of a problem that constantly confronts newsmen. Let some reporter with more enterprise, more imagination, or more luck than his fellows develop a news angle that they have missed and they are likely to fall in line, seize on it, and work it to a painful death. When a Philadelphia newspaper reported, in the socalled "flapper era," that a "bobbed-haired bandit" had taken part in a gang robbery, "bobbed-haired bandits" popped up on every street corner. There was a period not long ago when the number of flying saucers reported would have hidden the sun.

It is not hard to understand what causes news fads. For one thing, it's easier to follow a well-marked news trail than to blaze a new one. For another, audiences build up interest rapidly in the kind of oddity calculated to develop into a news fad (and often get sick of it as quickly).

A third reason is that merely reporting an odd event may cause its replication. Harassed college authorities as well as many newspaper readers and radio listeners recall the "panty raids" of the recent past. They might never have become a national phenomenon had not a newswriter used the term "panty raid" for a bit of campus hi-jinks that was not new and certainly not brilliantly imaginative. But the term and the idea caught hold, first in the news media and then among the sophomore boys, who felt compelled to do exactly what the other boys were doing. Before the spring of the peak panty-raid year had ended, there had been some 80 "raids" almost exactly alike, and all duly reported from ocean to ocean. It was proper to report them; an epidemic of mass raids on women's dormitories by college boys needs to be reported as much as an epidemic of measles. But newsmen need to keep in mind that when they seize on a news fad, they may bring about more of the same, and that in chronicling it they trace a circle that ends not alone in reader ennui but also in their own desperate boredom.

There have been many examples of this kind of news circle: flagpole sitting; marathon dances; goldfish, phonograph record, and straw hat eating; telephone booth stuffing. Occasionally the reports of soberer manifestations that come in cycles, such as efforts to control or prevent the sale of comic books or "obscene" publications, may not only incite public interest but also lead to further efforts, and to more news.

Stereotyped news practices appear, too, in lazy diction. Not all newsmen consider all college girls "pretty" and all divorcees "glamorous"; but they use the word "star" with carefree abandon. (A star may be of two kinds: any actor, of either sex, who has ever been in Hollywood—extra points for extras in the days of silent films; or any man who ever wore a college athletic uniform.) "Turncoat," after the Korean war, seemed about to lose its validity as a colorful term for one who switched any kind of allegiance, for it became the only name

America has chortled, and Americans critical of the press have taken satisfaction, at jibes by A. J. Liebling at the laziness, carelessness, and superficiality of much American journalism. Liebling, a one-time newsman who for years wrote "The Wayward Press" for the New Yorker, collected his commentaries in three books: The Wayward Pressman and Mink and Red Herring, collections of magazine articles, and The Press, a set of informal critical essays growing out of earlier writings. All are stimulating reading for any student of news; but any

by which it was journalistically permissible to refer to American soldiers who had "gone Communist" and later recanted. It is well known that express trains are "crack," police round-ups "dragnets," and sex deviates "perverts"; happily "kiddie" went out with Shirley Temple's youth. This book will have more to say about trite writing in later chapters.

Among the most hackneyed of news stereotypes is the one that lures newsmen into believing that any story about any domestic pet or any small child is worth major billing. As with most stereotypes, there is some pragmatic justification for the habit of glorifying news and pictures of dogs that flag trains or steal the neighbors' milk, canaries that whistle "Loch Lomond," and two-year-olds who are addicted to bare-bottom strolls. No one doubts that most men and women respond warmly to news of this sort (if the

student should watch for the free-swinging generalization in which Liebling indulges, and the occasional lapses into brilliant ridicule as a substitute for logic.

story has pathos, the size of the picture is doubled, and so is audience interest). The sin is in the overuse of this kind of news. There is nothing inherently wrong in a dog story; but when the same dog story appears for the nth time in a year, cynicism and boredom are appropriate responses. And the suspicion that laziness has penetrated the newsroom.

The Responsibility for News Decisions

No responsibility in any news medium is as heavy as that of the man who makes its news decisions. His dicta govern whether his newspaper or newscast serves its clientele effectively or poorly. If he has contempt for his audience, if he bases his decisions on expediency and circulation or audience figures, if he grows mentally fat and lets news stereotypes do his deciding for him, or if he fails to keep abreast of the impulses and yearnings and events of his time, he cannot fulfill the public's rightful expectations. If, on the other hand, his attitudes and judgments grow out of experience and sound background, out of human sympathy and a deep-seated recognition of society's dependence on being well-informed, he is likely to meet his responsibilities creditably, and his accomplishments are likely to bring credit to him and to his profession.

Who is the responsible news worker who makes the news judgments? Usually he is the city editor or the managing editor (sometimes working with the news editor and other news executives) of a newspaper; the burden is always heavy on the city editor as the man who directs the news coverage of the local community. He is the director of the radio or television newsroom or the network news service or the wire service, the editor of the news magazine, the planner of the newsreel. He may be a reporter, even a young and inexperienced reporter; if he is, his news judgments are likely to be subjected to review by more experience heads. Usually "he" is the appropriate pronoun, for there are few principal news executives who wear skirts (though some have achieved real distinction). The number of women reporters and copy editors in American journalism is slowly rising, however.

What qualifies a news worker to make decisions? Ideally, he should be gifted with intelligence, perception, and social purpose, as well as such special personality traits as curiosity, imagination, sympathy, and energy. He usually has specialized news training and education, and long years of experience. There are other roads; William Randolph Hearst was given the opportunity to put his remarkable journalistic talents to work by his father's millions; Edward R. Murrow came to radio with a background in education and public affairs. But for the most part, the men who decide which events have the makings of news and which don't are men well grounded in news experience. The responsibility for news decisions is one that calls day after day for what sometimes seem superhuman qualities. That mere mortals perform so consistently "in the public interest" is one of the notable facts of twentieth-century journalism.

PROJECTS

1. Procure five daily newspapers from five good-sized cities, all published on the same day. Analyze the similarities and differences in the news they emphasize, noting especially whether they choose to play up the same nonlocal news.
2. From the emphases you find on the same papers' front pages write a commentary on the relative importance of local and nonlocal news. Show your judgment as to the validity of the news editors' judgments.
3. Compare the front page of the paper you read regularly with those analyzed in the projects above; then, using all the news you think "your" paper might have used but didn't, remake the paper's front page to your own taste.

CHAPTER 4

The Channels of News

Charles Chapin, the salty city editor of the New York *World* in its brilliant days, is quoted as saying that the kind of reporter he wanted on his staff was "the one who knows in advance where hell is going to break loose and is on hand to cover it." Chapin meant by this pithy remark that a good newsman can often anticipate the events that the public wants, or ought to want, to know about. Laymen, however, are likely to assume he meant something more mysterious—laymen, taken in by the glamor-boy (and -girl) reporters Hollywood has helped to create, often believe that a newsman possesses an extra sense, a handy built-in news divining rod that automatically sets his nerves jangling when a transport plane is about to fall or a football coach to fire his star halfback. The legend, which Chapin's remark appears to support, would have you think that newsmen cover news events because, whether by lucky coincidence or sixth sense, they are on hand when the news is being made.

Happy coincidences do occur. One of the spectacular achievements of television news's early days was NBC's on-the-spot report of a fine big Chicago fire. But it was neither intuition nor advance knowledge that had led NBC executives some years before to place their studios high up in the building that looked straight down into the heart of the fire. Nor was it extrasensory perception that led Leonard Coatsworth, a Tacoma newspaperman, to drive his car onto the Narrows Bridge spanning Puget Sound on a certain November afternoon; he was simply following his daily route to his home. The mile-long bridge always trembled in a high wind; that day it started waving like a ribbon. When Coatsworth lost control of his car, he abandoned it and crawled along the bridge to shore, getting there in time to call his paper before bridge and car plunged into the Narrows. He was on hand to cover hell when it broke loose, and he had a thrilling story; but he got no credit for X-ray news vision.

Of 76 general news stories analyzed in a metropolitan morning paper (excluding special news such as that of sports, business, social affairs, and the like), only five were of a nature that would preclude expectation or preparation for them in advance; 71 appear to have come through regular organized news channels.

News breaks like these are obviously not planned; if the media depended on them, the public would be ill-informed indeed. It is true that the media depend on anticipation of newsworthy events for much of their news, but it is anticipation that grows from carefully organized planning rather than chance. Many events cast long shadows ahead of them, and many others worth reporting take place within well-defined "news orbits" or else are of such nature that the facts concerning them are readily available at identified and manned centers of news. Every news medium, newspaper, broadcasting, magazine, wire service, depends on following a scrupulous routine that provides not only thorough coverage of news centers but also advance information about most events that ought to be reported. News coverage, in other words, is organized, not accidental. The reporter gets the story because he plans for it, plans either to be on hand to observe or to ask the right questions in the right places.

The remainder of this chapter describes the usual patterns of such planning.

Newspaper Organization

In the usual daily newspaper organization, the managing editor is the executive charged with supervision of news coverage, the captain of the news team. It is his responsibility to make sure that day in and day out his paper presents a fair and complete picture of the major news, local and distant, of importance or interest to its readers. The detail work, of which he does little himself, is delegated to several lieutenants and sergeants and a whole company of Pfcs.

The managing editor is usually in the third echelon of the newspaper's chain of command. At the top is the publisher, the paper's owner or his representative. Next are the editor-in-chief (often titled executive editor) and the business manager. The editor is responsible for the entire editorial operation of the paper ("editorial" means everything in the paper that isn't advertising) ; the managing editor reports to him. The business manager is charged with the management and financing of the enterprise; his immediate subordinates are the heads of circulation, advertising sales, promotion, production, and other departments concerned with financial, mechanical, and distribution operations. Although this is not the only pattern of newspaper organization, it is typical of most, and similar to all.

On most papers, the managing editor's largest and most important platoon is under the direction of the city editor. The city editor directs the news coverage of the city or local community in which the paper is published. He may be responsible for covering an entire city and some of its suburbs, or a small town and several outlying communities, or a section of a city. However the area is defined, it is the city editor's commission to see that his staff finds and brings in the local news each day.

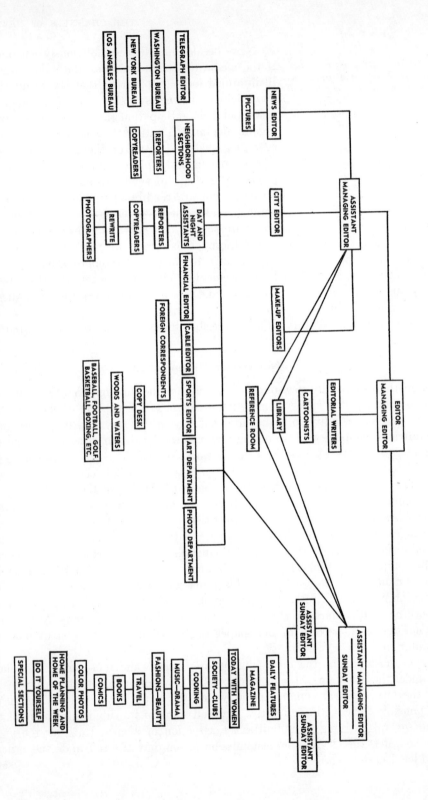

FIGURE 1   Organization of the news and editorial departments of the Chicago Tribune. Though it is exactly like no other pattern, it is similar to most. (Chart by permission of the Chicago Tribune.)

According to fiction and popular belief, a newspaper is a madhouse, and its city editor is tough, profane, harried, and always in a lather. Sometimes he is all of these, but more frequently he is a soft-spoken, businesslike newsman who gets results by careful control and thorough planning rather than by shrieks and shouting. Even Chapin of the *World,* who was both colorful and eccentric, was a master in organizing his news staff.

The heart of the city editor's force is his reportorial corps. The measure of his success is the skill with which he deploys reporters so that the major news of the day will be covered.

The city editor bases his planning on the fact that most news information centers in specific places. News of city government is to be found at city hall and other municipal offices. County news is gathered at the county building; crime news from police headquarters, from sheriffs, the FBI, and so on; business and economic news in banks, the chamber of commerce, trade associations, labor unions, businesses of all kinds; news of social welfare in the social service agencies and certain governmental offices. Sports news, transportation news, school and education news, church news, suburban-community news must all be collected through appropriate news centers.

To each of these news centers and to many others the city editor assigns "beat" or "run" reporters, sometimes several reporters to a large beat with many news sources, sometimes several limited beats to one reporter. No two papers have beat assignments that look exactly alike. Covering the waterfront is a difficult and important beat assignment in New York, Houston, Seattle, and Honolulu, but it's a song title in Butte, Phoenix, Indianapolis, and Calgary. The beat reporter must become thoroughly acquainted with every corner of his beat in order to gather all the publishable news each day. Chapter 7 describes the beat reporter's task in detail.

In addition to his beat reporters, whose work schedules remain about the same from week to week, the city editor has at his disposal a number of "general assignment" reporters to whom he assigns special stories. These stories arise often from sources not included in beats; or, if of beat origin, they are stories that demand more elaborate treatment than the beat men have time to give. As an aid to himself in such assignments, the city editor keeps a comprehensive date book or news calendar, so that he, as well as the beat men, can anticipate news events. Other news workers under the city editor's direction are a staff of photographers (picture reporting is an important adjunct of verbal reporting in twentieth-century news practice); several rewrite men, whose main job is to write stories from information telephoned into the office by the "legmen," the outside or beat reporters; secretaries, and office boys.

In some newspaper organizations two other departments are supervised by the city desk: the sports department and the women's or "society" department. On most papers, however, the sports department is jealously maintained as an independent division. Whether working through the city desk or not, the sports and women's departments follow procedural plans similar to that of the city desk; each has its director, its beat reporters, its unassigned reporters, its photographers.

This account of news-paper organization, though it applies to a metropolitan paper, may be readily modi-fied to fit almost any small paper. A daily in a small town may have no sports department; the city hall reporter may also cover sports, and business, and the airport, and even schools; the society editor may dou-ble as copyreader, and the city editor may write the editorials and cover council meetings. On the very small community weekly, one man is likely to do all these jobs himself, and sell ads and run the press as well. But the general outline is the same for all papers, for the differences are in scale, not in fundamental char-acter.

These news departments are organized primarily to cover local news. A second major division of the news operation is concerned with news from more distant points. Most large newspapers have a wire or telegraph desk, directed by a telegraph editor. This desk receives, selects, and edits copy from one or more of the press services: Associated Press and United Press International (and, in a few instances, the British agency Reuters and others). A major metropolitan daily may receive news not only from all these services but also from the Canadian Press, the Chicago Trib-une-New York Daily News Syndicate, the North American Newspaper Alliance, and other nonlocal or syndicated sources. Few daily newspapers can ful-fill their functions without at least one such service.

Many papers have a system of correspondents within their own circulation areas. Everybody knows of the "country correspondents" of the small-town weekly—usually women—whose weekly chore is to mail in "personals" and news of the "doings" in their own neighborhoods. Dailies often have state desks that direct large strings of correspondents. Many papers maintain correspondents at the state capital and some at the national capital, in neighboring states, in foreign countries. Simple or elaborate, county-wide or world-wide, systems like these must be directed, and the copy that comes in must be edited. Every news-paper must have an editor charged with this responsibility, whether by itself or sandwiched in with a dozen others.

The teletypesetter, a technological development of midcentury, has con-siderably modified the traditional wire-editing operation for hundreds of Amer-ica's smaller and some of its larger dailies. The electric telegraph device operates typesetting machines, often at great distances, without human intervention. Other developments such as new forms of typesetting are in the making. But all such changes affect editing and mechanical procedures more than they do those of the reporter.

Figure 2 shows one of America's most extensive and most successful city room operations. It is a complex organization. It shows each department respon-sible not only for gathering and writing its own materials but also for copy editing; the copy all flows to the big news executives' desk in the center of the newsroom. Most newspaper organizations would also show a copy desk—located just beyond the news editor in the procedure; in such organizations the news editor would decide on placement, size of head, and emphasis for a given story, and the copy desk would edit and write the head for it.

If newspapers contained only news, the city, wire, news, and copy desks would suffice to handle the entire editorial function. But newspaper content is designed not only to inform—to carry out the news obligation—but also to

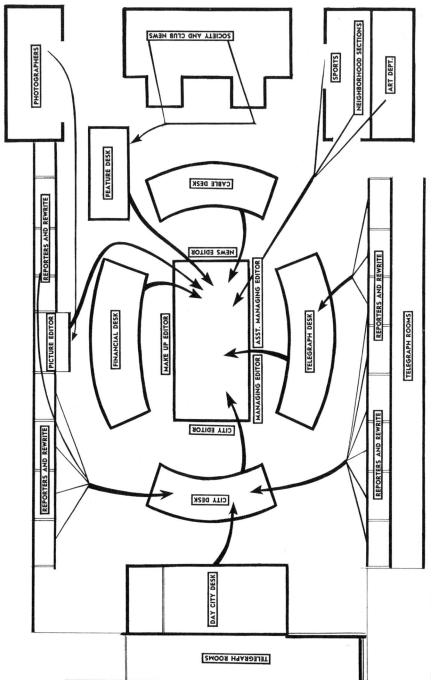

FIGURE 2   *The flow of copy in the* Chicago Tribune *newsroom. All copy passes finally to the managing editor's desk in the center. (Chart by permission of the Chicago Tribune.)*

express views and opinions, and to entertain. For these functions there are separate departments.

The views-and-opinion section of the paper is the editorial page and allied pages. An editorial-page editor, whatever his title, is responsible for this section. He is aided by editorial writers, research men and women, columnists, and special feature writers; many papers' charts of organization assign critics and reviewers to his department. The editorial-page editor is under the direction of the executive editor and usually bears no formal relationship with the news department; but a newspaper cannot be fully effective unless its news and editorial-page departments are able to work together. The editorial page may borrow reporters for research assignments, and the city desk may use editorial writers to do interpretive features.

Entertainment and service material in newspapers is of many kinds. Much of it is in the form of news features, either prepared by the city staff or furnished by the wire services. Much of it is syndicated material provided by outside services and often printed with little local editing or modification. Comic strips are in this category; so are many health and home-service columns, serial fiction, and Broadway and Hollywood gossip columns. The editing necessary for this material is sometimes the assignment of the copy desk, sometimes that of a special feature or syndicate department.

Papers with Sunday editions have separate Sunday departments with an editor in charge and a number of specialists; but much of the work for the Sunday paper is turned out by the regular city room staff.

Radio News

The newspaper organization provides the model for any kind of news-gathering operation, no matter how the news is to be disseminated. A radio newsroom that offers solid news coverage is, in most ways, a smaller version of the newspaper city room just described. Nevertheless, there are significant differences between the newspaper and the radio news systems, both in practice and intent, and great variations among radio newsrooms themselves.

Radio listeners prize news on the air. A number of studies of program preference have shown that news would be the last kind of program listeners would be willing to give up. But individual news "shows" rarely draw audiences as large as entertainment programs command. Several attempts at "all-news radio" have gone awry. But three well-manned and -planned all-news stations, as this is written in 1966, show prom-

The prime function of the newspaper is to present news, but for most radio stations news reporting is secondary. News gets a comparatively small portion of a day's broadcasting schedule even in the stations that take their news responsibility most seriously, spend the most money to support their news programs, and work hardest at competition with the other local news media. Traditionally the newspaper publisher takes great interest in the editorial effectiveness of the news his paper prints; but few radio stations are managed by men reared in the news tradition, and few hold that "news comes first." To most of the broadcasting industry, news is only one of several

ise of audience and advertising drawing power as well as of excellence in news offerings.

effective and profitable forms of programming. Almost no radio stations, however, get along without any news.

The amount of news and the number of words broadcast in any one day by any radio station constitute only a fraction of what a daily newspaper publishes. Even though radio has more "editions," any issue of a newspaper carries more words of news, and more individual stories, than most radio stations offer in a day. Radio must tell its news stories in fewer words, it can use fewer details, and it can offer many fewer news stories. A 15-minute sponsored newscast contains about 1800 words and 25 stories; one issue of a metropolitan paper may contain more than 100,000 words and hundreds of stories. Furthermore, radio puts the same story on the air half a dozen times; ordinarily a newspaper prints a story once only.

The average newspaper tries painstakingly to cover the news of its area for its readers. Whether it's a small-town weekly or a metropolitan daily, one of its prime purposes, and the task that demands more of its staff than any other editorial operation, is detailed coverage of its own precincts. In contrast, many broadcasters make no genuine effort to serve the local or regional news needs of their clientele; instead they "rip and read" the wire service news that comes to them from national or regional wire-service headquarters. Since the wire services must edit the news for scores or hundreds of stations, they pay relatively small attention to particular local or regional interests. Although a few small stations emulate the country weekly and broadcast news of local activity only, most radio stations do not cover local news as fully as the corresponding newspapers do, and some frankly develop no local news at all. It is significant that the FCC, in its "Standards of Practice for Broadcast Licensees," lists news broadcasts that are more than 50 percent drawn from the news wires in the same category as canned-music programs.

The distinguished former curator of the Nieman Fellowships at Harvard—fellowships to enable working journalists to improve the educational tools they bring to their work—stated firmly that "communication is all one job." In a report in the Atlantic Monthly on his 25 years as director of the Nieman program, Louis M. Lyons said, "Whether he reports for print or over the air, in newspaper, magazine, or topical book, or as an aid to public men in presenting public programs, [the journalist] is gathering and evaluating information, writing, editing on public affairs. The educational need is the same: to understand the issues in the great areas where a knowledge of history, government, economics, supplies the background to give meaning to the reports."

Size of station and size of home community do not in themselves determine the extent or quality of a station's news efforts. Some big-city stations (a decreasing number) have no genuine newsrooms and no qualified news personnel; on the other hand, some 500-watt stations in small towns have aggressive and well-manned news departments. Even a strong radio news operation, however, offers less news and more circumscribed types of news than does a competing newspaper.

Radio's basic news organization, as has already been said, is essentially similar to the press's. A news director is the "managing editor," responsible for managing the department, for making assignments,

•   •

Newspaper and broadcasting newsmen decry the "phony" newscasting that appears in some station schedules. They point out that some irresponsible broadcasters announce that they have "24-hour newsrooms" or that their news comes from "Mister News himself," although they have no competent or experienced newsmen on their staffs, no news-gathering or news-writing activities, and no balanced or complete news programs. These stations usually make no effort to give listeners an honest basis for understanding the news. Newsmen, knowing that professional news performance is not the product of ignorance and inexperience, feel that inadequate news offerings from such sources will reduce consumer confidence in all sources.

for establishing policy and news patterns. An increasing number of newsrooms maintain regular beat reporters who work alongside, and in competition with, newspaper reporters; but many stations think such extensive news-gathering effort unnecessary and overcostly. A well-financed station may boast a vigorous local news department with a dozen employes: news writers, editors, reporters, and "air men" who are sometimes the newsmen themselves, sometimes announcers who specialize in news. In small radio stations, the newsman is jack of every trade: he gathers local news, writes it for broadcast, selects and edits national and foreign news from the wire, and fits the pieces together for each succeeding air "edition."

Many stations have news specialists—sports specialists are most common, women's program directors second, and agriculture editors probably third. Specialized news programs usually occupy air spots of their own rather than portions of general news shows. In the stations that identify themselves strongly with regional areas, the newsman may have another type of news to deal with: news from correspondents in surrounding communities. A few stations boast as many as a hundred "stringers"; WMT Cedar Rapids boasts that it covers the whole eastern half of Iowa.

Almost all radio stations provide themselves with at least one wire service; the Associated Press and United Press International both furnish 24-hour teletype service for broadcasters, with news written and "packaged" for radio or TV purpose. In addition, many stations supplement their news broadcasts with network news; a few rely entirely on news from the networks (thus ignoring local news). The major networks maintain elaborate and expert news organizations, with reporters and commentators in news centers throughout the world, and special correspondents assigned to the scenes of important news events. In this respect the broadcasters have more news channels feeding their microphones than the newspapers offer; radio and television have the wire services *plus* network news forces. The press rarely has access to news the broadcasters develop for their own use.

Radio has developed some distinctive news procedures. Because speed is more important to broadcasters than it is to the press, which has already lost the race to be first with the news, telephone reporting is more common in air reporting than it is in news in print. Radio deadlines are usually more frequent than newspaper deadlines, and the telephone is faster than legs, autos, or buses. Radio has come to rely heavily on the telephone for local newscasts; a competent "inside man" can cover a whole city two or three times a day, and collect about as much news as his station can use.

The radio newsman also uses the tape recorder, a small battery-powered version which he carries about more easily than he could a portable typewriter. The tape recorder can be used for anything from a colorful sentence or a 30-second interview to a full-length speech. The enormous effectiveness of the tape recorder is that the exact voice and emphases of the speaker can be brought to the listener. Because many radio news departments are understaffed, the recorder has not been used as fully as its merits deserve.

Television News

It is natural that television news has grown up as a sister operation to radio news. Although some TV stations have no radio connection, the two kinds of news often come from the same newsrooms and even the same newsmen and announcers. The number of separate stories used in each 15-minute TV show is about the same as in the radio show; TV has, however, somewhat less total news "space" because it programs fewer news programs a day than radio does.

TV news, young as it is, has lost no time in outstripping its sibling in use of money and manpower. The anatomy of the television newsroom is vastly more complex than that of radio; because television must be illustrated, it needs cameras, dark rooms, editing equipment, and production crews. It has all the news handling facilities of radio—wire services, reporters, writers, editors, announcers—and adds expensive photography equipment, picture services, elaborate studios, and many more technicians than radio requires.

News practices vary widely from station to station in television, just as they do in radio. Some radio-TV stations have staffs of dozens of workers in their newsrooms. But one radio station making a start in TV news added one Polaroid camera to its radio news equipment, no additional personnel, no picture service, no mobile crew. And it put illustrated local news on the air.

The need for pictures is a factor that compels the TV newsroom to send crews to the scenes of news events. A radio reporter, or a newspaper reporter, could cover a fire or a parade fairly satisfactorily by telephone, without leaving his desk. TV pictures have to be made where news is being made. For this reason television has developed wide-ranging mobile units that sometimes give telecast news better local coverage than radio competition offers. But they also sometimes lead TV news to emphasize crumpled fenders and Sunday school picnics *ad nauseam.* (And competent radio newsmen are as insistent on effective on-the-spot reporting as their rivals.)

A difficult and unsolved problem for TV news is access for camera and sound equipment in courtrooms and other official quarters. The American Bar Association holds stubbornly to its insistence that picture making in the courtroom is likely to interfere with the processes of justice—a position that had more merit when picture-making techniques were clumsy and obtrusive than it has today. The Supreme Court has supported the ABA position by judging the Billie Sol Estes news "unfair" because of extremes of picture coverage. But the slow trend seems to forecast more and more freedom for TV cameras.

The News Magazines

News magazines like *Time, Newsweek,* and the *National Observer* (which appears in newspaper format), despite their differing deadlines and their broader range, maintain news-gathering and editing organizations similar in outline to the newspaper and broadcasting patterns. A look at the *Time* masthead, the list of its editorial and management staff, shows the far-flung character of the operation as well as the essential similarity to the newsroom plan. News magazines make wide use of wire and picture services; they have beat reporters in news centers throughout the world, and large staffs of editors in the headquarters offices. Since they always aim at national or international audiences, they do not face the local-news problems that newspapers and broadcasting stations must solve.

The three major magazines of Time Inc.—*Time, Life,* and *Fortune*—have developed a staff operation that their executives call "group journalism." Under this system, a single news or feature story may be the work of scores of reporters, researchers, writers, and editors; this is one of the reasons why you see no by-lines in *Time*. (The *National Observer* depends heavily on named reporters; *Newsweek* follows a middle course, combining group journalism with use of by-lined specialists.) An editor at *Time* headquarters may decide that a forth-coming issue is to carry a story on food resources in southeast Asia. He assigns reporters in the area to work on the problem; researchers at home and abroad begin digging into the facts; photographers start shutters clicking. Eventually all the information flows into the New York editorial office, where writers and editors, after filtering and refining the copy, produce the final story.

Some specialized news magazines follow similar procedures. *Business Week* maintains news bureaus and correspondents in more than 50 American cities; a few correspondents or a good many may contribute to the production of a single-column story for the magazine. *Time* maintains a large corps of specialists in the subject areas it reports, from foreign affairs to motion pictures.

The Wire Services

The news-gathering system of the international wire service is, in essence, another elaboration of the newspaper city room system. Although a war in Indo-china or an earthquake in Santiago presents more complex reporting problems than does a fist fight at Main and Center Streets or a cave-in at the old quarry north of town, and getting information about a war or an earthquake to thousands of newspapers and broadcasters is clearly more difficult than printing a story in the local paper, the basic operation follows the same lines. Just as the local news systems do, the news services station men at the nerve centers of significant news activity so that their reporters will be on hand when news information becomes available.

Press services send as many of their most competent men to foreign posts as they can afford. But students of foreign news coverage, recognizing that much of what the correspondents do is done excellently, point out that many reporters assigned to foreign posts do not remain at them long enough to master all their complexities and that, though major news centers like London, Rome, and Tokyo are well covered, lesser centers got more offhand treatment. The series of Middle East crises of the postwar period—off the main beats of foreign coverage— was reported in part by men rushed in from other posts, sometimes by men without adequate preparation and without knowledge of the tangled currents of Middle East history, politics, economics, and nationalism.

A careful study of the character and competence of American coverage of western European news in postwar years appears in The Foreign Correspondents *by Theodore E. Kruglak (Geneva: Librairie E. Droz, 1955).*

• •

Newspapers and broadcasting stations receiving news from the AP, the older of the two great American wire services, are AP "members"; the AP is a cooperative association rather than a profit-making enterprise. Those getting news from UPI, however, are "clients" or "subscribers"; UPI is a news-selling business controlled by the Scripps-Howard newspaper interests (United Press bought and absorbed International News Service, the Hearst wire service, in 1958). Nei-

A fundamental difference is that the newspaper or local broadcaster is primarily concerned with news of interest to a limited area. The wire service does not report news of strictly local impact; its function is to bring its members or clients news that develops beyond their ordinary spheres of operation. The great news services—Associated Press and United Press International in America, Reuters in England, Agence France-Presse in France, TASS in Russia—more often assign their enormous staffs to the world, national, and state capitals than to city halls. They put men on World Series baseball and national championship tennis, but not on the small-town high school games that are news only for the home-town papers. Their men usually cover news that is likely to be broadcast or published in a number of places, news that is of wide general significance or interest.

The Associated Press, as an example, maintains bureaus and correspondents in every major world capital; it has a big Washington staff, and it covers every state capital; it has a roving sports staff and a science department that reports scientific and medical developments wherever in the world they occur. AP carries the significant news about Little Rock, Arkansas, not for the Little Rock papers but for the papers elsewhere that are interested in the news because of its broad-scale impact. This does not mean that the AP's news about Little Rock or Chicago is never used by the Little Rock or Chicago papers that are members of the AP. Members get, and are free to use, whatever local news their AP bureau develops; indeed, they may ask the bureau for more thorough coverage of some events if they wish to. But in most cases they prefer to have their own staffs gather and write local news, with the detail and emphasis necessary to make it effective for local consumption.

Substantial differences appear between the news distribution system used by the wire services and that of the local news operation. The local reporter gets a story and writes it for his own medium, for his own audience—a short, swift operation. The wire-service reporter, however, writes a story that will go through quite a different process. Take a hypothetical case about an imaginary cloudburst and flood in Anderson,

ther agency may legally require an exclusive contract; a paper or broadcasting station may use as many wire services as it cares to pay for.

Every member of the AP is, by the association's rules, a news-gathering agent for every other member. Thus the AP is "protected" in Amarillo, Texas, for example, by the morning News and the Evening Globe-Times, its two local members. Any news developed by these two papers automatically becomes the property of the AP for whatever broader circulation AP editors decide to give it, and all member papers and broadcasters are obligated to "file" stories of more than local interests so that the AP can use them promptly. UPI generally maintains its own correspondents in Amarillo and elsewhere to cover such stories, usually members of local news staffs.

The wire services maintain well-manned bureaus in major cities.

• •

AP and UPI have been providing radio wire service to broadcasters since the 1930s. In addition to their basic news wires, the press services provide other types of material. They have telegraphic photo services, which provide pictures at electronic speed both for newspapers and television. The news services also furnish special features, columns, and other material, some of it by wire, but some circulated by mail.

Indiana. How would the UPI cover and report the story? Let us say that the UPI in Anderson employs a correspondent who gets on the job as soon as the story breaks. He writes a story and files it by wire or telephone at the nearest regional UPI bureau—in this case at the state capital, Indianapolis. At Indianapolis the story is relayed to the UPI's Midwest headquarters in Chicago. From there the story may be relayed again, possibly in rewritten or shortened form, to national headquarters in New York, where editors will decide whether it has national interest. If they decide it has, it goes on the trunk wire, and within a few minutes the story is in the newsroom of every UPI client in the United States. On the other hand, if UPI in Chicago decides that the flood is of interest to the Midwest but not the nation, the story is filed on the state wires of several states in the region, but withheld from the New York wire. If the UPI bureau in Indianapolis had considered the story of concern only within Indiana, it would have relayed it only to clients on the Indiana circuit.

Meanwhile, the story is rewritten in radio style for broadcast-wire clients, again with attention to its significance in various regions; it may go on the national, the regional, or only the state wire. When specially written services for radio were new, the newspaper story would usually be written and dispatched before the radio story; sometimes radio stations received the news some minutes after the newspaper did. The difference in time was rarely significant because, in most cases, radio could put the news on the air long before it appeared in print. In recent years, the wire services have tried to keep the time differential extremely small and to serve first, whenever a choice is necessary, the medium with the more pressing deadline.

At the New York headquarters the process of selection and distribution is repeated hundreds of times daily; it involves not only news from the domestic bureaus but also stories from UPI's foreign staff. All of these stories must be moved on national wires, perhaps rewritten or edited. The same procedure of selecting and distributing stories is carried out on a more limited scale in Chicago.

Word of Mouth

A book like this gives slight attention to one of the principal channels of news transmission—person-to-person communication. The reason is obvious: such communication, unorganized and unplanned, is not a topic one studies except as a socio-psychological phenomenon. There is no purpose to take a long look at it here. But some notion of its importance as a news distributor may be derived from facts found by a team of communications researchers at the University of Minnesota on November 22, 1963.

On that day, at a little before 1 P.M. an assassin murdered President Kennedy in Dallas. Beginning at 5:30 P.M., the researchers made 200 telephone calls in Minneapolis and its suburbs to find out by what means citizens had first heard of the shooting, and how much they knew of it. A summary of some of the findings will provide a student of news material for rumination. Among them:

1) Every respondent had already learned of the shooting. Three fourths of them had heard of it within an hour of its occurrence; all by 3:30 P.M.
2) Among men, half learned the news first from another person—direct personal communication; two fifths of the women did so. Most of the women were in their homes when they learned it, and most of them learned it from television. One person reported hearing of it from 60 other persons.
3) About half of the respondents told somebody else about the event. A quarter of the women telephoned others to report it.
4) Most of the respondents used only one mass medium for information, and TV was the medium most used. But those with college graduation had usually used two or three media by the time the interview took place.
5) Accuracy of information held by the respondents varied widely. A few knew the name of the man held in the Dallas jail; less than a fifth expressed reservations as to his guilt. A few described him as Communist, pro-Castro, even a Russian and a Cuban.

The point of all of this is that news, at least shocking news, travels fast by word of mouth. That it so often changes shape as it travels is an indication of the need for organized, dependable mass communication systems.

The Professional Associations

The two principal trade or professional organizations for working newsmen are the American Newspaper Guild, with 30,000 members, and the Radio-Television News Directors Association, with about 1000 members.

The Guild, a union organized in the depression years of 1933 and 1934, represents workers on nearly 200 newspapers in the United States and Canada (as well as in the wire services and on a few magazines). Its primary purpose is the economic protection of its members, who are not only news workers but often members of circulation, advertising, and other noneditorial departments.

It has raised salary levels and improved working conditions throughout the United States wherever it has had contracts with newspaper companies. Some newsmen believe that on many papers the establishment of "top minimum" salaries for Guild members who have been employed from four to seven years— the period varies from contract to contract—tends to make the required minimum, in effect, the actual maximum. But factual evidence seems to deny this. In many newspapers in which the Guild represents the workers, at least half the editorial employes are paid more than the "top minimum" would require.

The Guild has been criticized by those who think it pays too little attention to professional standards and the improvement of journalistic performance. When the Guild was established, its statement of purpose gave these matters serious priority. But as a result of economic pressure and the development of the "horizontal union" plan of organization, with noneditorial as well as editorial membership, the Guild, during its first two decades, gave principal attention to such matters as salaries, leaves, pensions, and severance pay. In recent years, however, the Guild, nationally and in some local units, has been increasingly active in efforts to raise the levels of performance.

The employers' objection to the Guild, more pronounced when the union was young than in the years since World War II, was based on the fear that a newsman's union affiliation might get in the way of his maintenance of objective, impartial attitudes and judgments in reporting news related to his union interests—news of employer-employe relations, for instance. Performance through the years has shown that this fear was unrealistic.

As its name suggests, the Radio-Television News Directors Association is an organization of the men who supervise radio and television news operations. It has developed along professional lines, with its efforts concentrated heavily on the improvement of news broadcasting. Although the RTNDA, organized just after World War II, is still a small organization—the number of truly professional broadcast newsmen from whom it draws membership is not large, and some broadcast management has little interest in supporting such a professional society—it has campaigned with some success to gain freer access to the news for both broadcasters and newspapers, as well as to gain wider acceptance in news-making centers for broadcasting as a news medium on a par with its printed competitor.

There are a number of similar newsmen's organizations on smaller stages: local press clubs in many cities, often more social than professional, and state and regional radio-TV news societies similar in purpose and program to RTNDA. The National Press Women has many state affiliates; one of its activities is a series of annual awards to newswomen for excellence in professional performance. Among other organizations of greater or less influence are the American Society of Newspaper Editors (daily newspaper editors), the National Editorial Association (mostly weekly newspaper publishers and editors), the American Newspaper Publishers Association (daily publishers), the National Conference of Editorial Writers (newspaper editorial writers), the National

Association of Broadcasters (station and network owners and administrators), and a number of similar state and regional associations.

Sigma Delta Chi, which draws its membership both from among college students intending to make careers in news or editorial journalism and from the ranks of practicing newsmen, cuts across media lines; unlike most other professional journalistic societies, it selects men from newspapers and news services, from broadcasting, and from magazine and free-lance journalism (its Greek-letter label is an anachronism dating to the day when it was an under-graduate "honor society"). A counterpart for undergraduate and practicing newswomen and professional writers is Theta Sigma Phi.

PROJECTS

1. From examination of all of the wire service stories in the first several pages of a daily newspaper, make a complete list of all the sources for the news information they present. (Note that a wire service—AP or UPI—is *not* a source of information; it serves the function of reporter.)
2. Ask 10 or more individuals how they first learned of some striking recent news event. Then write a comment on your findings.
3. Keep a week's "diary" of your own news consumption, showing both the amount of time you spend daily in the intake of news and the relative importance to you of the various media from which you draw. Write a commentary on what you discover.

CHAPTER 5

The Audiences of News

When Joseph Pulitzer was old and blind, the news from his New York *World*
and other papers was read to him every day by talented secretaries, who selected materials to serve his special interests and enthusiasms. Because the news
was distilled to suit the taste of one individual, the secretaries' choices would
probably not have served any other man as well as they served Pulitzer; their
selection would assuredly not have been the same, in quantity or emphasis,
as the selection made by an editor who aims at communicating with a "mass"
audience.

Although "good" news, as chapter 3 pointed out, must have personal meaning and emotional interest for each consumer, as well as significance for a
considerable portion of the audience at which it is aimed, news media never
select news to suit the interests or tastes of one person. News is the report to
a group, not to an individual, and editors and newsmen responsible for selecting news think in terms of collective audiences, often composed of many
thousands of men, women, and children. The theoretical goal of the news media
is to interest everybody to the maximum.

Newsmen know, however, that the audience for each medium and for each
particular story is peculiar unto itself, that the size and nature of each audience
is determined by many technical, geographic, economic, cultural, and social
factors, and that each audience is actually a collection of smaller audiences
and groups with different backgrounds, different needs and wishes, impelled by
differing influences. Newsmen are aware also of the paradoxical fact that the
"mass" audience must be reached only through the eyes and ears of the individual reader, viewer, or listener. Since no two humans and no two audiences
are alike, a single news story is unlikely to interest "everybody." In practice,
therefore, the goal of news is modified; newsmen try to interest as many people
as possible as much of the time as possible. Although a large quantity of "seg-

mental news"—news for groups within groups, news for specialists, news for minorities or minority interests—is often offered to relatively small audiences by newspapers and news magazines, and less frequently by radio and TV, newsmen always hope to make meaningful contact with the largest possible proportion of consumers within the mass audience at which they aim.

Audience Identification

If a news carrier is to serve its audience fully, it must know precisely to whom it is talking. Most audiences have well-defined limitations, interests, and characteristics. Many of a particular audience's characteristics are obvious even to casual observation; many are identified or described in standard reference works such as encyclopedias, histories, and census publications. Some can be described only by painstaking research. Geographical proximity is a prime factor in defining an audience, since an audience is usually the population within reasonable delivery distance of a newspaper's point of publication or within acceptably clear range of a radio or TV broadcasting signal. Although some media, the national broadcasting networks and the news magazines such as *Time* and *Newsweek*, reach beyond state or regional lines and describe their audiences in national and sometimes international terms, most media seek more sharply limited audiences.

GEOGRAPHICAL DEFINITION   A common newspaper and broadcasting practice is to provide area maps designed to show precisely where a medium's audience is concentrated. Newspapers speak of the areas in which they reach a majority of the homes as their "saturation areas." Radio and TV stations call the areas in which their signals are satisfactorily received by a majority of radio or TV sets their "primary areas." The maps defining these areas are often prepared for advertising sales purposes so that space and time salesmen can show advertisers the exact nature of the coverage the media offer. But since they show not only the physical extent of an audience but also the areas in which it is light or heavy, they obviously tell editors facts they need to know: Has the newspaper its share of audience in suburban areas? Do listeners in the industrial districts tune the station's signal in? or out?

When a radio or TV station is established, the extent of its primary area is predetermined by sending into the field engineers armed with voltmeters, instruments that register where the signal is strong and where it isn't. A station already on the air, however, knowing the electronic extent of its primary area, conducts house-to-house surveys to determine how many of the families that *might* tune to it are actually doing so, and why. It may decide to broaden its primary area, in effect, by broadcasting programs that will pull in listeners from its "secondary area," especially if such an area is weak in reception of other signals. Or it may decide to direct its appeal to only a part of the primary area it reaches, to the urban but not the rural area, for instance, or to a single community within an urban area, such as a foreign-language enclave.

Most broadcasting stations find the extent of their audiences conditioned by special and variable factors. One is that a radio signal carries farther at night than in the daytime. Station WHO Des Moines, a 50,000-watt outlet, designs its evening news shows to cover a much broader audience than its daytime shows, which are essentially Iowan in character. Another factor is that a directional transmitter—a transmitter that sends broadcast waves much farther in some directions than others—is sometimes required by the FCC to reduce interference. A third factor: The FCC grants some licenses for daytime—sunrise to sunset—broadcast only, or for greater power in daytime than at night.

Competition conditioned the news programming of a radio-TV station in Austin, Minnesota, in an unusual fashion. The physical area covered by its radio signal was larger than that reached by its television; but there were many radio competitors in the area, and, in the first years after TV went on the air, almost no television; so the station extended its TV news coverage well beyond the area it covered for radio.

All such mappings, measurements, and surveys show that audiences are limited and differentiated by technical and geographic factors as well as by particular interests. Imagine a big city with four radio stations (big cities today have many more than four): a clear-channel station of 50,000 watts and a regional station of 10,000 watts, both affiliated with national networks; an educational or noncommercial station of 5000 watts; and a "local" of 500 watts. The clear-channel station covers several states with its far-ranging signal; its audience may include residents in millions of acres of wheat and dairy land, a developing oil-well area, a desert or two, and half a dozen urban industrial districts. Its listeners are a microcosm of the nation; they include almost every occupation, every taste, every economic and social level. Such a station selects news of broad appeal; it cannot afford narrow concentration on its own city.

The less powerful stations usually have smaller, less diversified audiences; the 10,000-watt station may have a primary area no more than a fourth as large as that of its 50,000-watt competitor, and the 500-watt signal may reach only the receiving sets in its own county. The educational station, though its coverage may be about as wide geographically as that of the 10,000-watt transmitter, purposely limits its audience by omitting the commercial entertainment programs on which most stations build their appeal. Its programs, news included, are selected and treated more soberly than those of the neighboring stations. Its listeners, therefore, are selected not only by geographical and technical factors but, more sharply, by the special interests and the cultural and educational levels of the families within range of the broadcast signal.

Similar variations appear in television audiences, though TV audiences within an area are more nearly of the same geographical extent since the range of the TV signal is controlled by different electronic factors. A heavy increase in broadcasting power adds relatively little to a television station's range ("translators" that rebroadcast a station's signal and the development of "community antenna" systems, however, today extend the audiences of many TV stations beyond the few counties of their primary areas.)

The circulation range of the newspaper is comparable to the electronic limitation of broadcasting. What are the practical distances to which trains, trucks, or, in some cases, airplanes can take a paper in the relatively short period during which its news is fresh? The Des Moines *Register* considers the state of Iowa its territory; trucks and railroads lay down its papers each morning in every community between Moline, Illinois, and Omaha, Nebraska. The Chicago *Tribune* maintains one of the nation's largest newspaper circulations, about 1 million, chiefly because it is delivered at 7:00 A.M. daily not only in Illinois but also in neighboring Indiana, Michigan, Wisconsin, Iowa, Missouri, and even more distant points.

But most papers, particularly the smaller ones, do not attempt to reach such extended areas. Small papers cannot often afford the truck fleets needed for widespread distribution; and nearby areas within easy delivery range may have papers that provide adequate service. Some papers arbitrarily decide to concentrate their coverage on their own communities. New York has six general daily newspapers; but only the *Times* has significantly wide circulation outside New York's metropolitan area.

The size and nature of an audience are also limited by the extent of the medium's news-gathering ability. How far can its reporters and correspondents range? Should it, like station WBZ-TV Boston, maintain an ambitious staff of "stringers" throughout its primary area and attempt to cover competitors' areas more thoroughly than they do themselves? Or should it limit its news gathering to sources and events within local telephone reach? Are there reasons for supporting far-ranging foreign staffs like those of the New York *Times,* the *Christian Science Monitor, Time* magazine, and the CBS network? Should a newspaper maintain a state desk and a corps of country correspondents? Are reporters in the suburbs necessary? No two newspapers or broadcasters can give exactly the same answers to these questions, but every medium must answer them one way or another.

Radio and TV coverage, for the most part, is less ambitious than newspaper coverage, and radio and TV newsmen serve their audiences a more limited fare. They do not seek special or minority audiences as vigorously as the newspapers do, and they have fewer offerings for small groups. They highlight the significant news; but they present less news of crime and passion than the press does out of consideration for the "living-room character" of their audiences; some kinds of news are considered inappropriate for a portion of the eyes and ears that might be within reach. Another factor is that broadcasting is primarily an entertainment medium, and that both entertainment and advertising take precedence over news in the eyes of broadcast ownership and management.

Newspapers also have standard characteristics. Every daily paper uses one or two wire services, and all offer their audiences syndicated comic strips and service features that vary little from one paper to another. But every newspaper puts emphasis on news of special local or topical interest to the particular audience it hopes to serve. The smaller the newspaper, the less likely it is to be of interest to anybody outside its own pre-empted bailiwick. The American weekly newspaper continues to be successful in proportion to the degree to which it concentrates on matters exclusively of interest to its own locale.

Whether small weekly or great daily, in California or Connecticut, every

American newspaper offers its own well-defined audience a selection of news that would serve no other audience as well. It is obvious that the Hartford *Courant,* for instance, would not fare well if it were published in Sacramento. It may not be quite so obvious that the Duluth *News-Tribune* and the St. Paul *Pioneer Press*—both Ridder papers published in Minnesota only 150 miles apart—are edited for their audiences alone, until you examine them. Examination shows that the *News-Tribune* shouts "Duluth" from every page (advertising pages included): Duluth business, Duluth shipping, Duluth sports, Duluth politics; a feature reviews the year's developments in Duluth as a seaport, and a sports writer tells of bow-and-arrow deer hunting in the Quetico National Forest area.

"Why," asks the New York Times *or the* Christian Science Monitor *devotee in Tulsa or Tuscaloosa, "why can't we have a local paper that treats news in the same way? Why can't we have the completeness of news coverage of the* Times *or the interpretive treatment of the* Monitor?" *The reason is that there are not enough readers in either city who like the methods of the* Times *or the* Monitor *to provide a commercially profitable audience. Most Tulsans wouldn't buy a paper like the* Times *even if it carried a Tulsa dateline; they don't care as much about complete coverage as they do about Oklahoma news with strong local emphasis.*

When newspapers transcend the geographical limitations of their areas of publication, they usually do it by addressing special types of readers who are not geographically concentrated rather than by carrying regional-interest materials to many areas. The New York *Times* and the *Christian Science Monitor* of Boston are both called "national newspapers," but this does not mean that the *Times* would be a satisfactory paper for the whole of American citizenry, or even for the total news audience of Tulsa or Tuscaloosa; it means that a small group of readers in Tulsa, another in Tuscaloosa, and others all over the country are sufficiently interested in the *Times's* approach to news and its method of presentation to buy the paper. The *Times's* total weekday circulation, however, including its outside-New York circulation, is smaller than that of two of New York's general dailies, and larger than that of only three; the *Monitor's* circulation, including its Pacific, Atlantic, and Central editions, is the smallest among the Boston-published dailies.

Many audiences cannot be identified by geography: *Women's Wear Daily* carries news of the women's clothing trade to workers in that business; *Sporting News* aims for an audience of baseball players and fans; and the *Wall Street Journal* is published for the business and financial world.

OTHER IDENTIFICATION FACTORS   If every news event and every kind of news offering were of interest to everybody, it would mean that society had achieved psychological and biological uniformity; every reader of the Ottumwa *Courier,* every reader of *Variety,* and every listener to NBC would have to be a carbon copy of every one of his neighbors. Since, happily, the Aldous Huxley forecast of something like this does not seem likely to develop, though it would be a convenient pattern for newsmen, advertisers, and all the rest of the mass communicators, news will continue to offer different rewards and affect different news consumers in different ways. The degree of stimulation offered by any piece of news will vary with the number of consumers the news reaches, for no two of them have exactly the same origin, background, education, environment, taste. Since each audience is composed of groups of people, it is apparent that no two audiences can be the product of identical forces and influences. Every newsman needs to know what factors have contributed to the background and interests of the consumers in the community he serves in order to know how best to appeal to them.

Among the primary influences on a community are the economic and social conditions in which it exists. The audience of a newspaper or a broadcasting outlet in New England is concerned with shoes and textiles, metal goods, labor-management relations, and anything that affects industrial production. The people of a county in west-central Texas, however, find cattle and oil and the cotton gin more significant subjects for news.

National origins, religious traditions, political attitudes, and many other factors in a community's social and cultural environment help to identify audiences. Newsmen in San Diego don't forget that Spanish-speaking Mexicans are among their clientele; in St. Louis and Milwaukee and New Ulm, Minnesota, newsmen are aware of the German ancestry of thousands in their audience. News of the Catholic church, of Catholic activities, appropriately receives more emphasis in St. Paul than it does in Minneapolis, only two hundred yards distant across the Mississippi. The effect of political attitudes on the character of a community is readily visible in the American South, where the one-party Democratic tradition dominated political attitude, and therefore political news, for many years (the recent growth of Republican strength is demanding and getting recognition). The cultural and educational levels of an audience must be taken into account; a news medium in a small town whose chief enterprise is a state university clearly serves interests quite different from those of ranchers in central Montana. A newspaper in northern Wisconsin knows that its readers are concerned about the tourist industry, the prospects for good fishing, and the likelihood of an increase in governmental appropriations for highways. A Kansas radio station broadcasts the immediate and long-range weather predictions several times a day because it knows that its signal reaches a farm audience, for whom weather news is of great importance. The variations are endless.

Such factors, by describing audiences and their tastes and delineating a particular community's characteristics, guide news editors in selecting and emphasizing news. As long as there has been news, similar identifying guides have been used to suggest stories that have appeal and relevance for the community. Sometimes audience identification is self-evident. The man establishing a newspaper in California's date-rich Imperial Valley can decide, without having to reflect very deeply, that news of heavy industry will be of little direct concern to his readers. In Honolulu, a newsman can observe, without research, that Oriental nationalities are an element in the community with which he will deal. Frequently, however, exact, documented measuring guides are necessary. Data on the social composition of an audience must sometimes come from secondary sources. Census reports are useful for identifying the national, religious, industrial-economic, political, and cultural backgrounds of American communities, just as electronic measurements and audience-checking surveys help in establishing geographical and physical patterns.

Although the background and social composition of a community identifies an audience, all this description does not explain the inner individual responses to news or analyze the effects of news on the hearts and minds of the men, women, and children the media reach. A long generation ago a man named George Gallup —his name now a household word—began to think that the news media did not know enough about their audiences. Gallup was a teacher of journalism at Drake University, as well as a trained psychologist. From his own newspaper experience, Gallup knew that every newspaper office in the land discarded scores of news stories, hundreds of lines of copy, thousands of words of fact and opinion and human-interest every day because editors thought "readers wouldn't be interested." Gallup challenged the editors' judgments.

"You may be right," he said, in effect, "or you may not. But you don't know. You're just guessing."

Gallup persuaded the editors of the local Des Moines *Register* to play along with him in an experiment. He picked stories from the *Register's* discard, and the paper published them ("piffle-hook news," they called it in Des Moines). Then Gallup interviewed the paper's readers. He discovered that a good deal of piffle-hook news got more reader attention than much of the news more routinely selected; and he also discovered that individual readers were at least as varied as the responses to individual stories.

From this experimental study, aimed at discovering how much piffle-hook news (minor news, human-interest news) an audience would like to have, Gallup developed the so-called aided-recall method of studying reader response to different kinds of newspaper material. In its simplest form, the "Gallup method" is a formula for finding out how a public responds to given newspaper material by interviewing a "sample" of the individuals who make up the public. The interviewer, selecting an interviewee who has read a recent issue of the paper, goes through a copy with the reader column by column and item by item, asking whether the reader has seen an item and whether he has read it in full or in part. He records the response to each item. When the researchers think enough individual responses have been collected to constitute a satisfactory sample, they are tabulated and matched with identifying information: How many of those polled are women? men? children? Are they in upper, middle, or lower economic level? Are they well or poorly educated?

Since the development of this and other methods of modern audience analysis, the newsman knows more than he ever knew before about the impact and effects of news, and he can tailor his work with a surer hand than he had pre-Gallup. Specifically, he can order his news-gathering efforts so as to assure a minimum of lost time, of waste in collection of facts he will eventually discard because they are not relevant to the audience he seeks to serve; and he can select the emphases in the stories he writes with greater assurance that they will be the ones his readers or listeners will find significant or interesting.

Audience Response

There are about as many different responses to the stimuli of news as there are respondents. Though it is true that similar general patterns develop—most people who view a picture of the shattered body of a bomb-torn soldier respond with horror; most register approval at news of an advance in the "war" on cancer—no two are impelled to precisely the same thoughts or actions.

Some of the responses are anything but subtle or hidden. Let the radio broadcast the news that a fire has broken out of control at the corner of Main and Fourth Streets: in minutes police lines are swamped with spectators led by the news to go see the fire with their own eyes. Let the newspaper report that one type of cigarette is more "healthful" than another: the sales of "healthful" cigarettes zoom and those of other types slump. There is no doubt about the effect of news on audiences in large-scale phenomena such as these, and no need for costly research or elaborate analysis to show it.

More and more newsmen believe, however, that news can serve its public best when its effects are known with precision, when it is known exactly how given types of news handling affect given audiences, and how different approaches to news alter impact. Consequently, many researchers besides Gallup have developed techniques for analyzing the effects of news. A spate of specialized agencies for communications research have grown up since World War II: commercial agencies such as those of Gallup, Roper, Nielsen, The Pulse; academic or non-profit agencies such as those at the University of Michigan, Columbia University, and the University of Chicago; journalistic research agencies such as those at the schools of journalism at the University of Illinois, the University of Minnesota, Stanford University, and others.

The research men have investigated the effect of news on political attitudes and voting behavior, on the development of juvenile delinquency, on knowledge of public affairs, on conformity to current fads and fancies, on popular language. They have devised tests to find out which parts of newspapers and of newscasts hit their audiences hardest and are remembered longest, and what techniques of news presentation yield the greatest reader or listener comprehension. They have studied typography, rhetoric, and illustration. Although most communications researchers would say that studies in these areas have barely begun, that sweeping advances must be made before understanding can be achieved, it is apparent that a reporter, news writer, or editor can understand his craft and fulfill his obligations better if he knows of the achievements of communications research and something of the possibilities it holds for the future.

Through the years, many studies have been made of individual papers, some under continuing long-range programs, others in one-shot surveys. The Minneapolis Star and Tribune Company, a leader in the field, has been studying and analyzing reader response and reader characteristics for the two papers it publishes since 1944 (other leaders are the Des Moines *Register* and *Tribune* and the Houston *Post*). Many newspapers employ commercial research organizations to do some of the things these papers do for themselves. One could hardly list all of the things the newspapers have learned about their audiences and their own performance from such studies, things that were once only guessed at. A few of them from the findings of one major newspaper suggest their range at the time of one survey:

More than half of the readers were between 20 and 44 years old.

A third of the reader-families had incomes between $4000 and $5000 a year; and another 25 percent were in the $3000 to $4000 bracket.

The typical reader was a high school graduate. About a fourth of the readers had less than high school education; another fourth had gone to college.

Two thirds of the readers who had voted in the preceding presidential election had voted Democratic (though the paper is published in a state considered "normally Republican"—and though the paper had urged the Republican choice).

Two fifths of the readers were members of unions; most of the two fifths belonged to skilled-labor unions.

More than 90 percent of the readers had home telephones.

Two fifths of the readers read current magazines, mostly in the evenings. The most-read magazine was the *Reader's Digest,* by a two-to-one margin over the *Saturday Evening Post;* others high on the list were *Life,* the *Ladies' Home Journal, Good Housekeeping,* and *McCall's Magazine.*

Seven out of ten had listened to radio the day before the interviews; half had viewed television. They had spent 45 minutes with the newspaper.

Generalization about audiences drawn from such a highly specific study may be perilous; but the newspaper for which it was made can use the information to its own and its readers' advantage. Each of the facts, or sets of facts, suggests a larger body of information. For example, the paper not only knows that the bulk of its readers are in the "prime of life" period, it also knows how many are younger, how many older. It knows how many older readers prefer *Life,* how many the *Atlantic;* it knows that only a negligible few read the *New Yorker* (a favorite of the paper's editors). It knows how many of its male readers tend to be Democrats and union-affiliated; and how many women see the advertising pages.

Perhaps America's most extended study of reader responses to newspapers is the Continuing Study of Newspaper Reading, a research project begun by the Advertising Research Foundation just before World War II and continued through and well after it. During the period more than 140 daily newspapers were subjected to Gallup-method reader study. Sponsors of the study (Association of National Advertisers, American Association of Advertising Agencies, American Newspaper Publishers Association) were primarily interested in readers' responses to advertising, but the studies did not stop there. Reader response to every piece of news, every feature, every editorial in each of the papers was reported. Though the CSNR itself does not draw conclusions, some conclusions appear obvious. Any experienced newsman, examining the data given here, would form some opinions; he would form more from the full report of the study.

In the 15 years of the study the general news story that drew the highest percentage of readers of any of the 17,887 stories examined was one published in the Indianapolis *News* on May 7, 1945: "Hostilities in Europe End; Huns Sign Terms." Of all those who read that day's *News*, 94 percent of the men and 87 percent of the women read the story. This story had both extraordinary importance and extraordinary human interest; it impinged on some special concern of almost every reader—relatives or friends in service, business problems, daily pressures. Perhaps the wonder is that some 10 percent missed the story.

That an international-news story won top interest among men was typical of the studies' findings. In 138 studies, 18 of the 32 stories that scored highest among male readers contained national and world news; only 14 dealt with local news. Women, on the other hand, gave their highest attention, 91 percent, to a story in the Lima, Ohio, *News* about the death of a local judge. Of the 34 stories that drew most attention from women, 23 contained local news, and among all the stories women preferred local news by almost three to one.

This is consistent with the fact that women gave more attention to news about people than men did. Of the 32 stories most read by men, only 12 dealt primarily with individuals; of the 34 that women preferred, 25 dealt with identified individuals.

Some of the data support responses one might have expected, and others don't. One might not suppose that front-page news does not necessarily outdraw news on other pages, nor that "position" news does not always command most attention. Not many people are astonished that pictures receive more attention than any other one type of material, that sports news gets fairly heavy attention from men and little from women, or that "women's features" hold the interest of three times as many women as men. Men read the daily weather news more eagerly than the broadcasting listings or the obituaries; women put obituaries first among these three, weather second, the broadcasting log third.

Generalization from these data as from others may be dangerous. Men's and women's responses show some sharp differences; but 15 of the "most-read" stories, nearly half of them, appeared on both men's and women's lists. It is true that women paid more attention to local news than did their husbands; but women also read local columnists less than men, and Hollywood columnists more.

As in the individual newspaper studies described earlier in this chapter, the relationship between special audience characteristics and readership has been analyzed. The summary of 138 of the studies showed few differences, for example, among readers in four economic-occupational groups: business and professional families, salaried families, skilled laborers, and unskilled laborers. "Editorial page items" (columns, cartoons, features, editorials, letters) were read most frequently by men in all groups. Next for men came display advertising, which was a shade ahead of comics; sports news came fourth. Women in all groups put advertising far ahead of anything else; then came editorial-page material and society news and features. Although editorials drew only 29 percent of women and

43 of men, the extent of readership followed the economic-cultural pattern: business and professional men and women read them most, unskilled laborers least.

What a newsman does with this information about his customers is clearly up to him. One newspaper experimented by making two trial front pages, one entirely of news that scored high in feminine readership, one of news that men preferred. The results were not "good" front pages; in fact, the experiment showed how unsatisfactory would be a newspaper whose news was selected only on the basis of reader-attraction. Perhaps what this proves is that findings such as these can be used to determine what you shouldn't do as well as what you should.

If newspapers have done a lot of looking in the mirror, the other media have done it too. Indeed, magazines and broadcasting started studying their audiences and the effectiveness of their products before the newspapers did. Radio and TV news presentations have been modified, for example, after studies that showed what the optimum number of stories for a 15-minute newscast is, or what kind of audience is listening where, and at what time; farmers, for instance, listen or view at hours quite different from those favored by urban dwellers. CBS, with an elaborate research department, has studied both its audiences and its programs in depth. A confusing number of research agencies serve the broadcasting industry, both in the elaborate nose counting of listenership to individual programs and in audience response to questions about broadcasting. Both Congress and the FCC have taken long looks at what they think are faults in "audience-counting" by Nielsen, the American Research Bureau, The Pulse, and other agencies; and the industry itself, through the National Association of Broadcasters, is involved in efforts to improve this kind of research.

Not only must a journalist, as Ben Hibbs says, avoid trying to edit by statistics. He has also to be sure what the statistics really say. Three careful studies of TV audiences were reported in the winter and spring of 1965; they added up to superficial confusion. One "proved" that almost half of television viewers were dissatisfied with programing, and that a fifth called it "terrible," while only a fiftieth called it "great." Another reported that "public acceptance of television is now higher than at any time from 1959 to 1964." The third produced evidence to show that television was losing appeal to the well-educated, the upper income groups, and Americans leaving their teens, and gaining allegiance from those with limited education, low income, and fifty years or more of age. Similar apparent differences might be deduced from

Magazines have conducted intensive audience study for nearly half a century, at the cost of millions of dollars. The Curtis Publishing Company for years made regular studies of the readership of the *Saturday Evening Post*, the *Ladies' Home Journal, Holiday,* and other magazines. *Time* has mountains of data about the character and attitudes of its readers, and is constantly adding more. *Better Homes & Gardens* uses both its own elaborate research forces and the services of commercial agencies to keep abreast of the habits, the desires, the day dreams of what it calls "the middle majority," the vast body of Americans whose families provide *Better Homes & Gardens* multimillion circulation. Advertising agencies and advertisers, thanks to research, know a great deal about all these media and the support and responses of their audiences.

And with it all, no astute newsman, no editor, no wise media executive thinks that all he needs to know

statements about the appeal of news on the air. But the polls measured different audiences in different ways with different questions, and blanket indictment of all because of surface disagreement would have been as misleading as trying to show any one wrong because it seemed to deny another.

he can gain from quantitative data. "You can't edit a magazine by arithmetic," Ben Hibbs said when he was editor of the *Saturday Evening Post*. His illustrious predecessor, George Horace Lorimer, considered reading his mail and making personal contact with readers through wide travel the best method of knowing his audience. The expense, complexity, and magnitude of statistical procedures should never blind the eye to the fact that talent, intelligence, and personal editorial contributions can, and do, build great editorial enterprises.

No more may they be allowed to blind the reporter to his own responsibilities. The results of audience studies conducted by his own newspaper or his own broadcasting station may be open to him, and they will help him; so will the studies conducted in a thousand other contexts. But what he finds out is that on his own the questions he asks in the right places and the observations he makes on and off the job will help him at least as much. News must always be gathered, winnowed, and written to serve a highly particular audience; and the man who does it, the reporter, ideally ought to know more about the audience for each story he writes than anybody else.

PROJECTS

1. (a) Make a list of what you believe are the principal audience interests to which the news media in your community should give attention: political, industrial and economic, educational and cultural, religious, social, national or racial origin, and so on. (b) Check your subjective findings against reliable source books: census, encyclopedia, fact books, library reference materials. (c) Now compare the news, local and nonlocal, in your local daily paper or on the air against the audience interests you have identified. Write a report on your findings.
2. Interview 10 or more members of one of the prominent subgroups you have identified in the local audience, asking their opinions as to the effectiveness of local news coverage of activities of special interest to the group. Summarize and comment on their statements.

SUGGESTED READINGS

Among periodicals that often report the findings of communications research are the *Journalism Quarterly*, which says of itself that it is "devoted to research studies in the field of mass communications"; the *Audio Visual Communication Review*; the *Journal of Applied Psychology*; the *Journal of Marketing*; the *Journal of Broadcasting*; the *Television Quarterly*; and the *Public Opinion Quarterly*. Reports on research studies appear somewhat less systematically in *Advertising Age, Broadcasting, Bulletin* of the National Association of Educational Broadcasters, *Editor & Publisher, Printers' Ink, Public Relations Journal, Sponsor, Tide,* and other specialized or trade publications. A bibliography of current magazine articles on American and foreign journalism appears in the *Journalism Quarterly.*

Among more recent books dealing with mass communications research are the following:

Berelson, Bernard, Paul F. Lazarsfeld, and William N. McPhee, *Voting: A Study of Opinion Formation in a Presidential Campaign.* Chicago: University of Chicago Press, 1954.

Campbell, Angus, Philip E. Converse, Warren E. Miller, and Donald E. Stokes, *The American Voter.* New York: Wiley, 1960.

DeFleur, Melvin L., and Otto N. Larsen, *The Flow of Information.* New York: Harper & Row, 1958.

Klapper, Joseph T., *The Effects of Mass Communication.* New York: Free Press, 1960.

Schramm, Wilbur, *Mass Communication,* 2d ed., Urbana, Ill.; University of Illinois Press, 1960.

———, *Process and Effects of Mass Communication.* Urbana, Ill.; University of Illinois Press, 1954.

———, *Science of Human Communication.* New York: Basic Books, 1963.

CHAPTER 6

Organization of a Newsroom

Successful news coverage, as the chapter on news channels made clear, is a matter of careful organization and planning, organization and planning inspired by imagination, backed by factual knowledge, and activated by tireless effort and persistence. Reporters are not called "legmen" for nothing; news gathering requires energy.

In newspaper practice, news gathering normally begins at the city desk. Although radio, television, and the news magazines do not use the apt term "city desk," each has a director of news operations whose position corresponds to that of city editor. An examination of the city room operation of a typical medium-sized daily will show in outline how any kind of news-gathering system functions.

Take an afternoon daily, with a "final" edition printed at 3:30. Make its locale the county seat in an agricultural area, the trading center for a population of 100,000; say it has some light industry, several radio and TV stations, a small college. Make the city editor a man of 40, experienced on three or four papers. Call him Miller.

Miller gets to work at 7:00 each weekday morning—his paper has no Sunday edition. There's no newspaper competition in his town, but at breakfast he read the morning paper from a bigger city a hundred miles away. He has listened to two early morning newscasts, one while he was shaving, the other while driving to the office. Already he has a firm grasp on the major news of the day. Most of the news stories he has heard or read this morning are of nonlocal origin; he knows that his paper's wire service will provide coverage of them. But he has picked out two stories for special local attention: one about the Washington crop forecasts, the second about a new movie actor announced as the surprise lead in a major Hollywood production. He pegs these two for the day's work.

The City Desk

Miller's first task after he gets to his desk is to glance through the "overset," the long proof sheets of news that was put in type for yesterday's paper but not used. With a black pencil he quickly "kills" a number of stories no longer usable; in some stories he changes "today" and "tomorrow" to read "yesterday" and "today"; he clips some of the stories and puts them aside. The edited galley proofs go into the basket for the composing room.

Next he reads through the copy turned out by reporters after yesterday's paper had gone to press: a couple of speeches delivered last night and some features he had assigned after yesterday's deadline. He checks them rapidly, edits here and there, lays one aside for a new lead. The others he tosses on the news editor's desk nearby.

Now he outlines today's local news schedule. He uses a big diary-like calendar, with a page for each day, for recording "futures." (City editors use many kinds of "tickler"—dated Manila folders, sheaves of notes and memos, card files, desk calendars.) On today's page, Miller finds notes on a dozen stories that must be covered—two conventions, a style show, a visit by a senator, and other specific events—as well as several general reminders, such as "Check new bus depot." He clips yesterday's paper for stories that need follow-up today. He fishes in his coat pocket for notes he has written to himself. He may come up with 5 to 50 tips for today's news by the time the reporters and desk men come in.

Titles may not mean much on a small newspaper. "City editor" is an invariable term, but the wire editor is often called the managing editor and the copyreader the news editor, and so on. The duties of each job change from paper to paper and from title to title, too; each news system molds its own pattern. When all the functions are viewed at once, however, the total is about the same on equivalent papers, no matter how the jobs are described or the work is divided.

Miller's staff includes three men and a woman. The woman covers the college and the public schools and does society and club news, as well as feature assignments; one man covers county and other offices as well as special assignments; one doubles as sports and farm editor; the third is a recent addition, a photographer inevitably nicknamed "Click." Miller himself covers the city hall beat. "Man ought to get out on the street every day," he says, "if he wants to know what's going on."

In addition, there are a wire editor, a news editor-copyreader, and an office boy. The managing editor will be in later; one of his jobs is writing editorials, and he was able to do those yesterday afternoon. The elderly editor—"the Old Man"—who is also the publisher, has not been very active in recent years, but he'll look in for an hour or so late in the morning, bringing copy for the nostalgic column he writes for the editorial page.

The major early-morning task for the city editor is the assignment sheet (some city editors do it the night before). This may be a long memo posted on the office bulletin board, or a series of individual memos to reporters. Miller writes each reporter's instructions on a separate sheet. He keeps a carbon for himself so that as the assignments are met he can check them off. One set of assignments is for Don Finnegan, the young reporter who covers the county beat:

```
FINNEGAN
MEDICS' CONVENTION--Here's yesterday's clip. Follow
up for today. Cover Osborn cancer speech this A.M.--
we'll give it a play. Get something on the afternoon
panel if you can. See whether you can get the slate
of nominees for the elections (tomorrow). We can use
up to a column, or maybe two shorter pieces.
FIRKINS TRIAL--Anything on this yet? Is it on the
calendar? How jammed-up is the District Court
docket?
SWIM POOL--Doc Nelson told me last night he thinks
the pool in City Park is dangerously polluted. See
him; also park officials. Might be a pretty good
story if Nelson will talk. The park boys will prob-
ably be mad. Be sure to see Nelson first.
FEATURE--Seems to me there ought to be a good longish
feature on the number of non-municipal official and
quasi-official offices we have in town--federal,
state, county, etc. Don't forget Grange, Am. Legion,
and so on. Might start working on this after dead-
line this P.M. No hurry.
CONCERT--Could you take a look in at the band con-
cert this evening? We don't need a lot, but we ought
to have a short piece. Or a feature if you can dig
one up. This is a pet of the Old Man's, and he can
give you some background.
NEW BUS DEPOT--Check it again. Shouldn't we call it
"station"?
COVER YOUR BEAT.
```

Miller makes similar sheets for his other staffers. On the woman reporter's sheet he writes:

```
BY ANY OTHER NAME .... Check up on Jay Jensen, the
young movie actor who has just been picked for that
big film role. If I'm not mistaken, he used to be
Josiah Schuffelgruber from out on a farm north of
Elden Center. Get a picture of him as J.S. if you
can.
```

Miller writes to the farm editor:

```
CROP FORECASTS--See what the county agent and five
or six leading farmers think of the Washington
forecast.
```

Next Miller has a conference with the wire editor and the news editor-copy-reader, reporting to them what local stories he expects for the day; together they decide what the "play stories" are to be. They need a picture for the front page the news editor is planning. Miller amends the photographer's assignment orally: "Get a good shot of a lot of kids in the City Park pool. Finnegan is doing the story." A telephone call from the airport announces a flight of Air Force planes due for an unscheduled visit; Miller tells a reporter to get there later with the photographer or with his own camera.

"No news today," a newsman sometimes growls disgustedly. He doesn't mean it literally: the paper will be as full of stories as usual. He means that the news is dull, that the day has not brought news of great interest or importance.

There is no inhabited community which has literally "no news." In the modern world, the wire services always supply more nonlocal news than a newspaper or broadcaster can use. The local news may not be exciting, but only an abandoned ghost town in the Nevada desert has no news. When a reporter finds a shortage of local news, he ought to examine his own enterprise, imagination, or energy. The amount of publishable news is limited by a newsman's concept of news, but not by lack of newsworthy material.

Then Miller goes out "on the street." First, he has a cup of coffee at the Corner Drug where he chats with cronies and, as always, picks up story ideas; he moves on to his beat, the city hall—mayor, councilmen and other officials, the police and fire departments, other municipal offices.

Back in the office, Miller writes the stories he has picked up; he takes some scratched notes out of a pocket and composes his daily column of local anecdotes. The reporters return, one by one, to write their stories. They tell him when they have failed to complete assignments or when they are developing new stories. Miller's pencil cuts through the copy as it comes across his desk, paring, editing, sharpening. Then the copy goes to the copyreader, who writes heads for it and gives it final polishing before sending it on to the composing room.

Miller has had a fairly routine day. Some are vastly more exciting and vastly more confused—the days of the big blizzards, elections, the annual Harvest Festivals. At such times, routine may go out the window, and everybody from the Old Man down may be pressed into special service. Although some days are even more placid than today, the daily schedule usually follows the pattern of this one with its rhythm of locating the focal points of news, identifying particular events that must be covered, and seeing to it that staffers are where they ought to be, and when.

The main burden of the day's work, on a daily such as this one, is finished by noon. Most of the local copy is written; the principal beats have been covered; the wire news for the day has been selected, edited, and set in type. After a hasty lunch Miller and his staff check the last-minute stories; perhaps they make final runs over their beats. They telephone for late information. By midafternoon the last copy deadline has passed, and the presses roll. The paper is in thousands of homes before the family assembles for dinner.

A reminder of what has been said several times before in this book: The procedures of broadcast and magazine newsmen in covering news differ in detail from those of newspapers and the work of other newsmen; but in principle and in broad lines they are the same. The radio news director has to organize his staff and his day so as to report the day's events; he has to look ahead to future events; he has to decide what regular news sources to attend on a beat basis.

And before that hour the staff is at work on tomorrow's paper. Finnegan is starting work on that feature on nonmunicipal officialdom; the women's page editor is looking into the history of a farm boy named Josiah Schuffelgruber. The business editor starts planning next Friday's market page, which has to have roundups of food and produce news from half a dozen nearby communities. Miller checks his futures book, entering events that he must be sure to cover next week, next month, next year. He advises a reporter on the construction of a new lead that will get his story off to a quicker start, and he makes a list of assignments for the 50th Anniversary issue to be put out in six months. Perhaps he runs down the street to talk with a banker who has been refusing to help the business reporter with financial stories. He and the photographer plan a picture story on the backyard zoo some kids on the West Side have started. He's likely to be hard at it long after his staff has left for the day.

The city desk is the heart of most newspaper news-gathering systems; but it is surrounded by and works closely with other departments with similar purposes and often similar procedures. Among the principal ones:

THE WIRE DESK   This is a center of news reception rather than of news gathering, since its "reporters" are principally the wire services. Its function is largely to receive, edit, and consolidate materials that come by wire rather than to originate assignments; but from time to time a wire editor demands further coverage of an event by one of his services, or suggests coverage on stories the services have missed. The two chief points of contact between city and wire desks are in joint decision as to what news is to receive emphasis and in the relay of tips by the wire editor to the city desk concerning stories whose "local angles" must be locally developed.

The largest newspapers distinguish between wire desks and cable desks. Some also have separate state or regional desks.

THE PICTURE DESK   Most photographic assignments are made by or through the city editor or the editor of a specialized department, such as sports or women's. But pictures are edited and captioned by the picture editors; and picture features are largely planned by them. (Only the largest papers maintain separate photo desks.)

CORRESPONDENCE   Stories from a newspaper's correspondents, if they come by wire or cable, are usually routed through the wire or cable editor or the state desk. But the small paper that maintains wide coverage of the small towns in its circulation area must have a "correspondence editor," whether he gives full time to the task or splits his day between this and other duties.

SPECIALIZED DEPARTMENTS   Whether the paper (or the broadcasting news operation) is large or small, it is pretty sure to have news employes assigned to special fields of news. Most common, indeed almost universal, are sports and women's news fields. Others that are often given special attention are business, agriculture, entertainment, and science.

PROJECTS

1. Go through every local news story in one issue of a daily paper and determine the news sources from which the newswriters procured their information. Make a list of all the sources, showing how often each is used. Write a comment on what you have found.
2. From the local news stories in one day's issue of a daily, make a list of *all* the news events it suggests the paper should cover the next day. Then check the next day's paper to see how many of the events you identified were reported.
3. Using all the sources you can think of, write an assignment sheet for the next issue of your school paper.

CHAPTER 7

The News Beat

Newsmen have developed two ways to organize beats, both logical: the subject method and the geographical method.

The first, which asks a reporter to cover news in a clearly-defined subject area or in a group of kindred subjects, is common in large news gathering enterprises —large newspapers, large broadcast news operations, large news magazines. Most "routine" beats follow this pattern: police, city hall, school, church, federal, and business. It calls for reporters who become specialists, reporters who cover only news of education, or science, or aviation, or entertainment. The sports writer is a specialist; so is the political writer. When the newsroom is wealthy enough to support "experts" in special fields and when its community provides enough news-worthy activity to keep them busy, the subject pattern is extremely efficient. Much of the most effective reporting comes from men and women thus assigned to special beats.

When the writer of this book worked on the Hono-lulu Star-Bulletin—*his first out-of-college newspaper job—the shiny nameplate on his desk labeled him "Marine Editor." But when the city editor wanted him, he called "Waterfront!" The "Marine Editor" was at first assigned only to the waterfront beat, covering piers and ship movements, business that had to do with Honolulu's important ship-ping industry, the harbor-master's office, and such.*

The geographical method, in contrast, groups to-gether news centers that can conveniently be covered by a single legman. This is the more usual beat on the small newspaper and in broadcast newsrooms. A reporter, for example, may be asked to cover the news in the city's biggest industry, a meat-packing plant recently established as a branch of Swift and Company. This is a good-sized assignment in itself, with the plant's vigorous trade union, the demand for better housing for workers, the expected expansion. "Look," says the city editor, "the plant is way out there in the suburbs next to Brighton and Wilshire. You might as well cover suburbs too. And the Veterans' Hospital is on your way back to town." Thus a beat grows.

But the beat mushroomed. The post office was on the waterfront—why not have Waterfront cover federal news as well? So federal courts, customs, liquor control, immigration were added to the beat, even though some of their offices were far from the harbor itself. Next to one of the federal offices was the Hawaii Education Department office; so education was added. Visitors to Honolulu, who disembarked on the waterfront, went to hotels; by osmosis hotels became part of the beat. And so it went.

Often both methods are used in planning a beat. Miller, on the paper to which you were introduced in chapter 6, uses both. One of his reporters covers farm news and sports news—the subject-matter approach. Another man is assigned all local business news; but this subject assignment is not enough to keep him busy, so he is used for wide-ranging general assignments. The women's editor writes society and club news; Miller himself handles the city's official news—the subject approach again. But young Finnegan covers just about everything else; this means that he walks all over town to cover his beat. "Not very logical," you say, if he must range from one end of the city to the other. But in the small city major news centers are usually not far apart.

Suppose we follow Finnegan on a typical day on his beat, the day for which Miller gave him the assignment sheet in chapter 6. Before Finnegan starts out on the beat, he must finish his morning chores in the office. Most beat reporters have office assignments in addition to their outside work: bringing stories up to date for the day's paper, giving the copyreader a hand with overnight features from the wire, telephoning to check facts in the clippings given them for rewrite, making appointments for interviews, and checking signals with the photographer on the day's assignments.

Finnegan leaves the office as long before 9:00 A.M. as he can. As usual his first stop is the town's leading hotel, and this works out well today because the State Medical Association meeting is there. He rechecks the clipping of the story he had written yesterday. Then he stops at the reception desk for a moment's chat with the clerk. He checks registration cards for story tips.

"One man you ought to see," the clerk says. "I told him to expect a ring from you. He's a vice president of Greyhound—*I* think he's here about the new depot." Finnegan congratulates himself on his good fortune in having a hotel clerk who knows how to be helpful. A call to room 309 yields an appointment for 11:30.

Then he goes to the mezzanine, where he greets the Chamber of Commerce stenographer who is acting as receptionist for the medical convention. She helps him find Dr. Osborn, who is to give the talk on cancer. Osborn makes his task easier by giving him a copy of the talk, with the assurance that he isn't going to depart from script by one word. "This is too important to take any chance with ad-libbing," Osborn tells him.

Finnegan seeks out the chairman of the afternoon panel and gets from him enough material for a couple of summary paragraphs. He questions the secretary of the Association about the slate of new officers, but the secretary tells him brusquely that it won't be available before the voting tomorrow afternoon.

"We'll meet at two o'clock and vote right away," the secretary says. "But I can't give you results until we adjourn at about 3:15."

Finnegan explains that he must have the names as early as possible if the story is to make tomorrow's paper. He asks whether he may check with the secretary by telephone as soon as the balloting ends—or would the secretary call him? The secretary becomes more cooperative; a plan is set up so that the news will reach the paper with 10 or 15 minutes to spare before final deadline. If the voting is routine as usual, the slate will be accepted without change; Finnegan can write the story in advance and have it ready to roll, if the secretary will let him have the names now, in confidence. The secretary agrees.

The reporter has wrapped up one major assignment.

The county courthouse is across the street. The courthouse, a pile of dirty yellow stone in Rutherford B. Hayes design, sits in the center of a cool green park—cool inside, too, even when it's broiling outdoors.

The sheriff's office is quiet. "Don't ask me where the boss is," says the deputy languidly. "Said he'd be back at noon. Nothing doing today. Some farmers out by Penbrook say they're going to picket the dairy—but they've said that before."

Questioning reveals that the sheriff is probably out looking into the threatened picketing; Finnegan makes a mental note to check with the farm reporter to see who'll do the story.

He goes on to other offices. The county clerk, a cooperative source, hands him a typed list of marriage licenses. Finnegan exchanges a few words with the middle-aged stenographer about the TV show they both saw last night. Quick checks in the auditor's and engineer's offices develop a cluster of minor stories. He sticks his head in the county agent's door, and agrees quickly to the agent's request to "have your farm man be sure to call me."

"About the picketing?" asks Finnegan.

"Pretty smart, aren't you?" says the agent with a smile.

A clerk tells him that the county judge isn't in today. Finnegan asks whether there is anything new on the Firkins trial. "Nothing," says the clerk. "Probably get around to putting it on the November calendar in a few days."

Aware that he's given the county beat somewhat too fast a brush-off, Finnegan must nevertheless move on. The post office and other federal offices are barren of spot news; federal court's next term is two months away. But the postmaster hands Finnegan a routine printed announcement from Washington about the next set of civil service examinations for secretarial and clerical positions. "Just came in this morning," says the postmaster.

"Big news," says Finnegan a little sourly. The postmaster, who has known a lot of young reporters, chuckles.

"You're the one who's supposed to know," he responds. "But there've been seven girls in here already this morning to get the dope on it."

Finnegan's eyes widen. "How'd they know?"

"Heard it on the radio."

Embarrassed, Finnegan pockets the announcement. "My error—I missed it," he says. "We'd sure better carry it this afternoon."

As he turns to leave, a light strikes him. "I shouldn't think there'd be many people in a town this size interested in these federal jobs," he says, a question in his tone.

"Son, you'd be surprised. I'd say offhand there are two-three hundred holding this kind of job in town right now. And of course a lot of our kids go to Washington each year. Peace Corps and stuff like that, too."

"That," says Finnegan, "is a story. Can I talk with you next week about it?"

"Any time," says the postmaster. Finnegan leaves, planning the story as he goes. *Have to remember to tell Miller I'm doing it.*

At the board of education Finnegan gets the name and pedigree of the new social studies teacher in the high school. From the sidewalk engineers on the block where they're laying foundations for the new supermarket, he learns that proceedings were halted for half an hour this morning when a playful dog decided to romp in the wet concrete. A few questions develop a humorous paragraph that he can turn over to Miller for the local-anecdote column.

Though he's in a hurry, he decides on a brief detour to the bus station. The local manager is cautious about the new "depot," but he admits that he knows the man at the hotel is here about the project. He tells Finnegan that the man spent all last evening looking over the vacant lots a couple of hundred feet up the street.

At 11:00, Finnegan is back at the hotel, listening to Dr. Osborn's talk, following the speaker's words on the script he has been given. Osborn keeps his promise—he sticks close to his text. "Wish I could have taken a chance," Finnegan mutters. He gets away at 11:30, however, for his appointment with the Greyhound vice president.

At first the official is cagey and careful. But Finnegan finds that the tip from the bus station manager pays off. When he asks a direct question about the vacant lots, the Greyhound man grins. "Shouldn't try to keep anything from a reporter," he says good-naturedly, and he produces the whole story. The company is going to put in a new $950,000 station and convert the old one into a garage. "Sure—no reason why you shouldn't go ahead and print it."

Elated, Finnegan makes an appointment with the man for the photographer to come in and take a picture; then he telephones Miller. This is a bigger story than Miller had expected, and he and the wire editor will want to plan how to play it.

"Okay," says Miller laconically. "Click will be right over. Get back here and write it—we haven't got all day."

"I know it," Finnegan agrees quickly, "and I haven't touched the airport story yet. Mind if I do it by phone, and fix it up for Click to go out alone?" Finnegan telephones the airport at once, gets his information, and makes a date for the photographer. He calls Miller back, saying he'll be right in. He isn't going to get to the swimming pool piece for today, he reports apologetically.

He had had to skip his usual morning coffee at the Sugar Bowl today, but he stops now to grab a fast lunch and to say a word of greeting to the loquacious and friendly waitress who "knows everything that happens in town, whether it's her business or not"; she always has a lead or so for him. Ordinarily, Finnegan has a luxurious half-hour for lunch, on the days he's not covering Rotary or Optimist luncheons; but today he is more pressed than usual. He finishes his hamburger and coffee in ten minutes and dashes for the office.

Before he starts writing, Finnegan calls the sheriff's office. "No news," says the sheriff. "Just went down the county a piece to check a fool tale about a kidnaping. Nothing to it . . . Yes, I talked to your man about the dairy picketing." But questioning brings out a story of a frantic mother who had seen disaster in an hour's disappearance of a toddling daughter. She had roused a score of families before the child was found—asleep in an upstairs bed.

For more than an hour Finnegan writes quickly. First the medical convention; then the bus station story. The copy flows out of his typewriter; he has learned to plan his stories as he gathers the information, so that there's no sitting around waiting for the muse. When he hands in the story on the new station, Miller gives him an unusual "Good work, Don."

Then there are more phone calls. Some of them are repeats of the morning's calls—the sheriff's office and some of the county offices. He gets Dr. Nelson on the telephone and makes a late-afternoon appointment to talk about the swimming pool problem; Miller says the photographer has brought in a good picture, and they'll count on the yarn for tomorrow.

By 3:00, the copy deadline, Finnegan has hammered out a dozen stories. By 4:00 when he leaves the office he has made progress on two of the features Miller had assigned that morning, the swimming pool and the nonmunicipal-offices stories. Finnegan thinks this last story is dull, but he can see that it will make an informative background feature, even if it isn't exciting to write or to read. On the other hand, he is looking forward to covering the band concert that evening in the park. Ought to be some good color, he thinks.

Techniques of a Beat Reporter

Finnegan has been on this beat six months now. He thinks he knows it fairly well. When he tagged around with his predecessor for two days before he took over, he thought it a man-killing assignment. How a man could ever get to know everybody in the county building, let alone all the rest, he couldn't figure. Now he thinks he has the beat under control, if not entirely licked. Give him another six months or a year and he will know not only the idiosyncrasies of his own assignment but also a good many of the techniques of successful reporting.

If Finnegan is like most reporters, he may never verbalize all the things he has learned, he may never try to reduce them to formulas or even generalizations. This is unfortunate, for no learning process is as productive as telling somebody else exactly how to perform a task. Halfbacks, pastry cooks, artists of all kinds—reporters included, since reporting is both craft and art—are likely to do their work instinctively or by rule-of-thumb routine. Although masterly products may be turned out even when the performers can't explain exactly *how*, all would become better at their specialties if they were able to give careful descriptions of what they do; for continuing progress depends both on the giving and the receipt of knowledge.

If Finnegan, after he has mastered his beat, were to try to give his successor the advantage of what he has learned, and to do it in writing, he would come up with a mass of useful precepts and suggestions.

The cardinal rule, underlying all other rules, is *know your beat*.

There are all kinds of ways of knowing a beat. You've barely begun when you get to know the obvious things—the names on the doors, the principal activities of the offices, and the like. You can get control of this kind of knowledge of most beats in the first few days, just by digging into the beat and really seeing what you see. But the truly meaningful kinds of knowledge require time, thought, and a lot of pure hard work.

Take almost any of the major offices in the county building. In any of them you have a principal official—a county clerk, a recorder, an assessor, a sheriff—and a lot of subordinate employes. You have a certain number of activities and responsibilities that are obvious, and you might say that any kid in a high school civics class could name them. But the high school kid doesn't know anywhere near enough. You have to go deeper. You have to get into the official governmental manuals to learn what county organization is in your state. You have to read books on public administration; you ought to see whether each office may not have its own special table of organization. You better plan on time in the library, in your paper's morgue, wherever there are official records that might be helpful. And, incidentally, you better remember that no two states (and maybe no two counties in a state) have the same practices or laws, and that knowing one doesn't mean you know another. They don't even call official records and official proceedings by the same names from one state to the next.

Though all of this seems pretty evident, it's fundamental, and must not be ignored or undervalued. Even so, it constitutes only the surface trappings of the beat job. And the reporter has to live beneath the surface.

A beat reporter has to get to *know people*. He has to know not only the county recorder but also the whole staff, and sometimes he has to know the staff better than he knows the recorder. In almost every office there's one member, a stenographer, a clerk, the information girl, who not only knows everything that's going on but can talk easily. From such sources a reporter gets all kinds of tips, even though he often has to go to the top man or even an outside source to corroborate a story or to expand, amplify, or check facts.

A first step is to *make sure that your beat knows you*. A reporter is smart, on his first visit, to introduce himself so that the staff will remember him. Maybe he writes his name and telephone number down for each news contact—a good way of making a firm initial impression. He gets on informal terms with the staff if he can. Sometimes it's easier to arrive at a friendly, casual relationship with the stenographer than with the boss. It's no crime, incidentally, to be friendly with the stenos in an office—and with some it's no hardship.

A reporter has to rely heavily on the top man in an office, of course. This is the man who has the last word on almost everything, and the one who can hold back or release information. Moreover, however well versed you may be in an office's duties and procedures, the boss knows more, and you ought to depend considerably on his judgment. A beat reporter doesn't necessarily have to see the boss every time he steps into an office; but he ought to have a regular time, every day or so, to see him, arranged at a time convenient for the news source, but also a time when the reporter can surely be on deck.

Word from the boss, however, is only one road to *finding out what's going on in an office.* There are all kinds of ways. One of the best is chatting with people, obviously. But every bulletin board is a source of tips; sometimes the janitor or the man at the newsstand notices things that the regulars consider too routine to mention. There's no such thing as knowing too much. Get the boss, as a favor, to tell you what he thinks are the really important jobs he and his staff are supposed to do. You may not agree with his evaluation; but in cases when you don't, remember that he probably knows some things you haven't found out yet.

Another thing: You can't cover the county recorder this year without knowing what news his office yielded last year. Better *spend some time going through the paper,* recent issues as well as those of one and two years back. Often last year's stories give you material without which this year's would be incomplete.

You'll learn quickly to observe the signposts that will help you to *establish rapport with your news sources.* Suppose you see a creel and a fly rod in the recorder's office: You don't need a very high IQ to figure out that conversation about fishing will interest him. You don't even have to be very smart about it—a fisherman is always happy to tell anybody what a good fisherman he is. If you see that a secretary has a stack of literature about Mexico on her desk, you've got an opening. You might be surprised to find out how many questions you can ask about travel in Mexico and what a lot of plus values they'll yield, in good will, in news tips, and in easier access to information. (But be sure that you know that Mexico is *south* of Texas before you start talking. Ignorance will get you nowhere.)

All of this doesn't mean that you make yourself a phony. Maybe you're no fisherman and never expect to be one. You don't pretend; you simply use an obvious gambit. Don't forget that if the recorder wants something from you, he'll probably start talking to you about your collection of jazz records, or whatever special interest you've revealed to him.

Good manners are essential, a mandatory part of a reporter's stock in trade. If you know the play called *The Front Page,* or almost any play or movie about newsmen, you may have absorbed the idea that reporters are drunks, boors, or good-for-nothings. Well, *The Front Page* may have been an accurate picture of one kind of Chicago newspaper life in another era and another generation; it has little but jargon to do with the journalist of today. Reporters are people, and if they behave in civilized manner they'll get civility in return. Movie reporters seem to have their hats glued to their heads; real reporters take their hats off just as frequently as stock brokers or grocers or schoolteachers. Reporters say "please" and "thank you"; they don't sit down until they're asked to; they first-name their news sources only when it's clearly appropriate (though they know how valuable a first-name relationship can be). They behave courteously, and they get courtesy in return.

Being courteous, however, doesn't preclude being aggressive and stubborn when you're trailing a hard-to-get story. Sometimes you'll find a news source who doesn't want to talk—for a good reason, such as that he doesn't know the answers, or a bad one, such as that he's afraid he'll talk himself into trouble. Sometimes it may take weeks of asking the same question, in dozens of places and in many different ways, to "break" a story. But you'll learn that there is an answer to almost any question. If you *keep looking for the answers* long enough and hard enough, you'll usually find them.

Remember that *you are the expert on news*. Everybody thinks he can run a newspaper better than the editor, and everybody tells the reporter how to do his job. A news source may say that the paper "can't run such-and-such a story, or that it "had better" run the story or else. The reporter doesn't have to get rough, but sometimes he has to be tough. If he is entitled to the information he has gathered, if he has obtained it through acceptable channels and by acceptable methods, he and his editors make the decision whether the news event becomes a news story.

Reporters can increase efficiency and total production if they *obtain cooperation from news sources*. You will be asked often to hold off publishing a story for a few days. Sometimes the request is one that you cannot grant; but in some cases you can serve your readers just as well, and meet the news source's wish at the same time, by respecting the request. You have to use judgment.

Reporting has traditional responsibilities. Every reporter knows that *newsmen keep promises*. They don't break release dates; they don't print information entrusted to them in confidence; they don't reveal sources if they have promised not to. But these principles of behavior can be used against you if you're not careful. A news source can gag you by putting you on an "off-the-record" spot. If a reporter finds he's been had by this kind of ruse, he may even decide he must retract his promise, in the interest of publishing news that ought to be published.

If you're alert, you won't often be caught in this kind of trap. A Boston editor once said: "I make it a practice to refuse to let people tell me news facts 'off the record.' I know that I can virtually always get the facts through other channels. Moreover, in many cases the news sources say to me, 'Well, I'm going to tell you anyway, and you can use your own judgment as to whether to print it.' "

Responsibility means other things, too. It means that you *keep appointments,* and *keep them punctually*. It means that you return the stenographer's carbon copies when she lends them to you to save you a lot of note-taking, return them in good shape and when you said you would.

Follow routines that your news sources can count on. Regular habits will pay dividends. If your source knows that you're going to be in every day at the same hour, he'll get the habit of keeping things in mind for you and of being available for your purposes at the time you want him.

You don't have to see every news source on your beat every day. For one thing, the days aren't long enough. For another, not every source has news every day; some will pay off only once in two weeks or a month. Sometimes public officials or business or other executives are genuinely too busy to give you time daily. But you can usually check on prominent or busy sources through their secretaries or staffs. The busiest people are often the easiest to deal with; they will give their time gladly for legitimate news, though they'll resent your taking up their time for nothing.

One of the most practical pieces of advice an experienced reporter can give: *Don't ask vague questions*. Always try to be specific. People tend to think more easily and respond more fluently and with more detail when the questions they are asked are concrete rather than general or abstract. When a man is faced with a vague "Do you have any news today?" it is easy for him to give an equally vague and empty reply—all too often "No." If you ask a man "What do you know today?" or "What's new?" he'll probably reply

"Nothing"; when you ask the same man whether he has decided to accept the offer of a new position with the City Planning Commission, he'll probably give you the full story.

Most beat reporters find it a good idea to *keep a futures book* or calendar, somewhat like the one city editors keep. You're likely to be in trouble if you trust your memory for every upcoming date and event. It's much safer to write details down in a notebook or on a desk calendar.

The futures book is a good place to *jot down feature ideas* or hunches for special stories. Although a beat man's primary assignment is to make sure that the regular or routine news is covered, that the paper is informed of the day-to-day activities centering on his beat, he's doing no more than 51 percent of the job if he doesn't have an eye open for features, for stories that may take some extra time or extra digging. If you watch for such opportunities, you'll quickly have more work than you can handle immediately; but you'll want to note ideas as they come to you. It's easy to forget even the good ones. If they're really strong ideas and if you don't have time to work on them yourself, you ought to tell the city desk so that somebody else can be assigned to them.

Always remember to *keep the desk informed* of what you're doing. Sometimes somebody else is working on the same yarn you've dreamed up, maybe from a different angle. The city editor is the guy who knows. He can help you, the other fellow, and the paper to get best results if he knows what's going on. Moreover, he's the boss. If you have questions about writing a story or using your information, it's best to consult him. He's been around longer than you.

PROJECTS

1. Using as your "beat" some news center that you know well, a college or departmental office, a dormitory, the Union, a religious center, or something else, make up a list of all the news stories growing from its activities that a local newspaper might cover within the coming month.
2. Get the permission of a beat reporter for a newspaper or broadcast newsroom in your community for you to accompany him on his daily rounds. Write a report of your observations.
3. Get a professional reporter's consent to interrogate one of his principal beat news sources about the effectiveness of the news coverage of his newsworthy activity. Then discuss the news source's comments with the reporter.

CHAPTER 8

News Gathering:
Problems and Methods

No book is large enough to describe all the problems reporters face in gathering facts for the news they write; this book outlines some and hints at others. In a great many years of professional experience, no newsman could hope to encounter them all. But there are three obstacles to fact gathering common to all that deserve consideration here: getting to the news, recognizing the news, and digging out the news.

Access

The difficulty of gaining access to the news is the problem newsmen talk most about, and one that has received serious attention in the years since World War II. It has always been present, in colonial days, in the period before electronic communication brought speed to journalism, and in new forms in the twentieth century. It is a good deal more than the mere inadequacy of physical facilities; in fact, physical facilities for news gathering today are no problem. The problem of access today is a problem of persuading the men who control the sources of news, that is, the information that makes news, to permit reporters to get at it.

"Access" is, it seems evident, taken for granted under the First Amendment. The language of the amendment does not make this clear; but its meaning is that every American has the right to the information he needs to make decisions and guide actions, at least insofar as governmental interference is concerned. Government shall not get in his way; and this means that government shall not get in the way of the citizen's information agent, the newsman. The implication is, however, that the citizen has legitimate expectation of receiving all information of interest or importance to him, governmental or nongovernmental. And problems of access are serious both in gathering news of government and in reporting private nonofficial activities.

That news of government is sometimes hard to get is not a new problem. It is as old as government. Nor is it hard to understand that some official agents or agencies of the people like to make their own decisions as to how much to tell about their activities. But the American system of government open to public vision, criticism, and modification does not accept bureaucratic secrecy; and the news media, eager not only to serve the public but also to publish the news that will lead the public to buy papers or tune in broadcasts, have always opposed what they have considered unjustified withholding of information.

In early United States history it was not uncommon for national and state legislatures to operate secretly; but as news demands increased, and as confidence in the press grew, the closed doors began to open. Congress *may* meet in secret sessions under its rules, but in practice neither the Senate nor the House has barred reporters for years. Newsmen of press and broadcasting had freer access to news of most kinds by the time World War II started than ever before.

But the war set a new current into operation. During the war American news media observed a self-censorship system, a system whereby, under the wise counsel of newsman Byron Price, newspapers, radio, and other news agencies voluntarily refrained from issuing information whose dissemination was classified as detrimental to national interest. The phrase "national security" became the touchstone: "Withhold anything that would, if revealed, be harmful to national security." The news media, according to Price, achieved a record close to 100 percent; they reported virtually nothing that the Office of Censorship advised holding back.

This success established firmly in the popular mind the principle that information damaging to national security might properly be withheld from the public; and unfortunately, many official minds have seized upon the "security" plea for use in peace as well as in war.

The peace was not quiet, nor was it truly peace: the world suffered a cold and sometimes a shooting war. In the years following V-J Day, no patriotic American wanted the Soviet group of nations to gain information that might damage the interests of the Western world. And the supercautious in government, or the overzealous (in the eyes not alone of American newsmen but of the unfortunately small number of citizens who take interest in such matters) wanted to carry "security" far beyond the point of prudence or reality.

In accord with this kind of thinking, President Truman put into effect a "security" system under which many officials of many departments of government—minor officials as well as high ones, and departments seemingly distant from issues of national security as well as those close to them—were authorized to withhold governmental information. The news media protested (as they had, successfully, against an earlier Truman proposal of like intent), but the system was adopted. President Eisenhower modified the Truman system, but he did not abolish it. During the Kennedy and Johnson administrations it was extended in some areas. The information officer of the Department of Defense, after the public became aware that it had been consciously misled by the White House in the U-2 spying-on-Russia crisis and the perilous events revolving around the

Castro rise to power in Cuba, expressed the view that "management of news" was a governmental responsibility. This he took to mean that government might withhold news, or present news in what it thought to be appropriate light, at its own inclination.

The net effect was that the American public was denied information from areas of governmental activity into which it had formerly had clear view, or from which the curtain had been only partly drawn; and many critics thought that such concealment could not be justified as contributing to national welfare. "The elementary principle of democratic self-government," said these critics, "is that public business must be conducted in the public vision. A secrecy system, with authority for concealment vested in individuals far below the policy-making level, is just as likely to be used to mask mismanagement, stupidity, or corruption as to withhold information of value to the Kremlin. Moreover, the harm to the nation from occasional release of information that should, perhaps, be kept secret is likely to be far slighter than the danger of not letting the people know what their government is doing."

The system remains, nevertheless; it has been extended by the broadening of "security systems" within government departments such as the Department of Defense, and indirectly as other agencies have been encouraged to draw their curtains.

Growing sophistication about news procedures, in government and out, has buttressed the dams at the sources of news. Not only have governmental offices at all levels, from cabinet to coroner, learned that the best way to keep information from the public is not to release it; nonofficial sources of news have learned it too. And so the newsman faces a constant fight to overcome not merely physical obstacles but purposeful and unreasonable or selfish attempts to bottle up information to which the public has a right —or at least for which portions of the public have a need.

A clearer view of the ramifications of this problem may come from looking at some of its specific manifestations.

City and county officials decide, from time to time, to close their records to newsmen. It is common for county clerks, for example, to withhold news of the

The news agencies, press and broadcasting alike, have been vigorous in their denunciation of the tendency toward secrecy, and strong in their attempts to combat it. "Freedom of information" or "freedom of the press" committees have been given spirited leadership for the American Society of Newspaper Editors, the Radio-Television News Directors Association, Sigma Delta Chi, and other professional organizations by such men as J. Russell Wiggins of the Washington Post, *Herbert Brucker of the Hartford* Courant, *Jim Bormann of WCCO Minneapolis, and a score of others. Though they have not always succeeded in their attempts to break down unreasonable barriers to newsworthy information, they have at least kept the stream from dwindling to a trickle. At ASNE behest, Harold L. Cross described the problem and the attack on it in* The People's Right to Know, New York: Columbia University Press, 1953. *The views of newsmen have been echoed, supported, and given some implementation by the Congressional subcommittee headed by Representative John Moss, which for a decade gave vigilant attention to the trend toward official blackout. The Moss committee succeeded in getting Congress to modify federal agencies' rights to bottle up nonsecurity information, and in a number of specific cases opened doors that had been barred. But the war has not been won.*

issuance of marriage licenses at the licensees' request; somewhat less common, but nevertheless of repeated occurrence, is the holding back of information by police officials. In most such cases the information is legally public, and both moral and legal right are on the side of the newsman. The editor of the Moose Lake, Minnesota, *Star-Gazette*, denied access to public records by a county official, procured an opinion from the state attorney general that gained access for him (his long fight won him a national Sigma Delta Chi award for "courage in journalism"). The Norwich, Connecticut, *Bulletin*, when police decided to clam up, got news of a car theft from other sources, printed it, and brought about the recovery of the car (police soon after decided that the newspaper's position had been right).

Legislative committees and subgroups of city and county councils sometimes decide to hold meetings in secret. By tradition, most such groups hold hearings and take testimony in public, but often conduct deliberations and make decisions behind locked doors. In dozens of cases newsmen, merely by reporting that public actions are being taken in secret, convince the public that such secrecy is improper. Usually convincing the public is effective in convincing the news sources.

If public sources are troublesome when they decide inappropriately to withhold information, private sources may be more so. The law does not say that a businessman, or a physician, or a church official, or the operator of a bowling alley, a brothel, or a boarding-house must talk to a reporter about his affairs, even when they are charged with public interest. Every reporter has experienced difficulty in prying what he believes to be information the public ought to have out of news sources that are reluctant to talk. The news sources may seek to remain silent for defensible reasons: that release of information would be damagingly premature, that it would invade privacy, or that they do not have authority to release it. They may also remain silent for causes the reporter rejects: embarrassment about acts the reporter thinks the public has a right to know about, the wish to cover improper or even criminal behavior, or sometimes a misguided sense of "modesty." In any such case the newsman, if he believes he (and his audience) should not be denied the information, has to find ways to dig out the facts.

Sometimes there is no way better than to "make a good case" with the news source, to persuade him that he should accept the reporter's evaluation of the circumstances. But there are other ways:

The reporter may often find other sources for the required information. It is rare that newsworthy facts are corked up in only one bottle.

He may use the sometimes questionable device of publishing a story reporting the news sources' intractability. Often such a story is the news; but when it is used as a club, it may be misused.

He may bring other pressures to bear. One cub reporter, observing two businessmen in tête-à-tête that he had reason to believe concerned a commercial development of importance to his community, was turned away when he questioned the men. He quickly informed his city editor, a man of standing in the community; the city editor approached the business men and came away with the story.

He may invent other approaches suitable only for individual cases.

Dwight D. Eisenhower, speaking as a retired general rather than a retired President, told a group of newsmen at the Overseas Press Club in New York of his belief in the trustworthiness of the war correspondents with whom he dealt in World War II. During the North Africa preparation for invasion of Sicily, he said, "I took the reporters into my confidence . . . and they never let me down."

But Eisenhower also showed how to prevent reporters from reporting. "The reports were getting too close to the truth" in suggesting the coming invasion, he said. So he laid the plans open to them, off the record, "to shut their mouths—to stop them from writing. Later, some of them said to me, 'General, don't ever do this again.' They appreciated my trust, but they didn't want it repeated."

• •

A number of American states have passed laws requiring that public meetings be public, that is, that their doors be open to any citizen. This gives the newsman no greater privilege than anybody else, but it guarantees to him that, in states where the law exists, he can attend and report any legislative meeting and any other regularly scheduled session held by a public or governmental body. More and more states are adopting laws of this kind.

• •

A distinguished speaker at a Toledo luncheon, Norman Cousins, editor of the Sat-

Both governmental and private news sources have learned that so-called public relations operatives may often contrive to conceal information as well as to make it public. The fundamental purpose of a public relations man is to establish and perpetuate a favorable public attitude toward the activity or client he represents. It is not unnatural, though sometimes antisocial or even dishonest, that in some cases he may "forget" information harmful to his cause, or twist information to give it a better face. Newsmen have learned to be wary of "handouts" and other controlled information because they know they may be getting only part of a story, or a slanted story. But they have also learned that public relations men may often be of inestimable value to them, opening doors they could not pass through on their own, that many public relations men have standards as high as their own, and that some stories could not be covered at all without the help of the PR man who works from the inside out.

The "off-the-record" device, which has a legitimate place in news handling, can be used to stifle the newsman, as has already been pointed out. Off-the-record information is often given to reporters not for publication but to enable them to understand involved news situations and to evaluate and put into proper perspective the news events they cover. Astute and sophisticated news sources, however, knowing that the ethical principle almost universal among newsmen impels them to respect the promises of secrecy they make, have all too often trapped reporters by giving them in off-the-record conferences information that ought to be made public. This creates both a moral and a tactical problem.

Pressures are brought by interested groups and interested individuals to keep news out of the papers and off the air. The father who does not want it in black and white that his son was driving while drunk, the real estate speculator who wants to buy up property before plans for building a new factory to occupy the site have been announced, the civic group that thinks its program for park development will be hamstrung by premature news—these pressures, legit-

urday Review, *was aston- ished, in the middle of his talk, to see a man rise sud- denly from his seat and stalk angrily from the hall. The man was Paul Block, Jr., publisher of the Toledo Blade and Times. Later Block explained his abrupt act to Cousins: "You were making a public speech to an open, unrestricted audi- ence. But you announced suddenly that you would interpolate some off-the-rec- ord remarks. In other words, you were willing for a large audience to hear what you said, but unwilling for a newspaper to report that you had said it. The Toledo papers have ordered their reporters not to accept ma- terial under this restriction; for this reason, since you seemed to me to be taking advantage of your audience, I left the hall."*

Later Cousins responded to Block that his position "was wise and incontesta- ble." He added that he be- lieved Block had acted "in the best interests of respon- sible newspaper publishing."

imate and illegitimate, selfish and public-spirited, come daily in any reporter's life.

International news sources are sometimes the most difficult of any to penetrate. Not every nation holds, as do the United States and some of the rest of the Western world, to the principle that the public ought to know about, and the news media to comment on, na- tional and international affairs. For three years a United Nations subcommission on "freedom of in- formation" labored to bring forth a code for interna- tional exchange of news and other information. It dis- banded in despair, with little accomplished, because so many of the nations represented did not want any such exchange. Indeed, the interest of some nations was more in setting up a mandatory system of controls of information than in freeing news of its shackles.

Radio and television news have always faced spe- cial problems. One that has gradually dissipated, though it is not entirely wiped out, is a lack of public acceptance of broadcasting as a news medium pre- cisely as the newspaper is accepted. This does not mean lack of confidence in broadcasting, but rather an unawareness that broadcasters seek news as do the papers. It took some 20 years for news-of-the-air men to persuade the White House to adopt the term *news conference* in place of *press conference*, and there are still newscasters who, red-faced, find them- selves slipping into the older term.

Broadcast access to news events is sometimes hampered by the equipment without which news on the air would not be possible. In some cases the intrusion of the news camera, or even of radio's tape recorder, has caused problems. Coverage of court news and other governmental news by camera has been made especially difficult by the edict of the American Bar Association—expressed in its Canon 35, a section of its code of recommended procedures for bench and bar—that picture taking is not consistent with fair and orderly procedure. Canon 35 is not law, but it has the force of law when judges apply it to their courtrooms; and all but a minority of judges do apply it. Vigorous campaigns by newsmen's organizations, both print and air, have not persuaded the lawyers to change their views; the fact that picture-taking techniques make photography far less "intrusive" than it was when television was new has not assuaged their concern. Some judges permit courtroom photography; and some city councils and other official bodies do. Occasionally pictures may be made of certain types of Con- gressional proceedings. But the general problem remains.

Such shackles as these, in many phases of modern life, are so numerous that accounts of them could go on for many pages. The point is clear: news media often must fight hard for the information they carry to their audiences—and some information they cannot get by any means whatever.

And if you can't get to the news, you can't report it.

Seeing What You See

One of the tired, but still pointed, anecdotes about cub reporters—this one may even be true—tells of the young newsman who, assigned to cover a luncheon talk, reported to his city editor, "There's no story. Speaker had a stroke." He just may have been the novice working for the Detroit *News* during prohibition years; when this man was sent across the Detroit River one wintry day to cover a disastrous home fire he came back with the story but the added oral report: "The reason one of the kids wasn't in the house at the time of the fire was that he was out helping to push a sled load of bootleg booze across the river." The city editor's shrieks still resound.

The point of these stories is clear: One of the tests of a newsman's worth is his ability to recognize a newsworthy event when he meets it. Not many such obvious stories as the two in the preceding paragraph will be missed. But the kind of alertness that assures a reporter, young or old, that he won't let news slip through his fingers is primary in the news business.

Where does this alertness come from? What are the personal qualities that produce it, or help to develop it? There are no sure answers to such questions, or at best no universal answers. But from many newsmen who have puzzled over them come a few suggestions.

CURIOSITY   This is the skeptical, inquisitive, seeking attitude that leads a man forever to be asking, "Why? How? Who? What results?" A skilled reporter never wants to accept any event as routine. He is always trying to find in it the elements that differentiate it from any other event. He takes clocks apart mentally, if not with a jeweler's tool, to see how they run. He asks for proof of anything that is not to him self-evident. He demands that he be shown the broken switch that caused the wreck, rather than merely to be told about it. And he always wants to know more about an event he is covering than he needs to tell his audience. He's aware that it's easy to cut out nonessentials when he gets to writing the story, but impossible to invent missing facts.

IMAGINATION   The reporter needs imagination, not the fiction-writer's imagination, which builds life out of whole cloth, but the kind that looks at life and tries to put it into context. It is related to the curiosity just described; but it adds the reporter's own evaluations of an event, and his projection of it into whatever surrounding circumstances may be relevant. It says, "How will this event affect the man's family, or his job, or his society? Who can explain why it happened? How much of it will readers or listeners understand? and, if the answer is 'not very much,' how do I handle it, or add to it, so that it will become clearer?"

KNOWLEDGE   Recognizing a newsworthy event requires knowledge, often advance knowledge, the knowledge of an event and its context that permits curiosity and imagination to do their work. This kind of knowledge usually implies work, study or research or interviewing before the event, so as to be well prepared for it. The man who understands something about how computers work, and what they can and can't do will know what to look for when he is sent to report a demonstration of a new mechanical brain. You don't send an art critic to report a baseball game—you send a sports writer (preferably a baseball writer).

A payroll holdup at the Detroit News led to a dramatic interchange of shots in the street in front of the building. As the shots sounded, newsmen's heads popped from a score of windows looking down on the scene. The reporter assigned to write the story interviewed more than 50 members of the News staff, all of whom had seen some of the same action, all of whom were trained newsmen. He got from these observers no full agreement on all details of the event. There were four gunmen . . . five . . . six . . . eight. The murdered policeman wore a white rubber raincoat . . . a black . . . no coat. He fired six shots . . . 10 shots . . . no shots. He didn't even have a gun, and so on.

This is not to derogate the newsmen of the News— many of them were the best of their craft. Nor is it to say that accuracy can't be attained. It is, however, an emphasis on the difficulty of patching together a factual account when differing sources are used. No two observers see the same things.

ACCURACY   Alertness to a news event also requires the alertness to see and report facts precisely. A favorite reporting-classroom device is to introduce before a group of students a feigned fight, or some other colorful event, without warning, and ask students to report what happened. The number of students who saw a pistol when none was present (or called the automatic held by one man a revolver); the number who mistake the colors and character of clothes, hair, eyes, skin; the number who report remarks that weren't made—all of these underline the difficulties of truly accurate observation. How can accuracy be attained? First of all, by scrupulous attention to detail, by a self-imposed discipline which isn't easy to come by but that can be developed. Second, by taking careful notes; reliance on memory is notoriously undependable. Third, by checking and double-checking, by asking questions, by querying when in doubt, by making sure that you never leave the scene with anything left moot behind you.

There is more to accurate and effective observation than these four elements. But the reporter who possesses curiosity and imagination, or works at developing them; the reporter who never approaches a story unprepared; the one who salaams and raps his forehead thrice on the ground at mention of accuracy, this reporter is going to be more effectively observant than most.

DIGGING OUT THE NEWS   If you can't report news you can't get at, no more can you report news you fail to remove from its protective sheathing.

Its sheathing may be a news source's unwillingness to reveal the news. It may be a failure on the part of the man who possesses the facts to recognize that they are newsworthy (in which situation it becomes your responsibility to help him to see that they are). It may be weakness in your own powers of observation (see the preceding paragraphs) or in your methods of interrogation, your interviewing technique. Or it may be a concealing blanket that is a complex of these and other factors, often with the complexity in which so much of modern life is clothed as an added element.

The reportorial techniques to remove these covers for the facts you need are suggested elsewhere in this book, some in this chapter, some in the section on investigative and interpretive reporting, some in the chapter on interviewing. No repetition is needed here.

But there is no harm in saying, again, that facts that don't get into the reporter's notebook are facts that don't get into his story.

Methods and Tools of Reporting

The traditional reportorial tools are a soft black copy pencil and a wad of copy paper. Newspaper reporters are doubtless guilty of a certain amount of professional inelasticity, or self-conscious obstinacy, when they insist that these tools are superior to a ballpoint pen, for example, and a neat spiral-bound notebook. Reporters reason that four or five sheets of office copy paper seized from the desk drawer and folded into pocket size make handy and inexpensive note pads and that copy pencils furnished by the business office are convenient and cheap. The disadvantages are that copy paper is soft and perishable, and that copy-pencil longhand smears into illegible smog if it is handled much. Although use of a hard pencil or a pen on hard-finish paper would yield greater neatness and longer-lived notes, neither neatness nor longevity is a pearl of much price in daily journalism. If the newspaper or radio-TV reporter gathers his material in the morning, he almost always writes the story or telephones it to the newsroom by noon. The notes often get dog-eared and crumpled, but they go into the wastebasket within a few hours. The copy-pencil scrawl gets smudged, but usually not before the reporter has made full use of it.

The movie portrait of the reporter who begins an interview by waving pencil and note paper under the nose of the man he is questioning is not taken from life. Such procedure at the beginning of an interview would often have the effect of freezing the man being interviewed. Another favorite misrepresentation shows reporters with press cards ostentatiously stuck in hatbands when they wish to cross fire or police lines. Press cards are usually issued by local police headquarters, some-

When there is more time between the gathering of the facts and the writing of the story, there's more need for less perishable notes. A reporter working on a long feature story that may not be completed for several days, or on a radio documentary that is going to take a week to develop, or on a magazine article that may require fact gathering over a period of a month would be foolish indeed to use copy pencil and soft paper. The order and permanence of ink and a notebook or light file cards would be well worth the extra trouble. And it needs to be said that the copy paper tradition is becoming less honored than it used to be—you see an increasing number of notebooks in reportorial hands.

In the twentieth century the typewriter, the

times by other agencies, to help newsmen and to make sure that only qualified reporters gain privileged access to news events. Press cards are a real help to reporters, who always carry them; but they stay in wallets or handbags rather than in hatbands.

camera, the tape recorder, and the telephone have become prime reportorial tools.

TYPEWRITING   Every kind of news communication requires ease and skill with the typewriter. If you can't type 35 words a minute without having your eyes glued to your fingers, if your copy is badly marred by errors, if you haven't learned to "compose" on the typewriter, to typewrite a reasonably competent first draft that needs only a little pencil editing for final polish, you'd better take a course in typing.

THE CAMERA   The camera has been recognized as a reliable and sometimes an unsurpassed reporting instrument since Mathew Brady showed the world how. Brady's inspired photographs of the Civil War are among the most impressive and informative records we have of that period of history. Today every reporter, with the exception of the radio newsman, ought to be able to count on his camera as a supplementary tool. Every reporting student needs to have a basic knowledge of the camera and of photography not only because a reporter must know how to evaluate and edit pictures but also because he is likely to be asked to take them himself. This book, although it does not give instruction in photography, would be misleading if it failed to mention the importance of pictorial reporting in twentieth-century news communication.

The motion picture, the picture magazine, the television screen, often justify the saying that "a picture is worth a thousand words." This truism, however, and a companion aphorism that asserts that "pictures don't lie" are often misunderstood or taken too literally. The news photograph, like the news story, may be transformed by the flow of time and events, and camera reports may be as contrived and deceitful as the falsest verbal reporting. A photograph without the help of words, or at least of a second picture, tells only one side of a story; it cannot report the story that lies behind the facade. Yet what the camera can see it often reports superlatively. Fortunately, human imagination and experience enable the spectators to fill in the gaps left by any kind of pictorial or verbal representation.

THE TAPE RECORDER   Although radio newsmen think of the tape recorder as an instrument peculiarly theirs, and it is indeed a news-gathering implement of special value for aural broadcasting, it can be used in a somewhat similar manner by television news. Tape recorders, moreover, are no longer rare in newspaper and other news media reporting, and their obvious advantages promise wider reportorial acceptance in the future. Besides the important advantage of providing the reporter "live" interviews and the exact words, accents, and vocal emphases of a speech, a meeting, or an interview, the recorder, which misses no sound within range of its microphone, can hardly be surpassed as a means of assuring precise and accurate notes. More than one reporter has experienced the refusal of a sophisticated interviewee, aware that his words on tape can't be denied later, to permit use of a recorder.

It is partly thanks to the recorder that a "new" form of interview—full reproduction of both questions and answers, verbatim except for minor editing—has returned to both magazine and newspaper journalism (Bennett and Greeley both used it, without electronics, more than a hundred years back.)

THE TELEPHONE   The telephone has been called the enemy of good reporting, and it is easy to see why it is frequently unsatisfactory for news gathering. A reporter can usually manage an interview most efficiently when he is face to face with his interviewee. Although a fact is a fact, and a nonfact a nonfact, however it is communicated, there are subtleties surrounding the relationships of facts that may not be revealed by telephone. In most cases the telephone is an inadequate substitute for direct personal contact, but in radio reporting newsmen gather much of their local news by phone because speed is more essential to their work than subtlety, details, or quantity of information. (Tape-recorded interviews made by telephone have become a radio staple.) Most newspaper reporters gather news by telephone only when a personal interview is not feasible (or when they get lazy). A careful reporter uses the phone for checking simple facts, when speed is essential, or when distance or other factors make it impossible to reach a news source face to face. Sometimes a telephone call will bypass an office door when repeated knocks on it get no answer.

Newspaper legmen, including beat reporters, who need to meet onrushing deadlines use the telephone to reach their offices quickly, and rewrite men depend on the phone for information from legmen who have already collected the facts. In addition to beat reporters who phone in their stories because they are too far from their typewriters to meet their deadlines, there are some reporters who almost never write stories themselves: for instance, those who must never be long away from their beats, such as police reporters on metropolitan papers. These reporters use the telephone instead of the typewriter; after they have gathered the news, they telephone it to rewrite men waiting in the newsroom.

Newsmen have developed many "techniques" for phoning stories in, two of them more common than others. In both methods the outside reporter opens the phone conversation with a general statement that gives the rewrite man a view of the nature, tone, and substance of the story. In the less usual method the reporter shapes the story in advance and dictates a virtually complete story, with well-formed lead and well-organized body. This reporter is dictating, in effect, to the rewrite man's typewriter; the rewriter, listening at the other end of the line, should have a finished story when the receivers are back on their hooks.

Few American newsmen learn shorthand; in England it is the unusual journalist who doesn't know it. Many journalists think that American reporting suffers because reporters don't use shorthand. The validity of this view is hard to deny; the

The other method sounds more like the casual manner used to tell a friend about an event. The reporter departs from "pure" conversation by weeding out information that doesn't help the story; he may suggest points of emphasis; but he doesn't dictate the

more precise and complete the reporter's notes, the more accurate and meaningful the story based on the notes.

final form of the story. He gives the rewrite man the essential information; the rewrite man uses the information in whatever way he thinks most effective. A reporter using this method might sound something like this:

This is Thompson, calling from the police press room. Story here about a traffic smash a few minutes ago . . . one man killed. I'll give you his name first: William Sindwich. First name William; last name spelled S as in Sam, I as in Indiana, N as in Nebraska, D as in Denver, W-I-C-H . . . like sandwich except with an I instead of an A. He was 28 years old, and his home was San Francisco . . . Here's what happened. Sindwich was driving along on South Main Street, alone . . . cops think he was just traveling through the city. At the corner of Lincoln Avenue a car barged into Main without stopping at the stop sign . . . smashed into Sindwich's car and turned it over. Sindwich was dead when the ambulance crew got him free . . . Yeah, Sindwich was going south, the other fellow east. The cops arrested the other driver—name of Pike Kolasky. Pike, as in Pike's Peak. Kolasky . . . K as in Kansas, O-L-A-S as in Sam, K for Kansas again, Y as in Yellowstone. Or Yucatan. Kolasky is 19, lives in town at 419 South Madison. That's Street, not Avenue. He wasn't hurt, the cops say. He's going to get a negligent homicide rap, they tell me. Got no previous record . . . Yeah—at 2:15 this afternoon . . . Any questions?

Note the way Thompson reported the story:

1) He identified himself and the source of the story—the police press room.
2) He gave a quick summary: "Traffic crash . . . man killed."
3) He gave the principal name, and spelled it out carefully; he followed the spelling with more identifying information.
4) He gave a simple chronological account of the event.
5) He spelled out the name of the second man in the story.
6) He reported the official action expected.
7) He gave the rewrite man an opportunity for questions.

While Thompson was talking, the rewrite man was taking fast notes. Thompson probably told the story at normal conversational speed; the rewrite man did not try to record every word, but rather took down key words and phrases that would help him construct the story later. Most newsmen develop a kind of personal speedwriting, if they didn't know shorthand. They invent their own abbreviations, symbols, elisions, so that they can keep up with normal conversation.

The spelling technique is a device for insuring accuracy that is by no means peculiar to newsmen. Everyone who uses the telephone for relaying precise factual information has his own list of letter identifications; many workers keep such a list taped to their desks beside the telephone for ready reference. It is useful to identify letters by geographical names because they are easily recognized: A for Alabama, B for Buffalo, C for California (or Connecticut or Calcutta). Although geographical identifications are common, some reporters prefer standard given names: A for Alice, B for Barbara, C for Charlie. The purist uses the correct "A as in Alabama" or "A for Alabama," but the ungrammatical form "A like in Alabama" persists and is widely used by newsmen—even those who know better.

Although specific methods of news gathering differ because time and space schedules, forms of presentation, and audience requirements are different, the similarities of news media practice are more striking than the differences. All reporters use basically similar principles and practices in gathering news, whether they work for newspaper, news magazine, or radio or television.

PROJECTS

1. Interview a professional reporter working for a local newspaper or broadcasting station about problems of access to news. Write a report on what you learn.
2. Make up a list of specific questions about a newsworthy event you have observed recently. Go to five or more others who observed it and get their answers to the questions. Write a comment on the similarities or differences among their answers.
3. Select a five- or six-inch news story from a local paper. Break it down into its separate facts; then simulate reporting the facts by telephone to a rewrite man.

CHAPTER 9

Style in News Writing

"There is," wrote Christopher Morley, "no such thing as good style or bad style. The question is, Does it accomplish its intention?"

Morley, essayist, critic, and fiction writer, was talking about "literary" writing. He was saying, in effect, that what you always ask first is whether a piece of writing is effective, whether it does its peculiar job well, whether the author has combined his words and phrases and sentences to carry facts and ideas and emotional impulses economically, directly, and vigorously to the audience he has selected.

To put it differently: Morley means that there is no such thing as an absolute criterion by which to evaluate the style of all kinds of writing. Nobody would hold that a telephone book or a dictionary has "literary" style, but nobody could deny that the forms the compilers of such books have chosen are calculated to help readers take quick and sure advantage of their content. By this standard their style is first rank. It accomplishes its intention.

There may be a number of effective styles for a single purpose. Traditional books on English grammar and usage employ a carefully systematized style, straight-faced and straitlaced, without adornment, a style clearly suitable for such books' function. But a widely-admired book in this field, A Dictionary of Modern English Usage, *Second Edition, by H. W. Fowler, offers wit and caustic commentary along with its stric-*

What Morley said about writing in general applies no less to journalistic writing than to other kinds. Journalistic style may be effective; it may be ineffective; what is effective in one area of journalism may be grossly deficient in another. What does its work well on the sports page may be atrocious in the women's department. What is "good" for the *Christian Science Monitor* audience may not do at all for that of the Milwaukee *Sentinel.*

The fact that there is more than one road to a journalistic goal does not mean that the roadbeds are entirely different. Indeed, they may have more similarities than differences; and the similarities are funda-

tures on rhetoric, grammar, and diction. For many users penetrating and entertaining asides make the book more pleasing and helpful than similar works of more conventional manner.

mental. In almost any example of effective journalistic style, as of any called by another name—"literary," expository, narrative, technical, pedagogic—there are fundamental characteristics that must be present. The familiar tools are constant: simplicity, directness, economy, color and vitality, precision. The differences between writing effective for one purpose or audience and that effective for another are differences of degree, not of kind. What may be "easy" for one audience may be "hard" for another. But for any audience you set your planes of word choice and complexity of thought and structure according to the audience's characteristics, and then seek to write as simply on these planes as your skill, time, and patience will let you.

Conscientious journalists have become profoundly weary of a pair of common fallacies about journalistic writing: the careless assumption that emphasis on such primary qualities as simplicity and clarity means that writing with these qualities must be puerile (John Milton wrote with both simplicity and clarity), and the illogical generalization that because some journalistic writing is shoddy all journalistic writing is shoddy. Such conclusions are the products of lack of knowledge and of lazy thinking. That simplicity in writing is to be desired will be denied only by those who think that polysyllables spell elegance and that fancy rhetoric is synonymous with erudition and symbolic of high IQ. This chapter will have more to say on this subject.

The second criticism, though it does not stand up in syllogistic form, has more meat on its bones. A high proportion of journalistic writing, in newspapers, on the air, in advertising, is as *effective* as any writing anywhere, but it is a regrettable truth that too much of it is characterized by lack of precision, curbstone diction, careless grammar, and lazy acceptance of yesterday's tired phrasings. How much of this may be laid to the haste of journalism, how much to incompetence, how much to lack of self-respect and firmly held standards it is hard to say. All such forces contribute.

But it is no more reasonable to typify all journalistic writing by its blackest representatives than it would be to say that no movie actors can act because some can't or that all college football players have sinecure-job subsidies because some have. That much journalistic writing leaves a good deal to be asked nobody realizes more painfully than the large body of newsmen who take their craft seriously. Of them it is fair to say that they are their own severest critics. The fact that various agencies of the press have in recent years employed "readability experts" to help them improve their writing is one evidence both of awareness of the problem and of the desire to solve it. Scores of local and national awards, in individual newsrooms, in Newspaper Guild contests, through Sigma Delta Chi, under many other sponsorships, attest to newsmen's earnestness about doing their work better. A comparison of the press of recent years with that before 1900 shows that, for today's purposes, today's best writing is surer, sharper, clearer than its most illustrious ancestors.

In any case, there is no roof on the effectiveness to which journalistic writing may aspire, and there is no disposition in any responsible newsroom to erect one.

College journalists are sometimes told by writing teachers who have flouted opportunities to know better that "working in journalism will ruin your writing." Such counsel is like telling a 10-second runner not to compete with 10.5-second men because to do so will slow him up. This book has already suggested that some of the influences in some newsrooms must be fought by the man who hopes to write well. But some influences will help him: the demand for conciseness, the demand for accuracy, the demand for telling clarity and vividness, not to mention the competition with the man at the next desk. He can gain facility in the newsroom more surely than almost anywhere else; whether he gains it at the expense of effectiveness depends primarily on his personal "artistic integrity."

Newsroom men aware of the Hemingways, Lewises, Sevareids, and scores of others who have turned initial writing experience in newsrooms to profit rather than let their style dissolve under it are understandably impatient with the counsel that "it will ruin your style." They know that it will ruin no style but that of "writers" whose inability to withstand it suggests that they may not have been going anyplace anyway.

The Goal of "Reaching Everybody"

A significant conditioning factor in most journalistic writing is its character as mass communication. It is not often that any news story, advertisement, or magazine article is written in the hope that it will reach literally all 200 million of us. But most journalistic "messages" are designed with the expectation that they will have impact on at least a significant share of the defined audience at whose interests they are aimed. Some "messages" frankly attempt to reach audiences of many millions: news stories broadcast by the networks, for example; national advertising; the kind of magazine feature material that the *Reader's Digest* elects to publish.

This fact puts double emphasis on such contributors to effective style as simplicity, clarity, and directness. The broader the audience, the more desirable the use of vocabulary and grammatical patterns that will achieve an "easy" rating on the readability scales.

And this sometimes means, in the hands of incompetent or slovenly craftsmen, the inept product that critics of American journalism deride and fear. It can lead to vulgarity and oversimplification. It can lead to lazy acceptance of the cult of the lowest common denominator, the principle of choosing as target the lowest man on the totem pole.

But the search for simplicity need not lead to the shallow nor the crass, to lack of precision, nor cheapness, nor counterfeit workmanship. Indeed, journalistic writing that has meaning for the largest audience is likely to be that with the surest use of English, the most artful as well as the most artistic design, the most subtle and discriminating selection of fact and detail.

The writer of this sort of journalistic prose approaches his daily undertakings with respect for his audience and an informed and understanding desire to serve it. One of the emptiest of American clichés is a saying popular among those whose taste for esoteric writing and thinking is too often matched only by their scorn for the multitudes outside their circle: "The average American is fourteen years old." Whatever validity there may be in such a generalization is complex and involved; it is not the simple flat aphorism its mouther would have you think. Even if it were a substantial guide to audience evaluation, it would not justify "writing down," nor make such condescension an effective means to an end. Moreover, it would not make writing easy; on the contrary, it would almost always intensify the problem.

Pluses in Journalistic Style

Just as there are deadfalls to be avoided in newswriting (some of them are discussed in the next chapter), so there are guideposts that not only warn of dangers but also point toward a proper destination. The very terms that name the characteristics of effective news writing can be used to list these guides:

1) Thoroughness of reporting
2) Orderliness of structure
3) Precision of diction and grammar
4) Economy
5) Vitality, color, imagination

An additional bonus accruing from a reporter's mastery of his materials is defined by poet-critic John Ciardi in the Saturday Review *(July 20, 1957): ". . . obscurity is not at all the same thing as unintelligibility. Obscurity is what happens when a writer undertakes a theme and method for which the reader is not sufficiently prepared. Unintelligibility is what happens when the writer undertakes a theme for which he himself is not sufficiently prepared."*

KNOW YOUR STORY   No one has yet found a substitute for thorough reporting. For fairly obvious reasons, a writer must have full grasp of *all* the facts relevant to the story he hopes to tell. Without pervading knowledge, he cannot pinpoint the center of his material—he cannot, that is, decide on the theme of his story, its core, its essential summary. And without such knowledge he cannot decide on the flavor the finished story should offer. The newswriter does not depart from objectivity when he plans what primary effects he wants his story to produce on the consumer's mental and emotional sounding boards. Indeed, it is basic to the concept of objectivity that he make up his mind what effects the facts ought to have ("ought" not in a moral sense, but rather to mean that the consumer should get the sense of standing in the reporter's shoes). Without full mastery of his material, a full view of all facets of his subject, no writer can be certain he has achieved these effects.

And without certainty he cannot arrive at defensible decisions as to how to treat his material in order to carry accurate meanings to consumers.

For these reasons, among others, "Know your story" is the newswriter's first commandment.

CONSTRUCT IT RIGHT   Without orderly, logical organization, no piece of writing can carry the full meaning intended for it to an audience.

Turn to the stories on pages 154 and 161. Neither of these stories has been put together properly, from the point of view of logic of material and meaning; sometimes their facts have not been properly selected. No virtuosity of writing can overcome or cover up such defects.

Or, to put it the other way, skillful writing will help a newsman give maximum effectiveness to a set of facts he has mastered thoroughly, sifted, and organized properly.

Chapter 11 will go deeper into problems of news story organization.

THE GRAMMAR AND THE DICTIONARY   Your desk book of grammar gives you the rules of the road. They are rules that are based on centuries of experience, rules that, writing men and women have agreed, will help in the delicate task of building words into phrases and phrases into sentences so that they become most readily acceptable to human thought habits. Ignoring or fracturing them is a good deal like making your own rules for driving a car in traffic. Suppose you decide to turn left at the corner of Broadway and 42nd Street. You may get by with it. More likely you will end by snarling the purposes and tempers of a score of other drivers, and possibly end up with a bashed fender to boot. You have failed to achieve your objective, or worse. You haven't been effective.

A first-rate condensation of the most important "rules of the road" for writers is The Elements of Style, *by William Strunk, Jr., and E. B. White (New York: Macmillan Co. 1959). A one-dollar paperback, it has been a boon to thousands of journalists, student or professional. An excellent and more extensive book is E. L. Callihan's* Grammar for Journalists *(New York: Ronald, 1957).*

• •

One of the "reforms" credited to Basil L. Walters (affectionately and widely known as Stuffy) when he became executive editor of the Chicago Daily News *was the short-sentence-short-paragraph rule, a rule to which Walters had become devoted during successful years with Des Moines and*

There is nothing sacrosanct about the rules of grammar. Like traffic rules, they change as the needs of communication change; they bend and give way before appropriate stresses. There are times when the effect a writer seeks can be gained only by breaking them.

But in general "good English," English that observes the rules, is the clearest and most forceful English. It gives the eye or the ear what the reader or listener is accustomed to. It doesn't offer an unnecessary challenge to the consumer; it doesn't stop him with the realization or the uneasy suspicion that something is wrong. Ordinarily it provides the easiest, the most economical, the surest path to understanding.

The same comment may be made about precision of diction. The self-respecting craftsman takes up his tools with pride and tender regard. He wants them sharp and strong and delicate, and he knows that each time he or one of his fellows misuses them, each time someone lets slip a *flaunt* for a *flout*, a *literally* for a *figuratively*, a *good* for a *well*, a *nominal* for a *small*, a tool is blunted, a word is degraded. Each time the work of both writer and reader is made more difficult.

Minneapolis papers. One goal was the two-line lead, another the elimination of jargon, a third the reduction of even the most complicated news to man-in-the-street terms. Most newsmen agree that the paper gained in readability. But some, on the paper's staff and off it, thought that the reform went too far—"you can't do a diplomatic story or one on economic trends in nursery language." One of the Knight newspapers (the News at that time was under Knight ownership) subjected Walters editorially to the following gentle spoofing:

Stuffy Walters dropped by Charlotte the other week.
Visiting.
Nice fellow.
One of the boys.
One of the really great boys.
Big.
Almost a legend.
Maybe strictly a legend.
Who's to say?
Stuffy grew to size as managing editor.
It's a title.
Means "boss."
Nowadays they call it "executive editor."
New age.
Same meaning.
Stuffy does most of his bossing around the Chicago *Daily News.*
Nice, nonetheless.
A little peculiar, maybe.
Likes short sentences.
Terse.
Gets 'em.
We're glad he came by.
Glad.
Honestly.

TIGHT WRITING   A *mot* attributed to a businessman letter writer is that "I didn't have time to make it short." It has become a cliché, which means that it is a witty expression that has been exhausted by overuse. But the truth it expresses is untarnished. The leanness, the economy, the conciseness, and the terseness characteristic of "good" journalistic writing are not often easy to arrive at. They take time, thought, and a savage willingness to pare one's own beloved rhetoric to its marrow.

This too is something that is said in this book more than once. In the interests of tight writing, it will be said here as stingily as possible: Say it briefly. Say it fully and properly; but drop excess baggage, cut out the adornment that hides rather than amplifies. Speak your piece and stop.

It has been said that there never has been a piece of writing that could not be shaved to advantage. This may be overstatement; but most editors would argue for it. (So would most experienced writers. They sometimes find the surgery performed by editors on their products painful, but they do not often deny, when time has let judgment temper anguish, that their work is the better for the operation.)

The key to successful cutting is not in the wholesale elimination of paragraphs or sections of a piece of writing; if that earlier step in the writing process, selection and organization of material, has been properly managed there should be no major segment available for discard. Rather, it lies in the ability to run a firm pencil through a word here, a phrase or sentence there. The true professional is the one who guides his pencil by a relentless eye on the audience and the effect he seeks, who readily sacrifices the verbal gems he has created, no matter how pat his parental pride makes them seem, if the result will be to inform or move the consumer more surely, more quickly, more appropriately.

One aid to this process is not available in most forms of news communication: the advantage of "letting it cool." It is easier to identify the words and phrases you don't need when the writing is a day or a week old than when it is still smoking. The newsman, whose product never gets time to cool, rarely has this advantage. He must nurture fast, sure editing judgment.

BRING IT TO LIFE   Everything in this chapter, in an important sense, has to do with "bringing it to life." You guard your writing against the perils of haste, you avoid bromides, you watch diction, you slice out verbosity, and you use all the writer's arts to gain movement and vigor.

You go beyond these more or less routine measures. You remember the counsel of your composition teachers to use the active where you can instead of the passive: "Koufax fanned Mays" is more interesting, moves faster than "Mays was fanned by Koufax." You remember, too, that verbs are vigorous words because they connote action, and that concrete nouns are strong because they represent specific and readily identifiable concepts; conversely, that you can kill an idea by overdressing it with adverbs and adjectives (though this does not mean that you should avoid modifiers when they give vitality to fact or idea). The astute teacher and critic of writing, John Ciardi, advises, "Never send an adjective on a noun's errand."

You will learn other ways of gaining color. Underscore these suggestions:

First of all, select significant, meaningful, characteristic detail.

Seek the appropriately specific rather than the general. Say *scalpel* (when it's the right word) rather than *knife; dachshund* instead of *dog; scarlet* instead of *red; swamp* or *smother* or *outlast* instead of *defeat; dance* or *amble* or *saunter* instead of *walk.* But make sure that the term you choose is the most accurate you can find; be sure it is chosen because it is right rather than because it is interesting. If it is right, it is likely to be interesting.

Search for the simple word, the commonly-used word, rather than the esoteric, the erudite, or the fancy.

Look for the word that replaces a phrase. Keep sentences mostly short, direct, and simple in structure.

Seek colorful, illuminating figures of speech and illustrations—but never over-ornate or overcomplex ones.

The work of professional newsmen—stories chosen usually because they are effective, but sometimes to illustrate weaknesses—may be more helpful to a novice than any amount of exposition, if he examines it with critical and discerning eye. A few are presented in this book; but no journalist, young or old, can ever afford to give up picking his own clinical samples.

Here are excerpts from a Pulitzer prize story by George Weller of the Chicago *Daily News*—a timeless story even though it was written before some of the readers of this book were born:

"They are giving him ether now" was what they said back in the aft torpedo rooms.

"He's gone under and they're getting ready to cut him open," the crew whispered, sitting on their pipe bunks cramped between torpedoes.

One man went forward and put his arm quietly around the shoulders of another man who was handling the bow diving planes. "Keep her steady, Jake," he said. "They've just made the first cut. They're feeling around for it now."

"They" were a little group of anxious-faced men with their arms thrust into reversed white pajama coats. Gauze bandages hid all their expressions except the tensity in their eyes.

"It" was an acute appendix inside Dean Rector, of Chautauqua, Kan. The stabbing pains had become unendurable the day before, which was Rector's first birthday at sea. He was 19.

The big depth gauge that looks like a factory clock and stands beside the "Christmas tree" of red and green gauges regulating the flooding chambers showed where they were. They were below the surface. And above them—and below them, too—were enemy waters crossed and recrossed by whirring propellers of Japanese destroyers, transports, and submarines.

The nearest naval surgeon competent to operate on the young seaman was thousands of miles and many days away. There was just one way to prevent the appendix from bursting and that was for the crew to operate upon their shipmate themselves.

And that's what they did: they operated upon him. It was probably one of the largest operations in number of participants that ever occurred.

"He says he's ready to take the chance," the gobs whispered from bulkhead to bulkhead.

"That guy's regular"—the word traveled from bow planes to propeller and back again.

They kept her steady.

The chief surgeon was a 23-year-old pharmacist's mate wearing a blue blouse with white-taped collar and a squashy white duck cap. His name was Wheeler B. Lipes.

[*The story tells of Lipes' inadequate training; the grim courage with which he and his patient approached the operation; the tension aboard the sub as substitutes for anesthetic, antiseptics, surgical instruments were improvised. At length, the climactic point:*]

It took Lipes in his flapfinger rubber gloves nearly 20 minutes to find the appendix.

"I have tried one side of the caecum," he whispered after the first minutes. "Now I'm trying the other."

Whispered bulletins seeped back into the engine room and crew's quarters.

"The doc has tried one side of something and now is trying the other."

After more search, Lipes finally whispered, "I think I've got it. It's curled way up behind the blind gut."

Lipes was using the classic McBurney's incision. Now was the time when his shipmate's life was completely in his hands.

"Two more spoons" (*bent metal spoons had become surgical retractors*). They passed the word to Lt. Ward.

"Two spoons at 14:45 hours," wrote Skipper Ferrall on his notepad.

"More flashlights and another battle lantern," demanded Lipes.

The patient's face, lathered with white petrolatum, began to grimace.

"Give him more ether," ordered the doc.

Hoskins looked doubtfully at the original five pounds of ether, now sunken to hardly three quarters of one can. But once again the tea-strainer was soaked in ether. The fumes mounted, thickening the wardroom air and making the operating staff giddy.

"Want those blowers speeded up?" the captain asked the doc.

The blowers began to whir louder.

Suddenly came the moment when the doc reached out his hand, pointing toward the needle threaded with 20-day chromic catgut.

One by one the sponges came out. One by one the tablespoons bent into right angles were withdrawn and returned to the galley. At the end it was the skipper who nudged Lipes and pointed to the tally of bent tablespoons. One was missing. Lipes reached into the incision for the last time and withdrew the wishbone spoon and closed the incision.

They even had the tool ready to cut off the thread. It was a pair of fingernail scissors, well scalded in water and torpedo juice.

At that moment the last can of ether went dry . . .

[*The story then reports the operation's success and Rector's return to duty; it tells the reader finally that on a submarine shelf in a bottle "swayed the first appendix ever known to have been removed below enemy waters."*]

It does not take the eye of a Pulitzer-prize judge to see why this kind of news writing remains compelling years after the event. The excerpts—less than half the entire story—show the simplicity and guilelessness with which Weller wrote it, the classical directness of sentence structure, the telling selection of detail—not every detail, but only enough significant ones to bring the total circumstance to sharp reality, and the trenchantly specific facts that give the reader the sense of seeing and hearing, even smelling, the scene. They also attest the validity of the advice of Ted Bernstein of the New York *Times*: "One way of giving the reader a sense of immediacy in reporting . . . is to inject quotations—if possible, dialogue—into a story."

Another story, one that International News Service dispatched from Kansas in a tornado-torn year, shows many of the same values and devices:

This quiet town died in its sleep Wednesday night.

A tornado slashed across Udall like a sword. In less than a minute, 60 years of growing was cut down to the sod.

It was what they call a "tornado night" on the Southern Plains. In all, at least 115 persons died in four states, 62 of them in Udall. More than 1,000 were injured.

But Udall got the worst of it. Udall was wiped out.

It came at 10:29 P.M. Scott Mathews, 25, the town barber, was sleeping in a bunk at the rear of his shop. He can't be found. Neither can the shop.

There was a "social" at the town pool hall. Fourteen bodies were recovered from the wreckage.

There were three old peoples' rest homes in the little town of 500 people. Ten bodies were found in their ruins. There may be a dozen more.

The time of the catastrophe was set by the town's lone telephone operator. Operators along the circuit in other towns lost contact with her at 10:29 P.M. Her body was located at dawn.

Few residents can be found who actually saw the twister hit. Motorists stumbled on the horror when they found flat darkness where Udall should have been.

Nobody lives here anymore. Of the 500 people of Udall, not a one has been found who wasn't injured in some way. Everyone has been taken to neighboring towns. Only four battered buildings still are standing.

Aside from search crews, only the missing dead remain.

Udall's 35-year-old mayor, Earle Rowe, pitched into rescue operations and helped burrow through wreckage to rescue the screaming injured.

He himself was evacuated as a casualty. But he freed himself and tottered back to help.

He was evacuated three times before he collapsed. At a hospital in Winfield physicians said Mayor Rowe had a brain concussion.

Most folks were in bed, like Dean Riser, who taught vocational agriculture at Udall high school. He said: "The first thing I knew, the house was moving around. By the time I could do anything, the house was across the street from where it used to be."

It had been raining off and on for the last two days. Ray Binford decided it might be a good idea to get his aged mother over to his home "to get the whole family together—just in case." He was in his car with his mother when the wind came. He said: "We didn't have any warning. Not a bit. Something picked the car up, threw it across the street and I guess smashed us against another car or a tree or something. I was knocked out, and when I woke up I saw our car was on top of a neighbor's car.

"Mother was hurt and I tried to get help for her. But there wasn't any help.

"It was horrible. People were screaming in the dark, groaning and trying to locate their families.

"Finally, some help began to arrive and we got my mother to a hospital in Winfield. Then I found my wife and kids had lived through it. I guess you might say I'm lucky."

One of the first persons to reach Udall was Patrolman John Nail from the Sedgwick County sheriff's office in Wichita. "He said: 'The first thing I thought was, My God, the whole town is flattened.'

"It was about one o'clock and pretty dark, but I could see the dead and the injured laying around. I saw people mangled to bits. One boy had been smashed up against a tree. We couldn't find his head.

"A big grain elevator was demolished and there wasn't anything left of the railroad station. As we rounded up the injured, the ambulances began picking them up and took them to hospitals in Wichita, Winfield, Wellington, and the high school in Mulvane."

Lt. Col. W. W. Goodvin mustered 125 men of the National Guard and moved into the stricken area. Civil defense units, the women's disaster corps, the Red Cross, and other groups threw in their forces.

Wichita sent its third detail of 35 policemen, keeping only a skeleton crew for home operations.

Workers said it was difficult to determine where houses had been.

"Most of them didn't have basements, hardly any foundations," they said. "Maybe a rock of two where the house had rested."

Col. Goodvin, a Wichita real estate salesman, said: "The situation calls for martial rule—but there's nobody left in Udall. Everybody's been evacuated."

Later yesterday, a few people came home. Mayor Rowe was with them, released from the hospital, and they started talking of rebuilding. After a while they went back to their temporary homes in neighboring towns.

[*The story continues, describing the horrors at other towns in the area—"mopping up the story." At the* end, after reporting that "victims are trying to pick up shattered pieces of their lives," the story is tied to- gether with this paragraph:]

But not at Udall, Kan. Udall is dead. Nobody lives here any more.

The dangers of overwriting, and especially of deciding in advance of an event what clichés to apply to it (clichés either of thought or word), were displayed in some of the reporting of a "general strike" at Stamford, Connecticut. Some 10,000 organized workers planned a two-hour "sympathy walkout." Some of the New York papers, both "sensational" and "conservative," went overboard in reporting the event. One said that "industrial life was threatened with paralysis . . . by the far-flung walkout." Another reported that "Stamford reeled today under the impact of a general strike stoppage . . ." and some city desks pestered their assignment men at the scene for details of murder, mob, and mass fighting. The antilabor columnist Westbrook Pegler referred to the event in such terms as "Ku Klux Klan terror" and "a protest organized against law and government and in favor of rioting, assault, and anarchy." In fact, according to a punctilious reportorial analysis by Chard Powers Smith in Harper's Magazine, *there were no arrests, no broken windows, no fights; the demonstration, which was orderly and good-natured, tapered off short of the two hours planned for it. Smith says that the news magazines and most other news media covered it soberly and accurately, especially in stories that followed it. But some, both in concept and word, gave erroneous impressions.*

Readers found this a dramatically moving story. The writer has not "reached"; he has used memorable details simply and with restraint. He makes graphic use of quotations. He uses imaginative language where it will help: note that the hackneyed phrase *a tornado slashed . . .* has been brought to life by the addition of the appropriate *like a sword;* and that he says not that *the town was leveled* but that motorists *found flat darkness where Udall should have been.*

Like most stories, this one could be strengthened. It shows signs of the haste with which it had to be written; at times its rhythm stumbles. But its shortcomings do not pervert its sense of tragic urgency and drama.

Both of these stories, to be sure, are made from dramatic stuff. A moving, compelling story emerges readily from stirring material if the temptation to overwrite, to adorn, to try to make good material better can be downed. One of the marks of the "good" writer is that he knows how to spurn these allurements.

For a story from much more ordinary clay, look at the James B. Reston dispatch on page 156. The Washington correspondent rarely deals with materials that are so highly charged emotionally as the tornado story, at least on their surface, and this very fact tests his competence to "make his stuff interesting"— to bring to life events that for most readers would be dull, or at best routine. In this story, Reston has given such an event life and sheen by finding the distinctive in it and by skillful selection of detail plus direct and simple language.

The following short story from a small Midwestern daily deserves notice for imagination in form, but perhaps more for excellence of detail. It would be stronger if it were pruned by a few lines and one or two of its more far-fetched whimsies:

Local authorities have just solved this town's youngest crime wave.

Seven boys, ranging from 6 to 13, formed a "club."

Purpose: thievery from local stores.

Initiation fee: any stolen article—the bigger the better.

Dues: 50 cents a week, usually stolen from parents.

Privileges: wearing distinctive shoulder patches to signify outstanding achievement.

Old business: Jackknives, padlocks, model airplanes, holsters, neckerchiefs, and the like.

New business: more of the same.

First meeting: several weeks ago.

Suspension of operations: several days ago by alert sporting goods store owner.

Next scheduled meeting: probate court.

Science reporting is particularly challenging because most readers think themselves unable to understand scientific terms and concepts. Joseph R. Hixson, science writer for the New York *Herald Tribune,* faced a complex problem in reporting a speech by a medical scientist to a group of surgeons. To put the story into form for lay comprehension, Hixson wrote it with almost complete avoidance of scientific terminology; he used familiar symbols and "ordinary" language; he employed analogies and similes, as well as evocative descriptive verbs. Note the sparing appearance of adjectives, the reliance on simple direct sentences:

CHICAGO, Ill.—When surgeons decide they must cut a growing lump of cancer out of a patient, they know they face a cruel risk.

Just touching that ugly sponge of malignancy with fingers or scalpel can dislodge invisible cancer cells. In a few patients, those cells are picked up by the bloodstream and carried to remote parts of the body where they start new and more dangerous cancer colonies called metastases.

Thus the doctors may in some cases be making the patient worse by their treatment.

And so, surgeons here this week yearned to believe a preliminary report by Dr. Ward Griffen of the University of Minnesota, that the well-known plasma expander called Dextran may prevent the postoperative spread of cancer. Griffen found that the compound keeps wandering cancer cells from clumping together in a new site.

But no sooner had Griffen reported his experiments with mice than he said he also found that mixing Dextran with a tumor mass made the cancer grow much faster when he implanted the mixture in his mice. Medical men do not like two-edged swords.

At a session of the American College of Surgeons meeting here, Griffen and Dr. J. Bradley Aust explained that they turned to Dextran in their research because of previous reports that anti-clotting agents such as heparin cut down the spread of cancer.

But surgeons can't use an anticlotting agent before an extensive cancer operation because there would be too much bleeding.

So the Minnesota doctors turned to Dextran, which thins the blood but does not affect its ability to clot. The big molecules of Dextran stay in the blood vessels into which they are injected. There they attract water from all of the tissues of the body, thus enlarging the total volume of circulating blood.

Since doctors often use Dextran to restore blood volume after operations, Griffen and Aust saw no reason why they should not inject some before a gloved finger or the steel of a scalpel ever touched the cancerous mass.

When they tried this in mice, giving first Dextran, then an injection of breast tumor cells, they found that they were drastically cutting down the colonization of mouse lung by floating cancer cells.

Griffen says he has some evidence to suggest that the negative electric charge on all cancer cells is somehow increased by the Dextran molecules. When the charge increases, the cells repel each other more strongly, just as the same poles in two magnets do.

That could be the reason why fewer new cancers form. Or, Griffen speculated, the big molecules may change the lining of the blood vessels in some way so they keep the cancer cells floating in the blood and do not allow them to pass out of it.

Griffen is pretty sure he knows why injecting a cancer with Dextran enables it to prosper. He thinks the Dextran pulls fluid into the tumor just as it pulls water into the blood. That new fluid coming in brings more nourishment to the cancer cells, and they respond by growing faster.

A useful exercise would be to reread the Hixson story with a view to listing the "devices" he uses to make the story flow: similes ("just as the poles in two magnets do"), analogies (Dextran pulls fluid into the tumor as it pulls water into blood), figurative language ("Medical men do not like two-edged swords"), lay language ("lump of cancer," "wandering cancer cells"), and so on.

The following story was drawn from routine burial both by its suspended-interest pattern (see chapter 15) and its attention to revealing detail:

A man sat through two shows in a local theater last night—sat with unseeing eyes and ears that did not hear.

He was dead.

Through most of the second show, a city detective sat beside the body to prevent it from falling from the seat.

The detective was given the gruesome duty after the county coroner decided that course was best—so the audience in the theater would not be disturbed.

A woman patron of the theater seated beside the man saw him slump over. At first she believed he was sleeping. But after he remained motionless and silent for more than 30 minutes she became alarmed and told the theater manager.

A police surgeon slipped quietly into the theater, made an examination of the body in the dark, pronounced the man dead and called the coroner.

The detective took up his watch—his eyes on the screen, his hand gripping the man's coat.

He sat thus through the gay comedy and guarded the body until the last of the patrons had gone. The coroner took charge then.

The man, victim of a heart attack, was identified as . . .

The paragraphs below come from what might have been a routine police story. The first half of the story tells of the squad-car chase and capture of two teen-agers, a chase that involved dangerous speed and gunfire. Then it closes with this colorful description and explanation:

One of the young men, held for further investigation, gave the following account to a representative of this paper:

"We were gassing at an oil station and bragging about the car's power and speed. We thought we would give the station boys a thrill so we burned rubber going out and were spotted by these squad rod boys.

"Our borrowed rod is a 31 Ford full house, Merc head, double stacks, dual carbs, grooved cams, channel job —good for a hundred MPH, I guess.

"They tailed us for a few blocks at 70 or 75 miles per and then other prowl rods began to close in and they started pouring 38 specials our way. They nicked one of our rubbers and we said quits—this is for the chaplain.

"Now if you print this in the paper, don't be hard on us hot-rod crocks. We're just a bunch of fun-loving boys."

A newspaper photographer who is a sports car enthusiast translated the description of the car as follows:

"It is a 1931 model A Ford with completely 'souped-up' engine, made as 'hot' (fast) as possible.

"The 'double stacks' are two exhaust pipes. The car

has twin carburetors ('dual carbs'), the camshaft has been altered to keep valves open longer ('grooved cams'), and the floorboards have been cut down to make the car lower ('channel job')."

Restraint and simplicity of style that seems too natural to be artful (but that is usually attained only by painstaking effort) mark the following story. It is charged with pathos, and its writer might have let it become maudlin. But he kept his own emotions under control, and the result is that the event itself evokes the response in the reader that it did in him.

NEW YORK, N.Y. (AP) —The young doctor leaned back in the chair and smiled. "I'd give the patient another few weeks," he said. "A month or so at the most."

The doctor himself is the patient.

So Dr. Napoleão Leaureano, 36-year-old Brazilian physician, is going home to die. His plane was to leave this morning.

"A man ought to die at home," he said. "We have a fine new home. We've been making payments three years . . ."

He looked at his pretty 25-year-old wife, Marcina, and she said, "Oh, yes, it's lovely. Very lovely."

It has seas of flowers spilling over the wide yards that border on a shady street, and a patio and small pond in back. It's summer in Brazil, and the flowers will be blooming now. Their daughter, little 4-year-old Maria, will be there too.

"We're in a hurry to get back," the doctor said. "So much to do, and so . . . well, so much to do."

About a year ago Dr. Leaureano, a surgeon, completed a specialty course in cancer in preparation for setting up a diagnosis and treatment center in his home town, Joao Pessoa, Brazil. Shortly thereafter, he discovered he had the disease—the virtually unstoppable lymph cancer (lymph sarcoma) that spreads relentlessly through the body tissue.

Hundreds of his patients and friends, many of whom he had cared for without charge, scraped together a fund to send him to Memorial Hospital here, a major cancer research center.

But the hospital specialists here found it was too late to help.

"Yes, it's a little hard at first to reconcile yourself to it," he said. "But then, your perspective begins to change, and you're ready for it. You see things more clearly, more sharply."

And what, a reporter asked through an interpreter, do you see?

"Well, you see how very important work is, especially work that you want to finish. You cherish friendships more than ever. You recognize that affection, good will, and love are the main things . . ."

He glanced over at his wife, who now sat silently in a corner of the room. He added: "And family, the ones who are close."

He got up and walked stiffly across the room, and put his hand on his wife's shoulder. She stared down at the floor.

The reporter said to the interpreter: "Would you ask her how she feels to have such a courageous husband?"

"She's very proud," the interpreter said. "But I'm not going to ask her, because she's going to cry."

The next two stories show the dangers of overwriting. The first, by a male sob-sister widely known for his sentimental features, fails of conviction for a number of apparent reasons:

None lives who can quite understand it.

It isn't just death. Death can be kind as well as terrible. It's the taking of little children, cruelly, suddenly, almost as if some unknown power were striking in utter callousness. The crushing of the bud seems so needless, the heartbreak that follows so bitter a thing.

Little Melissa was 5. That is a tender age, the age that retains the fragile loveliness of babyhood and adds to it the wonderment of a mind and personality developing. To her the world was a bright and shining adventure, its winding ways safeguarded by love. It had been so since the very dawn of her existence.

[*The writer tells of the "must nots" Melissa had learned, among them the "must not cross the street without looking."*]

But this dreadful thing of Wednesday morning. There had been no violation of "must not." In the early springlike morning with its hint of bright days to come, with its bits of deep blue sky breaking gloriously through the clouds, she had gone for a walk, her little four-footed companion racing ahead and barking his delight at being alive and being Melissa's own particular property.

She had stopped, just as her parents had told her, at the corner. She had looked up and down. Far away was a car but her swift, flashing little legs could carry her to safety long before— The car, a ton and more of metal and glass, rushing through the day, its fenders flashing in the sun, rushing on and on, its driver hurrying, hurrying . . .

Our whole lives seem to be hurrying these mad days of this mad century. Hurrying for what? What is the aim, the goal, the end?

But how was Melissa to know? . . . Her world was a world of love and tenderness and safety. Not a place where cruel things rush down on little girls, screaming protests to clutching brakes, roaring the power that rises within them.

It was all so sudden. It had been a day of dappling sunshine and the promise of brighter days to come . . . And then it was a gray day, a dour and dull and tragic day, with a little figure in the dust, a voice that was still and a frightened little dog standing there with puzzled eyes. . . .

The long, long reach to make sure that nobody misses the story's pathos kills this story. Its details don't carry the ring of truth because they are not made specific, are not tied down by specific information (did the writer invent them? you ask). Moreover, the reporter was not satisfied to let the event make its own point; he injected his own comment into the story—another invitation for the reader to doubt. Any reader can be pardoned if, halfway through such a story, he asks whether a writer so deeply involved in the emotion of the event can be a trustworthy reporter, or even the more fundamental question of whether he is honest, whether he feels what he asks the reader to feel. Both his attitude and his reliability become suspect.

This approach to writing is likely to lead all but the sternest character into stereotypes: "dawn of her existence," "fragile loveliness of babyhood," "bright and shining adventure," "hint of bright days to come"—even the "little four-footed companion" that, inevitably in this kind of writing, ends up with "puzzled eyes."

The writer of the following story overwrote in a different manner. He tried valiantly to find a novel approach to his material. But he didn't know when to stop:

NEW YORK, N.Y. (AP) —Alors, mon enfant, shed a tear this mercredi for the French liner Flandre, très chic, très proud. What a day to weep for la patrie.

She ended ze maiden voyage here—mon Dieu—at the end of ze towline, twenty-four hours late. An official welcoming luncheon—ze paté, ze vin, ze works—she had to be called off.

And now, nom de chien, her bar run dry, its beer fini, its liqueur all but.

The 20,500-ton vessel left Le Havre July 23. Quel splendeur, so bright ze sun, so proud ze tricolor . . .

Sports stories, which all too often fall short of the possibilities of the events they treat, are sometimes as masterly as this one from the Cleveland Indians' spring training camp:

TUCSON, Ariz. (NANA) —"I hear you got control," said Oscar Melillo skeptically.

"Man, you didn't hear no lie," Satchel Paige replied.

"How many strikes do you think you can throw outa, say, 10 pitches?" Melillo asked.

Satch considered this carefully.

"Maybe not over eight or nine," he said, "I ain't throwed since October. Gimme another week an' I'll throw 10 out of 10, all of 'em curves."

"A Coke says you can't throw eight," said Melillo.

Satch grinned. "Man, you got yourself a wager."

Jim Hegan placed a shin-guard on the outfield grass to serve as a plate, and Paige recoiled at the im-plied insult.

"I c'n throw a thousand outa a thousand over that big old thing," he said. "Put a baseball cap down there. That's all the plate old Satch needs."

An audience had gath-ered, including Dick Roz-nek, the Indians' wild young left-hander. Roznek's eyes popped.

"Is he kidding?" he asked.

Paige withered him with a look.

"Sonny boy, you c'n get yourself a Coke, free for nothin', if you think I'm kiddin'."

He went into an elaborate windup and threw his first pitch, a sidearm fast ball that crossed the button of the cap-plate, waist high.

"Strike!" said Hegan.

"I gotto give you that one," Melillo conceded.

"Man," scoffed Satch, "you gettin' generous in your old age."

"Look who's talking about old age," Bob Lemon snorted, and Satch turned on this newest heckler.

"You talk like you pitch," he said. "Loud but not smart. What you know about anybody's age?"

"All I know," said Lemon, "is there was a colored man on that barnstorming team of yours out on the coast last winter. He told me he was 47 years old, and I heard you call him 'son.' "

Satch wound up and buzzed another fast ball across the cap. A plumb bob hung from the straight line of its course would have touched the cap's red but-ton.

"Two!" said Hegan.

"Two," Melillo agreed.

Five strikes Satch pitched before he missed the cap's edge by a hair. He cut the narrow strike zone with two more, then missed again.

It was seven strikes, two balls, with one pitch to go.

"You're in trouble," said Melillo. "You're in bad trouble. Because you want to know why? Because the other ball club just sent in a pinch hitter. A midget. He's only this big." And Melillo dropped to his knees. "To make it worse, he hits from a crouch. You only got about six inches be-tween his shoulders and his knees."

"Shucks," said Satch.

He tied his long body into a tortured knot and as he unwound his whip-like arm came down. It halted sud-denly in the familiar pattern of Paige's famous hesitation pitch. Then it resumed its motion and the ball left Satch's hand and whizzed across the cap.

"Strike!" said Hegan.

"I guess I used too big a midget," said Melillo.

"Gee," said Roznek, "I wish I had a million dollars so I could buy some of that."

Finally, a story told in two words—with the help of its headline, HERE'S THE LATEST NEWS ON ELIZABETH, and of nation-wide knowledge that England's queen was about to give birth to a baby: The complete story:

LONDON, England.—Not yet.

The "Ease-of-Reading" Formulas

News services and news writers have profited in recent years by the work of the readability researchers (see also chapter 12). The "formulas" that these students have developed have served as valuable tools for criticism. A study at Ohio State University, for example, showed that much of the foreign news presented to American readers by the press was such "hard reading" that "aver-age" readers could not understand it without more effort than they are usually willing to exert. This and other similar analyses, placing a red flag before the news media and their writers, have been an effective spur to efforts at more un-derstandable news presentation.

But emphasis in recent years on gradations of readability and the formulas for measuring them has led to certain confusions:

A newsman interested in exploring the readability formulas may do so through books on individual researchers' work, by the researchers themselves, listed at the end of this chapter. He may do so with less time and effort through a comprehensive study of the subject by George R. Klare, The Measurement of Readability (Ames: Iowa State University Press, 1963) or an earlier and less inclusive book by Klare and Byron Buck, Know Your Reader (New York: Hermitage House, 1954).

1) The readability scale or formula is a criterion, a tool for criticism or analysis, a measuring stick more than a writing or teaching tool. It tells you, usually in mathematical terms, whether a piece of writing, yours or another's, is "hard" or "easy," whether it contains high or low percentages of simple words, abstractions, human interest impulses, personal references, specificity, generalization. It does not tell you how to write a sentence; indeed, it does not tell you how to write. Instead it helps you to see, after you have written a passage, how clear or how foggy it is likely to be to readers of varying competences.

If you use such a scale persistently, if you apply it faithfully to many samples of your writing, you may find that you can adapt your style with some fluency to include more, or fewer, of the characteristics of "easy" readability.

But it is not a tool to be employed consciously while your typewriter is running fast; it can only slow or becloud your writing if you try to use it in the flow of composition. Its helpfulness comes principally in evaluation of finished work and in subsequent rewriting. Its principles may become part of your equipment; but chances are that you have already mastered them, for there is nothing new about them except their formalization. Teachers of writing, and writers themselves, have used the principles for ages.

2) A readability scale must be applied to a good-sized specimen. One authoritative source makes it clear that you need from three to 30 "samples" of a piece of writing (the longer the work you are testing, the more samples), each of a paragraph or so, in order to apply any of the major formulas (there are more than 30) with assurance. You can't use it, except in the most general way, on the single sentence you are writing.

3) To discover by formula that a given news story has an "easy" rating—that it tests at seventh grade level, for instance—is not to say that it is most effective for its purpose. A news story in a medical journal about a new use for antibiotics would offend its readers if it had been reduced to kindergarten prose; a review of a book on international politics should not be *oversimplified,* any more than the book itself should. The character and interests and information needs of the audience remain the prime criteria for the writer's choice of style and manner.

Can It Be Done in a Newsroom?

An empirical approach to improvement of news readability and reader comprehension was suggested in an experiment undertaken by a journalistic research "team" from the University of Minnesota. Two experienced news writers went to the city room of a "typical" small-city daily and, with the cooperation of the editors, rewrote a number of the stories that were to appear in that afternoon's paper. The next day trained interviewers visited 200 local families and, through interviews and carefully designed tests, compared the comprehension and retention of facts gained from the stories as published in the paper with those gained from the "improved" versions. The test showed significantly larger comprehension and retention from the rewritten stories than from the "originals."

So limited an experiment proves little. What it suggests, however, is that skillfully written news stories employing the art and craft of experienced news writers will render news easier for consumers to assimilate. The news writers in this experiment used no readability formulas; their guide was the judgment or the expertise that experience had given them. Their rewritten stories tended to be shorter than the original forms; they were cast in simpler sentences and often used simpler diction; they omitted details that seemed unlikely to add to (or even likely to inhibit) understanding. These characteristics do not arise from the formulas; the formulas, on the contrary, test the presence of the characteristics.

A question asked by a newspaper editor at a news executives' conference at which the experiment here reported was under discussion is legitimate: Can a man in a newsroom, under the pressure of deadline, turn out the "improved" copy that the experiments achieved? It seems reasonable to answer "yes." The experimenters were not supermen, but merely solidly competent news writers. They worked at newsroom speed. It is more likely that the faults in the "original" stories were the result of carelessness, or perhaps of lack of proper guidance, than of inability to do better.

Comparisons drawn from one pair of the stories used in the experiment shows the kinds of "improvements" that were made. The first version was published in the paper precisely as it had come to the city desk from the state highway department—a formal "release." The rewrite turned out to produce higher understanding and memory of facts than did the published story.

NEWSPAPER STORY	EXPERIMENTAL STORY
With axle load restrictions already in effect on highways throughout the southern and south central parts of the state, the Highway Department this week warned that northward extension of the restricted zone may be necessary at any time with the return of thawing weather conditions. Just prior to last Wednesday's snowstorm and its accompanying colder weather, highway field engineers had reported noticeable softening of grades and surfaces on a considerable number of gravel and bituminous roads in a belt across the north central part of the state, and the department was able to avoid putting these additional routes under load restrictions only because of the return of relatively cold temperatures.	*Maybe last month's thaw meant spring to you—but to the state's gravel and black-top roads it may mean a lot of damage.* *The thaw softened roads in a belt across the north central part of the state, just as it had done in the southern part.* *But now it has frozen up again. And that's where the danger comes.* *In fact, highway department engineers are watching those northerly roads carefully, to see whether they're going to have to broadcast a warning to trucks:* *"Cut down your loads!"* *This is the story:* *The thaw took a lot of the frost out of the roads. Then came below-freezing temperature, and the roads*

Surface freezing during the latter part of last week, however, was not of sufficient depth to relax any of the restrictions already imposed, as the frost had left the ground to substantial depths due to the protracted February thawing period and accompanying rains.

The Highway Department attempts to forewarn shippers, haulers, and truck and bus operators several days in advance of the actual necessity for posting load limits. This is done through newspapers, radio stations, and day-by-day information bulletins mailed direct to transportation organizations. However, sudden weather changes which reflect themselves in rapid changes of the load carrying capacity of gravel and bituminous highways sometimes make it necessary to impose restrictions immediately as an emergency measure to prevent undue and costly damage.

froze again. But not very deep. So heavy loads on trucks may very well crack the lightly frozen road surfaces, just as they would thin ice.

That's the reason highway engineers may send out that warning. Lightly frozen roads will carry light loads —they'll crack under heavy ones.

Already the engineers have put limits on loads in south and south central Minnesota. That includes Faribault, Rice County and the nearby areas.

Highway engineers have, they say, "quite a problem" in giving shippers, haulers, truck and bus operators advance notice on load limits.

"We send out word every day to newspapers and radio stations," they add, "and bulletins to various firms as well.

"But if the thaw comes in a hurry, we'll have to get out word:

" 'Cut down bus and truck loads—save Minnesota roads!' "

Many of the changes are evident. Some statistics, however, help underline the differences: The original story has a 45-word lead, 234 words, 4 paragraphs, 6 sentences; the second version has a 23-word lead, 247 words, 13 paragraphs, 16 sentences. The first story has a Flesch Reading Ease Score of 14.3, which rates it "very hard," and a college-level score on the Dale-Chall scale; the second has a "fairly easy" (sixth grade) Flesch rating, and a seventh to eighth grade Dale-Chall scale.

Can News Style Be "Personal"?

Questioning whether a reporter can develop his own newswriting style is something like asking whether two paintings of the Washington Monument by different artists will be identical. Similar in content, probably; identical, no. It is true that the conventions of news writing tend to reduce individual differences; If the subject matter, the design, of the event covered is routine, two or 10 or 100 news writers may produce stories that appear almost alike. But the writers will not produce identical stories. The more the event itself departs from the everyday, and the more the imagination and perceptiveness of each reporter are challenged and brought into play, the more the stories will bear the stamps of author personality.

In one definition, style *is* personality—in the sense that the distinctiveness of a man's style is the peculiar imprint that his attitudes, his personal skill, his curiosity, and his purposes make on his mode of expression. A fascinating but still little-developed area of psychological research deals with the revelation of a man's personal attributes through his writing; students in this field believe that biographical knowledge may be greatly enhanced as the new science takes on form and depth.

Individuality in news writing, were it to become an end in itself, might constitute a declaration of war on the news writer's purpose. He may not, as a responsible professional, direct himself in his writing at self-expression, as a primary goal; he must constantly ask himself how much self-revelation, how much personality he can allow to show through his work. No answer can be absolute; but it seems that as long as his imagination is governed by firm tenets of objectivity and responsibility, the effectiveness of his writing will be directly commensurate to the individuality he gives it.

For clarification, a distinction between "style" and "manner" as applied to newswriting for different media may be made. Both terms are general, and both could be taken to mean the same thing. "Style" here is the more general, applying both to broad characteristics of effective news presentation and to individual or personal particularities. "Manner" is taken to mean the individualisms of a single news medium or a group of media.

For example: The characteristic manner of the writing in the weekly newspaper is intimate, personal, "folksy." The weekly is typically the servant of a small and closely knit community, and its literary flavor reflects the fact. Weeklies or community newspapers do not today carry this manner to the familiar extremes of the turn of the century, for their audiences are more nearly the same people as "city folk" than they used to be;

Certainly it is writing with individuality that gains attention, that is collected in books, that is remembered. Note the Weller and Reston stories in this book; remember the *Thousand and One Afternoons* of Ben Hecht—brilliant personal views of Chicago through a *Daily News* repeorter's eyes—and the sketches of New York by Morris Markey, *New Yorker* writer (*Manhattan Reporter*), and Meyer Berger, the much-admired New York *Times* reporter (*The Eight Million*). These books might be described by the same terms; they report the glamorous and the drab, the comic and the pathetic, the obvious and the subtle in day-by-day occurrences in great cities. But the personal styles of the three writers could never be confused.

How achieve a personal style?

There is no rule of thumb.

You do the best reporting you can. You get complete control of your facts. You *cover* your subject—perhaps "uncover" would be the better word—so that no parts of it are unexposed.

You make sure of your audience, and of your understanding of it.

You select from the facts you *could* use the ones you *must* use in order to give the audience the extent of knowledge and understanding appropriate to the circumstances. You decide on a story organization (see

they have similar sophistica-
tions, similar interests, and
similar education and back-
ground. As the isolation of
the small community has
disappeared, the intimacy
of community interdepend-
ence has declined; and with
it the home-town informality
of the small town newspaper
has lessened. Nevertheless,
the manner of the weekly
is usually noticeably more
leisurely and casual than
that of the daily.

Broadcasting has devel-
oped a distinctive news
manner, one characterized
by "conversational" patterns
and a simplicity even more
marked than that of printed
news. Radio news writers
learned early that what was
good for the eye was often
unintelligible to the ear;
the ear is a less accurate
recorder than the eye, and
it does not have the advan-
tage of repetition available
to the reader (unless the
broadcaster takes precious
time for it). The ear can-
not assimilate details as can
the eye. Moreover, it is ac-
customed not to the formal-
ized patterns of written lan-
guage, but to the informal-
ity, colloquialism and ease
of face-to-face conversation.
Radio news copy, therefore
—and telenews copy as well,
since its goal is the ear even

chapter 11) consistent with the dominant theme, the central fact or group of facts.

Then, you write the story in whatever you think is the most effective way. You choose rhetorical forms and specific words because they seem to you the clearest and sharpest you can find to get the effect you want. You seek color where it is needed, and leave it out where it isn't. You stop when your story is told.

Inevitably the finished work will have "style." It may, as Christopher Morley would say, accomplish its intention or it may not; it may move or it may stand still; it may sing or it may mutter. And moving or singing may be appropriate for one story, standing still or muttering for another. Your own skill as a writer will control what impact it produces; and the degree to which you as a unique individual contribute imagination, an eye for distinctive detail, a nicety of rhetoric and word, will govern whether it is routine or whether it has a character that is its—and your— own.

though it accompanies vis-
ual messages—has acquired
a manner of its own. (The
effect of this development
on newspaper manner is de-
scribed in chapter 12.)

What is called "Time-
style" is a manner artificially
developed by the editors of
Time when it was young and
brash. This manner calls for
inverted phrases ("said
Jones" to introduce a quo-
tation), invented words
(cinemactress), and many

stereotypes such as tycoon
(a Japanese word meaning
"feudal lord" which Time
has made its standard term
for a financial or industrial
leader). Time is nearly 50
years old, and its manner
has softened with age. But
it is still distinctive and,
though American literati
have deplored it, it has left a
permanent imprint on Amer-
ican speech and writing.
Most critics think the result
is lively prose.

SUGGESTED READINGS

The books by Klare and Buck cited on page 122, bringing together descriptions of many studies of ease-of-reading, are strongly recommended. They may be supplemented by readings they suggest, especially such books by particular workers in this field as:

Flesch, Rudolf, *The Art of Readable Writing*. New York: Harper & Row, 1949; and Gunning, Robert, *The Technique of Clear Writing*. New York: McGraw-Hill, 1952.

PROJECTS

1. Using the facts in the "youngest crime wave" story, rewrite the story in a manner you think more effective. After you have done so, write a commentary on your reasons for the changes you have made.

2. *Reader's Digest* is the most widely circulated magazine in the world. After careful reading of an issue, write a statement of your beliefs about the reasons it comes closer than any other to being a "magazine for everybody."

3. Make as accurate a transcript as you can of a major radio news story you hear on the air. Compare this story line by line to a newspaper story on the same event. List the stylistic similarities and differences.

CHAPTER 10

Foes of Effective News Style

What are the barriers to effective style in news writing? What are the motives, pressures, or laxities that turn journalistic writing into "journalese," that trap reporters who know, and ought to do, better into writing that is pedestrian, precious, or worse?

Some of the foremost sinners can be named quickly:

1) Haste—the urge to speed
2) Laziness—the energy-saving shortcut
3) Carelessness—"the copy desk'll catch it"
4) Fads—the well-worn track
5) Overwriting—reaching for effect

The Urge to Speed

"Devoted wholly to a discussion of the conditions that affect newspaper writing," the April 1950 Nieman Reports *is a collection of articles by the reporters and editors studying at Harvard at that time under Nieman Foundation grants. The twelve articles by newsmen are as helpful to newsmen as they are critical, and as pertinent today as the day they were written. Equally valuable is the introductory essay by the noted Professor Theodore Morrison of the Harvard English depart-*

You were told in chapter 2 of the editor who decried the newsman "rushing through the ripe wheat fields grabbing handfuls of golden grain." His concern was the haste in daily journalism that may prevent thorough coverage or full illumination of the day's events. But his figure of speech applies, too, to the writer who, with a press or broadcast deadline driving his typewriter, has no time for the polishing, the nicety of word choice, the luxury of careful pruning that may save poor writing from futility and turn good writing into excellent. As a Nieman Fellow wrote in the April 1950 *Nieman Reports*, modern news is "history in a hurry." The haste that is today characteristic of news handling will always be an enemy

ment. Among Professor Morrison's penetrating comments: "Any purely literary skill that makes one piece of emptiness more adroit than another is too unimportant to bother about."

• •

Jack Lait wrote his brilliant story about the killing of gangster John Dillinger with INS editors begging for copy. George Hicks of ABC produced one of the greatest of war broadcasts —the story of the Normandy invasion—with shells and planes screeching over his head. Will Irwin's "The City That Was" was written while the fires were still reddening earthquake-ridden San Francisco. Russell Jones wrote Pulitzer prize stories from Budapest with revolution outside his door and twenty-four-hour-a-day UP deadlines spurring him.

A book such as A Treasury of Great Reporting, *edited by Louis L. Snyder and Richard B. Morris (New York: Simon & Schuster, 1949), presents dozens of stories written under pressure, most of them about events high in importance and high in conflict. But it should not be forgotten that deadlines press on lesser news, and that they may yield excellent "little" stories as well as "big."*

of maximum effectiveness in writing. Experience almost always reduces the casualties of speed—the more often a newswriter sweats under a deadline, the greater his relaxation as he watches its approach and the less nervous his fingers. Many an oldtimer in a news office boasts that pressure stimulates something in him to sharpness in writing that goes beyond his more leisurely work. "Best piece I ever did," you'll hear such a man say, "was the time they were holding the front page for me to wrap up a city hall fraud."

But what he can't say with assurance is how much stronger the story might have been had he had time to go over it with a pencil, perhaps to cut out a paragraph here and add one there. For there has rarely existed a piece of copy, journalistic, literary, imaginative, factual, that could not be improved by application of second judgment.

Chapter 2 pointed out that the emphasis on speed in newspaper production seems due for gradual decline, thanks to the pre-eminence of broadcasting in fast news dissemination. But deadlines are here to stay; and they occur in the weekly newspaper shop with one press time every seven days just as relentlessly as in the great daily with seven in one. In magazines, too; and in news broadcasting more often than anywhere else. And it is all too easy to let today's carelessness, indulged in the name of emergency, bloom into tomorrow's habit.

There is, that is to say, no quick cure for the disservices of journalistic haste. There is no avoiding the newsroom clock. The newsman must live and prosper with it, develop skill in advance planning, learn to make pressure a stimulant and not a shackle.

The Energy-saving Shortcut

A second kind of haste that may downgrade newswriting is perhaps better called something else: laziness. It is the haste of the man who can't give patience or time-consuming pains to his work, the man geared to the energy-saving shortcut. This is the tool of the I-don't-care man, the man who never finds time, the writer for whom it's easier to borrow another's imagination than to brush the dust off his own. Its stultifying product is called by many names, all coming to about the same thing: cliché, bromide, stereotype, triteness, hackneyed term, tired English.

It is easy to see how the cliché grows. Chapter 3 referred to the overwork to which the term "turncoat" was submitted at the end of the Korean war to refer to American soldiers who sought Communist sanctuary and then turned back. News writers everywhere found it easier to pick up the handy epithet than to seek new ones. The term had vigor and quick meaning when it was first used. But its repetition quickly rendered it tiresome and flat—a cliché.

Another example: In the dim past a sports writer describing a touchdown borrowed from gold-mining the meaningful term "pay dirt": "Jones plunged the last yard to pay dirt." Effective language, that first time; and sports writers recognized it, for they quickly came to use it ad nauseam (in one Midwest lawyer's office the weekly football pool was based not on scores but on the number of times "pay dirt" appeared in a local sports writer's stories).

Newsmen and their critics have for years been vocally aware of the feebleness and indeed the asininity of dependence on the cliché. City and copy editors have railed and threatened against it, thoughtful reporters have composed their own satires on it, and such writers as Frank Sullivan have turned it to use in a wryly amusing form of literary criticism (Sullivan's series about Mr. Arbuthnot, the "certified public cliché expert," were for years a recurring pleasure in the *New Yorker*). In their continuing war on lazy writing the Associated Press Managing Editors Association one year turned attack on the sports cliché, and as part of a long report on sports writing sins listed the "ten most disliked clichés, in order of detestation": *mentor* (usually *cagy* or *genial*), *inked his pact, pay dirt, circuit clout, gonfalon, roaring out* (or *back*, or *from behind*), *outclassed but game, clobber, gridder, cager.* (Author's note: Where was *cinder luminary*?)

The threadbare phrase is a threat to effective journalistic writing because, after it has become threadbare, whatever flash it had at first has faded. If its use doesn't come strictly out of laziness, it derives from lack of imagination, or boredom, of the illogical and thoughtless assumptions that (a) the fact that Ring Lardner drew laughs from "tenderhooks" means it will draw laughs in a thousand future uses and (b) practically nobody has read Ring Lardner.

An unfortunate stimulus to the growth of clichés in news journalism is the stultifying form of the American newspaper headline. Imprisoned between column rules less than two inches apart, the headline has to be written in short words, and the result is headlinese, a language in which verbs become nouns, nouns become verbs, and the five-letter word is king. From headlinese come such usages as the verb *probe* in place of the noun *investigation* (*probe* means "to explore"), *nab* (which is slang) for *capture* or *arrest*, and *gut* ("eviscerate" or "remove the insides of") for *destroy by fire*. These words and scores of their brethren, often imprecise as well as trite in headlines, have worked their way into news prose, almost always to the injury of what the writer is trying to say.

Editorial writers, too, frown on clichés of writing and thinking.
The journal of the National Conference of Edito-

Which is not to say that you should avoid *gut* if *gut* is what you mean. If the fire burned out the insides of the building, the building was *gutted*. Say so. But if it damaged the basement or burned through the west wall, say that, and say it precisely.

rial Writers sardonically offered its readers a "utility editorial" described as the most "altogether admirable aid to editors since the discovery of the adverb 'manifestly' and the verb phrase 'it appears.'" Here is its closing paragraph:
"We must all (get behind, oppose) this latest development in the (ever, never) changing rhythm of time, in order that the —— may continue to ——. On the other hand, as —— has so well said, '——.'"

•   •

From a post-Christmas issue of the New York Times' "Winners & Sinners": "'Telephone switchboards through the district lit up like a ——.' Complete the foregoing sentence in exactly two words. Mail your answer with two box tops to Dead Letter Office."
Two books of "winners and sinners" have been published, both by the editor-compiler of Winners & Sinners, Theodore M. Bernstein: Watch Your Language (New York: Channel, 1958) and More Language That Needs Watching (Channel, 1962). Both are well-described by the jacket of one: "a lively, informal guide to better writing." Bernstein is also the author of a more comprehensive guide to usage: The Careful Writer (New York: Atheneum, 1965).

To see the cliché in another setting, sample a story by James B. Reston in the New York *Times* during a presidential campaign. Reston scolds both major candidates for their bromidic patter. The Democratic candidate, says Reston, talked about "freedom and progress," "powerful selfish interests," and "the belief of the Democratic party in the people." The Republican depended on the need for "a rudder to our ship of state" and "a firm hand on the tiller"; he found the Democratic party "coming apart at the seams," and the United States facing not only a "rendezvous with destiny" but also "the crossroads of its history."

The advantage of this kind of language, of course, is that it doesn't make any difference what campaign or what candidate uses it. It is all-purpose, interchangeable, like the "utility editorial."

Q.—How does the newsman avoid using such clichés when the man in the news himself uses them?

A.—Often he can't. He can't give his audience an honest or accurate picture of the news scene without reporting them.

But this does not mean that they have to become *his* tools.

Look at some more examples—not all that could be dredged up, but enough to suggest the wealth on which the Frank Sullivans base their criticisms:

round into shape
leave no stone unturned
let the chips fall . . .
bend every effort
hand to the plow
blot on the escutcheon
dregs of defeat
bring home the bacon

face a severe test
no holds barred
ax to grind
nose to the grindstone
shoulder to the wheel
bandy names
hit the canvas
pretty coed

Let the AP Managing Editors committee summarize:

No one is so starry-eyed as to think that clichés can be stamped out. Remember that many [well-worn] expressions were vivid, fresh, and challenging when first used. Overuse has made them threadbare. . . . Some widely used words, in the right places, still carry impact: *scintillating, brilliant, superbly. Went down swinging* and *looked at a third strike* are useful within reason. In the art of writing there can be no hard and fast [Author's note: this is a cliché] rules. What is needed is common sense application of the principles of good English.

"The Copy Desk'll Catch It"

Precision, saying *exactly* what he means, is a hallmark of the competent writer. The English language is one of the most delicate tools man has invented. Employed with care and respect, it can inform and illuminate; it lends itself to economy, directness, and explicit meaning. It is also of such durability, such toughness, that it withstands and survives constant manhandling. Careless writers who are satisfied to use it to say something loosely in the neighborhood of what they mean or in the neighborhood of what the facts require are a deplorable blemish on the journalistic writing craft. They are sometimes like the *aficionados* of the cliché, the men who are too lazy to search for the true and unequivocal expression of their meanings.

They are also those who believe that "the copy desk'll catch it." Prominent in this group are the very young, the novices (sometimes of genuine talent) who believe that "good" writing derives mostly from inspiration, and that you get inspiration most easily when you live in Paris or Majorca or, in a pinch, in suitably uncomfortable accommodations in Greenwich Village or Carmel. These are the ones who scorn the effort to write sharply and truly on the ground that, as sophomores too often say, "they hire copyreaders to watch grammar." These are also usually the ones who do not become effective writers. A writer who deserves the name has too much pride in his craft and his art, and too much respect for the sensitivity of his tools, to leave it to somebody else to use them properly, or even to sharpen or adjust them, for him.

He knows, moreover, that he will never find writing "easy." Sharp-edged writing cannot be anything but hard work.

A hazard the dependents of the copy desk ought to face, but choose to ignore, is that the copy desk is not infallible. Sometimes the men there get lazy, too.

What are the principal kinds of writing errors that a writer as well as his copy editor has to watch for?

Despite the Associated Press Managing Editors' strictures on clichés, AP sports stories don't always avoid them. An otherwise well-written story about a world's record in the shot put by Texan Randy Matson used the tired "smashed the barrier" three times, and added that Matson also "sailed the platter" for a discus record. But the story used quotations from Matson and his coach effectively . . . in particular this one from the coach:
"I know what will happen one of these days. We'll see Matson standing on the middle platform at the Olympics, getting his gold medal. He'll peel off his Texas A&M warmup suit, and underneath he'll have on a cape and a

USAGE   First, one must watch for errors in word usage:

"The President plainly *inferred* he would ask a larger appropriation." Correct word: *implied*.

"She *flaunted* convention by wearing slacks to the theater." Correct word: *flouted*. (A fascinating recent variant: *flount*.)

"The speaker *expounded on* his topic . . ." You expound a topic, not *on* it.

"The coach said he would *platoon* Outfielder Briggs with Sanders . . ." *Platoon* came into sports jargon as a colorful and legitimate term to describe the

big S on his chest. Then he'll fly away, and we'll all wonder whether we really saw him."

squad of defensive players substituted for the offense in football. The word means a group. It does not mean "to substitute," and it does not apply to a single individual. Its use in the baseball story for "alternate" might be defended as acceptable and meaningful jargon; but to give it a second meaning when an apropriate word is available is unnecessary, and any such usage demeans the original word—takes the sharp edge off a tool.

"Women have *less* fatal accidents than men." A nonsense statement; what it means is *fewer*.

"An *estimated 200* were present . . ." *Estimated 200* combines a precise term and one used because precision is impossible. Better: "Spectators estimated at 200" or "about 200."

"Jones has a *possible* leg fracture." Not an *impossible* fracture? The adverb "possibly" should be used.

"The *general consensus of opinion* is . . ." *Consensus* is a word that needs no help; it means "agreement of thought." Write "the consensus is . . ."

"The second book is different *than* the first." *From,* not *than*.

"*Today marks* the anniversary of . . ." This says the opposite of what it means, that the anniversary marked today. Sports writers are particularly given to having todays mark events, or to using "marked" as a synonym for "was."

"Froehling *literally* blasted the Australian off the court." Another precise opposite. Should be *figuratively*.

"Jones paid a *nominal* price for the land." The writer probably means *small*. A nominal price is often small, but it doesn't have to be.

"The governor delivered a full-length message to the legislature." The writer probably means *long*. "Full-length" could be 100 words or 10,000.

"The man was convicted of *wreckless* driving." Most courts think this the best kind.

These examples offer a puny sampling of the abuses to which English is submitted every hour. They are not a catalog, but rather suggestions of the kinds of language traps a careful and decently prideful writer should avoid. This is not to argue against the constant search for fresh phrases and word usages that don't mangle existing meanings; we would have a static and eventually a dead language if it were not for the impulses given it by daily inventions. Listen to Ellsworth Barnard of Bowdoin College, who wrote to the *Reporter* (January 24, 1957):

You seem not to have heard of certain principles accepted by all competent students of linguistic science. The first is that a living language is organic and ever-changing, that therefore usage is the only ultimate determinant of correctness, and that lexicographers and grammarians record and do not legislate. The second is that there are "levels of usage," generally held to be three: formal written English; the informal spoken English of educated people ("colloquial" English); and the normal spoken English of nonprofessional people (called, with no implied disparagement, "vulgate"). Language is like dress: the question is one of manners and not morals, of what is appropriate and not what is legal.

GRAMMAR   This comment applies equally to a second category of errors, those in grammar. To give a catalog of "good" and "bad" grammar is not a function of this book (guides to grammatical usage are suggested on page 111). But a few principal problem areas may be quickly named:

> *The dangling modifier:* "*Now 200 years old, she* was dressed in a costume handed down from her great-great-grandmother." "*Riding a bicycle, the crowd* cheered the high-wire performer."
>
> *Verb-noun* and *verb-pronoun disagreement:* "*The effect* of these influences *are* to reduce accidents." "*The effects* of this influence *is* to reduce accidents." "*The newspaper* usually carries wire stories on *their* front page."
>
> *Wrong pronoun case:* "They gave it to the children, *whom* they thought would need it." "They gave it to the children, *who* they meant it for."

Since all of these errors are commonplace in what Professor Barnard calls the "vulgate," any writer needs to keep his guard high against them.

STYLE   Group three includes wordiness, clumsiness, and complicated sentence structure:

> "An official Royal Canadian Mounted Police receipt Galbraith gave Gray for $182.64, representing duty and penalties, said the sum included $35 penalty for using his car to bring the items into Canada without declaring them."
>
> "The three men ousted have 10 days within which to file with the public safety commissioner a demand for a hearing before the civil service board, failing that their discharge becomes absolute."
>
> "A statement issued by the Unitarian-Universalist Association, Boston; the Southern Christian Leadership Conference, Atlanta, and the American Friends Service Committee, Philadelphia, said they will receive contributions." So long a compound phrase, especially when it contains semi-colons, is rarely well used as subject of a verb. Recast the sentence.
>
> *People* and *person*—A good deal of stiff writing comes from misunderstanding of effective use of these two words. *People* in its classic usage means a nation or a race. Its colloquial modern use to refer to a loosely-defined group of individuals has become well accepted (note it in the second sentence of the quotation from Professor Barzun on page 136). But those who refuse to accept it often demand that *persons* be its substitute; and *persons,* or *a person,* is often stilted and almost always imprecise. Note this sentence: "Old drawings found in an attic here are adding laurels to a deceased artist whose prime job had been to make persons laugh." *People* would have served more effectively than the prim, pedantic *persons.* . . . Usually better than the singular *person* is a more specific noun: Man, woman, reader, mechanic, player—whatever identifying substantive applies precisely to the "person" intended.

Students of grammar and language apply distinguishing terms to groups of troublesome words or usages:

Solecism, an error in usage, grammatical or verbal: "He don't"; "the boy run down the street."

Barbarism, an "uncivilized" usage, one not accepted by careful writers and speakers: "secured" for "obtained," "a high-type singer," "host" as a verb.

Impropriety, improper usage: "infer" for "imply."

Vulgarism, similar to barbarism and impropriety; careless or common misusage.

Colloquialism, a usage accepted in everyday speech, or by a particular group.

Jargon, terminology of a specific group or profession not ordinarily intelligible outside the group.

Slang, word coinage or usage of vulgar or colloquial origin. Slang often becomes "good English" upon wide acceptance and use.

Sometimes it is desirable to recast a sentence that defies clarification. Note this clumsy construction: "The FBI agent said Taylor told Lindberg that he (Taylor) was a member of the syndicate." It may be that the sentence would be clear without the awkward identification. If it wouldn't, revision would improve it: "Taylor told Lindberg that he was a member of the syndicate, according to the FBI agent."

You will find in an example on page 161 the following sentence: "Firemen fought the stubborn blaze without masks or other precautionary measures until the arrival of firm officials who warned the buildings contained chemicals which easily could form poisonous gases." The omission of the word *that* in this example ("warned *that* the buildings") probably grows from an effort to obey the injunction "keep it tight." This commandment sometimes leads to confusion, which is more to be shunned than the long sentence. Note another, and more objectionable, kind of *that* omission: "Mr. Brownell said a District of Columbia grand jury returned the indictment last Oct. 13, but that the District Court had kept it sealed." Here the *but that* phrase demands an earlier *that* after "said."

As proof that many of these things do happen, note, and weep over, this paragraph from a small newspaper's sports page:

Littlefield was not particular who they revenged itself on. Bigtown Central was the team at hand and it was a swell basketball team but Littlefield was out to show the state that they played basketball cast of the mountains and they really showed some 7000 fans just that by downing the Bigtown champions 82 to 64 in a hotly contested game that climaxed the first day of play in the annual state tournament.

Another failure—the failure to write what you mean:

A lead spoke of "a fall of 13 percent in President de Gaulle's popularity"; the story adds that his popularity fell from 55 to 42 percent. The fall, therefore, is not of 13 percent, but of 13 percentage points.

"Capt. Mack A. Mitchell Saturday flew from Seattle to Los Angeles in two hours 14 minutes—960 miles at 450 miles an hour." But 134 minutes at 450 miles an hour would have taken him 1005 miles.

"Lillian Gish hearkens back to silent-movie days." *Harks* back.

"The incubator was taken to the hospital during the first week the twins were born."

"He was found guilty of wreckless driving yesterday."

"The population of Mexico City has burgeoned to more than six million." Look up *burgeon*.

"The policeman put his foot on Fay's stomach as Fay lay prone on the deck." Look up *prone*.

"The speaker gave fulsome praise to the team." Look up *fulsome*.

"Capt. Joe Doakes revealed that 64 less accidents and 21 less fatalities were reported during the first two weeks of April over the same period last year." *Revealed* should probably be *said* or *reported; revealed* suggests previous concealment. *Less* should be *fewer*. *Over* should be *under*, or *than in*.

The Well-worn Track

Jacques Barzun, the distinguished historian and critic, has this to say about care in writing (from his "English As She's Not Taught" in the December 1953, Atlantic):

"The contemporary mind . . . speaks with the backing of popular approval when it says: 'Stop it! You understand perfectly well what all these people mean. Don't be a dirty purist looking under the surface and meddling with democratic self-expression.' To haggle over language is quibbling, of course. All precision is quibbling, whether about decimals in mathematics or grains of drugs in prescriptions— fairly important quibbles. The question is whether in language the results justify the quibble. Well, the public is here the best judge, and it is evident that . . . it cannot understand what it is asked to read: the government blanks, the instructions on the bottle or gadget, the gobbledygook of every trade, the highbrow jargon of the educators, psychiatrists, and social workers, and—one must add—the prose of the literary critics. The great cry today is for improved communication, and yet under the pretext of being free and easy and above quibbling, those who do the most talking and writing

Language, like most phenomena of any age, has its styles and its fads. They are not to be ignored; but they are to be indulged with judgment. The "10 best-dressed women," whose annual nomination is a familiar promotion of the clothing industry, are selected partly because they possess abundant equipment, both personal and accessory, and partly because they make good use of contemporary thinking and design. Whatever else you may say of their distinction, you will not find them guilty of overdressing, or of kowtowing to fads merely because they have currency, or of belaboring last year's fads; indeed, you are likely to find their use of current fashion more in subtle and appropriate modification than in flat acceptance. By the time the box-pleated handkerchief, the stewpot hat, or the plastic heel is available to everybody on Main Street, it has long been discarded by the well-dressed woman.

The writer who hopes to dress his materials most effectively must keep his language up to date, current. But he avoids crowding it with worn patterns, and he uses neologisms, the day's slang, and the like only when they give his prose the surest meaning, the sharpest clarity, color, and vigor he can find among all the writing designs he can borrow, remodel, or devise.

More specifically: He guards against such artificial mannerisms as the so-called "Timestyle" (see chapter 9). Though *Time* finds its inventions useful, they have not been accepted into the spoken language (and likely never will be, for they are not easy or natural); they draw attention to themselves for the wrong reasons. Their attraction is in their glitter, and glitter sometimes obscures substance.

Unless you're working for *Time*, avoid them. And avoid other contrived language patterns. Leave Art Buchwald's style to Art Buchwald, who uses it better

indulge themselves in the very obscurities and ambiguities that cause the outcry."

• •

"The better the writer, or at any rate the sounder his style, the less will he be found to indulge in the vogue-word."

What is a vogue-word? A word that comes into sudden popularity and usually into painful overuse. "Image" became such a word in the 1960s; "motivation" another; "framework," "overall"—make up your own list. Nothing is wrong with most of these words, in themselves. But when they become fads, they become tiresome—and often they appear when more precise words are available.

The quotation above comes from A Dictionary of Modern English Usage *(page 107), the notable book by H. W. Fowler, brought out in an excellent new edition in 1965 under the editorship of Sir Ernest Gowers, London: Oxford University Press. No writing man should fail to have it on his desk. Others he could use profitably are the Bernstein books (page 13), the 1957 Dictionary of American-English Usage (a modification of Fowler) by Margaret Nicholson (Oxford), and two by Roy H. Copperud, Words on Paper (New York: Hawthorn, 1960) and A Dictionary of Usage and Style (Hawthorn, 1964).*

• •

That jargon colorful and effective in one place becomes nonsense in another appears from this passage:

"Evans glanced a ball from Johnson swiftly to Davidson fielding at fine leg a pitch's length or more from the bat. It was Bai-

than anyone else ever will. Self-conscious prose is likely to be ineffective prose.

Guard similarly against letting the habit of language-mangling get control of your writing fingers. Some of America's verbalists have seemed in the last quarter-century to be irresistibly impelled to a kind of vocabulary manufacture that is more often simpleton than simple—a mode that invents new words to express clumsily concepts already well and honorably represented, that makes nouns into verbs that are not needed, that ignores the logic of rhetoric and grammar, compares without comparison, and substitutes glibness for telling precision. Some examples of these tendencies:

The use of *-wise* as an all-purpose suffix to transmute a noun into a modifier: *saleswise, newswise, filmwise, problemwise,* et ceterawise.

Similar use of *-ize* to turn adjectives into verbs: *finalize, slenderize, actualize.*

The use of nouns and adjectives as verbs: Jones *contacted* the office to *firm* the agreement. The coach sent Smith in to *defense* the passing attack.

The comparative that compares something to nothing: Smoko, the better cigarette; Drinko, the fuller-bodied wine; Synthetico, the longer-lived tire.

The use of *de-* to form unneeded antonyms: *desegregation* instead of integration; *de-intermixture* instead of separation.

The misuse of *-type* in a bastard adjectival combination: a *flat-type* magazine (instead of a flat magazine, or a flat type of magazine).

It is no secret that much of this kind of verbal manhandling comes from the advertising offices. Why this is so, why advertising copy writers, as often on the air as in print, are willing to substitute vulgarity for the vigor of fresh and meaningful invention, is hard to understand, especially since much superbly lean, precise, stimulating writing is produced by American advertising. Whatever its source, language concoction that adds nothing to the richness of communication is to be decried.

So too is the habit of seeking substitute words where none are needed, perhaps the result of over-zealous or insensitive instruction in some composition

ley's call but Evans made off for the run; Bailey sent him back, Evans in turn fell, recovered quickly and threw himself for the crease."

The paragraph is from a cricket story in a London newspaper.

classes to the effect that word repetition is a writing sin. Note, for example, this too-familiar rhetoric: "Jones flattened Smith three times, once in the first *round*, again in the second *session*, and finally in the third *canto*." (Where would the writer have turned had the fight gone 10 rounds?) Similar wasteful straining appears here: "It will be the third time in *as many* years . . ." A sensitive writer would use the simple *three*.

Two other paths that bear "danger" placards are those marked *Jargon* and *Gobbledygook*.

Jargon is the specialized language common to, and appropriate in, any specialized field of activity: sports, business, science, religion, education, or other. On occasion it is not only permissible but markedly effective to write in jargon. When a golf writer covers a tournament for the sports page, he assumes that his readers will know the game and its idiom; he may write *eagle, bogey, stance, two-iron, hole-high, one up,* and *explosion from the trap* with assurance. But the White House correspondent covering the vacation of a golfing President has to be more careful in use of such terms in copy that is likely to end up on page one. A substantial percentage of his audience might find them puzzling.

And the newsman writing a medical story, or a record of the new discount rate ordered by the Federal Reserve Bank, or a piece growing out of horticultural research at an agricultural college, must be equally cautious. Casual readers who are likely to be lay readers in any field but their own will be floored by language that is kindergarten talk to the experts. More of the newspaper or the newscast is written for the layman than for specialists.

It is true that jargon often works its way into the common, idiomatic language. During World War II government offices in Washington developed a type of prose that, as a *Fortune* editorial complained, made a "perpetually ratcheting sound composed largely of terms such as *setup* and *offbase* and *cutback*." *Fortune* went on to point to such terms as *processing, task force, operator, directive, know-how, programing,* and *levels,* and to wonder whether "if any victory is to be achieved in the war, it will not be a victory over verbal ugliness." No admirer of meaningful expression can deny that overuse of such terms renders them shallow and ineffective. Many of them have come into colloquial use, and not always to enriching effect; too often they are merely weak substitutes for precise terms. It may be wise to remember Alexander Pope's warning, "Be not the first by whom the new is tried," and then to be careful not to contribute to its premature aging.

In the necessity to simplify technical material for presentation in mass media lies one of the newsman's most difficult puzzles. For the expert, the specialist, the technician who understands a special jargon thoroughly is commonly unwilling to have it "adulterated" or "diluted" so as to make sense to the multitude. The heart surgeon wants the grocery clerk to know about a new cardiovascular operative procedure—but he sometimes believes it can be described only in heart surgeons' terms. This is a language the grocery clerk can't understand. The reporter's problem may be, first, to persuade the surgeon to accept a presentation in lay language, and, second, to get help from the expert in telling the story both simply and accurately. Many reporters have found that experts will not accept such treatment. Their problem then becomes whether to flout the expert's wishes, or to write a story only the expert can understand, or, in extreme cases, to forget the whole thing.

Gobbledygook is a term that writers and their critics apply to the foggy, pretentious, diffuse prose in which so many governmental pronouncements have been cast. We have had it for centuries (writers of legal documents, for example, until recently made gobbledygook a religion). From the first "whereas" in a public meeting's formal resolution down through the mazes of military orders to today's "directives," pompous or humorless or tasteless writers have yielded to the temptation to substitute verbosity for concision and pedantry for clarity. One example—a "directive" from a state administrative commission—is enough:

> To all employes of this commission: Any employe who might be engaged in occasional outside activities and whose services are actuated by the experience or knowledge gained during the course of his or her employment by the commission or because of information available to him or her, the contents of which is directly or indirectly connected with said employment and by reason of such experience, knowledge or availability of information receives benefit which such employe would not enjoy if he were not gainfully employed by the commission.
>
> It is therefore ordered that no employe of this commission shall engage in any business activity as a private citizen which may or might in any way directly or indirectly involve any matter coming under the jurisdiction of this commission, or the outcome of which might be affected or influenced by the result of any action or duty performed by this commission.
>
> This order shall not be construed as taking away from any employe the right to work on his own time when such work is not contrary to the foregoing directive.

What this appears to mean is something like this:

> Employes of this commission are forbidden to engage in private business in which their connection with the commission might yield them profit, or which might be affected by commission decisions or actions. They may engage in other activities, however, on their own time.

The commission statement, 178 words; the revision, 43.

Happily, the newsman's chief concern with this kind of prose is in trying to understand it and to interpret it to his audience. It can't be said that gobbledygook is journalistic. One of its ancestors, legalistic prose, is being disowned by modern lawyers, and bureaucracy, both official and private, shows signs of losing patience with it.

Reaching for Effect

Overwriting is gilding the lily, laying it on thick, seeking the fancy or pompous or roundabout in place of the simple and direct. It may be spawned by lack of experience, or of competence, or of discernment, or of humor, by one or several or all of these. It is purple prose, it is pretentious and often precious, it is usually long winded. The best that can be said of it is that it is commonly earnest. It is almost never as forceful as a careful purge will make it.

Allegations that Academia is infected by gobbledygook are common, and not hard to substantiate. Samuel T. Williamson, in an early complaint he called "How to Write Like a Social Scientist" (October 4, 1957, Saturday Review of Literature) offered these six rules.

1) *Never use a short word when you can think of a long one.*
2) *Never use one word when you can use two or more.*
3) *Put one - syllable thought into polysyllabic terms.*
4) *Put the obvious in terms of the unintelligible.*
5) *Announce what you are going to say before you say it.*
6) *Look down on—not up to—clear, simple English.*

And critic Malcolm Cowley tells how a sociologist friend took 94 words to state his assumption that rich people live in good neighborhoods.

•   •

Aware that the Christmas season often stirs reporters to attempts at what the New Yorker likes to call "rich, beautiful prose," the Minneapolis Tribune put on its cityroom bulletin board one mid-December this notice:
"This is the time of year reporters and copyreaders can pay special heed to keeping sentimentality out of news stories. This, of course, has nothing to do

Newswriting today is relatively little marred by overwriting. Twentieth-century prose of all kinds shies clear of the self-conscious sentimentality that was a characteristic of much late-Victorian writing; and the very nature of news purpose and form demands straightforward manner and style. Most modern newsmen scorn fancy writing, and the men at most city and copy desks run searing pencils through the work of the forgetful or the inexperienced who become more interested in rhetoric than in reporting.

Moreover, the effect of news on the air has been salubrious. When you are seeking to attain a conversational style, to write words and sentences that an announcer can speak easily and thousands of ears can assimilate, you don't want the speaker to sound like a high school sophomore who has just discovered *Roget's Thesaurus.*

But every newsman comes now and again on a news event with honest emotional values, and if he's alert he will remember the virtues of understatement. The reader's or listener's imagination, sensitively stimulated by selection of detail and insinuation of mood and manner, is a valuable adjunct to every writer's equipment; and he can arouse it better by the delicate nudge than the free-swinging bludgeon. The hint is likely to strike harder than the haymaker; the hint has a subtle way of sneaking into the consumer's subconscious and there nourishing itself on whatever creative powers he can offer. But he can often see the haymaker coming. He may not dodge it, but he can put up the defense of skepticism.

The old-fashioned sob story (see the example on page 119) was often marked by overwriting. This form of overwriting grows out of scorn for the reader and lack of self-respect in the writer; it is dishonest in intent and inaccurate in reporting. But it is not the only form. Another is the overnice, the kind that the New York *Times'* Bernstein calls "writing with the little finger well out." An example Bernstein gives is somebody's report that "the Texan took things easily." The idiom, which is good English, is "took things easy." In the same basket is writing that a

with genuine qualities such as warmth and gentleness, sympathy and humility. We want to reflect the Christmas spirit in our pages, but even more than usual we want to put the blue pencil on overwriting."

man "felt badly," or that Mrs. Jones works as a "charlady."

Euphemism is a writing sin by no means the property of journalists alone. For years the critics of business pretentiousness have railed, with little effect, at such pomposities as *mortician, bootician, beautician, display engineer* (for window dresser), and *realtor*.

The apostles of accurate, direct, simple news writing have, however, put their fingers on scores of journalistic euphemisms. Common are those dealing with forms of asocial behavior, and most frequent the words referring to sexual acts. Such words as *bastard* and *prostitute* are on some newspapers' and broadcasters' proscribed lists, apparently on the hypothesis that the degree of offense in such terms is directly proportional to their accuracy, directness, simplicity, and vigor. *Nude* is somehow less revealing than *naked*, and to *disrobe* more genteel than to *undress*. The word *rape* was for generations on the prohibited lists; permitted in its place were such nice-Nellie replacements as *assault, criminal assault*, and *statutory crime*. (Newsmen take acid pleasure in telling of the story that reported, "After the lady escaped, she ran disrobed down the street shouting, 'I have been criminally assaulted.'")

Sophistication and candor are today clearing out such overgrowth. The impatience of newsmen with less than honest language, along with greater audience tolerance, has helped the cause.

A final form of reaching: attempts in insufficiently skilled hands to reproduce a dialect or a mood. The story about the French liner on page 120 is an example; here is another:

> It was a pretty bad cuttin'.
> Eddie Lee, of the Hiawatha Avenue S. Lees, got a shiv struck pretty deep in his neck.
> The knife belonged to Benjamin Franklin James Singleteary.
> It was on account of Ben's gal friend's double wooin' and there's some that says they can't blame Ben much—'cause of its happening twice, and all.
> Ben and Eddie ain't been friends for a long time.
> Once when Ben was courtin' a gal who worked out in one of big homes in the Lakes district, Ben and Eddie were pals. Real friendly like . . .

This kind of effort fails because of lack of restraint. The writer did not stop soon enough. Were the device used less laboriously, the story would have been stronger.

Inexperienced writers sometimes fall into a similar error in attempting dialect. This example, for instance:

> McGinty had this to say: "Begorra, an' it's shure Oi am that no girrul av moine wud dhrink loik that."

Dialect can best be suggested with a few sure strokes. An attempt at precise reproduction, like this one, not only fails to enlist the reader's imagination; it stops him in his tracks.

PROJECTS

1. From radio and television news- and sportscasts and from daily papers, make a list of 25 or more clichés you hear or read. Try to suggest effective substitutes in cases in which you dislike the clichés' use.
2. Using the facts in the overwritten story about the child's death (and supplying such "facts" as age, full name, and others you would use), rewrite the story to eliminate the mawkishness that it exhibits.
3. Select a news story from *Time* magazine in which you find what you consider "Time-style" mannerisms and rewrite it to eliminate them. Then write a commentary showing whether you think you have made the story more effective.

CHAPTER 11

The Form and Organization of News Stories

> A very *Tragical Accident* happened at *Water-Town,* the beginning of this Month, an *Old man,* that was of somewhat a Silent and Morose Temper, but one that had long Enjoyed the reputation of a *Sober* and a *Pious Man,* having newly buried his Wife, The Devil took advantage of the Melancholy which he thereupon fell into, his Wives discretion and industry had long been the support of his Family, and he seemed hurried with an impertinent fear that he should now come to want before he dyed, though he had very careful friends to look after him who kept a strict eye upon him, least he should do himself any harm. But one evening escaping from them into the Cow-House, they there quickly followed him, found him *hanging by a Rope,* which they had used to tye their *Calves* withal, he was dead with his feet near touching the Ground.

In 1690 Benjamin Harris gave this story front-page space in *Publick Occurrences,* the colonies' first attempt at a newspaper. No expert eye is needed to see that it is hardly a third cousin of the modern news story. It is vague about names, addresses, and dates; it is a good three weeks "old." It has no lead, no opening summary of principal facts; its news is in its final clause. It is loaded with the author's comment and moralizing innuendo.

Nevertheless, it is news, the report of an event of interest to the audience for which *Publick Occurrences* was designed. And it was reported in a form that, with little change, persisted in the American newspaper for 150 years. This news form suited the needs and moods of readers in a leisurely age, and the pattern of personal journalism as well. The failure to identify the "Old man" by name was discreet in a small, tightly-knit community, especially one with rigid religious concepts. The lack of a current time element was not important in a newspaper that was to appear only once a month. The relaxed pace suited the times: the readers felt no compulsion to get to the point in a hurry, for there were few competing demands on their attention. The editorializing—"Tragical Accident," "impertinent" fear, the allusion to the Devil—was part of an accepted journalistic tradition; the editor was expected not only to report facts but also to suggest the attitude the readers should take toward them.

Such editorial embroidery expanded to great lengths. Nobody who read the *Massachusetts Centinel,* published in Boston on July 6, 1785, nearly a hundred years after the "Tragical Accident," thought this story opening unusual:

> Monday last, being the anniversary of the ever-memorable day, on which the illustrious Congress declared the then Colonies of North-America, to be Free, Sovereign and Independent States, all ranks of citizens participated in the celebration of the happy event, and even Nature put on more than usual mildness, expressive of her joy on the occasion— Ere the Eastern ocean was yet bordered with the saffron hue, the feathered choristers sang their early matin, and to usher in the auspicious day, Aurora unbarred the ruddy gates of the morn, with sympathetic smiles.

A hundred years later, the Chicago *Tribune* of June 16, 1898, opened a story thus:

> GUANTANAMO BAY, Cuba—The first heavy fighting at close quarters between the American marines and the Spaniards took place here today.
> As usual, American pluck and discipline won. The little invading force showed splendid courage and spirit . . .

Though it too contained editorial comment, this turn-of-the-century story had several new elements: simpler rhetoric, with shorter and "easier" sentences; an air of currency; and a twentieth-century lead. In the nineteenth century, as suggested in chapter 1, a number of social and technological developments altered American journalism and changed the public's use of the newspaper. Technological progress had increased the speed of production beyond the dreams of a colonial publisher. The snail-paced artisanship that continued into the nineteenth century became high-speed mass production. Steam power and giant cylinders in the printing process meant that instead of a few hundred small papers printed in an hour many thousands of large ones could be printed. Technicians in paper and ink had made equivalent improvements. Ottmar Mergenthaler's typecasting machine, the Linotype—first used in New York in 1886—had already begun to supplant the laborious process of setting type by hand. Even before the Civil War the telegraph had not only made an increased amount of news available and outmoded last month's or last week's events as material for current news but had also emphasized, because of the expense of sending news by wire, the advantage of terseness.

Benjamin Day's and James Gordon Bennett's idea that all kinds of current events, many of them trivial, were worth reporting to large audiences meant, among other things, that there was an increased number of news stories and, therefore, that stories had to be written in fewer lines than before; this new practice showed that news stories could speak for themselves, without reportorial comment and interpretation. The new concept of news had further impact on news form. No longer were newspapers publishing "news" solely to achieve a political, economic, or social end; they were telling their readers about life as it developed day by day, for the purpose of informing them rather than of shaping their opinions. By the end of the century the Associated Press was a major factor in American news gathering and dissemination, and its emphasis on conciseness, objectivity, and accuracy was reflected in every paper in the land.

The creed of news journalism today abhors one-sided news emphasis and slanted news coverage; but there has never been a time when such practices have been entirely absent from news presentation, never a time when some news media did not seek to use news presentation as a means of influencing opinion. In the 1890s the Hearst papers seemed to prefer news that would push the United States toward war; in the 1930s the so-called isolationist press sought to publish news that would suggest to readers that the United States should stay out of war. Most readers of this book have known of Southern Americans who believe that the Northern press slants news against the South, or vice versa; most have heard political partisans declare that their side does not get a fair break in the news. These charges are hard to prove today because the evidence is so slim; but there are instances of purposeful use of news. Moreover, the so-called crusade is an open attempt to influence readers, not by unfair news treatment, but by piling up the evidence to support a view.
There is, however, a vast

As important as any of these influences was the change in the "average reader." By the last decade of the nineteenth century education had reached millions of Americans; nearly 90 percent of the people were able to read and write (in the next 50 years literacy rose to 97 percent). Though the horseless carriage was still a thing to be feared and Guglielmo Marconi was only beginning to send electrical impulses through the air in his father's gardens in Bologna, Italy, the average American lived a faster-paced life and had wider interests and activities than his grandfather. One evidence of this was the specialized magazine; in the 1890s the *Youth's Companion,* "the magazine for all the family," which at one time boasted the world's largest circulation, was beginning to fade as family interests began to lose their simple homogeneity.

All these permutations meant that the newspaper had to tell its reader more, and that it had to do so more succinctly. It had to help him select rapidly among its offerings, and to read rapidly what he chose.

Modern News Form

The news forms that evolved through the latter half of the nineteenth century were not always the outcome of self-conscious contrivance; no newspaper genius sat down and invented the modern news story. Rather, the interplay of experience and necessity made it possible for the newspaper to come into the twentieth century with a news form designed to help the reader and to assure him expeditious reading of the news. The principal agents were the newspaper headline and the lead-and-summary story form.

gulf between publishing news that sound news judgment says ought in the public interest to be published, whether it influence opinion or not, and publishing only news that attempts to influence readers to form the opinions the publisher wants them to hold.

The *headline* is the newspaper device (sometimes borrowed by broadcasting) for describing briefly and legibly the salient points a story is to make. It is the newspaper's table of contents and its showcase. It enables the reader to decide at a glance whether the story is for him. The delicate techniques of effective headline writing (and the confining shortcomings of the pattern) are not within the range of this book.

The *lead-and-summary* form of news story starts with a quick roundup of the major facts of the story, showing its central import, summarized for the reader's acceptance or rejection. Then it summarizes subordinate facts and arranges them in order of decreasing importance. This story form has been given various labels; the most apt is "inverted pyramid."

The newsman's expectation is that, when a reader's eye catches a headline, his judgment tells him in a flash whether he wants to read the story. If he decides to go on, he reads the lead, and the selective process continues. If the lead holds his attention, he continues with the elaboration. Perhaps after reading the few paragraphs summarizing the most important details he has had enough; the story provides convenient exits. If his interest persists he can continue through succeeding segments of the story, either to a break-off point or to the end of the story. The design of such stories appears in the following samples:

BIRMINGHAM, Ala. (UP)—An intoxicated surgeon started shooting at police Friday while holding his infant granddaughter in his arms. A policeman braved the fire until he put the baby down and then shot the doctor dead.

The lead paragraph summarizes the major facts. It uses two sentences rather than the one more common in leads, and gains clarity and force by doing so.

First exit

The slain surgeon was Dr. Abijan C. Fields, 49. Coroner Joe Hilderbrand called his death "justifiable homicide."

Summary of two important secondary facts.

Second exit

Police said Fields, for many years a prominent surgeon but lately less active, was paroled recently from a federal hospital for narcotic addicts.

Summary of less important background facts.

Third exit

Yesterday, police were called to the family home. There Patrolmen B. L. Buchanan and C. D. Guy found Fields holding his granddaughter, 11-month-old Marie Irene Montgomery. Fields started cursing them, the patrolmen said, and Guy went for help.

Before he returned, the doctor whipped out a pistol and fired three shots at Buchanan. The officer backed away rather than fire while Fields held the baby.

Fields then put the baby down and followed Buchanan downstairs, where he cornered him and announced, "We'll shoot it out here."

Buchanan drew his service revolver and fired five shots. Two struck Fields, who was dead on arrival at a hospital.

The last four paragraphs reconstruct the story chronologically for the reader who continued beyond exit three. But those who stopped sooner had already been given the important facts.

The mid-August heat wave will continue today with local temperatures expected to climb to 95.

A quick summary of major facts—and a quick answer to the reader's question: "How hot?"

First exit

Only relief in the state will be felt in the northwest portion, as a low pressure area moves eastward.

Highs today in the state will be from 80 to 85 in the northwest and 90 to 95 in the south and east.

Supporting facts summarized in two closely related paragraphs.

Second exit

The weatherman promised a little relief tonight with a predicted low of 70 in the city. A few showers are expected.

Yesterday's high in the city was 96 at 4 P.M. At 6:30 P.M. the relative humidity was 41 percent.

These two paragraphs might have preceded the two above. A concession to non-local readers?

Third exit

[*A final paragraph reports highest temperatures in neighboring states.*]

The "most expendable" facts in the last paragraph.

A local man and his wife were killed in a home fire today.

A quick, laconic summary.

First exit

Found dead by firefighters in a burned-out house at 417 16th Ave. S. shortly after 1 A.M. were John Doe, in his 60s, and his wife, Mary, 58.

The most important facts to expand on the summary lead.

Second exit

David L. Jamieson of the arson squad said he was told by neighbors Mrs. Doe was in the habit of throwing extra fuel into the oil heater. Under such circumstances, he said, sudden ignition of

Background or explanatory facts, elaborating on major facts.

the extra oil would blow open the heater door and flame and smoke would puff out.

Third exit

Doe's charred body was found under a pile of debris. Mrs. Doe was declared by the medical examiner office to have died of smoke inhalation.

Further elaboration.

Fourth exit

Neighbors said Doe was retired.
City Hall records indicate that the house and the one next door at 415 16th Ave. S. were built about 1867.

"Expendable" facts. Should they have been included?

The order-of-decreasing-importance or inverted-pyramid form helps both the copyreader who edits the story and the printer who puts it into the page form. The copyreader knows that in a well-put-together story the least important facts are in the closing paragraphs; if deadline is pressing he can usually cut an overlong story rapidly and sensibly by lopping off or paring the final paragraphs. (But he won't use this lazy device if he has time to work over the entire story.) When the story is in type metal or cold type, the man composing the page may be able to fill a 4-inch hole with it even though it's 5 inches long by cutting off its closing 1-inch paragraph.

This practice sometimes trips up careless printers, however. No printer can ever safely assume that the last paragraph is unnecessary. To do so without checking the copy may lead him to the kind of faux pas that the New Yorker likes to call the "Most Fascinating News Story of the Week." Here is an example (this one picked up, in toto, from the New York Herald Tribune):
"WASHINGTON, June 28 (AP)—An Army secretary stood it as long as she could. Finally this week curiosity got the better of her and she decided to see what was in the three large paper bags which were neatly tied and stuffed together on the top shelf of a storage closet.
"Each bag was expertly hand-lettered: 'Trash.' Above and below the word was the rubber stamp: 'For Official Use Only.'"

These examples show, among other things, that there is no iron-clad formula to guide the newswriter in inverted-pyramid construction. He often departs from pattern as he goes, deciding arbitrarily which subelements are to come first and which to follow. Two competent reporters arranging the same set of news facts may assess them differently, even when both are following the "standard" pattern.

Variation in News Story Form

A complaint sometimes directed at American news presentation is that it is overstandardized, that its enslavement to inverted-pryamid form deprives it of inventiveness and variety. News story patterns in other countries, the complaint points out, are not imprisoned in a single mold. Sometimes the casual and wandering form of the news story in a European newspaper confuses its reader, and certainly it asks more of him than does its American counterpart. A story in *Il Mattino*, Naples' principal newspaper, for example (the event was the NATO secretary-general's visit to Italian government officials), devoted its opening 35-line paragraph to a list of the officials' names rather than to the principal outlines of the news. Another, reporting the liberation of a young man falsely accused of murder, told the reader first that "innocence has triumphed against every machination of men and affairs." The London *Daily Express*, reporting the tears of a young Briton ("24 and pretty") after her husband had been arrested in Moscow on a "criminal charge," gave prime attention to friends' characterizations of the couple and their happy marriage.

But foreign reporting that departs from American patterns may be extremely effective. *Le Figaro* of Paris, in a page of news on an anniversary of V-E Day, showed sensitive recognition of the particular interests of Parisian readers in two stories: a dispatch from Washington was divided into halves, the first reporting Presidential comment of direct concern to France, and the second summarizing other elements in the event, and a story from Bonn with contrapuntal treatment of East and West German celebrations of the anniversary, alternating paragraphs from one scene to the other.

The tendency in many western European newspapers is to move closer to American newswriting patterns. The principal "new" newspaper of Italy's postwar period, *Il Giorno* of Milan, was designed after intensive study of American practices, and some of its success it attributed to skillful use of shorter and more direct news stories.

Decline in newspaper use of the inverted-pyramid form has appeared in the crystal ball of a top editor of United Press International. Roger Tatarian thinks the summary lead will appear less often, especially in stories reporting news that the reader heard last night by radio, and predicts that more and more news will be written in narrative form.

"The inverted-pyramid style . . . will remain a useful tool," he says, "but it is no longer the dominant monster it once was. . . . The narrative news story is going to be more fun for the journalist, and it is also going to be harder for him to do."

But if patterns across the Atlantic show readiness to change, so do those at home. The standard and traditional patterns still dominate, and they will continue to do so because they serve useful and logical purposes. Dissatisfaction with the inverted-pyramid strait jacket is not confined to lay critics of the press. Complaint at its monotony arises now and again at newsmen's conferences, and some news media—the weekly *National Observer* is a distinguished example—are seeking departures from restrictions that arise more from habit than from function.

The departures cannot be sharply classified; indeed, if they could be so clearly categorized, they would soon cease to be departures. Wide use of the suspended-interest form and the chronological or narrative story is a characteristic of the *National Observer* news manner. This can hardly be called "new," however; the form has been known and used since long before summary lead and inverted pyramid were invented. Their application to situations that for half a century were thought to demand "straight" handling is what is worth noting.

The weekly appearance of the *Observer* is without doubt one of the impulses behind its search for new patterns. In a weekly the news quality of immediacy is low and other points of emphasis and of reader attraction must be found. But other impulses push in the same direction. One is the increasing attention in American journalism to the particular needs of particular audiences.

Particular needs may be served better by one arrangement of story elements than another. (An extreme example is the presentation of stock-market news in column upon column of tabulation.) Two impulses come from broadcasting. Roger Tatarian points to one on page 149, noting that newspapers are learning to look for new approaches to news that radio or TV reported last night. But, as has already been explained in this book, the mere improvement in style and rhetoric forced on stereotyped news writing by the best of air-news writing is a significant force.

News writers who successfully break out of the shackles of news writing conventions do so because they apply imagination to material and audience needs. Their procedure is not to decide on a pattern and apply it to a set of facts, but rather to perceive that a set of facts can be most effectively brought to life through a specially contrived story structure or manner. The story that follows is an example of this procedure. Its form is more nearly that of a magazine article than of the standard news story. Its structure is almost episodic. It opens with an anecdote, and it proceeds in an anecdotal manner. It maintains unity by close adherence to its principal topic, but its informality permits the inclusion of quotations and of background material that would likely have been squeezed out of a conventional story.

"I'm the only brown child in my room," Joetta Harris told her mother on the way home from Groveland Park School in St. Paul Tuesday.

Mrs. Robert Harris' heart sank.

But it was all right, Joetta said. She had made lots of "best friends."

She did object to the pupil who sat behind her, however.

"Why?" asked Mrs. Harris, fearful again.

"He's a boy," said the 6-year-old scornfully.

The Negro mother laughed.

"Well, boys are people, too," she explained.

Joetta was one of 75 children from St. Paul's predominantly Negro Selby-Dale area who transferred to five predominantly white elementary schools yesterday.

The children rode in a private school bus. Nearly all paid at least part of the $35 fee. The rest was made up from more than $5,000 in contributions, said Mrs. Harry Bratnober Jr., 1175 Davern St., spokesman for Parents for Integrated Education, the sponsoring organization.

Joetta and her sister, Pam, 9, were among 15 Negroes who transferred to Groveland. Normally they would have gone to Maxfield School, which was more than 91 per cent Negro last year.

The Harrises, who live at 795 Central Av., decided last spring to transfer their girls.

Harris is one of four Negro firemen in the St. Paul Fire Department. He was brought up in an integrated neighborhood in the North End of St. Paul. He had seen Negroes from the ghetto fail when they were thrown in with whites on jobs.

"I think they should have this relationship with white kids early," Harris said Tuesday.

But, having decided, the Harrises were faced with a problem—how to explain their decision to Pam without spoiling the naturalness of the interracial contact?

Pam solved the problem when she came home from camp with her best friend and asked:

"Maggie's going to a different school this fall. Why can't I?"

Harris rejects the idea advanced by some Negroes that private busing is inadequate, saying, "It's a beginning, at least."

On the other hand, he doesn't accept as valid the objection of many whites that interracial dating may become a problem.

"I don't care what color their dates are so long as they come to the house to meet my daughters," he said.

There were no problems at any of the five schools yesterday, according to Robert Indehar, school social worker assigned to advise on the transfer project. Besides the 15 Negro students at Groveland there were 15 at Edgecumbe, 27 at Highland, 3 at Horace Mann and 15 at Mattocks, he said.

The greatest fear of the sponsors was that the Negro transfers would be alone and, in effect, segregated at noon when the neighborhood white children went home to lunch.

To avoid that, principals took advantage of a long-standing policy to urge parents of children living more than three quarters of a mile from the school to send lunch with their children.

The open enrollment policy that made yesterday's transfers possible is also a long-standing school board policy. Some Negroes say its only previous racial application was by whites to escape ghetto schools that became predominantly Negro.

Its use as a means to end de facto school segregation was urged last October by the Committee on Racial Imbalance in St. Paul Schools. But the school board could not afford to bus the students.

The idea of a privately sponsored bus originated with Mrs. Bratnober, a former school board member, and a group of her white friends. Together with Negro parents like the Harrises, they formed Parents for Integrated Education.

Other stories that depart from routine appear on pages 112, 121, 247, 249, 260, and 263. The influence of human-interest material on story form receives attention in chapter 15.

News Form on the Air

Examples of broadcast news stories will show both similarities to and differences from news written for the eye. In the story below (the stories here presented were broadcast by WCCO Minneapolis, a 50,000-watt station covering a broad territory) the summary-inverted-pyramid pattern is followed closely. But style is carefully controlled: a "soft lead" gives the listener an instant of preparation for what follows; the sentences are short, straightforward, and simple in construction; most sentences open with strong noun phrases; words are familiar (with the striking exception of some in the last sentence of the third paragraph— an inexplicable lapse into jargon that most listeners won't understand). The story also illustrates the use of the pre-recorded tape interview:

```
     The White House announced this noon that four-million
dollars will be spent by the National Aeronautics and Space
Administration at the University of Minnesota. A new build-
ing, to be constructed near the Institute of Technology on
the University campus, will be a part of the new space-
science center promised by Vice President Humphrey last
fall.
     Congressman Joseph Karth of St. Paul, who heads the House
Committee on space sciences, talked with NASA administrator
James Webb. He asked Webb to explain how the four-million
dollars will be spent at the University. . . .
     Webb (on tape): We have had a policy of trying to find
those means through which we could strengthen the University
and bring it into closer relationship with industrial growth
and development in Minnesota, building on the strength
you've already demonstrated. So this new building will house
increased work in engineering, in mathematics, in physics,
in chemistry, in bio-physics, bio-medicine and bio-engineer-
```

ing, and in the behavioral sciences. And of course, all of
these relate to much of the work of your industries--to
the study of economics and how use of this can go beyond
the space industries.

Karth (on tape): Mr. Webb, just how big is this building
that's going to house the computer and do work in these very
sophisticated disciplines?

Webb (on tape): Well, this will be a six story building,
with 83,000 square feet of space, very near to the Institute
of Technology, and close to the College of Biology and the
College of Medical Sciences. And of course the computer will
be in this building or near by--the one financed by the
National Science Foundation. (END TAPE)

The new building, itself, will cost two and a half million dollars. An additional half-million dollars per year
will be spent on various scientific programs to be taught
there in relation to the overall space program. The computer, referred to by Dr. Webb, represents a 400-thousand
dollar grant by the National Science Foundation. It is known
as a major hybrid computing facility--a large analog, linked
with a small digital computer, plus inter-face equipment.

The multi-million dollar project has been in the works
for several months. Vice President Humphrey, Congressman
Karth and Senator Walter Mondale have led the fight to obtain for Minnesota a bigger share in the nation's multi-
billion dollar space program.

The next three stories show three steps in radio reporting of a fast-breaking
spot news story. The first is a bulletin that interrupted a non-news program. It
shows signs of haste; its opening sentence is abrupt, and the nature of the news
is not made clear until the second sentence:

NEWS SOUND

WE INTERRUPT THIS PROGRAM FOR A BULLETIN FROM THE WCCO RADIO
NEWS BUREAU . . . .

All available ambulances and doctors have been summoned
to the village of Maple Plain on Highway 12 about 25 miles
west of Minneapolis. There is a report of an explosion and
fire at the Molded Plastics Company there. Rescue workers
at the scene of the blast have put out a call for asbestos
suits to withstand the heat of the fire. Sightseeers are
warned to stay away from the area where rescue work is now
under way.

Stay tuned for more details as soon as they become available.

The first story was broadcast at 9:55 A.M. Seventeen minutes later it was followed by a second, a story more nearly "usual" radio news copy than the bulletin:

Here are more details on the explosion at the plastics plant in Maple Plain.

It is now known that at least two persons were injured in the blast at the Molded Plastics Products Company about an hour ago. Both were workers in the plant, which manufactures plastic toys. One was identified as Mrs. Alice Sohns (SEWNS). The other was a workman whose name is not immediately available. Both have been taken by ambulance to the hospital in nearby Watertown, Minnesota.

According to an eye-witness, Gust Giese, an oven for heating the plastics material exploded when it was lighted. Giese said the force of the blast shattered one wall of the plant, and blew off a portion of the roof. The plant is located on Highway 12 in Maple Plain, about 25 miles west of Minneapolis.

Fire which followed the explosion has now been brought under control. WCCO Radio Newsman Bill Arp is on his way to Maple Plain, and we'll have his complete report in the Noon News. Road blocks have been established to seal off the area from sightseers.

The story was wrapped up two hours later by an on-the-spot broadcast promised earlier:

This community of Maple Plain, about 25 miles west of Minneapolis, was rocked by an explosion this morning when gas ignited at a plastic toy manufacturing plant. Three workers were injured in the blast and the fire which followed at the Molded Products Company. Those injured in the explosion were Mrs. Alice Sohns of Mound, Rose Nagel of Watertown and Allen Sullivan of Maple Plain.

None of the injured is in serious condition this noon, though Mrs. Sohns is still under treatment at the hospital in Watertown. All three were working in the plant near the plastics heating oven when the gas was ignited. The plant owner told me that highly volatile fumes develop when the oven is lighted, and he believes the blast was touched off in that ignition period.

The Maple Plains assistant fire chief, Helmar Anderson, said the damages would amount to several thousand dollars. A cinder block wall was broken and a portion of the roof was

destroyed by the explosion. Fire followed the blast, but the
flames were brought under control within thirty minutes.
The plant, which employs about 50 persons, will be out of
production for several weeks.
    This is WCCO Radio News at Maple Plain.

Note the care with which both first and second stories warned sight-seers to
stay clear of the explosion site. This is a caution not always observed when news
breaks fast. Police and firemen have all too often been hampered by radio-drawn
crowds that get in their way.

Unity in News Stories

The principle of essential unity helps to meet the problems of story organization.

Briefly and simply, unity in news writing means that a well-organized story
makes one central point. A unified news story is planned and composed around
a principal idea, fact, or closely-related set of facts; it attempts to tell the reader
only one basic story. Its details are carefully selected for their relevance, and
tangential material that may confuse rather than reveal is rejected.

There are many ways of achieving unity in a news story. Look again at the
story of the drunken surgeon (page 146); every paragraph but one, the third,
relates directly to the principal event, and the exception provides relevant background. Note especially that the last four paragraphs of the story are presented
chronologically, the facts of the event recounted in order of their occurrence.
For some news situations the chronological pattern, starting at the beginning
of the event and narrating it in simple time sequence, is a most effective
method of gaining unity. Although the form is used more often in human interest
stories than in straight news, variations of chronological structure may be successful, as in the story just cited; or they may not, as in the following story, a
story exceedingly hard to understand with the one reading that most news gets.

An early-morning 90-mile-an-hour chase that had all the ingredients of a movie thriller today resulted in the capture of a suspected young auto thief, minor injuries to two local policemen and the wrecking of a police squad car.

The summary lead confuses by including too many elements. The "movie thriller" phrase promises something that the story does not deliver.

First exit (but later exits are hard to identify).

Figuring in the chase were at least a half dozen squad cars, directed by Sgt. Paul Ridley, dispatcher, who carried on a two-way conversation first with the squad car before it was wrecked and then with another that continued the chase.

Secondary detail, some too trivial to deserve second-paragraph position. The multi-idea sentence diffuses attention; and you never learn how the squad car was wrecked.

Held at the Public Safety building is David Satoiw, 19, of Milgrim's Landing, who police say admits stealing the fleeing car Thursday night.

Important detail. (But how do you steal a fleeing car?)

Patrolman Gerald Hangge, 29, of 1248 Farr Street, suffered knee cuts. Patrolman Leonard Marsch, 23, of 427 Fulton Street, is nursing a forehead cut and bruises on his leg and hand. Both were treated at City Hospital.

Is this secondary detail properly placed in the story? Does "both" refer to bruises, patrolmen, or "leg and hand"?

Within 11 minutes after the play-by-play account of the chase was broadcast to the chasing squad cars, the suspect was captured.

Confusing language ("account of the chase" broadcast to "chasing squad cars") and confusing position in the story.

After the first squad car had been put out of the chase, the police dispatcher carried on his two-way signals with Squad Car 303, with Patrolman Lawrence Swanson at the wheel and Patrolman Joseph Carchedi at the car telephone.

Chronological sequence is not clear; identification of Car 303 is not clear.

Although the radio part of the chase did not enter into the picture until 6:44 A.M., the chase actually started several minutes before.

Again the time sequence is not clear. Why name the precise hour?

Detectives Frank Yose and Stanley Pehosky were cruising at University near Hamline when a car sped by in the opposite direction at 50 miles per hour. The detectives turned and gave chase, not knowing it was a stolen car.

Apparently a new chronology begins here. (Opposite to what? and what is the antecedent of "it"?)

Not recognizing the detectives' car, the police squad car gave chase to it.

How did the squad car get into the picture? (And how does a squad car "recognize"?)

At St. Anthony at Cleveland the suspect's car pulled into a filling station with the detectives' car right behind, followed closely by the squad car. Recognizing the police squad car, the suspect immediately pulled out of the filling station. The squad car occupants also recognized the detectives' car so they took up the chase of the speeder.

Though the narrative continues, it is nearly lost in excessive detail. Since a map accompanying the story showed the route the cars followed, some of the verbal detail could have been omitted.

The suspect headed north on Cleveland to University with the police car right behind him. On University the chase went east to Fry and south on Fry to St. Anthony and east on St. Anthony to Victoria. From Victoria the chase went to Rondo and it was here that the two-way radio signals took up the pursuit. It went like this:

6:44 A.M.—"Car 326 chasing car on Rondo with license number 198-114, going east on Rondo from Victoria at 90 mph. Head him off . . ."

Is the confusion of the reporter's account lessened or compounded by the radio reports that follow?

[*The story concludes with the squad cars' radio reports.*]

This story is hard to follow because the attempt at chronological pattern is confused and because detail is excessive. For these reasons, it lacks the essential unity necessary for effectiveness. (Its careless writing, another shortcoming, should be noted.)

Three particular factors in its composition are worth observing. The phrase "ingredients of a movie thriller," which is gratuitously inserted in the lead, introduces an idea that is not developed later in the story, either by specific reference or by implication; the emphasis in the second paragraph on the two-way radio conversations suggests to the reader that the radio conversations are important for understanding the event, but the story's closing paragraphs show that they are not; and the superfluous detail—the route of the chase, the nature of minor wounds, the fact that a patrolman was "at the car telephone," the vague "at least a half dozen squad cars"—confuses more than it clarifies.

Contrast the auto-chase story with a Washington report by the New York *Times'* James B. Reston, a story that loses nothing in charm or unity by the fact that the name of its chief figure dates it:

WASHINGTON — the usually solemn Secretary of State Dulles was in a mood of relaxed good humor at his news conference Tuesday.

He expounded to the reporters the glories of being fingerprinted, disclosed that he is the first pistol-packin' Secretary of State since Cordell Hull, and announced he is going off on his first two-week vacation since taking over the State Department almost three years ago.

The opening paragraph establishes the story's unifying theme, the "relaxed good humor" of the news conference. The theme is supported in the second paragraph by introduction of topics not usual subjects of a State Department news conference (note that it's "news," not "press").

First exit

This last point may have explained his sense of well-being, but the real reason probably is that his foreign policy ideas are back in ascendancy in Washington.

A carefully-designed transitional paragraph to move from the story's structural theme to a more sober subject.

[*Nine paragraphs now develop the subtheme just introduced. Then back to the original theme:*]

As for the lighter portions of the conference, it went like this:

Dulles said he himself gets fingerprinted a couple of times a year. Why? asked a correspondent.

Return to the opening theme holds the story together and satisfies the reader's curiosity.

Because, said the secretary, he has to be fingerprinted in order to get his pass to the State Department building. And also, he added with a rather sheepish grin, in order to get a permit to keep his pistol. This drew considerable interest.

Fortunately, said the secretary, he hasn't had to use his gun at all. Apparently aware that he had dashed the hopes of the whodunit fans in the news corps, Dulles explained that his revolver is one he was given in 1917 when he made his first trip to Central America. He has kept it ever since.

Reston has tied the news elements in a not-very-productive news conference into a unified package by a contrived but skillful and convincing use of a major theme.

Here is an example of unity in the brief story:

MEXICALI, Mexico (UPI)—A fissure in a cotton field spewed sulphur, hot rocks and boiling mud today, raising conjecture that a new volcano was being born in Mexico.

Though its rhetoric is clumsy, the lead establishes the dominant fact—"a new volcano."

First exit

Mexicali police reported 14 fissures split the earth suddenly starting Saturday and one began rumbling and throwing debris 70 to 80 feet into the air 14 miles south of this border town, 170 miles southeast of Los Angeles.

Sulphurous gases belched forth and steam shot out.

Secondary facts support the main idea. (The first sentence, however, contains at least twelve ideas.)

Second exit

A group of volcanologists from Mexico City reportedly was flying to the scene today to determine whether this is the third volcanic eruption in the last decade in Mexico.

Development of an aspect of the main idea. Since it relates so closely to the lead, this might have been made the second paragraph.

Third exit

Mexico's most famous volcano of the twentieth century is Paricutin, which first burst forth in a cornfield in central Mexico near Morelos.

Background information. It could be dropped without major loss.

Everything in the following story belongs there, probably in the order presented. That some of its writing is pedestrian does not destroy its unity.

Radio pickups were broadcast Friday for 26-year-old Leslie Douglas Ashley after persons in Wharton and Houston reported they saw a man resembling him during the afternoon.

All of the leads turned out to be false, however, in the search for the one-time female impersonator, indicted on a charge of murder, who escaped from a San Antonio state mental hospital early last month.

A long-winded two-paragraph lead, one that delays reporting the major fact— that no arrest was made— until the second paragraph. There are at least five major ideas in this lead.

First exit

Wharton County Sheriff H. R. Flournoy said that about 12:30 P.M. a woman in a Wharton dress shop called to say a man who looked like Ashley and a blonde woman were shopping for women's clothes and fled all of a sudden when they saw they were being stared at.

A check proved that the man was definitely not Ashley, Flournoy said, after the Department of Public Safety had broadcast a statewide pickup.

This is the first of three instances offered to support the lead idea. The three are offered chronologically rather than in order of decreasing importance, since they are all of about the same weight.

Second exit

Four hours later, a television station porter in a company car thought he saw Ashley getting into a small light-colored compact car

outside a store in the 700 block of Travis.	
The porter told police that when the man spotted his car, which was marked with the station's call letters, he jumped back into his own auto and drove away with two others, a man and a woman.	*Second instance.*
	Third exit
Sometime later, a woman who works at a cleaning plant in the 2700 block of Montrose thought she spotted Ashley driving around in a light-colored car, and called police.	*Third instanre.*
Four police cars, two Harris County Sheriff's Department units and about 40 newsmen flocked to the scene, but quickly dispersed after it was learned that the man in the car was not the one they sought.	
	Fourth exit
Ashley is under indictment for the gun-torch slaying of Fred A. Tones, a Houston real estate man, in 1961.	
Convicted and sentenced to die in the electric chair, he was granted a new trial. Before he could be tried again, he was found insane and committed to the hospital at San Antonio.	*Summary of earlier facts of the case, presented for those who are not familiar with it.*
His attorney, Lloyd M. Lunsford, was out of town, but an associate of Lunsford said Ashford has not yet communicated with his lawyer.	

From these examples it is possible to arrive at several generalizations about the attainment of unity. A news story is unified when its central idea or theme summarizes the reporter's selection of facts (usually the lead presents the theme), and the supporting facts develop the theme. In straight news writing, the first step is the selection of facts, a process that requires decision making, since elements that do not contribute toward understanding, or that actually distract attention from the main point, must be rejected; the second step is putting the facts into focus in a summary statement.

AXIOM: *Better that the news consumer see the forest than every individual tree. Better that he grasp the* The writer may also contrive unity, however, by establishing a framework or mood—in the Reston story, the relaxed-good-humor mood—and then relating the elements of the story to it. This rhetorical ap-

broad outlines and the significant meaning of a news event than that he be given a maze of secondary detail.

• •

A "sidebar" is a secondary story that develops minor facts or a related angle of a news event whose major aspects are presented in a relatively important story. If unity is to be maintained, it is often impossible to present all the facts in one story, especially in stories of events involving many participants and many activities—a national convention, a catastrophe, a university Homecoming. Newsmen have invented the sidebar to meet this problem.

Sidebars frequently deal with human-interest subject matter. When the carnival comes to town the local paper carries a lead story with the major facts. It may also offer sidebars: seven heat prostrations in the first day's crowds, more visitors to the city than at any time since the President made a campaign speech here, the fat lady absent because she's honeymooning with the mayor of the last town the carnival visited. All such angles could be separate paragraphs or sections of the main story. But they gain clarity and emphasis by separation, and they keep undue clutter out of the main story.

For one example: On a day when a principal front-page story dealt with anniversary observances of the atomic bombing of Hiroshima and Nagasaki, a newspaper also carried four sidebars: a propaganda broadcast from Peiping Radio, the comments of the chaplain who had counseled the crew of the plane that dropped the first bomb, the refusal of the plane's pilot to

proach is more often found in editorial or feature writing and news commentary than in straight news stories in which the reporter uses only factual material. Yet even in straight news story structure a newsman frequently frames a unifying theme to tie disparate elements or events together: "Seven drownings occurred in three state boating accidents yesterday." Radio, with its need for condensation, uses this device constantly: "Foreign trouble spots are quiet today for the first time in a month."

Even when details are logically related to the theme, essential unity may be diluted or concealed by their unskillful or inconsequential use, especially in the lead. In the auto-chase story, as has been said, the reader is confused because the lead contains an idea that is not developed later and because the story introduces dimly related facts that obscure its major outline. Such details detract from the impression of unity because they are not shown to be essential. Often such nonessentials—the route of the chase, the policemen's two-way radio chatter—may be well presented in "sidebars."

A story may also lack unity when a minor fact is selected for lead emphasis, even though it carry marked interest. Unity requires that the major facts, as well as the central theme, be established in the lead, with minor supporting facts coming later. When minor facts are overemphasized it becomes difficult, sometimes impossible, to organize a balanced and unified inverted-pyramid story. Lack of balance is observable frequently in speech reports in which the speaker's parenthetical aside is made the lead. Such asides may be laden with reader-interest and even real news value. But when the reporter emphasizes a minor statement at the expense of the true tenor of the speech, he may destroy the story's unity and mislead the reader, who assumes from a statement's position in the lead that it throws emphasis on a principal characteristic of the event. This distortion of emphasis, which is both bad reporting and bad story structure, is a pitfall that traps both novice and experienced reporters. (The problems of reporting speeches receive attention in chapter 13.)

A story may lack unity if the reporter fails to

to comment, and the wreath placed at the Unknown Soldier's tomb at Arlington by a Hiroshima survivor.

Another example: Accompanying its story about V-E Day celebrations in Bonn and East Berlin, Le Figaro used a paragraph about West German annoyance with the Soviet embassy in Bonn for its "bad taste" in staging a giant cocktail party on the anniversary day.

•   •

Careless handling of review material in a running story concerning the question of free speech and free thought on a university campus caused needless anguish to the news figure involved and embarrassed shame to a lot of reporters and editors. In the course of the dispute, a professor upholding the need of untrammeled intellectual curiosity and free expression of views, even "wrong" views, remarked that he would approve the formation on campus of many groups with which he would not associate himself. He mentioned as examples among such groups a "society for the promotion of free love" and a "nudist club," along with many others of vastly different character. In the abundantly-reported follow-up stories, the summary statements of the professor's position frequently declared that he had advocated free love and nudism, a totally false description of his meaning and intent. Though attempts were made by most of the media to correct this error once it was brought to their notire, the false impression was never eradirated. Both in his own state legislature and in neighboring Canada, where

make his lead inclusive enough to cover facts that he develops in later paragraphs. Both this weakness and its opposite, including in the lead details not subsequently developed, are illustrated in the following story:

A special alarm fire which sent a pall of smoke over the Hadway district Wednesday night caused an estimated damage to the A. B. McMahon Co., 693 Filpott Avenue.	*The lead suggests that both the special alarm and the pall of smoke are to be emphasized. Try to find them later in the story. (And note a cliché, a barbarism and an incomplete statement.)*
Firemen fought the stubborn blaze without masks or other precautionary measures until the arrival of firm officials who warned the buildings contained chemicals which easily could form poisonous gases. Although the fire was almost out, Chief William Mattocks ordered his men from the area until they had donned masks. A number of the firemen who had been exposed to the fumes were administered oxygen at the scene.	*A clumsy second sentence introduces a new element, the chance of poisonous gas, which provides the basis for most of the rest of the story.*
The McMahon firm manufactures neon and other illuminated tubing for electric signs.	*Background information. Is it useful?*

This next story is constructed so as to let the reader know that, although major emphasis is to go to one set of facts, he will be given detail of another set before he finishes reading:

Rejection of a civil rights ordinance ended a six-hour City Council meeting last night. The Council voted 9 to 4 to table the proposal whose purpose was to make racial and religious discrimination illegal in employment in any business in the city. The Council also turned down a proposal that all schoolchildren must carry identification cards. [*The next fourteen paragraphs develop the major theme, the civil rights ordinance; the remainder develop the second topic.*]	*This two-section, three-paragraph lead plots the order-of-decreasing-importance structure of the story; it gives the reader a unified view of the news the story contains. If paragraph three were omitted, or inserted only after the first topic had been covered, the reader might well ask, "How did this subject get in here?"*

an immigration inspector denied him permission to cross the border, the misrepresentation of his views cost him pain and reputation.
The fault lay in failure of news writers to add the few extra words needed to make the background paragraph accurate and clear.

A story constructed as carefully as this one provides an effortless solution to the problem of transition. The fact is that the use of transitional devices as they are taught in essay- and theme-writing classes is rare in news writing. Yet a *sense of transition* must be present even though actual transitional phrases or sentences are omitted. Such a sense derives from the very unity of the story—from the facts that a dominant theme has been selected, that secondary topics are flagged near the lead, and that the reader never needs to say to himself, "How did this passage get in here? I wasn't warned that it would be coming."

This does not mean that straightforward rhetorical transition is never found in journalistic writing. In feature stories and in longer pieces not constructed in the "standard" news form the frank device to say to the reader "change of topic" or "change of emphasis," or even "different aspect of the same topic," must be used.

Time for Review

Often a news writer must take precious time and space to brief his audience, or some members of it, on what has happened before. Not every reader saw yesterday's paper, or heard yesterday's newscasts. Those who didn't will not understand today's developments without being told the background. And this means that in the "running story"—the one that continues from day to day—at least a few lines must go to retelling the parts of the total series of events without which what happened today wouldn't be comprehensible.

Usually this review of the background should come fairly early in a story, a fact that poses an additional problem, since it slows up the recital of the new developments. But including it is a necessity. The experienced news writer knows that the best way to do it is to hold it to a paragraph or so, in broadly summarized form, to keep its writing tight, and to exclude all but the salient facts that must be told. Even when these precautions are observed, some readers will be annoyed at "old stuff." These are the constant readers, the ones who don't need to be told again. But the risk must be run, for the sake of the uninformed.

Beginning the Story

Only the novice in news writing has time to sit and ponder at his typewriter before getting his story under way. A mark of the professional is the dispatch with which he starts writing. He gets at it fast because he has used the time between gathering the facts and arriving at his desk to plan what he is going to write. Usually he has decided what to put in the lead and how to write the opening paragraphs, and often he has outlined mentally the rest of the story. The pro is able to follow this businesslike procedure because experience has equipped him with a good many rules for lead writing—likely more rules than he has consciously articulated. (Some of the guides for lead writing are outlined in the next chapter.)

Before he starts his lead he has decided which elements are most meaningful, what the major facts are, and how they should be organized. He has done this, knowingly or not, by applying the principle of essential unity to his facts. He has asked himself: What is the point of this story? What is its central idea? What is the appropriate focus for emphasis? What in this material will be most significant and most interesting to my audience?

He may, in making his decisions, have come up against the continuing conflict between the significant and the interesting. In many news stories the conflict takes care of itself—in those stories in which the interesting *is* significant. But in many events it is the insignificant that has magnetic interest for the audience. If an Iron Curtain ambassador forgets to wear his suspenders when attending the first Presidential reception since the Cold War started, his forgetfulness would be less significant than the fact that he attends the reception at all—but much more entertaining. The reporter has an embarrassment of choices. He could emphasize the ambassador's absentmindedness and his red face; he could build around the significant fact that the ambassador broke his rule and attended; he could seek a way of tying the two aspects of the story together; or he could ignore the suspenders story altogether. The third choice might be the most likely, but a choice defensible as "best" is often hard to make. Although the press is often criticized for emphasizing reader interest rather than significance, careful observation and several research studies show that the news media more and more consistently report the news in its true perspective.

Look at a minor news event in which the significance-versus-interest choice must be made. This event involved fire and theft in a building across the street from both the sheriff's office and a fire station. The element of significance lies in the attempt at burglary and arson and its failure. The element of special interest (aside from the omnipresent interest in violent crime) comes from the criminals' thumbing their noses at authority. Which element should the reporter emphasize? or should he stress both? Answer the questions for yourself before seeing how the reporter who wrote the story solved them.

Brazen thieves got by with burglary and arson within eye-view of the county sheriff's office and a stone's throw from fire department headquarters at 1 A.M. today.	*The lead attempts to combine both significance and interest.*
The thieves broke into the Weston Engraving Co., on the third floor at 415 S. Fourth Street. From its windows you can look down into the sheriff's office on the ground floor of the courthouse across the street.	*This paragraph throws some doubt on the first. The thieves could see into the sheriff's office—but could the sheriffs see them?*

However, the sheriff's office was unoccupied. During night hours, the sheriff's radio tower is the nerve center of patrol activities.	*Now you learn that no sheriffs were on hand.*
Firemen were first on the scene, summoned by an ADT alarm that was set off by a sprinkler, which in turn was set off by a fire set by the burglars.	*At this point the story leaves its main theme—the thieves' brazenness—and goes to minor detail.*
Investigators found evidence they had started three separate fires—one in a trash container, one under a desk with papers pulled out of drawers, and a third among papers in an open area between the safe and a desk. Detectives who were called in said the burglars probably became disgruntled when they were unable to open the safe. The dial had been knocked off but no entry made. Fire damage was almost negligible, with sprinklers checking the blazes and firemen finishing the job. However, water damage was heavy in the engraving firm and in the second floor office.	*The fact that the last five paragraphs could be omitted shows that the story has observed well the inverted-pyramid form. But the three paragraphs about the setting and extinguishing of the fires invalidate the phrase "got by" in the lead. The thieves failed in both attempted burglary and attempted destruction.*
The firemen's cleanup job lasted an hour and 45 minutes.	*Why include this paragraph?*

Analysis of this story shows what happens when a reporter overplays a minor fact in order to capture audience interest. The facts did not justify the phrase "got by" in the lead; the reporter labored to justify it but ended up with a confused and unsatisfying story. Perhaps he would have fared better had he opened his lead thus: "Brazen burglars failed in attempted theft and arson . . ."

The Reston story (page 156) approached a similar significance-interest conflict in a different way. Here the reporter seems to have decided that the news conference he was covering was not of great significance, but that the human-interest developments were interesting enough to use as a point of departure (and to provide a theme). Reston therefore built his story around this element, establishing the "relaxed good humor" mood in the lead and relating most of the rest of the story to it.

No blanket rule can be written to help the news writer make all such decisions. He has to approach each new story with whatever judgment and experience he can contribute, and each time come to a new conclusion about organization and emphasis. There is no problem in understanding the rationale of the inverted-pyramid form, the form used in all media for straight news stories. The difficulties arise because the facts must be arranged in order of decreasing importance, an order that is suggested by the lead but rarely fully outlined by it.

The reporter can help himself and his consumer if, in planning the story before he starts writing, he decides:

1) The story's theme; its central fact—its unifying element;
2) How the facts can be grouped so that first things come first, and secondary sets of facts arranged to conform to theme and decreasing importance.

A story has a long headstart toward sound construction if its writer remembers always that in unity there is strength.

PROJECTS

1. Reread the auto-chase story and the comments on it in this chapter. Then rewrite it —insofar as you can with the facts given you—so as to equip it with a one-idea lead and more unified treatment.
2. Select three or more news stories from current newspapers that seem to you to violate the usual rules for straight news story structure. Rewrite them to make them conform to the standard pattern. Comment on the validity of your changes.
3. Select half a dozen local news stories from a newspaper or news broadcast, and rewrite them for "foreign" consumption—that is, for use by a wire service that is reporting them to other communities. Note the changes you have made in leads or structure, or both, and defend them.

CHAPTER 12

Leads: Design and Content

On June 9, 1864, readers of the New York *Times* had to labor through four columns of agate type (14 lines to the inch) before they learned that President Lincoln had been renominated. On June 19, 1896, the *Times* opened its story of the Republican convention thus: "William McKinley of Ohio was nominated as the candidate of the Republican party for President, and Garett A. Hobart was named for Vice President." The modern news lead had taken root.

The comments and advice this book has offered about effective news story organization and its dependence on unity prepare the way for writing the lead as well as the rest of the story. They point to two elementary guides for writing leads:

1) An effective lead (used especially when the significance of subject matter is the story's strongest element) opens with a brief, sharp statement of the story's essential fact, the theme around which the story is unified. (The "suspended-interest" lead, which defies this rule, is discussed elsewhere.)

2) The lead should limit itself to one central idea or concept, a concept that emphasizes the theme and content of the story. A one-idea lead is certain to be more effective than a multiple-idea lead, both because it starts the construction of a unified story and because most readers can take one idea readily but find it difficult to comprehend several at once.

The emphasis in today's news writing is upon brevity, and the standard news lead, to draw from an earlier sentence, is a "quick roundup of the major facts of a story." Whether it consists of a one-sentence paragraph, as nine tenths of today's leads do, or of two or more sentences or paragraphs, competent news writers always try to keep the lead as short as reason lets them.

The Straight-news Lead

Rudyard Kipling may be taxed with having set back by a good many years the development of today's news-story lead. Kipling put into doggerel the formula for the AP lead; easy to remember, it was also too easy to apply:

I keep six honest serving men;
They taught me all I knew.
Their names are What and Why and When
And How and Where and Who.
Were Kipling alive today, he might find it challenging to put a more modern formula into a couplet.

When news story form jelled at the end of the nineteenth century, the dominant characteristic of the traditional straight-news lead was its painstaking, and often painful, comprehensiveness. The Associated Press, under the careful and determined Melville E. Stone, was in large part responsible for developing the rule that every "good" lead must answer the questions *who, what, when, where, why,* and *how.* Soon every newsman was saying that a good lead must contain five Ws and an H. A lead with all these components is customarily called an "AP lead" because for many years Stone and the AP insisted on it. The five Ws and an H made the lead complete, but they also made it frequently long, heavy, and confusing; it is, in fact, sometimes referred to as the "clothesline lead" because everything hangs on it.

An example of an AP lead will illustrate both its virtues and its shortcomings:

> Two men, Joseph E. Hastings, 24, 1119 Woodhue Boulevard, Centerdale, and Dominic Tucci, age unknown, of Elmira, New York, were killed at 4:30 A.M. today at Fourth Street and Skystone Avenue, when a tire on Hastings' car blew out and caused the car to overturn on the two occupants.

This lead supplies answers to

who?   Hastings and Tucci named and identified
what?   two men killed in an accident
when?   4:30 A.M. today
where?   Fourth Street and Skystone Avenue
why?   tire blowout
how?   car overturned on occupants

The lead unquestionably summarizes the entire event for the reader. But note its characteristics: enough words to fill 10 lines of newspaper type; 18 specific facts, none sharply emphasized; a general air of ponderousness and confusion.

The AP lead remained the model for American newspapers until the period of World War II. At that time a number of influences combined to turn newsmen against it. A leading cause for the change was competition. For the first time the newspaper had a serious competitor in the presentation of current news— the upstart radio. Radio news was young, unfettered by tradition. Radio practice quickly disclosed that the long-winded lead neither held nor adequately informed a listening audience, and radio newscasters were eager to find inventive news patterns that would be effective for aural rather than visual communication. A reader's eye could retrace a complicated lead if he had missed a fact or failed to make a connection, but a listener might lose the story entirely if he missed even a syllable of the lead. Radio newsmen realized that their news offerings must have simplicity of structure, of language, and of sequence of facts. Abandoning the AP lead, they soon developed their own distinctive rhetorical form. A radio story about the automobile accident (page 167) might open thus:

> Another pair of auto deaths today--two men were killed in an accident in downtown Centerdale.

This is vastly different from the clothesline lead. It has seven facts and 15 words; it makes no pretense at using all of Kipling's serving-men. Yet radio newsmen could maintain with reason that it gives all the *essential* facts and that it introduces the story more clearly to the ear than would the longer version. It is readily understandable, and it permits the listener to take in the details of the story smoothly and easily. It has prepared him for the kind of information the story is to give.

Radio's claim was undeniable. It started newspapermen wondering whether the simplified lead might not have something for them, too. Readers were devoting fewer minutes a day to newspapers as news competition grew stiffer and more demands were made on their time—not only by radio, and after the war by television, but also by increased leisure, more money for recreation, more opportunities for diversion. Newspaper editors realized that news writing style should be made more readily comprehensible, easier to take, faster to read. The Associated Press hired Rudolf Flesch to analyze its prose style and suggest improvements; the United Press hired Robert Gunning. Individual newspapers put analysts and researchers to work seeking new approaches to readability. In 1954 the managing editor of the New York *Times* posted a memo in his city room: "We feel it is no longer necessary, and perhaps it never was, to wrap up in one sentence or paragraph all the traditional five Ws."

Results of all this interest in simpler writing are unmistakable. A dozen years after the Flesch report on its style, the Associated Press announced that the ease-of-reading level of its prose had reached the point it sought. And with the simplification of news style in general came the virtual abandonment of the clothesline lead. An up-to-date version of the lead on the accident story would run like this:

> Two men were killed early today in downtown Centerdale when their car overturned on them.

Contrast the number of words and the number of facts in the three leads.

When Dr. Flesch reported to the Associated Press on his study of its copy in 1950, he recommended that it reduce its habitually long sentences to an average of 19 words. An analysis of AP copy in 1964 showed its average sentence length to be 18.7.

The lead paragraphs of all the front-page stories in two metropolitan papers (picked at random) in 1924 averaged 53.2 words. Those of a 1955 paper averaged 26.4. Those of two 1965 papers averaged 25.9. With one exception, the 1924 leads were longer than the longest of 30 and 40 years later. The exception—shortest on any of the stories—was a 14-word paragraph under a famous by-line: Elmer Davis.

This sample lead is shorter than most of today's newspaper leads; indeed, the radio lead is one word longer partly because, in good radio style, it repeats a major fact, the *what*. Incidentally, the newspaper lead would be entirely acceptable for radio.

The move to a simpler lead pattern does not make the task of the news writer simpler. He can no longer follow the ready-made five-W-and-H formula. From the six elements he has to choose those that most truly catch the flavor and meaning of a news event. He has to compose a lead in half the number of words his predecessors used. In seeking shorter leads many papers give him firm office rules. One paper says that "no lead paragraph may exceed 35 words." A number of papers limit their leads to three lines of typewritten copy.

Today's news lead, then, is no longer ruled by the five-W-and-H formula. Yet the writer who designs the lead and the story that follows it refers to the formula constantly. From among its six elements, he must choose those that define the essential meaning of the event. Which elements, the writer asks himself, *must* be included in the lead? Which may be presented later in the story? Which may be omitted entirely?

The simple clothesline lead at the beginning of this chapter uses all six elements. The "modern" rewrite of the lead contains the *what* and the *when*, abbreviates the *who, where,* and *how,* and omits the *why*. Because the modern lead does not try to tell everything at once, some elements must be presented later. Although time and place (*when* and *where*) elements of a story can usually be given in a phrase, and the *who* in two or three words, the *what, how,* and *why* cannot be so easily compressed. When these elements are used in the lead, they must be given in sharply summarized form as mere suggestions of material to be developed later.

For quite different reasons, the *what* and the *when* are almost invariably included in any news lead. They deserve first attention.

WHAT   Since the primary purpose of news is to communicate what has happened or is about to happen, the *what* is the element that appears in straight news leads more often than any other. The lead cannot include all the relevant facts, or even suggest all the highlights; but it must give the *what*—what the story is about, what the main facts are, so that the reader can decide whether he wants to spend his time continuing the story. (The suspended-interest story uses a different technique to emphasize the *what*.)

Once the facts of the story are organized and the theme established, writing the *what* into the lead imposes no very difficult problem. Look at the news section, especially the front page, of any newspaper, or listen carefully to any news-cast. You will discover many examples of effective *what* leads, most of them simple in construction. A brief statement that summarizes the event or defines its principal meaning or characteristic usually suffices.

A pitfall peculiar to writing the *what* (or any element) into a lead may develop if the writer, in his zeal for brevity, condenses too much. A reporter who has been covering a field of news or a specific sequence of events month after month runs the danger of assuming too much knowledge on the part of the reader. He may forget that few readers know as much about the field as he does, and that some may be completely ignorant of any relevant facts. Note that in the following lead the reporter has taken for granted that his readers have specific knowledge before they begin to read:

> The long-range capital improvements committee Tuesday appointed ten task forces to make sure its 196-million-dollar public improvements program doesn't stall before it gets started.

> *Does this committee represent a city? a state? a corporation? the Chamber of Commerce? What kind of improvement is it interested in?*

Leads that omit essential facts may be permissible if the news circumstance is so widely known that nobody could be puzzled. It would have been appropriate, for example, to write in 1965: "A great Englishman was buried today." Most readers could supply the missing facts; few Americans did not know that Winston Churchill had died. But it is unsafe to rely on this kind of public knowledge in any but the most important or the most spectacular of news events.

WHEN   The time element is firmly and properly established as a major factor in news, and the straight-news leads of experienced professionals don't omit it. Leads that neglect specific, explicit references to *when* usually do so only if the time element is implicitly present. As earlier chapters made clear, the time element must be included; in the high-speed world of the twentieth century, it is frequently necessary to place an event in time in order to convey its full meaning. A second reason, of less weight, is that today's audiences have been conditioned to think that only "hot" news can have much importance.

In a news story the primary time element is the time at which the facts became known to the reporter; but stories may have more than one time element. The news that announces a future event often has a past-tense time element because the announcement of the event had been

The basic time element of any news story is the time when the news becomes available. This means that, in one sense, every news story is in past tense: a reporter must necessarily have found out what he is going to write about before he begins to write—the event had occurred, or the information had been released.

These examples show typical use of the time element:

made before the story was written: "Mayor Johnson said this morning that the Council will meet Tuesday . . ." Each time element must be reported.

Retired commanders of American Legion Post No. 24 were banqueted last night in the Paffrath Hotel.

Centerdale does not have enough policemen, Mayor Wilcox said today.

"Last night" is the time element—the time the event occurred.

"Today," when the mayor made the statement, is the time element.

The time element does not alter the essential nature of either of these stories. Both the Legion banquet and the mayor's statement could stand by themselves without the "last night" or the "today." But the reader finds the story about the Legion more satisfying and possibly more revealing if he knows that the event occurred "last night," for he can relate it to his own evening, his own life, and the life of his friends and his community. When the reader knows that the mayor made his statement "today," he can react to the immediacy of the lack of policemen in Centerdale; perhaps the "today" tells him that the mayor's concern was prompted by the recent wave of burglaries in the city's business area. If the time element had been omitted from either story, the relation of the event to the reader's environment would not be clear.

In this example, the time element is implied:

The Centerdale Yacht Club's "Electra" is leading in the Chicago-to-Mackinac race.

This lead omits the "today" because the time is clear; the race *is* under way. The implicit time element is common in radio and TV news, whose stress on immediacy is stronger than that of the press.

The following lead, from a Midwestern daily, illustrates how a story can be made misleading by omission of the time element:

Four German students who spent six months at a local university studying American educational techniques reported that controls imposed on American students are "shocking."

[*The story goes on to detail at length the Germans' comments. Its last paragraph reports that the comments were made in theses the students wrote after their return to Germany.*]

The casual reader assumes that this story reports a current event, that the students' comments had just been received or just been made public. This was not the case. The report had been received more than two years earlier, and its contents had been reported at that time by a campus newspaper. The story as published (it came to the newspaper through a wire service) does not make this clear—perhaps by inadvertence. But to informed readers it opens the reporter and his wire service inescapably to the suspicion of concealment of a significant fact. In any case, it presents its facts incompletely and out of context.

An "old" event, however, may acquire legitimate current interest. Twenty years after Franklin D. Roosevelt's death the American news media used a story about an event that had not been open to reporting during his lifetime. The Associated Press newspaper lead said, "President Roosevelt opposed the return of Indochina to France at the end of World War II, according to historical papers published *Monday*." A 1944 act became news in 1965 because it became public in 1965; the *Monday* is the spot news element. Facts about the private lives of the pharaohs are duly reported as news 4000 years after their occurrence, because penetration of Egyptian tombs brings old information to new light and new publics: "Archeologists learned *yesterday* that the rulers of ancient Egypt . . ."

Thus there may be two (or more) *when* elements in a story. Those just cited are examples. Most future-tense stories have a past time element as well; and the past element is in most cases the one that gives a story its timeliness. For example:

> Centerdale will hold its Fall Festival Sept. 19 to 24 next year, according to a committee decision announced today.

Note that this story could be written with the "today" further subordinated:

> Centerdale will hold its Fall Festival next year on Sept. 19 to 24.
> This decision was announced today by . . .

Two time elements. But the "next year" is not only a time element but also part of the what. "Today" is the element that makes the story current news.

This lead treatment has virtues of brevity and simplicity that spotlight the story's main fact, its "theme."

When should the time element become the opening phrase in a lead?

Look at the news columns of any newspaper and you'll find that the answer is apparent: "Rarely." Seldom is the *when* a story's most meaningful element. And since a tenet of good lead-writing is stress on its strongest element—more on this principle soon—the time element rarely opens the newspaper lead. (It is more common in broadcast news leads, however, again because of radio and TV emphasis on immediacy.)

But on occasion the *when* is the focus of the story, and deserves prominence:

> April 15 has replaced March 15 as the date on which income tax returns are due.
>
> Jan. 29, for the third year in a row, was winter's coldest day.

WHO AND WHERE   Though the *when* element should be in every lead and the *what* is rarely absent, the *who* is frequently the opening element. This is true sometimes even when the *who* actually carries less weight than other elements. The reasons are manifest: *who* is the human element in the story, and it may introduce the characteristic *prominence*.

When, for example, the name of the President of the United States appears in news material, chances are nine in ten that it will open the story. The name has audience magnetism; it not only attracts attention but suggests something about the nature of the story; it seems to many a news reader to concern him personally in one way or another.

That this pattern may depart from logic is evident. Sometimes *what* the President says, or the action in which he is involved, would provide a better opening than his name. Which, to look at cases, of the following six would you argue for?

> President Roosevelt today asked Congress for, and was given, a declaration of war against Japan.
>
> The United States is at war with Japan.
>
> Congress declared war to-day, following . . .
>
> Congress today declared war against Japan. The declaration followed . . .
>
> War against Japan was declared today by Congress, following . . .
>
> War!

When the *who* is not prominent, when it has no attraction value in itself and lends no distinction to the story, it should rarely open the lead.

Special *who* characteristics may sometimes justify opening emphasis on this element even though specific identification is not included:

> An 11-year-old boy smashed his violin and tried to hang himself today after being scolded for practicing the wrong lesson.

> A one-armed driver was named Centerdale's "safest" in today's annual County Fair competition.

Some leads may be written with no *who* element:

> Seven cars were involved in a series of rear-end collisions on the highway south of town this morning.

> The city's heliport will be located only two blocks from the City Hall.

> Rain so far this month has exceeded Centerdale's average rainfall for an entire year.

> Enough polio vaccine to inoculate every child in the county has been received at the City Health Office.

When to put prime emphasis on the *who*, when to subordinate it, when to delay its appearance, and when to omit it are matters for common sense and editorial judgment, guided by experience and the best interests of the news consumer.

Somewhat the same thing may be said of treatment of the *where*. Proximity, or its absence, is one of the factors influencing audience response, and a statement regarding it may be essential to understanding. The location of an event, when it is not specifically stated, is always implicitly suggested. In wire stories, the dateline usually serves.

Like the *when*, the place element does not often open a lead. Yet it may take first place in some stories:

> Chicago has been chosen as the site of next year's national Republican convention.

> A billiard table in a saloon became an emergency operating table this morning.

How and Why   *How* and *why* do not share priority with *what, when,* and *where* in the lead. Like the *what*, they cannot always be briefly summarized; and since the modern lead does not try to tell everything at once, they are often left for development later in the story. The clothesline lead (page 167) gave all six elements by prescription, but note that the modern rewrite of this lead on page 168 contains the *what* and the *when*, abbreviates the *who*, the *where*, and the *how*, and omits the *why* altogether. Sometimes it is enough to tell the reader, in the body of the story, how the event developed. A story about a panic in a burning night club describes the course of events and in so doing suggests the causes of fear and hysterical behavior. But it may take much more than fast on-the-spot investigation, and often more than one follow-up story, to bring to light the genuine underlying causes, the real *why:* faulty fire-prevention laws, lax enforcement of good laws, inadequate fire inspection, venality, coincidence, or what not.

The burning need to inject more *why* into modern news coverage is urgently recognized in America. A later chapter deals with this problem.

Writing the Lead

Every newspaper newswriter should paste two rules of thumb, mentally or physically, above his desk:

1) Open the lead with a brief expression of the story's strongest element.
2) Follow the one-idea-to-a-sentence principle as far as materials and effective rhetoric permit.

"STRONGEST ELEMENT"   Another way to put the first rule is this: Get the "best" facts of the story into the lead's first group of words.

What are "best" facts? They are those that most sharply express the theme of the story; those to which everything in the story will relate; those that can be briefly summarized to state the significant meaning of the story. Here are examples:

> Repavement of Centerdale's streets will be debated at . . .
>
> Joe Doakes was acquitted of murder by the jury in . . .
>
> Two hundred Tampico citizens died when hurricane Ione hit . . .
>
> Homes for 175 families will be built next fall by . . .

In each of these leads the opening group of words summarizes quickly the story's key facts—four words in one case, five in one, six in one, seven in one. In each lead, on the other hand, most other arrangements would not summarize so immediately or succinctly:

> A debate on the question of repaving Centerdale's streets . . .
>
> Whether Centerdale ought to repave its streets . . .

These rephrasings, it may be argued, are *almost* as strong as the original. But the first gets the nod because it has the key word "repavement" in the eye-catching, attention-commanding lead position. In these and the other examples the prime element is significance—the choice rests on the set of facts that do most to make the story affective to readers. In some cases, the "eternal conflict" may be resolved in favor of interest rather than significance, however:

> A quarrel over a recipe for chili sauce upset a Latin American government today.
>
> Dollar bills showered from what looked like a clear sky on a Centerdale home this morning.

And sometimes, in the interest of gaining reader attention, the news writer takes advantage of the element of prominence:

> Queen Elizabeth will attend the races at Epsom Downs today.
>
> Rock Hudson, movie actor, will open the annual United Fund drive here today.

ONE IDEA TO A SENTENCE   Rule of thumb no. 2 is no more than a restatement of what has been said about the modern simplified lead in contrast to the antiques of another era. One of the articulate advocates of the one-idea sentence, Ted Bernstein (see page 131 and other references), has this to say about it:

> Don't take this as a rule or formula, but generally the one-idea sentence speeds reading. At any rate, three or four or five ideas in a single sentence make for tough reading. Here is a sentence that surely would be better broken into two or perhaps three: "While the board deferred decision until April 29, its members left little doubt that they favored the change but believed the New York City Omnibus Corporation was entitled to relief because it would lose some riders as the result of the new pattern." Another example: "Junior Gilliam hit two home runs off Allie Reynolds, who gave up all the enemy runs in the first four innings, and Billy Cox hit another one off the Chief as his team won its fourth straight game and its 21st of the spring—all against major teams."

Bernstein is talking about any news-story sentence, not merely the lead sentence. But the one-idea lead sentence can hardly help being stronger than one that asks a reader or listener, "cold" as he comes to the story, unprepared for what it is to offer, to grasp several ideas. Note the contrasts in the two groups of leads that follow—a somewhat stacked contrast, since the first two are classics of their kind (the second group are chosen from one edition of a metropolitan paper):

OLD ORCHARD, Me.—July 12 (Special)—Captain John A. Smuts, the present husband of May Yohe, musical comedy star of the long-ago and former wife of Lord Francis Hope, once owner of the internationally known and ill-fated Hope diamond, interviewed exclusively here this morning as he left for an unannounced destination, replied to the broadcast reports concerning Hazel Potts of Waukegan, Ill., and indicated that a personal statement will be forthcoming from his wife in the near future.

A man who left a revolver in a rooming house here as he departed in a large limousine which took him to Municipal Airport where he boarded a Mid-Continent airplane is being held by authorities at Tulsa, Okla., for local police who seek his arrest on a charge of obtaining money under false pretenses, Chief of Detectives Kingsley B. Shotwell said today.

The National Football League may add two teams to its roster within two years.

The first cotton plantation strike since the 1930s began to flounder Thursday.

Variable cloudiness with occasional showers and thunderstorms were predicted for this area today and tomorrow.

Some federal jobs in the Administration's "youth opportunity program" are being distributed as Congressional patronage.

Two attorneys disagreed Thursday over the role lawyers should play in juvenile court cases involving parent-child welfare matters.

Five children younger than 16 don't keep Mrs. Raymond Plank out of the air.

"Strong" Lead Openings

In a general way, the first rule in the preceding section says all there is to say about getting the lead off to a running start.

But there are specifics to support the generalization. One is that strong leads usually open with the subjects of simple declarative sentences, nouns or noun phrases. Another: the verb or verb phrase should not be long delayed. As examples, re-examine the leads you observed on page 175:

Repavement of Centerdale's streets will be debated . . .	*Lead opens with the word naming the story's "best" fact. The verb phrase begins with the fifth word.*
Two hundred Tampico citizens died . . .	*The first five words include both the significant facts and the verb.*
Joe Doakes was acquitted of murder . . .	*The name opener is presumably strong because of audience familiarity with a crime of violence. Six words complete the summary.*
Homes for 175 families will be built . . .	*Four attention-catching words form the noun-phrase subject; a three-word verb completes the summary.*

Any reporter could arrive at scores of other arrangements of the words in these leads, and scores of other emphases on the facts in the events from which the stories grow. It is often possible to argue that Reporter Jones's choice of emphasis is sounder, or weaker, than Reporter Smith's; but the "strongest" rhetoric, even when there is no argument as to appropriate emphasis, is a matter of critical judgment. Once an emphasis is chosen, however, the number of vigorous alternatives may be limited.

NAMES   "Names make news," says the newsman's bromide; names frequently make strong lead openings. But the mere presence of a prominent name in a news circumstance does not necessarily style the lead. When a tornado strikes a prairie town, for example, and counts among its 100 dead a senator who happened to be driving through, should his name be given lead emphasis? Probably not, unless the lead can be devised to move instantly from the name to the broader character of the disaster:

> Sen. John Doe lost his life along with 100 others in a tornado here yesterday.
>
> A senator and 100 others were killed by a tornado yesterday . . .
>
> Sen. John Doe is one of 100 dead here today following yesterday's tornado.
>
> One hundred deaths, including that of a United States senator, were counted here today following yesterday's tornado.

A dozen other patterns, or a hundred, could be developed. But it seems clear that in two of the leads above the senator's name slows up arrival at the major fact: 100 tornado deaths.

(Incidentally, note that the longest of the four leads is confused by the ambiguous term "were counted." Exactly what does it mean?)

A name should open a lead, in brief, when the name itself is clearly dominant among the facts of the story (what, for example, if the senator in the tornado had been a leading candidate for the Presidency?), or when the attention it gains for the other facts of the event is great enough to overbalance the fact that it is *not* dominant. (A punctilious newswriter would say that the second justification for leading with a name is not consistent with responsible news presentation, that it is misleading, and his position would be a strong one.)

QUOTATIONS   Quoted opening words, phrases, or clauses, with quotation marks, are often effective both in attracting attention and in adding meaning. For example:

"Fog" from a broken
steam line caused two auto
collisions . . .

"Crime doesn't pay," an
ex-convict told an audi-
ence . . .

"The Pajama Game" will
be presented by home talent
here Nov. 19 . . .

"The three musketeers" of
Centerdale were arrested
last night . . .

"Fog" is appropriately, and interestingly, quoted as a quick way of saying to readers, "It wasn't really fog." "The Pajama Game" must bear quotation marks as a play title, according to most style sheets; the marks add to its interest. "Crime doesn't pay" appears to be not alone what the speaker said but also a fitting summary of his talk (faulty use of direct quotation leads in speech and interview stories will be examined in the next chapter).

"The three musketeers" is a reporter's device for identifying and character-izing quickly a group that has broken into the news. It is a lead opening that is both attractive and, if well used, meaningful. But it might be mere reaching for a catchy phrase. If the facts that follow don't justify the metaphor, the reader feels cheated and the story is weakened.

QUESTIONS   Question leads are sometimes excellent choices.

Will Centerdale get its
outdoor movie?

Will the rains ever stop?

Is polio really licked?

"Who won the turkey?"
was the question everybody
wanted an answer to.

A question lead, you'll note, meets excellently the criteria suggested at the beginning of this chapter: It states the major fact of the story in its opening words, and it limits itself largely to this idea. But it may have a deficiency that must be corrected immediately. If the reader is not to be left dangling by the question leads above, a quick answer or explanation must be provided. The reader must be told that the promoter proposing the outdoor movie hasn't made up his mind; that the weather bureau can't promise an end to the rains; that some members of the county medical society, at the meeting yesterday, expressed severe reservations about polio vaccines; that five citizens held "winning tickets" for the one turkey at the raffle.

A trap for the unwary seeker of a "bright" lead: to devise a question lead where no legitimate question is asked. "Is polio really licked?" is a sound lead if the flavor of the debate was one of indecision, if there was no consensus at the meeting, or if the consensus was one of doubt. But if there had been substantial agreement that the victory had been won, a better lead might be: "Polio has been licked, according to . . ."

Should you use "you" in a lead?

A proper answer, as to any question about lead effectiveness, is, "Whenever you gain clarity, interest, emphasis by doing so." The tendency in news writing of all kinds, on the air and in print, is toward informality and ease. If the newswriter thinks he can help the reader or listener to "identify" with the story, to apply its meaning to himself, by using the second person, he is usually wise to do so.

When the "you" is used, it means that the news event is one that can be treated informally or personally. It ought to be one in which readers or listeners can picture their own participation. The weather lead suggested above, for example: "Are you thinking the rain will never stop?" or "You may have given up on the sun," or "Don't plan picnics for this weekend." But this informal flavor would be unsuitable for some kinds of news.

SHORT LEADS   What is often called the "cartridge lead"—because it packs power into a small parcel—may be just right on "big" news:

> The war is ended.
>
> The new mayor—Richard Roe.
>
> The President is dead.
>
> Rain today ended the drouth.

Such a lead must be used, clearly, only for a news event requiring little background or explanation. The writer banks on having readers know, when he says "the President is dead," what president he is talking about. He assumes that the recent election campaign is so deep in audience consciousness that the placard-like announcement of the new mayor's name will be enough.

Because the cartridge lead demands special circumstances, it does not appear often. Only a few news situations justify the reporter in the assumption that every consumer will have enough fill-in information. The device should be used jealously; overuse or improper use would quickly debase it.

LONGER LEADS   Sometimes a newswriter finds himself with so much meaningful material that a brief, quickly summarizing lead would be inadequate. To meet this problem, newsmen have learned, the usual rules may be broken. Some leads may go to two or more sentences, or two or more paragraphs. Analysis of these examples may suggest to you other news situations in which departure from the standard pattern will be justified and effective.

> The most controversial welfare program of them all —aid to dependent children —was the topic of a public legislative hearing at the capitol yesterday.

> The result: controversy.
> • •
> Suffolk will have two new fire stations next year. This decision was made this morning at the fifth stormy

> Council meeting in three days.
> • •
> School enrollments will rise 30 percent within five years.

Finding teachers will get harder and harder.

The school building program is already "10 years behind time."

These three warnings came today from the State Education Bureau . . .

• •

Rochester, which hasn't recovered from the trauma of riots last summer, must now live with a new phenomenon in race relations. The Negroes of this city are organizing and their goal is power —so much power that they need not ask, but can demand, change.

The result, at the moment, is a serious breakdown in communications between whites and Negroes. No one can predict what will happen here, but events of the next few months—how well the Negroes succeed in their drive and whether violence erupts again—will influence events in many another Northern city.

Rochester Negroes are being organized under the guidance of . . .

[*This uncommonly long lead opens an uncommonly*

long interpretive story in the National Observer. *It suggests a trend in this kind of journalism.*]

• •

Two players who didn't have a chance topped the state amateur golf meet that ended today.

One had played in every such tournament for nine years, but never before came out better than sixth.

The other, though he has golfed for 30 years, never before entered a tournament.

Their names: . . .

Leads for Radio and TV

Leads on radio and television news stories vary from those in print in two important particulars (both suggested earlier): they are often more leisurely, and they are commonly less detailed. The man getting his news by ear must be "eased into the story" more gently than when he reads it. He is not accustomed to the quick plunge that a printed lead necessitates, and he, or his ear, is not accustomed to details in quantity. He *is* accustomed to the looseness and generalities of casual conversation. His friends don't say to him, "Centerdale will have two new fire stations next year," nor do they talk to him in the pattern of the three short paragraphs opening the school-enrollment story. Rather, they say, "They're going to put a new fire station downtown next year—and another out by the river" or "there's really trouble ahead for the schools." Radio and television take their cues from these conversational patterns.

(You were told on page 168 how this type of news treatment on the air has affected newspaper leads, and how it has worked to everybody's advantage.)

In spite of the differences, however, many of this chapter's observations about printed leads ought to be gospel to the writer for the air. It is not so often true that a strong summarizing phrase opens the radio or TV news story:

Well, the President is back at the White House.

In the Middle East, however, hope for peace is higher.

But radio writing ought to be simpler and less involved than writing for print. It follows newspaper lead practice in use of names, of softened summaries, of questions, and of "cartridges." It rarely uses long leads; and it avoids opening a lead, or any sentence, with a quotation for the obvious reason that the listener can't tell who is being quoted.

Watch for the Booby Traps

One of the sure signs of the novice as writer is that he strains to find verbal devices whose single virtue is that they are "different." Seeking substitutes for such simple, meaningful words as "said," "outfielder," "meeting," or "investigation," he succeeds often only in distracting and confusing the reader with words that don't say what he means (this problem gets attention in the chapter on news style).

This is the place to add that the same impulse, sometimes abetted by laziness, often causes inexperienced or careless newswriters to mangle their leads. There seems no other explanation for the use of weak or misdirecting or wandering leads that occasionally find their way into print or newscast time. There are too many ways to write leads badly to count or name; but some of the common faults are readily defined.

THE PREPOSITIONAL PHRASE   A lead that almost always falters is one opened with a prepositional phrase. Samples show how:

> At a meeting of the Kenworth Keglers last night, a six-team bowling tournament was . . .
>
> For the first time in ten years, members of the Kenworth Keglers will . . .
>
> With a burst of enthusiasm, the Kenworth Keglers decided last night to . . .
>
> In an unprecedented decision, the Kenworth Keglers voted last night to . . .

The first of these is both the commonest and the weakest. It says nothing of real moment to the story's theme beyond the club's name; worse, it is a "label" lead that might be used to open a dozen stories in every issue of any newspaper. Yet it appears again and again in poorly edited papers, and at the head of countless stories by beginning newswriters.

The other examples, though not so stereotyped, nevertheless waste words and readers' time and do little to advance reader knowledge of the substance of the stories. Note that if an "unprecedented decision" is the appropriate lead fact for one of the stories, a noun-subject phrase linked closely to a verb would emphasize it with vigor, dispatch, and clarity.

THE PARTICIPIAL PHRASE   A useful exercise would be to rewrite the leads below, revising them to get rid of the opening participles:

> Meeting at the Downtown
> Alleys, the Kenworth Keg-
> lers . . .
>
> Faced with certain defeat,
> rebels in the Atlas Moun-
> tains . . .
>
> Cheering as it took the
> final vote, the Senate yester-
> day . . .
>
> Bringing its membership to
> 479, the League of Women
> Voters closed . . .

Application of the suggestions earlier in this chapter for simple, direct lead construction will show ways of strengthening each of these leads. Chief among their
weaknesses are wordiness and wandering. It takes them too long to get to their
points.

It can sometimes be properly argued that a participle makes a strong opener.
A participle is a verb form, and verbs provide action and color. In the four samples just given (three present participles, one past), one opening participle says
something instantly to the reader: "Cheering." The verb itself has specific meaning, and it has interest; it may well signalize a prime factor in the news event.
But the other three, by themselves, say nothing.

THE DEPENDENT CLAUSE   Use of a noun clause, usually introduced by
"that," seems stilted and formidable to most readers, for it is distinctly pedantic
in tone. Yet it is sometimes an effective device to throw emphasis on a major fact:

> That all schools should
> long ago have been inte-
> grated was the conclusion
> of a Students Forum meet-
> ing on campus last night.
>
> That modern America is
> drifting away from funda-
> mental spiritual values was
> the contention . . .

The usage has the virtue of avoiding a journalistic solecism that makes some
grammarians moan:

> Schools should long ago
> have been integrated, a Stu-
> dents Forum meeting on
> campus last night concluded.
>
> Modern America is drift-
> ing away from fundamental
> spiritual values, the Ladies
> Aid decided at . . .

The first two forms are grammatically defensible; the second are technically incorrect, for they transform dependent "that" clauses into principal clauses and ignore the quotation marks that would justify the usage. But it cannot be denied that they are widely used and readily understood. Their establishment as an accepted rhetorical practice seems assured.

The most that need be said about the "that" clause opening is that it should be employed sparingly and only when it is sparkling in clarity.

WEAK "FOLO" LEADS   Often the most businesslike lead for the short prelim (the brief story announcing an upcoming event) is the one that gives principal facts fast and then stops:

> Maj. Henry Oakes will speak on bomb defense before the Kiwanis Club at the Center Hotel this evening.
>
> Bomb defense in industrial areas will be Maj. Henry Oakes' topic before the Kiwanis Club . . .

But often such a lead, though it *could* be used on the "folo" story with tenses and time phrases changed, is the worst opening a lazy reporter could devise.

In almost all cases the "folo" lead is effective only if it throws its emphasis on a factor not available for the prelim. What the man said, or the fact that somebody threw a plate at him, is pretty sure to be a more meaningful and more attractive lead than mere repetition of yesterday's story.

CLUTTERED LEADS   Leads should be as neat—though not as severely barren —as the top of a vice president's desk. They should not be cluttered. They should present only essentials. They should say the things that *have* to be said to key the story and get it moving. Things that could just as well be left until later should be left until later.

Before-and-after examples of several types of cluttered leads and their rewrites will show how clutter can be swept away. First, the overlong identifier:

Before	After
Walter Hoe, shop foreman at Metallics Industry, Inc., and winner of last week's fish story contest, is the new president of the local Inventors Club.	*Walter Hoe is the new president of the Inventors Club.* *Hoe, shop foreman at . . .*
Vice Adm. Shean Flaherty, who has been in the Navy since before World War I, will be grand marshal of the July 4 parade this year.	*Vice Adm. Shean Flaherty will be grand marshal of the July 4 parade this year.*

The unnecessary credit line:

Before	*After*
Work on the new high school will not be complete in time for school opening, according to Principal Walter Emmors.	*Work on the new high school will not be complete in time for school opening.*
Sunday's 97-degree temperature made it the hottest June 10 since 1942, Martin Williams, weather bureau director, said this morning.	*Sunday's 97-degree temperature made it the hottest June 10 since 1942.*

A combination of these two faults:

Before	*After*
Because of the increased demand upon the local blood bank, the list of blood donors must be greatly expanded, Newell R. Zieler, director and professor of bacteriology and immunology, said yesterday.	[*Close the lead sentence with the word "expanded." Or rewrite it:*] *Increased demand on the local blood bank means that many new donors must be found.*

Excess baggage—secondary facts:

Before	*After*
The Permanent Representative of Cyprus complained today to U Thant, Secretary General of the United Nations, that Turkey's representative had been trying to "create an atmosphere of tension and alarm" by false allegations that Greek Cypriotes were preparing a mass armed attack on the Turkish minority on the island.	*Cyprus complained today about Turkish allegations that Greek Cypriotes were preparing a mass armed attack on the Turkish minority on the island.*
The New York Yankees beat the Chicago White Sox 4 to 1 last night in a game played under the lights in Chicago before 14,207 fans, half of them kids.	*The Yankees beat the White Sox 4 to 1 last night.*
Approximately 20,000 Bellevue telephone numbers will be changed tomorrow as the Sunset Telephone Co. completes its modernization program, according to P. L. Fittens, manager.	*Some 20,000 Bellevue telephone numbers will be changed tomorrow. The change will complete . . .*

To some copy desk men the lead opening with an article—*a, an,* or *the*— is anathema. They'll stand a lead on its head to avoid an *A* opening. The difficulty with this approach is that leads standing on their heads may be as ungraceful as humans in the same posture. For example:

A ton of dynamite exploded this morning at Old Fort Quarry.	*Explosion of a ton of dynamite occurred . . .* *Two thousand pounds of dynamite . . .* *Dynamite amounting to a ton . . .* *Old Fort Quarry was the scene of . . .*
The Stadium will be enlarged next year by the erection of 2,000 bleacher seats.	*Stadium will be enlarged . . .* *Enlargement of the Stadium will be . . .* *Two thousand bleacher seats . . .* *Erection of 2,000 bleacher seats . . .*

Simple, unostentatious use of the article is often less an obstacle to reader interest than the artificiality of manipulation. Some writers avoid using the article simply by omitting it (note the first revision of the Stadium lead). This is no solution at all, for its clumsiness is obvious to the reader accustomed to referring to the Stadium as *the* Stadium. Writers who like the usage might take note that writers for the air, seeking "natural" prose, wouldn't think of letting it into their copy.

SUGGESTED READINGS

No two writers on getting news stories moving offer precisely the same points of view or precisely the same advice; but most are significantly similar. You'll note both likenesses and contrasts if you compare the counsel in this book with the helpful passages on newspaper leads to be found, for example, in:

Bush, Chilton R., *Newswriting and Reporting Public Affairs*. Philadelphia: Chilton Company—Book Division, 1965.

Emery, Edwin, and Phillip H. Ault, *Reporting the News*. New York: Dodd, Mead & Company, Inc., 1959.

MacDougall, Curtis D., *Interpretative Reporting*. New York: Macmillan, 1964.

Books on radio and television news with attention to comparable practice in broadcasting:

CBS News. *Television News Reporting*. New York: McGraw-Hill, Inc., 1958.

Charnley, Mitchell V., *News by Radio*. New York: Macmillan, 1948.

Siller, Bob, Ted White, and Hal Terkel. *Television and Radio News*. New York: Macmillan, 1960.

White, Paul, *News on the Air*. New York: Harcourt, Brace & World, 1947.

PROJECTS

1. Select from a daily paper six news stories each emphasizing a different lead element in its opening (who, where, why, when, what, how). Rewrite each lead to throw the emphasis on a different element. Then write a criticism, showing your judgment as to whether your rewrites are to be preferred.

2. Cover a speech or meeting for which you have read a prelim in a paper. Write as many leads for the "folo" story as you can—all varying from the lead on the prelim.

3. Make a tabulation of leads on news stories in a local paper that illustrate lead characteristics described in this chapter as weak. Write a commentary about such usages.

CHAPTER 13

News of Speeches and Meetings

People are always talking; and many of the things they say make news.

What they say makes news when they say it before public audiences, in speeches or in meetings or on the air. It makes news when reporters have asked them to talk, in interviews. It makes news when they talk before legislative sessions or committee hearings, during news conferences, through the medium of formal "releases." Sometimes what they say privately becomes news when it reaches reporters at second hand.

More than half of all news stories are directly or indirectly derived from spoken words. Some stories do not reflect oral sources; a report of a football game, for example, or of the vote of a legislature, or of the arrival of a famous visitor at a resort. This kind of report, since it is strictly "quantitative," built of flat, unqualified facts, needs no supporting authority, no *he saids*. But even this kind of story may draw some of its material from the spoken word, though it does not credit the source:

American Mutual Life Insurance Company has approved an 18 per cent dividend increase for ordinary policies.

Policyowners will receive a total of $750,000 in addition to the $3.85 million previously estimated for the year. The increase becomes effective July 1.

• •

The 11th annual Lake Forest Kennel Club dog show will be held Saturday at the community center.

Some 700 dogs from 36 states and Canada will be shown. Obedience trials will begin at 8 A.M. Admission is 90 cents for those over 12; others free.

• •

ROME, Italy (AP)—If you're looting any 2,000-year-old Etruscan tombs this season, beware of the patient shepherd and the eager bird hunter.

Italy's police have added them to the hazards for the illegal excavators who annually supply hundreds of thousands of dollars worth of Etruscan art work to museums and private collectors around the world.

[*The story continues to describe at length the thieves' devices and the police maneuvers, all without attribution of any kind.*]

In a week's issues of a metropolitan paper: 40 percent of the news stories had no direct reflection of spoken-word sources (many were one-paragraph announcement stories); 60 percent specifically named oral sources.

Of the 60 percent: 12 percent were interview stories; 7 percent were speech reports; 38 percent were stories in which speeches, interviews or other necessarily credited statements were important (though not the only) elements; 3 percent were based entirely on formal testimony.

None of these stories *shows* that its writer interviewed anybody, for none of them credits any of its statements to a specific source. But in each, it is clear that some kind of source had to be consulted: an official of club, union, or insurance company, an informed secretary, or perhaps a publicity release.

This chapter concerns the reporting of speeches and meetings; the following chapter is concerned with interviews. Both kinds of reporting use the spoken word as the primary news source.

Stories About Speeches

America has unlimited tolerance for speeches. Civic clubs, women's clubs, schools, churches, commemorative ceremonies, all offer speeches, scores and scores a day. The news media cover many of them, for good reasons: (1) As group events, they concern organized interests (wide or limited) within the community, and they merit some notice, if not always extended report: (2) Usually a speech is arranged because it illuminates a topic of current interest, one in which readers or listeners or viewers, some if not all, may have a stake: (3) The speaker may have something new or vital to contribute: (4) The speaker may himself be newsworthy, so that a report of what he says deserves public notice even if the substance is zero.

On the third and fourth scores newsmen are often inclined to skepticism. Many speeches are banal, and some would be better unheard and unrecorded. But it is often as meaningful to let the public know that a speaker has said nothing, or that he has merely played a familiar tune, as to report genuine contribution to public knowledge or understanding or thinking. Reporters often label speech assignments the dullest part of their work; many would scoff at the statistic that only 7 percent of their stories report speeches. (Because speech stories often "run long," and sometimes include full texts, they frequently use more than 7 percent of a newspaper's news space.)

However onerous the chore may be, covering speeches is fundamental among the skills that a reporter must master. To examine the process, consider a typical case in the experience of Reporter Don Finnegan (whom you met in chapter 6).

Finnegan, we will say, is told on a Tuesday morning that Dr. Arthur Prympton, psychiatrist, is going to talk before next Friday's State Chambers of Commerce Association convention on "Freud and Modern Business." "Might be a pretty good yarn," says the city editor. "Write a piece that even *I* can understand." Finnegan casts back into his college psychology courses to recall what he learned about Freud. A dimmed memory, he finds. "The father of psychoanalysis"—yes. But exactly what does that mean? And what's the relation to modern business?

Finnegan recognizes that he doesn't know enough about the subject to approach it at par. He takes steps, in the three days available to him, to bolster himself.

He calls the local Chamber of Commerce secretary and chats for 5 minutes about the kind of talk Prympton has been asked to give.

Does a reporter go through all this preparation for every speech story?

The answer is clearly "no." It isn't always necessary; often there isn't time for it.

But frequently a speaker has been invited to appear solely because he is able to talk on a technical or specialized topic to an audience of laymen; and the reporter may no more qualify as "expert" than do the listeners. The quality of reporting in all the news media would improve if specially-equipped reporters were always available—labor experts to report labor, science writers to report science, military specialists to report military matters. The news media (particularly the large newspapers) are moving in this direction. But there never will be enough experts to go around. The kind of thing Finnegan has done is essential if reporting is to be understanding and understandable.

He goes to the public library and finds two books that he thinks will be helpful: one a popular book on Freud, the other a nontechnical work on psychology in business. He races through the Freud book in an evening, scans the other; he comes up, he thinks, with some understanding of the Freudian approach and some questions about its bearing on business practice.

He calls a psychologist at the local college, and by him is referred to a local psychiatrist. "I used to know Art Prympton in medical school," says this source. "He's going to give a sensible talk—you can be sure of that. But watch for what I'd call overemphasis on the influence of the subconscious. Art's always loved the subconscious."

Finnegan is now reasonably well equipped, he thinks, on the purpose of the talk and its subject. He needs to know more about Prympton himself. *Who's Who* provides biographical data, and the information that Prympton has written two books on subjects that sound like his speech topic. Married, two kids, belongs to three yachting and two golf clubs as well as a handful of professional societies. All of this, combined with what the local psychiatrist has told him, gives Finnegan a solid preparation for covering the talk.

He tries one more step: an interview with Prympton. He'd like a preview of what the man is to say, and he'd like a copy of the talk. He learns by telephone that he can get neither—Prympton talks from scribbled notes, and he won't have time to see a reporter before the meeting. But he'd be glad to talk with him afterward.

With this background, Finnegan presents himself at the convention session and settles himself for the talk.

Finnegan belongs to the take-plenty-of-notes school of reporting. Not all reporters do. Some prefer high-light notes, points of chief emphasis, aphorisms, witticisms, structural outline, and dependence on memory for fill-in. Finnegan and his coworkers argue about this after deadline.

"You get so involved in scribbling notes that you hear only half of what the speaker says," admonishes one reporter, "if you try to write it all down. You can't see the forest for the trees."

"Not so," insists Finnegan. "You learn to follow what the man is saying as you write; you use his major points as your subheads, and you take down enough so that you rarely have to say later, 'Now just what did he mean here?' You don't put down every word, just key phrases, emphatic or colorful statements, and especially specific facts, figures, names, dates, and the like. These you have to have—memory isn't good enough."

The two schools are likely to continue to argue. But much may be said for Finnegan's thoroughness; he's less likely to be caught short than the man with high-light notes. "I'd rather have too much stuff than too little," Finnegan says. His position is not built on sand.

Had an advance copy of the talk been available, Finnegan's note-taking would have been simplified. Following a script as Prympton spoke, he could have underlined points the speaker emphasized, scribbled notes in the margin or between lines when the speech departed from text, blacked out phrases or sentences that were dropped. He could have made note of bursts of applause or other incidents paralleling the talk.

The advance script of a speech does not always say what the audience hears over the lectern. The more ceremonial the occasion, the more likely it is that the speech as written will be the prototype of the speech as spoken. When the President makes a foreign-policy statement, it is vital that the words he utters are precisely those he and his advisers have worked out.

But in more cases than not, the speaker departs here and there from what he has prepared. Sometimes he throws the script out of the window and starts anew.

One of the timeworn fables newsmen tell deals with this problem. It relates that a young reporter, assigned to cover a Sunday-evening sermon, procured an advance script, wrote a story from it, went on a date, and turned in his neat copy first thing Monday morning. The city editor said somewhat too gently, "Nice story. But what about the fire?" "Fire?" gasped the reporter. "The church burned down just before service last night," replied the editor.

"Incidents paralleling the talk," reporters know, often become important parts of speech stories; sometimes they steal the floodlight. If the speaker grows so heated that he steps off the stage, if a portion of the audience, in anger, walks out in the middle of things, if an audience in stitches at the speaker's wit appears to miss his moments of sobriety, if the floor collapses, such "parallel incidents" may either become the heart of the story or take enough prominence to dilute emphasis on the speech itself.

Finnegan will tackle this problem a little later. The talk ended and the meeting adjourned, his first obligation is to get a brief story into the office for the late afternoon edition. He telephones a quick summary to a rewrite man.

But he's glad that he has arranged for an interview with Prympton—some of the talk seemed obscure. He meets the man in his hotel room, and a half hour's conversation not only clears up the obscurities but yields material for an interview story Finnegan can write for Sunday publication.

Finnegan was fortunate in finding that his post-speech questions could be answered by the speaker himself. This is not always the case, unhappily; for often the conscientious reporter must clarify points by himself, or even add to his background, *after* the event. This may be merely to increase his understanding of what he has heard. But it may also be to find out whether what he has heard is responsible. As Elmer Davis put it, a reporter must be on guard against false

Churches don't often burn down, but speakers often fail to observe their blueprints.

or misleading statement so that his story will not be one "with no indication that what the speaker said was lie from beginning to end" (see page 26). It is today a part of the reportorial burden to try to let the news consumer know whether what the speaker said may be trusted. And often the reporter can do this only by painstaking fact-finding *after* he has heard the speech.

Back at his desk, Finnegan is ready for the writing job.

He is primed to start as he sits down because, on the way to the office, he has reviewed his facts and decided on both lead emphasis and general structure. How has he charted his course?

He starts with the fundamental assumption underlying all reporting: the reporter is the personal representative of each member of a vast absent audience. His obligation is to put the story into a form that will enable most of his paper's readers (but especially those with particular interest in psychology's relation to business) to take from it the essential impression they would have gained had they been present. This means objectivity—a reporter reports, he doesn't comment; it means scrupulous accuracy and balanced summary, and equally careful selection and rejection, so that the reader will get an overview of all the parts of the event that hold meaning for him; and it means decision as to what parts of the event not in the speech itself are to be reported. Finnegan's thinking, on his way to his typewriter, might go something like this:

"A serious talk—the audience took it soberly and without squirming. And Prympton made a number of points of concern to businessmen. Better make the lead on the three kinds of profit he said business can get out of the right use of personnel psychology . . . What about the Freud angle? He didn't give that more than a nod—it really was just a come-on to furnish a good title. I'll ignore it. . . . Lead with those three points, then develop each one in some detail.

"What about incidental color? There wasn't much, except that the audience sat tight and paid attention. Ought to get something to show that he made them chuckle now and then—probably by giving a couple of examples.

"Should I mention that he's an impressive-looking guy? Wish the desk had sent a photog, to show how he towered over the lectern. Guess I'll mention it."

With thinking like this, Finnegan is ready, when he sits down, to start writing fast.

Before he starts, however, he reports to the city desk:

"I've got three quarters of a column for tomorrow on Prympton. Pretty good talk. And an interview for Sunday—stuff on how he thinks business psychology ought to be taught in high schools. Maybe you'll want a later follow-up—something on what the high schools think of the idea."

SPEECH STORY FORM   American newspapers have developed a functional pattern for the speech story, one that permits both extensive use of directly quoted material and summary of parts of the talk that do not demand extended presentation. The pattern belongs to the straight-news form: summary lead followed by development of significant detail, usually in order of decreasing importance. More specifically, it involves:

1) A lead of one or more paragraphs, usually in indirect (unquoted) discourse.
2) Passages in direct quotation whose purpose is to present in considerable detail major points or those that justify elaboration or verbatim reporting. These passages alternate with:
3) Passages in indirect discourse, usually summarizing parts of the talk;
4) Attention to circumstantial detail—time, place, pedigree of the speaker, sponsorship of the talk, and other such related matters—and to "parallel incidents" as defined earlier in this chapter.

To see how these generalizations work out in practice, study the case history of an important speech by a President of the United States.

The speech was made by President Lyndon B. Johnson at a time when the legal protection of the civil rights of Negroes was a matter of national concern. Congress had in less than a decade passed three "landmark" civil rights bills, and a fourth was in the making. President Johnson, making a Commencement address at a university whose enrollment was predominantly Negro, took the nation by surprise when he asked for further steps to help Negroes attain "true racial equality." Briefly, his speech was divided into these principal subsections:

An introductory passage stating his theme: That Negroes in America remained a deprived minority, the doors to true equality closed to them;

A review of recent actions of Congress and the Supreme Court that had made initial attacks on the problems of Negro rights and status;

A review of progress in Negro education, social and economic position;

The statement that these "impressive achievements" did not alter the fact that for most Negroes society had not provided hope or opportunity;

A review of the area in which Negro communities and Negroes individually were falling behind the national norms;

The statement that "we are not completely sure why this is," followed by a suggestion of presumptive causes—prominent among them the decay of Negro family life;

A declaration of the intent of the Johnson administration to make definition and solution of the problems "a chief goal," and announcement of a plan to call a White House conference within a few months to move toward the goal.

It had not been generally known that the President would make a policy speech of this scope or on this topic; but no public appearance of a President is ignored. The event was widely covered. The broadcasting networks, the news magazines, the wire services, and correspondents for many American and foreign newspapers were present. Newscasts that evening and the next morning emphasized the story, and most morning newspapers front-paged it.

How did reporters' treatment of it correspond to the speech-story outline on page 193?

The outline does not prescribe the order in which its four elements are to be presented (except that a lead always leads); it does not insist that all be present. And no two reporters see any complex of news facts in just the same way. Yet similarities are more striking than differences in news stories from five major American newspapers (Minneapolis *Tribune*, New York *Herald Tribune*, New York *Times*, St. Louis *Post-Dispatch*, Washington *Post*), the Associated Press newspaper wire and the United Press International radio wire.

In the newspaper leads, three put prime emphasis on the White House conference, and three on the President's demand for "true equality." But their flavor is the same; the phrase "true equality" appears in three and the phrase "fulfill the rights" in two. The sixth is a brief paraphrase of the same idea.

Here are the leads:

Minneapolis *Tribune*:
President Johnson, asserting that despite the great advances of recent years Negroes remain "another nation" inside the United States, called Friday for massive new efforts to translate legislative and judicial progress in civil rights into true racial equality.

New York *Herald Tribune*:
President Johnson announced here last night that he intends to call a White House conference on civil rights next fall to try to determine how "to help the American Negro fulfill the rights which he is finally about to secure."

New York *Times*:
President Johnson declared tonight that legal freedom and equality are "not enough" to guarantee Negroes their full share of American justice and American plenty.

St. Louis *Post-Dispatch*:
A White House conference will be convened this fall to study the plight of low-income Negroes who are losing ground in the battle for true equality, President Lyndon B. Johnson has announced.

Washington *Post*:
President Johnson announced last night that he will call a White House conference in the fall aimed at fulfilling the rights of the American Negro.

Associated Press:
President Johnson has called for a new civil rights effort to achieve true equality for the American Negro —"not just equality as a right and a theory."

The radio lead is similar:

President Johnson said tonight that race hatred and white indifference have made the American Negro "another nation."

Now compare several of the stories. Note that all depend heavily on verbatim material. Paraphrase of the words of a President is something in which reporters indulge sparingly (in most speech stories there would be more passages quoted indirectly).

First, Edward T. Folliard's story from the Washington *Post*:

President Johnson announced last night that he will call a White House conference in the fall aimed at fulfilling the rights of the American Negro.	*A brief lead makes the White House conference the story's principal theme. (The* Post *published the full text of the speech on another page.)*
	First exit
In a commencement speech at Howard University, the President said that no act of his Administration will give him greater satisfaction than signing the right to vote bill now moving through Congress. He said this bill will be the latest in a long series of victories but not the end. Quoting Winston Churchill, he said it would be "the end of the beginning."	*General elaboration of the theme. This paragraph contains the only mechanics development in the story ("commencement speech at Howard University").*
	Second exit
Mr. Johnson said that although American Negroes have made great strides in the United States, a majority of them are poor, unemployed, uprooted—"still another nation." He went on to cite figures showing that the rate of unemployment for Negroes is twice as high as that for whites; that during a period when the number of white families living in poverty has decreased 27 percent, the number of colored families living in poverty has dropped only 3 percent; that the infant mortality rate among non-whites is 90 percent greater than for whites, and that the isolation of Negroes from white communities is increasing rather than diminishing.	*Two paragraphs develop the President's thesis that much remains to be done to "fulfill the rights" of the Negro. The unusual length of the second paragraph is compensated by the easy sequence of dependent clauses, all in the same grammatical and logical form.*
	Third exit
The Chief Executive said he would dedicate his Administration to correcting this situation if possible and is calling a White House	*A long passage bringing the story back to the conference theme.*

conference in the fall as part of the effort. The conference will bring together scholars, experts, Negro leaders and various Government officials.

The President said the theme and title of the conference will be: "To Fulfill These Rights." He went on to list the objectives of the conference:

"To help the American Negro fulfill the rights which—after the long time of injustice—he is finally about to secure.

"To move beyond opportunity to achievement.

"To shatter forever not only the barriers of law and public practice, but the walls which bound the condition of man by the color of his skin.

"To dissolve, as best we can, the antique enmities of the heart which diminish the holder, divide the great democracy, and do wrong to the children of God.

"I pledge this will be a chief goal of my Administration, and of my program next year and in years to come.

"I hope it will be part of the program of all America."

Mr. Johnson said there is no "single easy answer" to the problems of Negroes, and that for many of that race and for others in groups that also have suffered intolerance, the wounds are always open.

Perhaps the most important wound, radiating into every part of life, he said, is the breakdown of the Negro family structure.

"For this, most of all," Mr. Johnson said, "White America must accept responsibility. It flows from centuries of oppression and persecution of the Negro man. It flows from the long years of degradation and discrimination which have attacked his dignity and as-

Note its clumsy opening sentence.

A long unbroken quotation, introduced by a "he went on" credit line.

Fourth exit

After a transitional paragraph, the reporter moves to development of a sub-theme, the breakdown of Negro family life.

saulted his ability to provide for his family."
    The President said this is
something that is not pleasant to look upon but is
something that must be
faced by those seriously intent on improving the life
of all Americans.

A longer story by James Deakin of the St. Louis *Post-Dispatch* gives more attention to "parallel incidents" than do any of the others:

A White House confer-
ence will be convened this
fall to study the plight of
low-income Negroes who
are losing ground in the battle for true equality, President Lyndon B. Johnson
has announced.

First exit

    In a speech last night at
a graduation exercise of
Howard University, Mr.
Johnson said that despite
the gains of middle-class
Negroes "the great majority
of Negro Americans" are
falling behind in a time of
prosperity.

Mechanics—time and place.

    Terming this an "Ameri-
can failure," the President
promised that one of the
chief goals of his Administration would be to help
Negroes achieve the opportunities that they are guar-
anteed legally.

*A careful transitional para-
graph that returns the reader
to the lead idea, taken up
again in the next paragraph.*

    He said he would call a
White House conference of
scholars, experts, Negro
leaders and government officials to discuss the theme,
"To Fulfill These Rights."
The title is a variation of a
phrase in the Declaration
of Independence, "to secure
these rights."

*Background information
added by the reporter.*

    Mr. Johnson used the
forum of the predomi-
nantly Negro university in
Washington to paint a grim
picture of the economic
life of low-income Negroes.

*The scene is again men-
tioned, this time with more
detail.*

    The "proud and impres-
sive achievements" of
American Negroes, he said,
"only tell the story of a
growing middle-class minority steadily narrowing the

*The quotations that close
this paragraph and open the
next are not consecutive in*

gap between them and their white counterparts."

"For the great majority of Negro Americans—the poor, the unemployed, the uprooted and dispossessed —there is a grimmer story," he said. "They still are another nation. Despite the court orders and the laws, the victories and speeches, for them the walls are rising and the gulf is widening."

the speech as written. Consequently the reporter has separated them by his use of quotation marks.

A possible exit

The President told the 928 graduates and about 12,000 guests that these "are some of the facts of this American failure:

"Thirty-five years ago, the rate of unemployment for Negroes and whites was about the same. Today, the Negro rate is twice as high.

"In 1948, the 8 percent unemployment rate for Negro teen-age boys was actually less than that of whites. By last year it had grown to 23 percent, as against 13 percent for whites.

"Between 1949 and 1959, the income of Negro men relative to white men declined in every section of the country. From 1952 to 1963, the median income of Negro families compared to white actually dropped from 57 percent to 53 percent.

"In the years 1955 to 1957, 22 percent of experienced Negro workers were out of work at some time during the year. In the 1961-1963 period, that proportion had soared to 29 percent.

"Since 1947, the number of white families living in poverty had decreased 27 percent while the number of poor nonwhite families went down only 3 percent.

"The infant mortality of nonwhites in 1940 was 70 percent greater than that of whites. Twenty-two years later it was 90 percent greater."

More facts about the scene of the speech.

A long passage of directly-quoted "evidence" presented by the speaker.

Mr. Johnson said that "Negro Americans as well as white Americans have shared in our rising national abundance. But the harsh fact of the matter is that in the battle for true equality, too many (Negroes) are losing ground."

A possible exit

He said that the White House conference would explore ways to help low-income Negroes "move beyond opportunity to achievement."

"The next and the more profound stage of the battle for civil rights," he said, will be to translate hard-won legal rights into actual opportunities for better jobs and living conditions. The goal, he said, must be "not just equality as a right and a theory but equality as a fact and a result."

Careful use of credit lines as the quotations move back and forth between direct and indirect.

Exit

[*The report of the speech ends at this point. The story adds five paragraphs about honorary degrees awarded to Mr. Johnson and others, the press of the crowd around him at the end of the ceremony, and another commencement address he is to make the next day.*]

The Associated Press story (as it appeared in the Buffalo Evening *News*) is the shortest of the six. The original story as it moved on the AP wire was longer; *News* copyreading trimmed it:

President Johnson has called for a new civil rights effort to achieve true equality for the American Negro—"not just equality as a right and a theory."

Mr. Johnson, delivering the commencement address at predominantly Negro Howard University here, said the great majority of Negro Americans "still are another nation."

The wire service story, compressed into much smaller space than the others, does not divide itself into sections as easily. A break occurs between the fourth and fifth paragraphs; at this point the story moves into the conference, which has not been mentioned earlier.

"Despite the court orders and the laws, the victories and speeches, for them the walls are rising and the gulf is widening," the President said.

Citing statistics on employment and income to show that Negroes, in some ways, are faring worse today than five or ten years ago, Mr. Johnson said this represents an "American failure."

The President took the occasion to announce plans for a special White House conference next fall "to help the American Negro fulfill the rights which—after the long time of injustice—he is finally about to secure."

Mr. Johnson said the conference, bringing together scholars, experts, Negro leaders and officials at every level of government, will have a theme: "To fulfill these rights."

There will be additional objectives, he said. One will be to move from opportunity to achievement.

Another will be to "shatter forever not only the barriers of law and public practice, but the laws which bound the condition of man by the color of his skin."

And a final one will be, the President said, to dissolve "antique enmities of the heart which diminish the holder, divide the great democracy and do wrong to the children of God."

Note that a 23-word phrase (beginning "citing statistics") does the work of six paragraphs in the Deakin story.

The UPI radio wire story—part of a "world news roundup"—condenses even further. Note that each of its four sentences opens with a credit line.

President Johnson said tonight that race hatred and white indifference have made the American Negro "another nation."

Mr. Johnson said the "chief goal" of his administration will be to correct this situation.

The President—in a commencement speech at predominantly Negro Howard University—said he will call a White House conference this fall. He said the object of the conference will be to help Negroes achieve the rights that have been denied them through, quote, "endless years of hatred and hopelessness."

Some comments on these stories and their techniques are on following pages:

DIRECT-QUOTATION LEADS   Experienced reporters seldom lead speech stories with direct quotations. The speaker does not often provide a neat sentence summarizing his talk as tightly and effectively as would a reporter's careful paraphrase. When he is obliging enough to do so, or when an aphorism or a striking statement presented verbatim rings a note representative of the talk, the direct quotation may be extremely effective.

Not to be confused with the writer who uses quotation marks with a too-lavish hand in speech stories (where, after all, they are legitimate) is the one who showers them in his copy (a) to apologize for his writing or (b) to let you know he doesn't really mean what he says. This is the man who, because of inexperience, incompetence, or insensitivity, thinks he must quote every word he uses figuratively. All too often, to their detriment, sports pages are hosts to such writers. Examples:

The pitcher seemed "predestined" to lose.
Not everybody who doesn't comb his hair is a "beatnik."
She had a "gypsy" air about her.

One guide to punctuation says that quotation marks may be used for "words used in an unusual sense; or for coined words for which the author offers slight apology." True. But if your usage is so unusual that you have to say, "I know this is unusual," or "I know better," or "Don't take me seriously," you'd do better to rewrite.

•   •

Here is a case of reportorial paraphrase for analysis:
In a Senate committee hearing into the activities of

QUOTING WORDS AND PHRASES   Some stories overuse quotation marks around individual words and phrases. The device is useful to assure the reader that a colorful or qualitative phrase is the speaker's, not the reporter's (note "no single easy answer," fifth-from-last paragraph of the Folliard story). But over-abundant quotation of separate words or short phrases often serves no useful purpose.

VERBATIM?   The most common meaning of quotation marks is that the words within them are taken from the source verbatim, precisely as they were spoken or written. In the Johnson speech stories one assumes that they mean exactly that.

Whether this rule must be followed religiously is one of the topics of newsroom argument.

"You have no right to use quotes unless they mean precisely what any literate reader takes them to mean —that they enclose the exact words the speaker used," says one side of the dispute. "You are deceiving, and thereby forfeiting the right to reader confidence, if you put into quotes anything but verbatim quotations."

"But the important thing is to give the reader the right impression, and to do it economically," says the other side. "As long as your paraphrase gives the reader the right meaning, you have license to depart at least mildly—from the strict wording of the statement. If you don't use this freedom—always with great care—your stories are likely to run too long. Fact is, you can sometimes help the speaker to say what he means better than he said it. That's a favor to both him and the reader."

Many reporters believe in the second interpretation, and practice under it. They cannot escape an awareness, however, that it is hazardous. Some news-

a witness, the committee chairman used these words in the course of a formal statement:

". . . This witness in my opinion has shown utter contempt for this committee, for the Congress of the United States, and for his government.

"Whether that contempt is actionable or not, I am not at the moment prepared to say, but this committee will give consideration to the question of whether it is actionable.

"If it is found to be, I have no doubt what the judgment and action of the committee will be . . ."

A long news story about the session paraphrased these three sentences thus:

"This witness has in my opinion been contemptuous of this committee, the Senate, and his government," the chairman declared. "Whether this contempt is actionable, I can't say, but, if it is, I have an idea that this committee will do something about it."

Does the newsman's paragraph say what the senator said?

• •

Alfred Friendly, managing editor of the Washington Post, is the author of a most helpful set of suggestions to reporters about handling the delicate problems of attribution of news. He wrote the suggestions for the news staff of his paper; under the title "Memo to All Hands" it is published in the July 1958 issue of Nieman Reports. Unfortunately it is too long for inclusion here; but it is worth any news student's time (including the time to find it in a library).

Careful criticism of faults in news handling and news

men fear it enough to advocate the British system which calls for stenographic accuracy and completeness in speech reporting, even though the grammatical form is that of indirect quotation. A one-time editor of *Editor & Publisher*, Arthur Robb, said that a story written thus "contains a lot of the verbiage, by-passes, and repetitious figures of speech with which most of us adorn our spoken words, but no man on earth can impugn its accuracy. The question is, will anybody except the hero of the speech read it in its printed form?"

GUIDES TO CREDIT-LINE USAGE

1) Every sentence of indirect quotation ordinarily requires a credit line. Without either credit or quotation marks, it is not clear to the reader whether the speaker or the reporter is talking. That this rule should be followed closely means that a news writer must not let his indirect passages run too long. When he does, he finds that "he said," "he added," "he went on," and other such attributions become montonous or offensive.

There are exceptions to the one-credit-to-a-sentence rule. One appears in the fifth paragraph of the Folliard story: the first sentence is credited to "the Chief Executive," but the second carries no attribution. It flows so logically and unmistakably out of the preceding sentence that misunderstanding is unlikely. In comparable cases in which an uncredited sentence is clearly covered by a neighboring attribution the line may sometimes be omitted. But never if there is even distant possibility of misunderstanding.

2) One credit line suffices for any one continuous direct quotation (within quotation marks), no matter what its length . . . one phrase or 20 paragraphs. In the Deakin story, one credit line ("The President told the 928 graduates . . .") serves for six successive paragraphs of direct quotation.

Again, there are exceptions. In a long continuous quotation of several paragraphs the writer may find the meaning clearer if he inserts additional credit lines: "the speaker continued," "he explained."

3) In direct quotations, the credit line should always be attached to the first sentence of the quoted matter, usually at its close or in its body. It confuses

writing will teach as much as study of examples of excellence. The stories on the Johnson speech are all competent, but they are picked as being typical rather than outstanding. All could be sharpened in one way or another. Critical examination of them is urged; editing them would be a useful exercise.

a reader to ask him to read two or more sentences before telling him who is speaking. (All of the Johnson speech stories follow this pattern.)

Opening quoted passages with the credit line is often clumsy. It occurs frequently in the Johnson stories, probably because of the attention value of the speaker's name. The credit line is part of the mechanics of the story, and should be kept unobtrusive. Inserting it at the middle or end of its sentence is one way to play it down.

The inversion "Said Johnson" to open a sentence—spawned but not legitimatized by *Time*—is a rhetorical trick avoided by careful writers. It is unnatural and usually obtrusive.

4) Few words of attribution are as effective and as unostentatious as "said." There are still high school composition teachers who urge their pupils to seek elegance by substituting "stated," "declared," "averred," and the like; but competent writers think them pretentious and distracting. On occasion an "added," a "went on," or an "explained" may fit a passage's rhythm as well as its meaning. But such substitutes as "revealed" or "announced" may be used only when the speaker actually did reveal or announce. To write "revealed" is a mild form of sensationalism (perhaps subconscious) if "said" is the right word; "announced" unless the statement may properly be called an announcement is pompous.

Note both the strengths and the weaknesses in the story that follows. It possesses a brief, clear lead; several convenient "exits" for the reader who has had enough; excellent attribution; an adequate statement of the circumstances of the talk; and orderly arrangement of subsections. But note a potential confusion in its sixth paragraph (is the $15,300,000 to be needed for salaries? or for all costs?), and the fact that there is no enlargement on the speaker's second demand —the element with which the story opens. (Possibly a careless copyreader, in shortening the story, eliminated supporting material on this point.)

Personnel improvement and adequate financing are now the major problems confronting the local schools, Dr. W. L. Printess, new superintendent, said Wednesday night.

Addressing a dinner given in his honor by the Chamber of Commerce, the Citizens' Committee on Public Education, and the Council of Civic Clubs, the superintendent outlined school problems as he has found them since his arrival here and gave his forecast of the future.

"There are two chief problems from the administrative point of view," Dr. Printess said.

"One is providing on a high level opportunities for self-improvement. We want to make it possible for each person in the school system to gain still clearer insights into the education of our children and to enrich himself with understandings and techniques for reaching the highest educational levels.

"Problem No. 2 is finding sufficient money to main-

tain our present excellent teaching staff and to employ 900 or 1,000 new teachers needed in the next five years."

The superintendent said the city has $36,000,000 invested in 93 school plants. It employs 3,500 persons in the school system, and pays them $12,000,000 a year. Its needs for the next year have been set at $15,300,000. Of this amount only $11,825,500 is in sight from present revenues, Dr. Printess said.

Three major possibilities for assistance on school financing were enumerated by the superintendent: increased aid from the state legislature, a new school charter amendment, and deficit financing.

The legislature, he pointed out, could give assistance in three different ways: by creating an independent school district; by granting more basic aid for all schools, including those in this city; and by granting local schools a greater proportion of available educational monies.

The superintendent said he is aware of the great differences of opinion in the city on all three possibilities.

"It may be that I am just naive, or that I am enjoying the honeymoon stage so intensely that I don't see the realities," Dr. Printess said, "but I have the abiding conviction that when the public is sufficiently and accurately informed in regard to the real needs of our school system, it will vote the necessary funds. Therefore I feel that the most crucial requirement for the success of the school program is the expansion of our hardworking Citizen's Committee on Public Education."

EVERY RULE HAS EXCEPTIONS   Now and again a reporter finds himself with a speech story that denies the conventions, one that can be told most effectively only by invention of its own distinctive pattern. Those that follow show how unorthodox treatment meets particular situations.

The first, written shortly before Gertrude Stein's death, took its cue from the fact that Miss Stein was best known for her "rose is a rose is a rose" poem and her sometimes obscure prose. The New York *Times* had this kind of fun with an appearance of Miss Stein at Princeton University:

PRINCETON, N. J.—Gertrude Stein, author and poet, delivered a lecture here tonight to an audience of 500 professors and students of Princeton at McCosh Hall. At the close of her address she asked: "Are there any questions?" There were none.

A hit and miss consensus taken unofficially after the lecture disclosed that few if any even came close to assimilating Miss Stein's literary theories. The audience was amused but otherwise unaffected by the obscurities which Miss Stein considers axiomatic.

She spoke, as far as could be ascertained, on the subject "The Making of the Making of Americans." It seemed to be, according to vague reports, a trilogy of excerpts from three of her books in an attempt to show the transition from the relatively harsh language of the first books to the softer combination of words in the last.

Several of the students took notes on the lecture hoping to be able to explain it later to their friends who were refused admittance because of Miss Stein's mandatory limit of 500 persons at her lectures. The notes were destroyed promptly at their first reading after the lecture.

When the doors of the hall were closed after the audience assembled, a detachment of police was necessary to keep in order those who had been barred. Several hundred persons crowded about the entrance.

Miss Stein, garbed in a tan jacket, fawn-colored tweed skirt, and square-toed tan shoes, walked out on the platform and began her lecture without introduction or any of the preliminary functions ordinarily in evidence.

She thanked the audience "for controlling yourselves to 500" and said she was sorry to set that limit but felt that she could not interest more people than that at one time.

After the lecture, which was under the auspices of the Spencer Trask Fund, Miss Stein left the platform and her listeners left the hall apparently with the realization that their education, their education had been sadly neglected, neglected.

A reporter for the Niagara Falls *Gazette* realized that he must bring movement, color, and restrained comedy into his story about a luncheon speech:

Rotarian expectations of a sedate talk on chemistry took to the hills yesterday as a popgun-wielding Princeton professor darted about Hotel Niagara's ballroom amid bubbling cauldrons, blinding multicolored bursts of flame, and intermittent explosions that kept club members in a state of tense amusement.

Dr. Hubert N. Alyea, a rapid-fire lecturer with more than a flair for the dramatic, twice dashed out among the luncheon tables to spray Rotarians with a fire extinguisher as smoke ascended from his vials.

In a highly illustrated summary of the principle of atomic explosion, he told the Rotarians that the atomic bombs dropped in World War II were of two kinds. The explosion at Hiroshima was caused by the bombardment of an atom of Uranium 255 by a neutron, while that at Nagasaki resulted from the bombardment of plutonium.

Splitting the U-255 atom, said the professor as he fired a popgun at a rubber ball that had been cut in two, releases three additional neutrons plus energy. In the bomb, the rate at which the energy is released is phenomenally rapid and causes an almost immediate explosion, whereas the rate of energy-release in the atomic pile can be retarded by use of graphite "anchors" which remove the danger of the pile's mushrooming heavenwards.

The atomic pile, the professor said, has three main peacetime uses. It can generate power, produce direct electricity, and change elements into more valuable elements such as radium and radio-active phosphorus—the twentieth-century realization of the medieval alchemist's dream of transmuting lead into gold.

"Bombs release 200,000,-000 electron volts," he said, precipitating a sudden searing explosion in a paper cup followed by a white-hot flow of molten metal. "This," he told the club members, many of whom were still blinking their eyes, "only released 10 electron volts. . . ."

Dr. Alyea cited the discovery of the rate at which radioactivity in uranium disappears—by halves every four billion years—as an extraordinary step forward in aiding scientists to discover the age of geological deposits and consequently the age of the earth. This, he said, has now been estimated as 4½ billion years—the time since the uranium rocks began radiating.

Radioactive carbon, too, he said, deteriorates at a fixed rate, thus making it possible to date archeological finds such as the flaxen wrappings of Egyptian mummies.

"Why, it's as exciting as dating a Harvard man," he exclaimed.

"Let's have another explosion?" he asked, looking up at the high ceiling of the hotel ballroom. "Oh, my, this is a challenge!" With that the professor injected some ordinary household flour into a closed milkcan. An ember was placed in it, and the lid went smashing against the ornate ceiling.

The professor departed from his teach-by-demonstration method to observe that with the weapons now at our disposal 40 million people could be wiped out overnight. He suggested that for each dollar spent on atomic weapons another dollar be given to the social scientists and humanists to work out a better order of life—one in which war will not be possible.

The following story (from a university daily) also puts the emphasis on the color of the event. The coed reporter took liberties with objectivity; she made the story a personal reaction. Though the critical reader may scorn her doggerel, it gives the treatment of the event appropriate distinction:

Oh, I went to Convocation with no banjo on my knee—
It was just a staff assignment—and a dull one, I could see.
No, Frank Warner—don't you sing to me,
For the day is hot and sultry; you don't mean a thing to me.

There's not much fun connected with hard labor in the summertime, particularly a Minnesota summertime. But before Convocation was out yesterday balladeer Frank Warner had his audience pretending they were cotton pickers, lumberjacks, gandy dancers and canal boatmen.

Looking more like a well-tailored utilities man than someone who had combed the Southern hills for American folk songs, Warner cocked his foot on a chair, rested a homemade guitar on his knee and spun yarns and sang songs.

Warner spurns hillbilly music. He brushes it off as "cultivated corn," and sticks to his genuine love of old American folk tunes. In these songs, which still survive in the South and in parts of New England, Warner finds American socio-economic history reflected. "These songs built our railroads, planted our crops, and dug our canals," he asserts.

He sang several work songs, beckoning the audience to come in on the chorus. It did so with vim on the tragic lament of the Erie canal boatman who sang, "The Erie is rising, and the gin is gettin' low."

But for a lumberman's song, Warner had to take one from New England, not from the Paul Bunyan country.

Not all the folk songs of the Upper Midwest have

been collected; Warner sternly reported, "Of the 20,000 folk songs in the Library of Congress, only one is from Minnesota."

Oh, I went to Convocation with no banjo on my knee—
But I stayed and liked it plenty—sounded awful good to me!

Oh, Frank Warner, you can sing for me;
Even on a day that's sultry, you make swing that swings for me!

The reporter who wrote the next story decided that a direct quotation summarized the flavor and intent of the speech. He found an unusual way to put the credit line ahead of the quotation:

A volatile Episcopal priest, recalling what happened to him in Jackson, Miss., vowed Wednesday: "I'll rot in prison before I give in to that kind of fascistic treatment."

The speaker was the Rev. James Jones, one of a group of Episcopal clergymen who were jailed last September for "breach of the peace." They were on a "prayer pilgrimage" in support of peaceful integration in the South.

The treatment that irked the 36-year-old Chicago priest was an order from a Jackson policeman to "move on" because he was sitting in the white waiting room of the Jackson bus station with a Negro clergyman.

But Father Jones' subsequent arrest—and the 30 days he spent in jail—provided valuable insight which helped him in his work.

His work is the operation of a successful Chicago "halfway house" for ex-convicts.

Father Jones was in the city Wednesday to explain the operation of the home—St. Leonard's House—in a talk before the annual meeting of the State Corrections Association.

[The story continues to recount the talk in anecdotal fashion that jibes with the informal manner of the opening.]

ONE WAY TO MISUSE AN ADVANCE SCRIPT   Formal speeches are often composed in formal language, language that at times becomes stuffy. When a reporter is working from an advance copy of such a speech, he may end up with a piece of copy as stilted as the original. The writer of the story below fell into this trap; his managing editor offered pungent comments:

The Story as Published
Wilmer Dodge, state budget administrator, told the state education commission today that the state has "ample financial resources for an orderly and effective attack on its many serious problems."

Because of this, he said, "Our educators have a clear and challenging mandate to expand and improve the system at all levels."

The committee held its first fall meeting today at the state capitol. High on

The M. E.'s Comments

Here is the type of news copy this paper can do without.

Note the pattern of linking high-sounding phrases into a chain.

Note how removed those quoted phrases, and some of the others, are from common language.

You may conclude, as I did, that the only hard news is in

its agenda was a report from a subcommittee assigned to evaluate the objectives and structure of the full group.

Dodge praised the governor for what he called "courageous" insistence on refusing to be deterred by financial problems in improving the standards and services of the state's schools.

He said "it would have been easy for the governor to turn away from the full reality of the educational problem because the scope of the need obviously meant that appropriations would have to be greatly increased."

Dodge pointed out that the program approved by the legislature provided 59 million dollars more for the current biennium than was appropriated for the preceding two years, an increase of 32 percent.

the last graf. (And even that news is not fresh news.)

What can we do with such stories?

A copy editor can point out to the copy chief that a story is all wind.

A copy chief can ask news desk whether the story should be spiked.

The news editor may consult with the city desk regarding the importance of the story. (They may decide to run the story despite its faults.)

The city desk may discuss the story with the reporter who prepared it.

If the story came from the wire services, the city editor may address his remarks to the wire services.

SIDELIGHTS SHOULDN'T BE BLINDING   The unwary reporter may sometimes be misled by the striking but minor sidelight. For example: A candidate for the mayoralty of a small Western city was making a campaign talk before a luncheon club. He talked soberly and informedly for 45 minutes on campaign issues; then he asked for questions. "What you going to do about those chiselers on relief?" demanded one of his listeners. The speaker warned his audience that he had not studied the relief problem and was not factually informed on it; he went on to say that "reports that thousands of families in the area are getting Aid to Dependent Children assistance fraudulently" should be examined carefully, and that he would do so were he elected.

A reporter made the lead on his story say: "Thousands of chiseling families in this area getting ADC relief" would be a target of the candidate should he be elected. Here are some of the things he did with that lead:

1) He gave the reader a faulty impression of the talk, the impression that it had been largely devoted to the theme of the lead. (Careful story construction, plus more careful rhetoric, could have avoided this impression.)

2) He misrepresented the speaker, for he made him say something he had not said and let it look as though he claimed knowledge he had said he did not have.

3) He presented the event in false perspective to the reader.

4) He made himself look foolish; for there were only two hundred families in his area receiving ADC funds at the time, a fact he should have discovered before letting his story reach print (especially since the speaker had warned that he was not sure of the facts).

Senator Joseph H. Ball, a competent political reporter before he was appointed to the Senate, commented on a mistake of this kind in a story about a talk he gave to a group of veterans:

> I spoke for a half hour on my political philosophy, and that was followed by an hour's question period, during which almost every current issue in domestic and foreign policy was covered. Yet the whole story was built around my answer to a question as to why I opposed retroactive terminal leave for enlisted men. That, in itself, is a serious distortion of the meeting . . .

It is often mandatory that a reporter select a relatively minor element in a speech for emphasis. When a man speaking on "The Future of American Industry" tells his audience that "the largest atomic reactor in the world will be producing this community's power within five years," the reporter can hardly be blamed for seizing on the statement as his lead. But he is not a competent reporter if he does not make it fully clear that the remark was a sidelight, offered casually against a much broader talk. (And he probably won't remain a reporter long if he doesn't persuade the speaker, once the talk is ended, to develop the important news tip he delivered in passing.)

Meeting Stories

Recall the statistic that 38 percent of the stories in a week's issues of a paper made the spoken word an "important (though not the only)" element.

A large proportion of these stories reported what the newsman calls generically "meetings": group meetings, formal or informal; committee meetings, club meetings, school meetings, PTA meetings, and the interminable like. It is true that most such meetings in a metropolitan area are allowed to go uncovered by the news media; there are too many of them, many of interest to only a few of the audience. In the small community, where any meeting touches a larger proportion of the residents, the local paper and the radio station give such events faithful attention.

Meetings usually provide one, or both, of two kinds of news material: the business or group action they develop, and the formal or informal talks that are parts of many. The reporter's obvious problem, when a meeting includes both kinds, is that of emphasis. Is the business transacted at the meeting, the election of officers, the decision to stage a fund drive next fall, the lead of the story? Or should he play up the outraged criticism directed at local "radicals" by the Congressman from the next state?

The decision may be to leave out one element or the other, in which case the construction of the story is simple. If it is to include both, the two-element lead suggested on page 180 may be useful:

> Local "radicals" will block
> industrial progress in Hop-
> kins if their political pro-
> gram succeeds, Congressman

Wilfrid Korlaski told the Agrarian Club last night.

His talk followed the club's election of officers and its decision to stage a fund drive next fall.

"You can't have booming business along with the kind of government these fellows want," Korlaski said. . . .

Or:

Decision to stage a drive for funds next fall followed the annual election of officers at last night's Agrarian Club meeting.

The two actions came after Congressman Wilfrid Korlaski had told the club members that local "radicals" will block industrial progress in the city if their political program succeeds.

Funds for next year's activities program must be raised . . .

Either such approach brings essential elements into a two-paragraph lead, and makes logical their orderly development as the story continues.

The meeting story that follows is one in which the reporter appeared to find no formal business to report. His concentration is on the response to the speech that was its principal planned element (but that the reporter leaves virtually untouched). Analysis of the story shows a careful and easy-to-follow structural pattern.

A meeting of the Mayor's Human Relations Commission ended in a shouting match Thursday after a Negro woman member said most whites don't know what integration means.

"It does not mean one group 'coming up' to the other group," said Mrs. Hannah Empter, 2417 Index avenue.

"It means two groups coming together into something new."

Until human relations committees learn this, "we are going to keep on talking at each other instead of to each other," said Mrs. Empter, a special service worker at Neighborhood House.

[*Note how the reporter parallels the next four paragraphs against the five that follow.*]

Mrs. Empter was set off by three things:

The suggestion by the speaker, Alexander F. Miller, an official of the Anti-Defamation League of B'nai Brith, that Negroes were left without a culture by slavery.

The suggestion of Stephen Fligelman, president of the Council for Civil and Human Rights, that minority groups need special treatment in employment but that it is offensive to the white community to say so.

The suggestion of Sam Scheiner, executive director of the Jewish Community Relations Council, that newspapers should run stories of successful Negroes to improve the Negro image.

To Miller, Mrs. Davis said: Negroes have put together a culture combining their African heritage and "our European ancestors," the slave-masters.

"It's not a white man's culture," she said. "Not even the integrationists have taken the time to understand this."

To Fligelman she said: "We don't need special treatment like you give your children. I don't want your help. Just get out of my way."

She said Scheiner exhibited a patronizing attitude about white culture in claiming he wanted a "better life" for minority groups.

"YOU want it. What about what THEY want?" she asked.

The discussion flared after the lunch meeting at the Protestant Center as Scheiner and Fligelman attempted to explain their positions to Mrs. Empter.

To a comment about law and order, Mrs. Empter cried, "Whose law and order? Your law and order." Discrimination hides in Northern law and order, Mrs. Empter said.

"I'm out of Alabama, and if I had the choice, I'd go back. I can see it there. I can fight it."

"Did you lose 6 million Jews in concentration camps?" Scheiner demanded.

"Comparatively I lost that many hanging down there," Mrs. Empter snapped.

Later Mrs. Empter said she had seen six Negroes hanged, including her 14-year-old cousin when she was 12. He looked at a white woman in her bathing suit, in Prichard, Ala., she said. "And they hung him then. Not later—then."

[The reporter now supplements the meeting story with an interview in which Mrs. Empter explains her position more fully—and more calmly.]

PROJECTS

1. Make a study of all the credit lines in a number of speech stories printed in your local paper. Check them against the guides to credit-line usage described in this chapter. Write a commentary on the skill—or lack of it—with which they have been handled.
2. Analyze the similarities and differences in two treatments of the same speech, one on the air and the other in print. Compare the approaches, the leads, the content, the length, the credit-line usage, and anything else you think germane.
3. Attend a meeting whose program includes a formal talk as well as other business. Write two newspaper stories, one of 50 to 75 words and a second of 500 words or more. Does the difference in length affect the structural lines or the emphases of the stories?
4. Write a radio news story about the same meeting. How does it contrast with the stories written for print?

CHAPTER 14

Interviews

Newsmen make an arbitrary distinction between stories that are merely *based on interviews*, wholly or in part, and *interview stories*. The nature of those only *based on interviews*—stories for which the facts are gathered by the interview process but in which the reporter does not need to credit the interviewees—is described at the beginning of chapter 13.

(see page 9).

Today's journalism the world over takes for granted the interview as a prime tool of news presentation. Yet it had to be "invented," and not so long ago. It came into use in the middle third of last century. James Gordon Bennett is commonly given credit for the first interviews, the outgrowth of his questions to Rosina Townsend, madam of a "fancy house" in New York City in which, in 1836, a sensational murder had occurred (see page 9). Bennett wrote many of these interviews in question-and-answer form like that of court testimony. Nearly 25 years later Horace Greeley used the same "new" form to report an interview with Brigham Young.

The interview at first met more scorn than favor. The Pall Mall Gazette of London said that "this American interview is degrading

The *interview story* itself is, in contrast, one that grows directly from a series of statements by an individual news source (or a number of them) and that *takes its significance from the fact that it comes from this kind of source.*

Though interview stories are of many kinds, three types that dominate in modern journalism deserve special attention:

1) The *news interview,* a form that gives the consumer competent or "expert" comment and illumination on a subject current in the news.

2) The *personality interview,* whose purpose is to let the interviewee reveal his character, his personality, through his own words.

3) The *symposium interview,* in which the views or attitudes of a number of "respondents," sometimes a large number, are reported.

The News Interview

Suppose in your community word gets to the news media that a new paper mill, employing several thousand workers, is to be established. The prime story

to the interviewer, disgusting to the interviewee, and tiresome to the public." James Russell Lowell derided the newspaper interviewer; and Godkin's liberal and intellectual Nation *said, in 1869, that "the interview is generally the joint product of some humbug of a hack politician and another humbug of a newspaper reporter."*

All of that was in the infancy of the interview. Edward Price Bell, the respected Chicago Daily News *foreign correspondent, reported these nineteenth-century criticisms in a talk to the American Society of Newspaper Editors in 1927. But he went on to say that the interview had become a tool of major journalistic importance, "bridging the gulf between genius and the common understanding."*

is the straight news announcing the fact, the story telling who will build it, how much it will cost, where the new plant will be, how many it will employ, when it will open. All of these are "simple facts," and most of them may be presented without individual accreditation (though any such story should show sources of information). The facts are "simple" in the sense that they are flat statements of unadorned circumstance, without subjective qualification: If the new plant is to be built on the old McGregor farm along Willow River just east of the county fair grounds, the reporter may say so without comment or attribution.

But no alert newsman will be satisfied to stop with this "simple" treatment, especially if the community is small enough so that most of the lives in it will be affected by the new industry. The newsman asks himself a battery of questions:

How much new take-home pay will the mill bring into the community?

What will be the housing problems if three hundred new families come to town? Will there be a major home-building program?

Why did the firm select this community?

What does the Chamber of Commerce think the mill will mean to the local economy? Might this be the start of an industrial boom?

Will Willow River provide enough water for a paper mill? Are transportation facilities adequate both to bring in wood and pulp and to ship paper out?

These and many more news questions suggest themselves. To develop them into stories, the reporter has to find informed interviewees and ask the questions. He goes to officials of the new company, local businessmen, bankers, the city water superintendent, builders and contractors, and others to find his answers.

And when he writes the stories, he packages the information in what newsmen call the *interview story*, the story that would have no validity if it were not possible to credit its offerings to competent sources.

What he has developed is a news interview, the type of interview with three dominant characteristics:

1) Its subject derives from a current news topic.

2) The source of its material (the interviewee) is specially qualified to comment or provide information on the particular topic—a source in whom reader or listener will have confidence.

3) It adds significantly to the public's knowledge or understanding of the subject. It illuminates, expands, debunks, explains, or in some other way offers more depth than the original "simple fact" story did.

The importance of this type of news effort is clear. No man in the complex twentieth century knows more than a little about his world; no newspaper reader or listener to a newscast can bring to the bewildering mass of facts laid before him enough relevant knowledge to evaluate, explain, or understand more than a little of it. More and more it has become the news medium's responsibility to help its customer by providing the background that the "average man" lacks.

When, therefore, a revolution explodes in a new republic across the world, the reporter goes to a qualified student of foreign politics for a competent interpretation of it. When the home town baseball franchise is sold down the river, the leading sports promoter in the community is asked for comment. When fire kills a score of elderly patients in a "rest home" in the next county, views and facts about comparable dangers locally are sought from county, city, fire, welfare, and hospital authorities. When a speaker at the state university commencement declares that parents are responsible for declining reading competence among school children, half a dozen elementary school principals are asked to say whether, in their opinion, he knows whereof he speaks.

These are the reportorial efforts that develop news interviews. Note the three characteristics: The stories take their tips from subjects in current news; they seek material from interviewees whose competence will be generally accepted; and they help the consumer to see puzzling, clouded facts against a background that throws them into visible and understandable relief.

THE TECHNIQUE OF THE INTERVIEW   Return to hardworking reporter Don Finnegan, who finds this note on his assignment sheet:

```
Dr. Franklyn Silcox, an urban sociologist from the
U. of California, is going to be visiting here next
week.  Get to him and see whether he'll talk about
the effect of moving 300 new families into town.
Does this dislocate the business or social balance
of a city this size?  Since there isn't decent
housing available, what would Silcox think the best
possible plan--suburban subdivision, condominium,
scattered apartments, or what?
```

Finnegan groans and goes to work.

His first step is like that he took to start the Prympton speech story. He needs to know his subject. Perhaps, from college sociology, he has some background for this kind of assignment; perhaps he has to do a good deal of library digging. He's likely to want to find out, first of all, what plans the management of the new mill has made for housing the families it proposes to import. (This may yield several advance stories.) He may make a trip to the newspaper's "morgue" for information about the city's housing problems in recent years. He calls up real estate dealers and contractors to learn their views and plans (more advance stories?). He digs into recent magazine and book references to Suburbia and Exurbia. He equips himself with a solid knowledge of his city's peculiar problems and of the broader aspects of the subject as well.

Remembering how useful he had found advance knowledge about the psychiatrist, Prympton, Finnegan realizes that similar acquaintance with the man he is to interview will be even more helpful. The interview situation is not impersonal like that of the speech, but face-to-face, sharply personal; the success of the interview may depend on establishment of rapport between interviewer and interviewee. Rapport can be built best by a newsman who knows what kind of man he is going to meet.

"Obit" is newsman's argot for "obituary." In newsrooms any biographical account of a man's career is an obit, whether its subject is alive or dead. The usage has grown out of newsroom practice of writing obituary notices of newsworthy figures in advance of death, especially when death seems imminent, so that the copy will be instantly available when it is needed.

So Finnegan works diligently at learning about Dr. Silcox. From reference books, from the "morgue," from telephone chats with Silcox's host-to-be and other local acquaintances, he provides himself a thorough "obit." He learns that Silcox is 47 years old, has traveled widely abroad, has degrees from four universities, has written twelve books (Finnegan reads hurriedly through a recent one called *The Doom of the City*). He's now on leave from his university post to act as consultant to several cities on housing projects; he sometimes has been vociferously annoyed at reporters who, he says, have quoted him inaccurately. He was the Pacific Coast golf champion for two years in college. He has exacted from his host a promise that there will be "no cocktail parties with more than six guests."

With this background, Finnegan can plan. He finds questions taking shape: How does the hypothesis of *The Doom of the City* fit the fact that this community is going to have a good-sized population growth? Can such growth be absorbed by normal school, trade, and social facilities and processes? What specific problems have other communities faced in like circumstances? What about the Realtors Association suggestion that the new families be scattered throughout the city and in the suburbs rather than concentrated in one new subdivision? How long does it take a group like this to become assimilated into community life?

These and similar questions are going to lead to the meat of his story. But there remains the problem of persuading Dr. Silcox, who has sometimes been less than cordial to reporters, to answer them.

Finnegan decides on the direct approach. He telephones Dr. Silcox's prospective host:

> This is Don Finnegan, of the *Herald*. We'd like very much to talk with Dr. Silcox about what all these new paper mill families will mean to the city . . . Yes, it's a puzzling problem. We think Dr. Silcox will have a good many of the answers. . . . Yes, I know this is a social visit. But if I could have about an hour—at his convenience . . . Yes—I'm aware of that. My hope is that I'll be one of the reporters he finds reliable. . . . Perhaps an hour before he goes to the golf links? I'd be glad to put it up to him myself, if you'll let me know when he's to arrive . . .

Thus the groundwork for Finnegan's interview is laid.

A matter to which Finnegan gives some thought: The setting of the interview. Where should he stage it? From experience, he has set up some rules of thumb:

A paradox well known to reporters is that it's often the "little" man rather than the "big" one who makes things hard for newsmen. Public figures of stature are accustomed to contacts with newsmen, and usually they have confidence in the treatment they will receive and an understanding of the importance of sound relations with the public through the news media. The man who has never before been asked for an interview, the one just promoted to his first executive position—or just elected dogcatcher—is more likely than the "arrived" business or political or professional figure to be suspicious, overcautious, or self-important.

1) It's best to make the interview a twosome. If others are present, there may be disturbances; and the interviewee may not be as relaxed and direct in what he says as he would be without listeners—maybe not so honest, if he's the kind who likes to impress people.

2) But in some cases it's a good thing to have witnesses. Sometimes people don't like what they've said when they see it in print; some deny it.

3) Interviews over a cup of coffee or a mug of beer, in a restaurant or cafe, may be good, or they may not. It's usually easy to get into relaxed conversation in this kind of setting. But you're subject to many interruptions: the waiter, friends, music, noisy kids in the next booth.

4. A private home or a hotel room is probably best. Something like the golf club is relaxed, but the interviewee isn't there to be interviewed—he's there to play golf. He may resent your taking even 10 minutes of his time.

Thinking like this leads Finnegan to decide to try for a meeting with Dr. Silcox at the home of his host. Normally, Finnegan would telephone for an appointment, soon after Silcox's arrival. This time he decides on a note to break the ice:

Dear Dr. Silcox:
We're going to have three hundred new families in this community next year, and the *Herald* would like to let its readers know what this will mean— to the new families and to the present residents. *The Doom of the City* seems to me to suggest that everybody may be in for a hard time if we don't plan new housing exactly right.
I'm going to do a story for the *Herald* about this, and I'd like very much to talk with you about it. I'll telephone you on Tuesday, to see whether we can arrange an interview.

With this approach, which, Finnegan hopes, will arouse Silcox's interest and persuade him that he'll be talking with a reporter who knows something about the subject, Finnegan telephones Tuesday. His petty stratagem works: "Come over at 9:30 tomorrow morning—we'll have the house to ourselves for an hour," Silcox says. Then he adds, "But I've got a golf date at 11."

At 9:30 the next morning Finnegan is seated in a comfortable living room, facing a keen-eyed man in slacks. Finnegan takes his initial lead from the costume:

"You've kept up your golf," he comments. Silcox responds heartily.

"Yes indeed—my heart attack insurance." He smiles at Finnegan's quizzical eyebrow. "My doctor says it's the man who never leaves his desk chair that's in danger," he explains. "So it's easy for me to justify a couple of rounds a week."

Finnegan holds the conversation in this theme for a minute or so, to establish the easy atmosphere. The mood confirmed, he shifts to indirect attack on his subject.

"Dr. Silcox, I've noticed that you've been retained by a number of cities as a consultant on housing and city planning. We were wondering at the paper whether you might be here on such an assignment."

Silcox is in the city strictly on a personal visit, he says. "Fact is, I don't know much about your local situation."

This is a cue for the reporter to describe what is happening locally. Finnegan talks for five minutes, answering occasional queries; he pulls a city map from his pocket and refers to it, to Silcox's apparent satisfaction. Finally:

"I see what the problems are," Silcox says. "Doesn't look as though they would be too tough, provided that the city council . . ."

The interview is launched, and Finnegan thinks that he may have the theme for his story: *Problems won't be too tough.* Careful exploratory questions confirm this. Silcox develops the theme, under the reporter's lead, in a manner to tie it down to specific local cases. The reporter's task now is to keep the flow of information and comment coming, to hold it on course if it should tend to stray, to ask questions that will draw understandable and quotable answers. In his pocket Finnegan has a set of prepared questions; he's glad that he doesn't have to fall back on them because any such artificial move might slow or dam the stream of conversation.

As the interview gets well under way, Finnegan draws folded copy paper from his pocket and starts to jot down notes. He watches closely to find whether the interviewee is distracted by his moving pencil. At one point when Silcox is giving statistical data, Finnegan notices that he hesitates and appears to be watching the note-taking. Finnegan employs a time-tested device: Handing the notes to Silcox, he says, "Would you check the figures?" Silcox glances over the notes, nods approvingly, hands them back; from now on he pays no attention to the pencil.

Finnegan keeps an eye on his watch; as the hour expires, he prepares to close the interview. Would Silcox say that such-and-such points are the ones to emphasize? the reporter asks. Are there significant subtopics they hadn't touched? Would Silcox be willing to check some of the points by telephone if the reporter finds himself in doubt?

Promptly at 10:30, Finnegan leaves. "Thanks again," he says. "I hope you break par."

"Your honest interview,"
Edward Price Bell told the
ASNE (see page 212), ". . .
is a stranger to everything
but the desire to reflect
without refraction the heart
and mind, the sentiment
and the opinion, of the interviewee." He offered a
series of precepts for the
"major" newspaper inter-
view. Among them:
   Currency of interest and
weight of subject are indis-
pensable.
   The interviewer's success
is likely to be proportionate
to his knowledge of the subject.
   The interviewer's strategy
grows out of thoughtful
preparation for logical questioning. Tactics must await
the scene of the interview.
   "If your man does not
talk . . . you must try to
kindle him with your own
enthusiasm.
   "If note-taking as the talk
proceeds is inadvisable, note-
making as soon as possible
afterward is of the highest
importance."

His interview presented no unusual problems, and there are none in writing the story. Thanks to his preparation and to checking with the interviewee on appropriate emphases, the elements of the story fall smoothly into place. The form of the story is substantially that of the speech story: summary lead, usually in indirect quotation; development of individual subtopics, in order of decreasing importance; alternation of direct and indirect quotation, the direct for elaboration of points of emphasis or for especially forceful or colorful language, the indirect for summarizing passages. (In her small book *Some Observations on the Art of Narrative*, the British writer Phyllis Bentley describes the use of similar alternation. Miss Bentley calls it "scene and summary" in fiction writing. No writer of any kind can lose by spending a half hour with this book.)

Even more than in the speech story, the personal mannerisms, characteristics, and appearance of the interviewee deserve attention. Finnegan's problem: Will his story be more understandable, more meaningful if he shows what Jones looked like, that he spoke good-naturedly, that he was holding a golf club as the interview took place, that he occasionally thumped a chair arm to underline a point? Will the story be more readable or more interesting with these details?

The gain in readability is likely to be greater than that in comprehension in a story of this kind (in the personality interview the gain is doubled). Most reporters writing major interview stories think this kind of detail is worth the space it costs. In routine interviews it is rare.

Finnegan, in his notebook about reportorial practice, has recorded some of the things he's learned about interviews and interview stories:

> Don't ask general questions. *Always* make them specific. If you ask for a generalization, that's what you'll get. Don't say, "Do you think a sudden influx of population will hurt a city?" but rather "Can a city the size of this one handle housing for three hundred new families?"
>
> Don't talk too much. You're not the interviewee. Your job is to lead the conversation, to keep it on the beam, not to monopolize it.
>
> On the other hand, don't let the interviewee wander or talk too long about his operation or the time he bid seven spades. Hold him on the track. Be persistent; but try to be courteous about it.
>
> Remember that you're the seeker and the interviewee the giver. This means that you are, in a sense, indebted to him. You don't impose any more on his time than you have to. Usually if he's a man who has anything to say, he's also one with plenty of other demands to meet.

All this doesn't mean that you let him shove you around. You're entitled to as good treatment as you give.

Watch for the man who's overeager to be interviewed. He may have ulterior motives. Be sure to look carefully at the special interests or prejudices of an interviewee. He may let them throw a false light on what he tells you—purposely or not.

Two examples of reportorial malfunction—neither one fatal, but both embarrassing and both avoidable—illustrate the need for alertness in news interviewing:

A reporter in a news conference with Minnesota Governor Orville Freeman (later Secretary of Agriculture) asked Freeman how he planned "to open Eastern markets to Minnesota milk." It would have been a good question two days earlier. But Governor Freeman responded acidly, "If you had been reading the papers, you would know very well how I plan to do it."

A reporter was interviewing Albert Einstein when Einstein was a very old man. He describes his faux pas thus: "I had one lousy pencil; it broke at the outset of the interview. Einstein had a fountain pen in the V-neck of his sweater, and I asked to borrow it. With a shattering look, he unscrewed the cap slowly and reluctantly gave it to me. I started to scratch away with it, but he asked me to excuse him, took the pen, screwed the cap on, put it back in his sweater V, and said he would get me a pencil. He returned with one in five minutes. . . . I had the impression he disliked reporters anyway, and I must have made it worse for all who followed."

• •

Should a reporter "check back" with his news source?

SOURCES OF INTERVIEW ERROR   Finnegan's last comment shows recognition of a fundamental of any kind of interviewing: That the interviewee doesn't always tell the truth, or that he may present truths in such a way that they come out false. False statements may be planned and intentional, or they may be unplanned and unrecognized. In either case, the reporter's challenge is to spot them. It is not an easy challenge to meet.

In setting up his detection system he can draw help from the social psychologists. Here is a compendium of suggestions from such sources about potentialities for errors in the interview (modified in some cases for journalistic relevance):

Intentional Falsehood   Hundreds of impulses, mostly connected with personal benefit or self-protection, may lead an interviewee to lie. For example:

A woman charged with luring a man into an alley so that accomplices can slug and rob him may tell a false story to cover herself.

A man may be ashamed to admit that he has been on relief rolls.

He may fear that the truth will hurt him with his family, his friends, or his employer.

He may seek to satisfy personal vanity by making himself appear wealthier, or more traveled, or richer in experience or education, than he is.

He may be a "publicity hound," for any of many reasons.

He may distrust the interviewer, or the use to which the interview is to be put. On the other hand, he may work too hard to please the interviewer, to say the things he thinks the reporter wants to hear.

Faulty Memory   The interviewee may be so distant from the facts or events he is describing that his "positive" statements are unintentionally false. He may have taken little interest in an event at the time he observed it, so that even an honest effort at

The answer is "yes" whenever he has doubt about accuracy of fact or meaning, or whenever, in response to an interviewee's request, he has promised to do so.

"Checking back" raises some problems. On occasion the interviewee makes suggestions or demands that the reporter can't accept. He doesn't like the wording of the story . . . he wants this element emphasized, that one played down. He may, especially if he's a scientist or some other variety of specialist, object to the use of lay instead of technical vocabulary.

The newsman's obligation is essentially to make sure of accuracy of fact and impression in his story; beyond this there is no compulsion to accept the news source's suggestions. If his judgment differs from that of the interviewee, he must ask himself: Is the source's opinion valid, or should his own prevail (since he is a representative of the public he hopes to reach, and a specialist in the means of reaching it)?

In this kind of dispute there are a thousand shadings, and decisions may not be easy. Often a news source sees a news story, however competent and accurate it may be, not as an instrument to inform a broad public but rather as a means of impressing his fellow experts. When he does, he is denying both the purpose of mass communication and the propriety of effort to express complicated or esoteric concepts in everyday rhetoric.

There is also a matter of tactics. When newsman and source cannot agree, the newsman may have to risk his source's annoyance or anger; and this may block-

its reconstruction may be faulty. He may have been so deeply involved emotionally in the event that he has become the victim of wishful thinking.

Lack of Information   A man may have less information than he thinks he has. Or he may not think it worth while to recall distant memories, or to take the pains to produce precise facts.

Misunderstanding   The interviewee may not grasp the meaning of the questions he is asked, or he may not have put the questions into the right context. Here the responsibility is the interviewer's.

Interviewer's Errors   The reporter may use jargon or difficult terminology that throws his respondent off. He may have personal bias that misdirects the answers or misinterprets them. He may lack interviewing skill, so that he does not dig deeply enough, or he may make the interview "hard" or uncomfortable for the respondent. He may fail to establish rapport with the respondent.

Your experienced reporter knows these sources of error and keeps persistent watch to avoid them.

He knows, too, that a man who finds it difficult or distasteful to answer correctly in some areas may be quite dependable in others. Few man are entirely truthful in telling you how much money they earn. They often conceal what they consider shameful facts in their family or personal history. They are likely to be weak in recalling precise dates, the years in which they took specific vacations, for instance.

In contrast, most men and women respond accurately to questions about their own ages, their education, their nationality, their professional or business careers. They can tell you the names of their children, even though they can't always recall the ages. They know the make (though not always the model) of the cars they drive. In short, they are likely to be accurate and dependable when giving information that is precise and of constant intimate and personal interest to them.

Now study samples of the news interview.

The first, unusual in form, is an ideal story because it combines its news peg (a speech by one man) with its news interview (answers to reporters' questions) in one story. This version (from the Paris edition of the

ade an information channel he'd like to use in the future. The decision rests on the importance of the story to the public and the degree to which following the source's suggestions will make it less meaningful.

In any case, the evident gains in the reliability of checked-back stories outweigh the perils in disagreement.

New York *Times*) is shorter than the version in the New York edition, and less clear because it fails to show specifically that the first five paragraphs report a speech and the last three an interview. It is not often that the news basis for the interview and the interview itself can be combined in one piece of copy. The public would be better served if this could be accomplished more frequently. The prospect that it may occur more often depends on the degree to which the "urge to speed" can be resisted.

MILWAUKEE, Wis.—Donald B. Strause, chairman of the Planned Parenthood Federation of America, said yesterday that the increased availability of contraceptives confronts the birth-control organization with a moral challenge.

"The availability of contraceptives for all, which is our objective, is having a profound effect on the sexual attitudes and behavior of our time," he said at the annual meeting here.

Contraceptives are not the only factor, but to pretend they have no effect is to ignore the obvious, he said.

"We must now seek the greater assistance of religious leaders in helping to interpret this moral revolution into which we are inevitably drawn," he said.

"The two great supports of sexual morality in the past—fear of disease and fear of pregnancy—have now happily been largely removed . . . ," he said. "This, I submit, leaves our generation of parents with a problem that remains largely unsolved."

[Here the news interview begins.]

Alan F. Guttmacher, the federation president, said in answer to reporters' questions that contraceptives contributed relatively little to the sexual revolution. He pointed, instead, to the disappearance of the chaperone, dating in the early teens, "going steady," the accessibility of the automobile to young people, and the disappearance of the double standard. He said the strongest deterrent remains the attitudes formed in the home.

He conceded that contraceptives account for encouragement of between 5 and 7 percent of extramarital sexual intercourse, but he said that is a small price to pay for the elimination annually of 250,000 illegitimate births and 1,000,000 abortions.

Dr. Guttmacher said a leader in the Roman Catholic Church had told federation representatives that it is possible that in six or nine months the Vatican position would be clarified in the direction of a more liberal view.

The next story also exhibits the "normal" news interview pattern—more typically than the first, indeed, since it quotes only one source. Its summary lead introduces the story's one major topic; it alternates direct and indirect quotations; it credits every quoted statement. Its news peg is the conference to which it refers; its interviewee is an authority; its effect is illumination and interpretation.

Nursery schools and day care centers for small children may soon be as customary as the public school, an expert in the field predicted Monday.

Mrs. Dorothy H. Beers, New York City, consultant to the Child Welfare League of America, predicted, too, that the nursery school—which will enroll children from the age of three—eventually will be a part of the public school system.

She spoke to delegates here to attend the regional conference of the League.

"There are more mothers working now than ever before," she said. "Estimates are that something like four million mothers are employed."

This figure probably will increase, Mrs. Beers added. A large number of these mothers are working because they have to, and there must be some supervised care for their children, she said.

This care should be up to decent standards, Mrs. Beers added, and the standards should be set by the state.

"Some states have no licensing requirements," she said. "As a result, you find nurseries in fire traps—on the fourth floor without fire escapes. Or you will find places with large, open fire places, inadequate heating, inadequate food. You will find cruel and sadistic persons running these centers."

North Carolina and New York City have two of the best licensing laws, she said. But the law in this state—while good—is not tight enough to assure children the best protection, Mrs. Beers added.

She pointed out that a "great many" privately operated nurseries have no trained staff.

"Corners are cut so the operator can make a better profit," she said. "While I have no objection to a private nursery school owner's making a profit, I do want to point out that you can't afford mink coats in this kind of children's work.

"The average cost for an adequate program of this type is $15 a week per child. In New York City, many of the good private agencies charge from $80 to $100 a month."

Because most parents cannot afford to pay such fees, these children's centers will have to be subsidized by community or federal funds, Mrs. Beers said.

The Beers story has a significant fault: it does not reveal unmistakably that it is an interview (the preceding story is also weak in this respect). Reporters and copy editors sometimes omit or delete the phrase "in an interview" or its equivalent because they think it unnecessary, or because emphasis on the mechanics of newsgathering may pull the consumer's attention away from its essence. In this example, however, the statement that "she spoke to delegates" suggests—wrongly—that the story is reporting her speech. The "in an interview" phrase (which the reporter had written into the story) should not have been deleted.

In the long multiple-interview story that follows there is no such question. No event such as a speech or a meeting is involved; clearly the reporter went to six competent sources to procure comment on a current topic. The story may be said to move slowly because its first eight paragraphs are devoted to establishing the news situation, describing the problem; it does not begin its interviews until paragraph nine.

Strong opposition to more corporal punishment in local schools was developing Wednesday night.

Many school officials, especially at the senior high school level, were firmly opposed.

Corporal punishment was labeled a "retrogression," "a confession of failure," and a "return to the middle ages."

Instead, counseling, "talking things out," and in extreme cases psychiatric aid appeared to be the preferred methods of discipline.

Meanwhile, the Federation of Men Teachers, which has said there is "an urgent need for a forceful and real-istic policy within the limits of state law" (which allows corporal punishment), prepared to ask for a conference with Dr. Gladys Welles, superintendent, on questions of discipline.

The federation has charged a "real breakdown in classroom discipline" in the schools and has said the counseling system "is nowhere near adequate to do the job alone." The federation has also called attention to the Detroit system of discipline in which corporal punishment is used.

That the federation will run into difficulties if it pushes any demands for corporal punishment (which it has not yet done) was plainly indicated yesterday.

Dr. Welles was already on record against any such move. Top level administrators in the school system joined the opposition.

[The summary lead and the background now presented, the news interviews begin.]

Typical of the reaction at the high school level was that of Alfred A. Busco, principal at Edger high school, who declared himself flatly opposed.

"I don't believe in it at all," Busco said, "and I think by far the majority of our teachers and principals would be opposed. When youngsters are of high school age, if they haven't already learned to conduct themselves properly, you don't accomplish anything by corporal punishment. I don't approve of it even when it is administered by the parents.

"When you have a disciplinary problem at high school ages, you have to work to modify a mental attitude," Busco continued. "You have to reason with the youngster. You can't accomplish a mental change by corporal punishment."

Henry T. Monstrom, assistant principal at Hughes high, who handles most of the disciplinary problems in that school, also was in opposition.

"I don't believe you can use corporal punishment in high schools," Monstrom said.

"By the time a youngster is of high school age, he considers himself and wants to be adult. You have to deal with him as such. Furthermore, most youngsters are good sports. If you deal with them fairly and squarely, if they know what the rules are and what the penalties are, you get along with them all right. I've got a lot of faith in these kids."

Monstrom said that in some cases of extreme incorrigibles psychiatric care is needed. These, however, are few and far between. Monstrom also said that he doesn't believe in the threat of corporal punishment as a disciplinary measure.

[Four more interviews with school officials—all to the same effect—round out the story.]

(A sidelight: The headline over the story above used the word "spanking," likely because "corporal punishment" is not good headlinese. The story does not use the word. The reporter was careful to talk in general rather than colloquial or familiar terms. Would the story have been improved by more "common" language?)

The next story also states the problem at some length before getting to the answers or the answerer. Its three provocative opening paragraphs, however—none longer than eight words—move the reader rapidly and interestingly into its soberer statement of topic:

Do you like love scenes in the movies?

Are you content with your sex life?

Do you think Christ performed miracles?

More important, do you think questions like those ought to be asked of persons applying for jobs with the Peace Corps, the State Department, or other government agencies?

The State Department and Peace Corps apparently no longer think so, though they've asked such questions as part of psychological personality tests in the past.

Recently, however, it was decided some of the queries did a little too much prying and were "objectionable," so curbs have been placed on such tests, among them the well-known Minnesota Multiphasic Personality Inventory (MMPI).

One of the men who helped develop the MMPI nearly 25 years ago—Dr. Starke Hathaway—disagrees. And he came to the defense of the tests Friday.

If the tests are competently administered and used, they offer one of the best ways of looking at an individual's personality, said Hathaway, director of clinical psychology at the University.

Hathaway conceded that many people, "perhaps rightly," feel that personality is an individual's own business, a private thing.

"But I don't think you can live that way today," he added. "I believe that in a society that has to work together our personalities impinge on one another. We all make decisions about what kind of people we like or don't like. Tests are merely tools to help in such decisions."

The basic thing you must decide is whether people who work for the Peace Corps or other agencies should be examined as to personality, said Hathaway.

"If it is agreed that the personality should be a part of determining the appropriateness of the person, then should we not use the best, most modern means?

"Once you admit that jobs like these are not really appropriate for the terribly maladjusted or the highly prejudiced or others—once you decide that a selection must be made—then you ask how will you have your professional people make a good selection.

"Will you prevent them from investigating so-called personal items? If you do, you'll simply tie their hands as the hands of the doctors were tied years ago because of the prudery that would not permit examination of the body."

Hathaway asked if it isn't better to have trained authorities look at an individual's personality by direct questions rather than by secret signs or indirect, seemingly meaningless queries.

He pointed out that if the MMPI is properly given, the person taking it is told that he can skip questions he doesn't want to answer. Valid results still can be obtained.

Answers are tabulated by machine, and attention is paid to the over-all picture,

not to the replies to specific questions, said Hathaway.

He also stressed that a psychological test is just one of several aids in deciding about a person. "Decisions never depend on the tests alone."

Hathaway noted that personality tests have come under fire many times in the past, although the items objected to have varied.

"One person may not want to tell about his sex life, while someone else doesn't mind that, but won't say whether he believes in God.

"Some of the early objections were to tests with very innocent questions."

Hathaway is confident the MMPI and other well-administered tests will weather the current criticism as they have that in the past.

A common reportorial problem—as well as the danger of using verbatim quotation as a lead (see page 201)—appears in the opening paragraph of an interview story:

"In Israel everyone starves equally. In Iran, 99 percent of the people starve while the rest drive Cadillac convertibles."

[*The story that follows shows the basis on which the interviewee made this statement. The story appears to suggest that the statement was a figurative rather than a literal observation.*]

The day after the story was published, a letter from the interviewee explained at length that the opening paragraph—which, he said, "purported to be a direct quotation"—conveyed a false impression because of its emphasis. He went on to explain that in Israel "no one lacks the food essentials" and in Iran "no one is really starving"; he then said he expected "great strides" in the future in both countries.

The reporter offered this comment:

I had a rough time getting an angle for this story because I thought the interviewee had nothing new to offer—his stuff was largely familiar. But he did use the precise words given in the lead paragraph; I have them in my notes, in quotes—which means that they are verbatim. I think, however, that he used them in hyperbole—to make a point; I think the story would have protected him if it had said, in the second paragraph, "That was the *figurative* impression . . ."

I think his complaint legitimate, for he did not intend the quoted lead statement to be taken literally.

When should a reporter appear in a story? How?

It is fair to say that the most effective reporter, most of the time, is the invisible one. He represents the news consumer, and in effect he tries to achieve the illusion that the consumer saw and heard what he reports. When a story says that "the reporter asked" or that the news source "told this writer," some of the consumer's attention is forced to the mechanics of the interview, an aspect of the story which he should normally be unaware of.

In general, reportorial intrusion is justified in two situations (1) When a reporter takes actual part in an event—when he helps rescue the child from the river, when the visiting celebrity singles him out for comment; (2) When he is a featured writer so well known that the audience is interested in him as a personality. It is the sure mark of the novice to write the story about himself rather than about the event.

The key to self-reference is: Make it as unobtrusive as possible. A comparatively unostentatious term is the third-person phrase "the (or "a") reporter." The simple first-person "I" is less intrusive than the self-conscious "we" or "this reporter," and much to be preferred to such worn and labored circumlocutions as "this scribe," "this writer," "yours truly," "the author," and the like. Competent writers now rarely use the "editorial we" except for whimsical effect.

An effective device for presenting questions unobtrusively—and without steering the reporter into the center of the stage—is exemplified in the excerpt of an interview that follows:

> The man stood looking at a rubble-filled hole in the ground. He stopped to pick up a crumpled mail box. As he turned to his visitor, he spoke.
>
> "That was on the road— 100 rods away," he said. "How it got here . . ." You could make out a name on the box: George B. Linsson, Route 7.
>
> Did the tornado leave you anything else, Mr. Linsson?
>
> "Just what you see. We weren't at home. When we got back, we didn't have any house . . . didn't have anything."
>
> How about your neighbors?
>
> "We were right in the path. Seems as if we got it harder than almost anybody . . ."
>
> Ever have any previous experience with tornadoes?
>
> "Not in this part of the country. But we used to live in Kansas, and . . ."
>
> [*And so on.*]

Occasionally newspapers employ the direct method in reporting interviews, the question-and-answer pattern resembling the reproduction of court testimony. This has the advantage of completeness and literal accuracy, but the disadvantages of excessive use of space and, more important, of lack of emphasis, selection, and concentration. It is ordinarily used only when its high human interest or its great importance will guarantee that readers will wade through it. An example of its use in a human interest story:

[EDITOR'S NOTE: *Al Nakkula,
Rocky Mountain News
writer, interviewed John Gilbert
Graham in County Jail
Thursday. This is the first
interview with Graham.*]

John Gilbert Graham
flatly denies planting a bomb
on an airliner which killed
44 persons, including his
mother. He hints his mother
herself might have planted
the explosive.

My questions were direct
and straightforward. Graham
looked straight at me with
his penetrating gray-green
eyes when answering many
of the questions.

But when it came to such
questions as to whether he
had experience handling explosives,
Graham would turn
away or look down in his
lap, his heavy lips pursing
in annoyance.

Graham, dressed in the
gray denim coveralls of the
jail, sat with his hands folded
in his lap in the office of
Warden Gorden Dolliver.

Q: Jack, I understand the
FBI obtained a signed statement
from you, admitting
you placed a bomb on that
plane . . .

A: Yes, I signed a statement.
But it's not true. They
told me they were going to
put my wife in jail, and I'd
better get it straightened
out, myself.

Q: You mean, they used
duress—they kept questioning
you until you confessed?

A: Well, they started
about noon that Sunday and
didn't stop until I signed a
confession about four A.M.,
the next morning. Oh, they
took me out for dinner once
and gave me drinks of water
and such . . .

Q: They say you forged
the insurance policies on
your mother that night when
the plane crashed. Can you
straighten that out?

A: I didn't. My mother
signed them. I made out
three—one for myself, one
for my sister and one for my
aunt.

Q: How much were they
for?

A: I don't remember.
There was a foul-up on the
machine . . .

Q: Did you put a present
—or a bundle of dynamite—
in your mother's luggage?

A: I didn't put anything
in her luggage. I only bought
some straps to put around
the luggage. . . . I don't
want to discuss the present.

Q: Did you have a premonition
of your mother's
death before you had been
formally notified of it?

A: I didn't—she had. She
called everybody she could
think of before she left. . . .

Q: Do you mean your
mother might have planted
the dynamite in her own
suitcase to take her own
life? Has your mother ever
mentioned taking her life?

A: I won't answer that.
. . .

Q: Look, Jack, you've had
a couple of years in college
—you're no dummy. Do you
think the FBI is lying when
they say they found evidence
to show the dynamite
was in your mother's luggage?

A: I don't know. You'll
have to talk to my attorney
about that.

Q: Did you know a timing
device has been traced to
you—you bought one, found
it didn't work, and bought
another?

A: I don't have anything
to say about that.

Q: When did you learn
how to handle explosives?
In Alaska?

A: I was a civilian laborer
there. I did a little bit of
everything . . . I'm not saying
any more.

Q: What is your opinion
as to how that dynamite got
on the plane—in your mother's
suitcase?

A: I don't remember.

Q: You don't remember—

A: I don't have any theories
as to the cause of the
crash or what happened.

Q: Do you realize that
there are 44 people dead?
The FBI says you caused
their deaths. You've been
charged with murder—

A: Sure, but I didn't do it
and I don't know what happened.

Q: May I ask you frankly:
You say you didn't do it.
The explosives have been
traced to your mother's luggage.
Are you saying your
mother killed herself by carrying
the dynamite on the
plane, herself?

A: I have no idea.

Obviously this kind of treatment is unsuitable for radio or television.

The Symposium Interview

Full membership in the news interview family is held by the symposium or
group interview, the kind in which the reporter gets his information not from
one or two or a handful of sources but from a dozen, a score, or a hundred.
Almost always the topic for this kind of story is one of current interest, one
so prominent in the news that finding random interviewees to comment on it
is as easy as interesting readers in its topic. Typically, the topic has direct

impact on the man in the street; it is of the kind that affects everybody's pocketbook or personal comfort or general security. Such a topic is the new state withholding tax: do people like it or don't they? Or the hottest week in the last 30 years: how do you keep cool? Or the end of a threat of a general strike: would you have struck if it had been called?

The symposium interview differs from the model news interview because its interviewees are selected not for their authority on the story's topic, but as ordinary citizens whose views are worth reporting: they show how a news situation is typically affecting the community or a group within it. The story so developed may be fluff, pure entertainment—the purpose of the "how do you keep cool?" question is not to develop scholarly hints for lowering body temperature but rather to try to laugh a little at summer discomfort.

But often such a symposium brings out opinions of importance, as for example the story on page 228 about laboring men's reactions to charges of misbehavior by union officers. Sometimes the average man's response to a situation tells more than all the official comment in the *Congressional Record*, not the response of *one* man but of enough average men to give some overview of a general reaction.

(The distinction between *expert* response and *average* response—not that between the story with a single respondent and that with several or many—is the one that separates standard news interviews from symposium interviews. Thus, though the story on page 220 has two respondents and that on page 221 six, they are not classified as symposium interviews because their respondents are "expert." The distinction is an arbitrary one.)

Several observations on the characteristic problems of developing the symposium story are in order:

1) Finding interviewees is usually no problem, even though you don't know the name of a single one in advance. If you're working on the keeping-cool story, you station yourself at your city's busiest street corner and query the first 25 passers-by you can buttonhole. This would do for the withholding tax story, too. But the general strike story calls for a different approach—going to a labor mass meeting, or visiting a big industry, or finding some other locale where you can be sure that you won't waste time querying nonunion men and women.

2) There's no fixed rule as to how many responses you must get. If your purpose is no more than to report what a few people say—as in the familiar "inquiring reporter" column—without any attempt at generalization, you can stop with, say, five. But if you propose to develop a story that will properly reflect a public attitude, you decide that you must question 50 or 100 respondents. If the purpose is strictly entertainment, you probably continue questioning until you have enough "good" answers to make a good yarn.

However many you include, it is always necessary to let your reader know how extensive a survey you've conducted. If you say that "four fifths of the local citizenry believes that taxes ought to be lower" on the basis of interviewing ten local citizens, you're writing nonsense. But if you've interviewed 50 and find 40 holding the same view, you're justified in writing that "a majority of a small sample of local citizens indicated today that . . ."

3) In order to arrive at a justifiable conclusion, you must ask all your respondents substantially the same question in substantially the same words and manner; thus you draw comparable answers. If you approach interviewees in different ways, you'll get responses to different concepts, and you'll end up with an amorphous mass of comments from which you'll hardly dare generalize.

You'll learn not only to ask the same questions, but to make them simple. You don't say, "If the authorized agents of organized labor, by the constitutional rights conferred on them, issue a manifesto directing all members of affiliated associations to absent themselves from their places of employment, would you have the probable inclination to conform?" Rather, you ask, "Would you go on strike if a call is issued?"

You design nonleading questions. The previous one does not suggest either a *yes* or a *no* answer. But to say, "As a union member, you'd be obligated to strike if the call were issued, wouldn't you?" might make it hard for many respondents to answer objectively.

4) The simple summary lead is often the most effective for the symposium story. When your interviewees show substantial agreement in views, a summary is easy and obvious. It's not much more difficult when they disagree, for it's as newsy to say that "union members disagree on support of a general strike" as to report their agreement.

When the story is a light one, an entertainer, the lead ordinarily reflects it:

> A week of torrid weather has driven local citizens to everything from drink (usually lemonade) to six baths a day.

Near the lead, if not in it, should appear the news peg, the event or news development that occasions the story (this is also true of standard news interviews):

> And there's no let-up in sight. Yesterday's 95-degree peak will be repeated today and tomorrow.

At some place in the story should appear a brief explanation of the circumstances of the fact gathering:

> The things people are doing to avoid the heat, or moderate its effects, were described by 20 local residents asked this morning by a Herald reporter, "How do you keep cool?"

5) One of the virtues of the symposium interview is its high specificity. Its purpose is to report what men and women think or feel or do, and nothing makes this kind of reporting effective so quickly as talking in terms of real men and women you identify. This means that you:

(a) Identify respondents precisely whenever you can. Names and addresses are often used, not necessarily those of all 50, but certainly of the "typical" examples whose quotations are given. If it's inappropriate to give name-address identification, bring respondents to life by writing that "a blond workman in a sports jacket said . . ."

(b) Use direct quotations freely.

(c) Support generalizations with specific evidence.

6) In general, follow the same patterns throughout the story. If you start giving quotations in a formal manner, continue doing so:

> Joe Antonio, 2179 Robisdaile Avenue—I wouldn't strike if they gave me the plant.
> Tom Tripp, 423 S. Pittern Street—I'm ready to strike at the drop of a pickax.

But if you decide on a less formal pattern, stick to that:

> "I wouldn't strike if they gave me the plant," said Joe Antonio, 2179 Robisdaile Avenue.
> But Tom Tripp, 423 S. Pittern Street, differed. "I'm ready to strike at the drop of a pickax," he said.

Two symposium interviews illustrate the suggestions. The first is drawn by one writer, A. H. Raskin, from materials gathered nationwide by the New York *Times* correspondents:

NEW YORK. Sentiment for the ouster of Dave Beck and other key officers of the International Brotherhood of Teamsters is growing among the rank and file of the giant truck union.

But the sentiment is far from universal and even those who are strongest for a cleanup emphasize their belief that they are powerless to bring it about without help from the AFL-CIO or the government.

These were the major findings in a man-on-the-truck survey made Wednesday by correspondents of the New York Times in 25 major cities from Boston to Los Angeles.

The comments of union drivers and warehousemen ranged from angry demands that the Teamster high command be jailed to an assertion by one New York driver that he would have taken "even more" if he had had access to the union treasury.

A truckman delivering ceiling fixtures at the Empire State Building said Beck ought to be strung up on a lamp post. But a driver double-parked in the warehouse district in Minneapolis took a more detached view. "Everybody is out to get what he can," was his comment. "Let the big boys fight it out on their own. I'm doing all right."

Conspicuously few had any good word to say for their union president. A union shop steward in Jersey City said Beck was "tops" in his book. A unionist with more than a quarter-century of trucking behind him in Chicago asserted that Beck was doing "a wonderful job."

But for every defender Beck appeared to have a score of critics. On the loading platforms of truck terminals, from the cabs of long-haul vehicles, from doorsteps where they were leaving milk, and in the delivery sheds of waterfront warehouses, Teamsters voiced in language too earthy for repetition in a newspaper their belief that Beck had disqualified himself for union office.

"He had no business helping himself to our money," was the way a deliverer of paper boxes put it. "Men like Beck get millions; we get peanuts. If he was a poor man, he'd be in jail without all this fuss."

Fear was a deterrent to comment by many drivers. They said frankly that it is "not healthy" to sound off about grievances against their leaders. Others denied they were afraid, but insisted there is no way to make their voices felt effectively in the choice of top leaders.

Many of those who were most bitter about the high command were quick to exempt their local union chiefs from criticism.

A substantial segment of those interviewed took a "wait and see" attitude. There was a general disposition among them to admit things do not "smell good," but they urged that judgment be suspended until all the facts are in.

A few said they felt it is no business of anyone outside the union to inquire into its affairs. Most said they welcome the investigation by a senate committee, even though they fear it might hurt labor.

In Denver, rank and file Teamsters made no secret of their hope that the senators would look into their complaints against local Teamster chiefs after they "clean up the mess at the top." Insurgent members of the union in Denver have been trying for two years to get action on petitions calling for local reforms.

Widespread sentiment was voiced for action by the AFL-CIO to purge the Teamsters' top echelon.

Few ideas were put forward on methods of insuring greater democracy inside the 1,400,000-member union. Several members said they felt a secret referendum on international officers is the best way to ward off re-election of the present leaders or to prevent the handpicking of successors at the next union convention, in Miami Beach later this year.

[*The story continues for another column, its burden to show how widely Teamster members differ in their views.*]

A more common use of the symposium interview method appears in this story:

Students in the three local high schools appear to have no doubts as to whom to blame for teen-age "delinquency."

"Blame the teen-agers themselves," they say.

At least that's the opinion of 72 out of 100 of them queried this week by the Courier.

But they don't think it's a black-and-white matter. Here are some of the differing views they offer:

Most teen-agers are "all right." They shouldn't all be held responsible for the misbehavior of a few.

Parents have to share some of the burden of their children's misconduct.

"More understanding policemen" could help to cut down on instances of violence.

There isn't nearly as much drinking among teen-agers "as people seem to think." The "blame-the-teen-agers" theme, expressed in one way or another by nearly three fourths of the students interviewed by Courier reporters, was well summarized by a senior girl at Foster High:

"You can't tell me that the kids who get themselves into trouble don't know better," said Caryl Pitson, 18, president of her school's Student Council.

"Most of us come from good homes, and our parents have told us the score," she went on. "I've never seen a teen-ager who was misbehaving—maybe drinking, maybe driving too fast—who didn't know he was acting foolish."

Why do they act "foolish"? Sixteen-year-old Fritz Apfchen of Worthington High has some answers.

"They like to look big," said Fritz. "They think it makes an impression on the girls."

Tony Karnak, 17, also of Worthington, qualified this. "Girls like to make impressions on boys, too," he said. "I don't think we're much different from older people, as a matter of fact. Don't adults ever do things they're sorry for?"

From Fannie Fergus, 17, of Horace Mann High came this angle: "Our speech class had a debate on this last week, and we all thought the affirmative won. It supported the question, 'Resolved, that juvenile delinquency must be controlled by juveniles rather than by school, church, or city.'"

But Fannie expressed the second most common theme: "I think the kids who have the best home life—the ones who get along best with their parents—are the ones who get into the fewest jams."

About a third of the students interviewed supported variants of this view. Another third asked that the city's policemen "try to help high school kids keep out of trouble, rather than just show how tough they can get when we make mistakes."

Drinking, it seemed generally agreed, is not a major problem.

"Sure some of the students do it at times," said one Horace Mann senior boy. "I've done it myself a couple of times—not that I'm very proud of it. But I don't think I'm going to do it again for a long time. And neither is the gang I go with. We've talked it over, and we know it gets us no place."

Another Horace Mann senior pointed out that there have been no local charges of illegal sale of liquor to minors in the last two years.

The questions were asked of a random sample of students at the three schools—33 each at Foster and Worthington, 34 at Horace Mann. Three Courier reporters conducted the survey, with the approval of the three principals.

Here is a breakdown of the answers to specific questions. . . .

The Personality Interview

Newsmen have invented no more effective tool for revealing personality than the "personality interview," the interview in which the reporter lets his subject show the reader what manner of man he is strictly through what manner of thing he says.

The reason the pattern is effective is easy to see. To let a figure in the news, or an individual who is interesting, in the news or not, discuss his likes and dislikes, his attitudes about diet and dictatorship and doodling on the telephone pad, his hopes and enthusiasms and frustrations, and to let him do it himself in his own words, is to put the news consumer squarely into the reporter's vantage point.

This virtue underlines the distinction between the personality interview and the biographical sketch. The sketch, written usually at a respectful distance from its subject, tells you *about* him: where and when he was born, number of children, date on which he became an ambassador, and so on. It has its uses, one of them being that it serves as the structural pattern for most obituaries. It *describes* personality, at the same time offering a readable substitute for *Who's Who*. But it rarely achieves the warmth, the interest, the intimacy of the interview, through whose devices a skillful reporter can let a man's words and manners bring him vibrantly to life.

The personality interview may be used with any subject with whom a reporter can communicate. Not every such subject, however, is worth giving space in the paper or time on the air. Newsmen have two principal clues that help them to decide whether a subject is likely to offer any breadth of interest:

First clue: that a man or woman is a news personality, that for one reason or another he has gained a place in the stream of ongoing events. He has been elected mayor; he has made his fifth hole in one; he has refused to accept a million-dollar bequest from an uncle he detested. She is managing the Christmas Seal campaign for the eleventh year; she has been awarded the blue ribbon for her cherry pie at the state fair; she is to succeed her late husband as mayor. That is to say, public attention is already centered on the individual; the reporter comes to think of it as natural progression that he should have a chance to show the public, in the man's own way, what kind of human he is.

Second clue: That a person entirely outside the news orbit is made newsworthy by a trait of personality, an eccentricity, a hobby, or an oddity of habit or work or play; something has set him apart from his fellows. This kind of individual would be the teen-ager whose collection of samples of tree barks now contains 409 specimens; the professional foster mother who has given homes to a battalion of children; the old man who has read every book on the sea in the local library and is now starting over. None of these is involved in a newsworthy *event;* but an out-of-the-ordinary habit or practice gives him special audience interest.

Fundamental differences in the purposes of interviewing exist among the various professions for which the interview is a major tool, even though the techniques of all have similarities. A number of professions use the interview to gain information to be used primarily for the advantage of the person interviewed: social workers, physicians, lawyers, clergymen. From this fact grows the accepted social principle that most such interviews are confidential. The industrial employment officer uses the interview essentially for advantage of his employer.

The newsman uses interviews not for the interviewee's purposes, nor his own, nor his employer's, but to discharge his obligation to the public. He is the representative of his audience. His responsibility is to provide useful information to it—in the same pattern the audience's members themselves would have gained the information had they had the opportunity and the skill. This is not only his justification for seeking the interview but also his guide to the kind of questions to ask and to the pattern of presenting what he learns.

• •

Interviews on tape—usually brief ones—are commonplace in radio news. The tape recorder as a news

Interviewees identified by the first clue are likely to be not only interesting but also to some degree important. Those in the second classification are usually given attention largely because of their human interest.

The development of the personality interview differs little in technique from that of the news interview. Advance preparation is necessary, especially when the subject, as a figure in the news, is aware of his eminence (it's amazingly easy to offend some newly-newsworthy men and women by not knowing they were born in Flagstaff or Terre Haute or Kennebunkport). Moreover, a news figure is likely to be a busy figure, and anything that will conserve his time is an advantage.

The suggestions about techniques of interviewing earlier in this chapter can be applied to personality interviewing almost intact, but you may note some additional pointers:

1) It is clearly good tactics to steer the interviewee to the subject that has led to his selection: the fact that he has been made chairman of the board (what does he think about it? how did he get that way?) or that he has never seen a movie (does he consider this a plus or a pain?)

2) More than in the news interview, the verbal and physical mannerisms of the interviewee are worth reporting. In the news interview, the emphasis is on *what* a man says; in the personality story, on the *how* as well. That a medical researcher constantly repeats the phrase "Know what I mean?" is of no significance if the story is intended to let him clarify the meaning of his new theory of cancer identification. Properly used, it may be an aid to the reader trying to find out what kind of man he is.

gathering tool has not had broad acceptance among newspaper reporters, but it is gaining adherents. It is widely used by writers for magazines, both as a replacement for pad and pencil in interviews and as a means of recording entire conversations for later publication. Such publication has occurred in the Paris Review, Harper's, *the* Atlantic, *and other magazines. Newspapers have made no more than a beginning in the use of material so gathered, but the obvious advantages—as newsmen learn better how to use them, as the sources of information themselves become more accustomed to being interviewed on tape, and as the emphasis on news in depth grows more insistent—make it safe to predict that the tape recorder will be used more and more widely.*

● ●

Magazine journalists express some scorn for what has been called the "single-interview syndrome" of newsmen. They refer to the fact that newspaper and broadcast reporters under the pressures of time and space usually try to wrap up a story in one interview. "Newspaper reporters have a lot to learn from magazine writers," says one magazine man. "Some metropolitan reporters and feature writers seem to understand that interviewing the subject of the personality piece is not the beginning and the end of this kind of research. But many small-town reporters don't know that they ought to interview beyond the subject. My magazine experience suggests that no competent magazine article writer would allow himself to become the prisoner of

3) The reporter writing a personality story ought to help his reader see his subject as well as hear him. Artfully interpolated lines of description belong in personality interviews. They are not always easy to tie in, and when they are injected with a heavy hand they are liabilities. But it is helpful to the reader trying to understand what a man is like to know that there are overcareful creases in his trousers, that he has a middle-age bulge, that he scratches the bridge of his nose when he's thinking. Such details help to accent individuality.

Similarly, details of the environment of the interview—particularly if they relate to the interviewee's habitual surroundings—may help to establish personality and at the same time give vitality to a story. But observe these cautions: Don't load the story with excess detail of this kind; don't use color for color's sake alone, but rather for the sake of what it adds to the effect you're seeking; don't put all the detail either of setting or personal appearance in its own paragraph, but rather sneak it in in small touches through the story; and don't overwork the descriptive bromides (*pretty coed, sparkling blue eyes, beaming smile, pearly teeth, mane of snowy hair, vine-covered cottage*).

4) Remember that, though your purpose is to reveal personality and, if you can, character, you are rarely justified in causing your subject personal annoyance or injured feelings in the name of thoroughness. For example: to reproduce the language mannerisms of the interviewee exactly, down to the last "he don't," is good reporting and likely to be revealing of personality. But if the interviewee is a high school teacher, this kind of reporting would be embarrassing and might bring incommensurate penalties (Presidents of the United States have made syntactical errors in public). The reporter has to ask himself: Is the gain from literal reporting sufficient to offset the injury? When public obligation and personal values collide, which one do I protect? Sometimes, indeed, he has to ask a more drastic question: If I cut out the bad grammar and the bad manners, I'll make the story misleading. Is it worth printing if I leave these things in? Or should it all go into the waste basket?

anything his subject says."
The man makes sense.
Magazine writers, working
with more time and space
may spend weeks or months
gathering material for per-
sonality articles—"profiles,"
as the New Yorker *calls*
them. Nathaniel Benchley,
unable to persuade the se-
clusive Greta Garbo to talk
to him, went to more than
30 interviewees for material
for what turned into a re-
vealing article about her.
Newsmen work under cir-
cumstances that often deny
the possibility of this kind
of extended research. But
effort to approach it would
improve their product.

Examples of personality interviews will emphasize some of these observations, and suggest others.

The story about the young socialist, a long Minneapolis *Tribune* Sunday feature, reproduced here only in part, successfully acquaints its reader with a figure modestly in the news. It uses standard devices, direct and indirect quotations, descriptive phrases, background information. Its theme is stated in the second paragraph, that Miss Flodquist "is dissatisfied" with the world she sees around her; and this theme is the key to the personality the coed reveals through her words. Though the story is neither tightly written nor tightly organized, it achieves its purpose. It might do so more effectively if an exacting copy pencil had been applied throughout.

Greta Flodquist is an inquisitive girl, a slip of a socialist with wide eyes who is president of the controversial W. E. B. DuBois Club at the University of Minnesota.

Looking at the world from round, Little-Orphan-Annie blue eyes, Miss Flodquist, at 20, is dissatisfied with it.

"I am committed to taking part in things," she explained last week. "The Peace Movement, for example. I believe that socialism has much to offer us in solving our country's problems.

"But the DuBois Club is very broad. There are many people in it who are not socialists."

If Miss Flodquist could vote, she would vote Democratic. She considers herself an independent spirit, however; 45 years ago, she "might have been a suffragette."

"I suppose you've read Betty Friedan's 'The Feminine Mystique,'" she said. "Some of the things the suffragettes did were very interesting to me. The facts that they weren't masculinized women and that their cause got women into politics are very important."

"Women have unique qualities and there is no need for us to emulate men."

And then, with a beguiling smile, Miss Flodquist added, "But I'm not a man-hater."

Miss Flodquist is aware that men don't often listen to the political views of pretty women.

"I have to really fight sometimes to talk politics to people," she said. "Today, if a man sees a girl with a dress on, he assumes she's not 'political.'

"You don't have to wear sneakers and slacks and be unwashed to think."

Miss Flodquist knows she's oversensitive about her looks and her age. "I just don't look as though I care about Viet Nam and the Dominican Republic," she said.

[The flow of the story is broken here by three paragraphs describing the Du-Bois Club—its purpose "to encourage the development of the United States as a socialist society"—and identifying the man for whom it is named as a Communist.]

"DuBois is important to us," Miss Flodquist said, "because he symbolizes the growth of thinking throughout life. He was a Socialist in the 1930s.

"Even my thinking has changed in only two years at the university." Miss Flodquist is a farm girl who grew up near North Branch. Her parents, Mr. and Mrs. Carl Flodquist, still live there.

"I didn't know what it meant to get people in a community to work for something, for example, until I came here.

"I think of the DuBois Club as an action group. It is interested in student problems at the U—student housing, for example. I'd like to see students have a say on housing rules. They should be allowed, too, to evaluate the courses offered them if they're unhappy with the quality.

"And that's why we participated in the sit-in against the rise in tuition fees. We were faced with higher tuition without consultation. There are other areas—food prices for students, book prices—that need study by student groups."

Miss Flodquist, a theater arts major, is a representative-at-large in the student government association of the university. "The university is a little United States," she said, "and there are many students who don't take part. Only the involved students participate and work on these problems."

She said she thinks the recent sit-in on tuition remained peaceful because university officials were wary after student riots last spring at the University of California. "We sang and we had a quiet study area and we slept," Miss Flodquist said, recalling the 24-hour sit-in in the administration building. "No doors were locked and the campus police brought us coffee. The administration said they didn't care how long we stayed, but I think they really did."

Looking at the world beyond the campus, however, Miss Flodquist, a former 4-H girl and high school cheerleader, said, "The reason I'm involved is that I don't feel I can do what I really want to do without changing things first."

What Miss Flodquist really wants to do is become a modern dancer, with her own dancing company. This summer she will study modern dance at Colorado College.

[A long passage now lets Miss Flodquist develop her belief that wide national support of the arts is a need of society.]

Miss Flodquist, who said she couldn't express herself properly as a socialist or a physicist, believes she can serve important causes through the dance.

"My main concern is peace," she said. "That's why, when I was 16, I took my savings and went to Helsinki, Finland, to the World Youth Festival.

"For a farm girl of 16, it was an exciting thing to go to Europe and speak to foreign people on an individual level. Of course, I went as a typical American expecting everyone to speak English. And they didn't. My parents weren't for it at first, but they relented."

Miss Flodquist said she takes the advice of her parents often, and she doesn't think of herself as a rebel.

When Miss Flodquist thinks about marriage, she doesn't think she will seek out a fellow socialist or even a man with liberal political ideas.

"My husband might even be a Republican," she said. "It might be interesting."

A wrestler whose movie exploits were attracting attention was shown by the following story to be a man of parts. The writer, Mary Blume, seems to have a lady-like tongue in cheek at times; she permits herself the luxury of such asides as "that's show business" and "Maybe there will be a rematch." Permissible in a by-line story, they supplement the quotations and the abundant background facts in a way that adds to the personality picture the story gives.

PARIS—Harold Sakata rose politely to say good-bye to one team of reporters and signaled another team to wait. Considerately, he made his handshake as pulpy as possible, then he pointed to the steel-plated derby on the table.

"This is the hat I throw in fillum on pretty girl's neck," he explained.

The fillum was, of course, "Goldfinger," in which Mr. Sakata draped his sumo-esque shape in an Arthur Treacher outfit and skimmed his derby off his enemies' spinal columns.

Mr. Sakata is 5 feet 9 inches, 37 years old, and 228 pounds. He has a villainous moustache, a baby-like fuzz of black hair, and a very amiable manner.

"I like to be as gentle as possible," he said. "If you're thought of as a villain, then you show the good side in interviews. It's contrast that makes news."

"Goldfinger" is Mr. Sakata's only major film (he tested for the role by breaking the producer's chair with his bare hands) but he has had fifteen years' acting experience as a professional wrestler.

"I'm always the top of the bill," he said. "I give no quarter. I wrestle mercilessly, viciously. I like to beat my opponent down as quickly as possible. I provide very good entertainment."

At the moment he finds his wrestling is more thrilling than ever:

"The difficulty in pictures is that waiting fatigues the bones. In wrestling we have the quick action and opportunity to let off steam."

"My name is nice now. They want to beat me. If they win me they get my good name from me." (Mr. Sakata tends to lapse into Oddjobian dialect when talking shop.)

Last night in Paris, to a fine roar of boos, he wrestled at the Palais des Sports. His opponent was a young hero type. Sakata lost, but that's show business.

Is it harder to perform in films or in the ring?

"That," he said, "is too hard to say. To do both is marvelous."

Harold Toshiyuki Sakata (Toshiyuki, he explains, means rugged and poetic) was born of Japanese parents in Hawaii. He used to call himself the Great Tosh Togo and wear a kimono and Japanese clogs into the ring. Now he is known as Mr. Oddjob and wears the derby, striped trousers and black jacket, with his 19¾-inch neck wrapped in a wing collar. Business has picked up beautifully.

"I get three times more for wrestling than I used to. Since 'Goldfinger' everything I touch has turned to"—he smiled apologetically—"well, gold."

His real estate firms in Honolulu and Los Angeles are booming and he has a Mercedes 300 SL for speed and a Cadillac for comfort. He is thinking of buying an Aston Martin and going into politics.

He turned down a TV series, is considering a fillum in Rome, and recently murdered several people for the Kraft Suspense Theatre. He has a small yearning to play romantic roles.

But he is a sensible man

and it is villainy, he knows, that pays—"people take me as a villain and I gratefully accept it."

On the other hand, he doesn't like being a dead villain. Although Oddjob is electrocuted in "Goldfinger," Mr. Sakata is convinced that he does not really die.

"Under fair conditions James Bond would not stand a chance with the indestructible Oddjob," he affirms. Maybe there will be a rematch one day.

From the following example you may deduce that the personality story does not have to be all revealing. Its writer, a feature writer for one of the news services, appears to have been guided by the question "What would the TV audience want to know about Mrs. Kreitzer?" Had the story been written for the house organ of the naval supply depot in which Mrs. Kreitzer worked, or for a neighborhood newspaper, or for local radio, it would have taken different direction.

Before she won $32,000 on a television program last July, Catharine Kreitzer was a brittle, talkative woman with a deep respect for the Bible and little use for such earthy rewards as fame and money.

Today she is brittle and talkative, and the Bible is still her closest companion. But though she insists she hasn't changed "a whit," there is evidence of a subtle transformation.

A candid conversation in her four-room house just outside Harrisburg, Pa., would indicate that the quiz-show spotlight taught Mrs. Kreitzer a few facets of life that she might—without fame or cash—have been spared.

For one thing, she has discovered that the world has its hand out.

"Most of the mail I get," she admits wearily, "is from people wanting some of that money."

For another, she realizes that it's difficult to get a taste of wealth without wanting more. She has just finished recording a series of five-minute scripture read-

ings for TV and radio. Ask her why and she admits, sheepishly, "For money."

They still live in the little frame home in Possum Hollow, Pa., the "Bible lady" and her husband, James, and two of their grown sons.

"We just go on in the same tenor we did before. I don't see any point in going out and buying things just 'cause you've got a little money."

But she did give some of her winnings to her sons and friends, didn't she?

"Oh, sure," she snapped, waving her hand in the air as if to brush away the whole topic. "I gave $3,600 away. I think it'd be downright stingy of me to use all that money myself.

"After all, everybody can use money. It's a nice gift, don't you think?" she said with a little chuckle.

Mrs. Kreitzer took a seat on a tweedy sofa under a vivid print of "The Last Supper" and said that she hadn't been troubled with press agents or fabulous offers to go to Hollywood, as had been rumored.

"Y'know," she mused, "I used to say I believed about

half of what I read in the papers. Since I was on that show, I don't believe much of anything. I'm surprised they don't have me dyein' my hair red, I'll tell ya."

Actually, Mrs. Kreitzer's hair is almost black and lightly streaked with white. Her face is creamy and almost unlined, and her eyes' quick-flashing quality indicates an alert mind and possibly a quick temper.

She answers almost every question with a sharp, good-humored downdraft of air through her nose—a sort of nasal substitute for the old-fashioned word "pshaw!"

Mrs. Kreitzer became vehement when asked how much mail she gets.

"Barrels!" she says. "The post office over at Camp Hill says I cost 'em an awful lot of money. Most of 'em want some of the money, and most of the rest of 'em want to know what church I belong to."

She explained that she belongs to no church, though she is obviously religious and attended a Bible college in her youth. The reason she does not belong to a church, she said, "is not anything I want to explain."

As for the letters, "what appeals to me, I answer. What don't, I don't." The pleas for money she definitely doesn't answer.

The girls at the office (Mrs. Kreitzer works from 7:30 to 4 in a naval supply depot at Harrisburg) are always telling her to quit. "They say if they had as much money as I had, they wouldn't stick around the joint."

She can't see this reasoning.

"I figure," she says, "a person might as well work while she's healthy."

Meanwhile, the money is stowed away in a bank, and

Mrs. Kreitzer is making regular trips to Baltimore, Md., to make her Bible-reading transcriptions so she can earn more.

She was on relief with her family in the depression, her husband has been laid off work with a pleurisy condition and her government job pays only $3,100 a year.

This combination of elements prompts her to say:

"It's important to have a nest egg. That's all money's good for as far as I'm concerned."

Mrs. Kreitzer conducted a two-room guided tour on the way out, pointing out that upstairs in the white frame house are two bedrooms and

down in the basement is an extra bath. Out back is the winding Condoguonet Creek, and out front is the road back to town.

"Have you noticed any change in your wife since she won all the money?" I asked Kreitzer.

"Her?" He gave the male version of the Kreitzer snort. "You couldn't change her!"

One person tried, his wife conceded.

"I got a phone call from a man in New York who said he would like to take over and handle my affairs. You know what I told him?" she snapped.

"I said I just wasn't going to have any affairs."

Ask yourself some questions about the Kreitzer story: Does it gain or lose from its lack of time element, and by the fact that it moves back and forth from "says" to "said"? Is the writer justified in letting Mrs. Kreitzer say "What don't"? Is he justified in injecting himself close to the end of the story? Does his story support the promises of the second paragraph?

A story tailored for its particular audience, readers of the *New Yorker*, and that would probably seem suitable to no other is this one: [1]

We've met some formidable charmers in our time, but none to surpass the great couturiere and perfumer Mlle. Gabrielle Chanel, who came out of retirement three years ago to present a collection of dress and suit designs that have begun to affect women's styles (and, apparently, women's minds) every bit as powerfully as her designs of thirty-odd years ago did. We met Mlle. Chanel in her suite at the Waldorf Towers, just before she flew back to Paris. She was fresh from three strenuous weeks here and in Dallas, where she went to receive an award as the most significant designer of the last fifty years. At seventy-four, Mlle. Chanel is sensationally good-looking with dark-brown eyes, a brilliant smile,

and the unquenchable vitality of a twenty-year-old, and when, giving us a firm handshake, she said, "I am *très, très fatiguée*," it was with the assurance of a woman who knows she can afford to say it. Since the Chanel look is causing such a stir these days, we took particular note of what its begetter was wearing: a natural-colored straw sailor hat; a natural-colored silk suit, with box jacket and straight skirt; a white silk blouse, with gold cuff links; low-heeled brown-and-white shoes; and plenty of jewelry —a pearl hatpin, pearls and diamonds in her ears, ropes of pearls about her neck, and, on her jacket, an enormous brooch of antique gold studded with rubies, emeralds, and diamonds.

"The brooch is of my design, and the dress is nothing, *très simple*," she said when we congratulated her on her appearance. "The cuff links were given to me by Stravinsky, thirty years ago. The occasion? Admiration, of course—the admiration I bore *him!* You see this ring?" She extended the little finger of her left hand, and a topaz suddenly blazed in the light. "I would trade all my other jewels for this. It was given to me when I was sixteen, in my home province of Auvergne, by an old woman who liked me. She handed me the ring and said, 'Here, *petit Coco*'— let me explain that all my life I have been called Coco; when I was born, my father was away and I was named Gabrielle, which he didn't like, and he made me promise that if anyone called me by that name, I wouldn't answer, and I never have— 'petit Coco,' she said, 'wear this ring always. Never, never let it leave your finger. It will bring you luck, your life will be magnificent.' What she said then, so long ago, has proved true—my life is magnificent."

Mlle. Chanel said that she had been too busy in Texas to do any shopping but had managed to buy a lot of Texas shirts and hats right here in New York, which she was carrying back to Paris to give friends. "In America, it seems to me that people look at me in such a nice way," she said. "In Europe today, it is as if people had no more time to be nice. I liked very much Texas. The people of Dallas, ah, *je les aime beaucoup! Très gentils, très charmants, très simples.* Never in the least haughty." Mlle. Chanel did a skillful and funny pantomime of a haughty person. "I had the stagefright when I went to Dallas, and no wonder, for in truth I was afraid it would be like a huge movie stage, but I found everything real and the people real, like a big family, and the fright went away."

We lighted a cigarette for Mlle. Chanel and asked her how she had happened to be in retirement so long. Her brown eyes flashed. "Never was I really in retirement in my heart," she said. "During the war, nobody thought any more of making beautiful clothes, and after the war I watched the couturiers, the young men, to see what they

were doing. I traveled. I enjoyed life at my country place in Switzerland. But I was bored not having anything real to do. Always, I observed the new clothes. At last, quietly, calmly, with great determination, I began working on *une belle collection*. When I showed it in Paris, I had many critics. They said that I was old-fashioned, that I was no longer of the age. Always I was smiling inside my head, and I thought, I will show them. In America, there was great enthusiasm. In France, I had to fight. But I did not mind. I love very much to fight. Now, in France, they are trying to adapt my ideas. So much the better! But when I see some things they call 'after *la mode Chanel*,' I protest vigorously. There are no potato sacks among my dresses!

"I must tell you something of significance. Fashion is always of the time in which you live. It is not something standing alone. The problem of fashion in 1925 was different. Women were just beginning to go to work in offices. I inspired the cutting of the hair short because it goes with the modern woman. To the woman going to work, I said to take off the bone corset, because women cannot work while they are imprisoned in a corset. I invented the tweed for sports and the loose-fitting sweater and blouse. I encouraged women to be well groomed and to like perfume—a woman who is badly perfumed is not a woman! The problem today is *très dif-*

ferent. Nearly all women work, and if they don't work they want to work. So many women in France have a little car. This you cannot do with a crinoline skirt. Many of the big fortunes today have crumbled. In former years, rich women did not go shopping themselves. Now they do. Today people travel a lot. The clothes must be light in weight for the flying. But the grand problem is to rejuvenate women. To make women look young. Then their outlook on life changes. They feel more joyous."

Mlle. Chanel flicked the ash off the last inch of her cigarette, which she held pinched between the thumb and forefinger of her left hand. "As for myself," she said, "I am not interested any more in this year. It is gone for me. I am more interested in next year, and the next, and the next. Women have always been the strong ones of the world. The men are always seeking from women a little pillow to put their heads down on. They are always longing for the mother who held them as infants. Women must tell them always that *they* are the ones. *They* are the big, the strong, the wonderful. In truth, women are the strong ones. It is just my opinion. I am not a professor. I am not a preacher. I speak my opinions gently. It is the truth for me. I am not young, but I feel young. The day I feel old, I will go to bed and stay there. *J'aime la vie!* I feel that to live is a wonderful thing."

This story departs from some of the conventions of news writing, but any newsman can take from it hints to follow in personality interviews. Among them:

1) The careful description of the interviewee—more detailed than in most such stories

2) Skillful use of simple French expressions easy for the *New Yorker* audience to understand

3) Sparing and subtle use of French expressions in English—enough to give the appropriate flavor: "I like very much Texas," "light in weight for the flying," "the grand problem," and others. The effect is achieved with few rather than many such expressions.

The News Conference

"News conference" is the term for a twentieth-century newsgathering device developed to give newspapermen access to news sources not available individually to all of them. President Theodore Roosevelt was one of the first to give the news conference respectability; some of his successors in high places, and hundreds at other levels, followed the pattern. Typically, a conference of this kind brings together a group of newsmen to face a major news source—a government official, a business leader, a public figure—whom many newsmen would like to interview. Sometimes the "host" to the conference offers newsmen nothing more than a prepared statement or a set of prepared answers to questions submitted in writing in advance. More commonly, however, the news conference offers opportunity for relatively free give-and-take of questions and ad lib answers; this pattern, established by the second Roosevelt, has prevailed at Presidential news conferences most of the time since.

Significant changes in Presidential news conferences occurred in the years following the advent of television. Under the hand of James Hagerty, news secretary to President Eisenhower, the conferences were opened to tape recordings and to sound motion pictures for use by broadcasting and newsreels. Under the Hagerty system, complete tape and film records of a conference were edited and made available to all media soon after the conference ended. Thus the traditional inhibition on direct quotation of a President was virtually swept away; and a much more intimate look at the President and the newsgathering process was provided to the public.

Under President Kennedy the process was extended to live television—a possibility only when the President was supremely confident of his ability to say the right thing (for no editing was possible). This extension, though not considered fully successful, either by the White House or the news media, seems likely to continue in a form modified as individual presidents wish.

The news conference at a less exalted level has become a fixture of the American news-dissemination process; public figures of every kind, from nuclear physicists to Hollywood starlets meet the press in groups. Often such a conference is arranged at the newsmen's wish to enable all interested reporters to have access to a news figure on a basis of equal opportunity. Sometimes the news figure himself sets up the conference, and sometimes newsmen look cynically on such opportunities when they think the self-interest of the news figure is more at stake than the news that is likely to develop. But they rarely miss attending, even when they're skeptical, for they know their competitors will be there.

Rivalry between newspaper and radio-TV reporters has led to some difficulties in news conferences, and some absurdities. When the newsmen of the air were inexperienced in news conference practice there was some substance to the newspaper reporters' complaint that their rivals asked no questions on their own but simply took advantage of newspaper skill. However, this complaint has little merit today; indeed, the professional competence of radio and TV reporters often reverses it.

The introduction of cameras, recorders, and such technical gear raises thorny problems. Some especially good-natured news sources hold two conferences, one for newspaper reporters, another for radio and TV. But as both technical equipment of the broadcasters and their professional competence develop this absurdity will disappear.

A final complaint made by experienced reporters about news conferences is that they are likely to be superficial. "A reporter isn't going to reveal his ideas for a really good story in front of a dozen competitors," a Midwest radio news director has explained. "Not only that, but the news personality isn't likely to talk as fully or candidly before a group as he would in a one-to-one conversation. I go to news conferences, but if I have something really 'good' in mind I try to set up a private interview." (The use of the news conference by sophisticated news sources to block the use of news information is suggested in chapter 8.)

SUGGESTED READINGS

Interviewing is a major tool in a number of professions: social work, psychiatry, law, medicine, and personnel work of all kinds. In some of these fields intensive studies of the uses, techniques, and problems of the interview have yielded knowledge directly helpful to news workers. Among useful reports on such studies:

Garrett, Annette, *Interviewing: Its Principles and Practices.* New York: Family Welfare Association of America, 1942. A manual on social work interviewing, with many suggestions that apply directly to journalistic interviewing.

Kahn, R. L., and C. F. Cannell, *The Dynamics of Interviewing.* New York: John Wiley & Sons, Inc., 1957.

Maccoby, Eleanor E. and Nathan, "The Interview: A Tool of Social Science," in Gardner Lindzey, ed., *Handbook of Social Psychology.* Reading, Mass.; Addison-Wesley Publishing Company, Inc., 1954.

Merton, Robert K, Marjorie Fiske, and Patricia L. Kendall, *The Focused Interview.* New York: The Free Press of Glencoe, 1956. The "focused interview" is very much the typical news interview—an interview of those with known information on a defined subject on which the interviewer can make advance preparation. The book is especially helpful on opening the interview, evaluation of responses, and the group interview.

Interviewing for NORC. Denver: National Opinion Research Center, 1945. Concrete suggestions for interviewers, along with instructions on designing samples, opinion studies, and the like.

PROJECTS

1. Drawing from current newscasts and newspapers, select a number of local news topics to which the news interview process would lend understanding or illumination. Name the appropriate interviewees and appropriate leading questions for each.
2. Following the procedures outlined in this chapter, develop two or more of the interviews suggested in project 1. Write the stories as you think they should be used by a local newspaper or broadcasting station.
3. Select two subjects for personality interviews, one chosen because he is a current news figure and the other because some trait of personality, occupation, or habit makes him worth portraying. Write each of the stories, after conducting the interviews, for local consumption.

CHAPTER 15

Human Interest in News

What Is a Feature?

The term *feature,* one of the most common among newsmen, is one of the least precise. It has become a newsroom catchall. In the scores of contests every year for news story excellence, the category *feature,* or *news feature,* or *short feature*—or more than one of them, or something else with *feature* as part of the description—is pretty sure to be included. Rarely is there a definition with the term; and the wide range of the entries shows that newsmen have no consensus as to what the label means.

Facing the problem because he was so often asked to judge such contests, the publisher of the Denver *Post,* Palmer Hoyt, asked for help from Alexis McKinney, a veteran of 30 years in the newsroom. McKinney came up with a definition that said in part:

> A feature finds its impact outside or beyond the realm of the straight news story's basic and unvarnished who-what-where-when-why and how.
> The justification, strength and very identity of the feature lie in its penetration of the imagination—not in departing from or stretching truth but in piercing the peculiar and particular truths that strike people's curiosity, sympathy, skepticism, humor, consternation, or amazement.
> Writing a feature story is not just recitation of facts, . . . but rather an adroit presentation of facts and associated ideas so as to spotlight that which is significant but not apparent to the casual observer.

The McKinney definition is a sound start; but it stops too soon. The term *feature* also blankets in many kinds of material of nonimaginative, nonemotive content. In its broadest meaning it is safer to say that it is material selected for presentation by a mass medium primarily because of some element other than the timeliness of its materials. This approach eliminates neither the McKinney

241

emphasis on emotional values—indeed, it emphasizes it—nor the element of timeliness. It does mean, however, that the recency of the material is not the dominant characteristic, either for the medium or the consumer. The peak of interest comes from one or more other elements.

More specifically, newsmen would refer to all the following types of materials—some news, some not—as features.

SIMPLE HUMAN INTEREST STORIES

The man who ate 15 pies on a bet and ended in the hospital

The girl who forgot to attend her own wedding because she was having her hair set

The ambulance attendant who discovered the boy in the auto accident was his son

These are stories that fit the McKinney definition. They get into the news because of their oddity, their pathos, their entertainment value, rather than because they contribute significantly to knowledge of ongoing community life. Some of them would be reported because they are *also* spot news; others wouldn't be granted a nod were it not for the human interest element. In any of them the recency factor would be included; but it would not be the point of emphasis or the reason for their selection.

SIDEBARS OR SECOND-DAY STORIES

The fact that nobody in town could get water pressure to sprinkle his lawn during the big fire downtown

The resentment of the young man that his fiancée, just chosen Miss Jaycee, can find time for only one date a week with him

The pitcher's glumness—or his laughing it off—when the third batter in the ninth spoils his no-hitter

The factual listing of all this year's heavy rains that made yesterday's downpour doubly disastrous

Stories like these combine a sense of timeliness with their function of adding something to understanding of an event reported elsewhere. Usually they are strong in human interest; but they may serve only to illuminate or supplement the major facts of current news events.

NEWS FEATURES   These stories might be called "featurized news." They are similar to sidebars in their dependence on timely news events; but the distinction is that they treat news of some importance or news that must be reported for a reason other than its human interest though with emphasis on its human interest. Sidebars and "pure" human interest stories are usually brief; news features are often long. For example:

The story about the pistol-packin' secretary of state (page 156)

A story detailing the horrors and fears of a pair of elderly women when, finding themselves locked in a burning house, they feared they couldn't escape— and how they did

A story narrating the experiences of a ski-equipped search party trying to find climbers lost in a mountain snow slide

Background or Interpretive Stories

A story showing that old-timers are more common offenders in traffic court than first-timers

The story analyzing and explaining the use of personality tests (see page 222)

The story evaluating local housing problems in view of an influx of new families (see page 213)

A physicist's explanation of why he thinks the public should (or shouldn't) be concerned about the possibilities of nuclear radiation

These are stories that would not be developed if the newspaper or broadcaster were interested only in reporting "news that occurs." They add importantly to public understanding of current news.

Color Stories

The reaction of the crowd at an auto race when a fatal smashup occurred

The behavior of all the girls who didn't get crowned when the beauty queen was picked

The atmosphere of a college campus at 2 A.M. when nobody is around but watchmen and night-owl students and researchers in a few offices

The color story is one that attempts to put the reader or listener squarely into the setting it is describing. It is essentially a descriptive story, but one descriptive of a scene or the surrounding circumstances of an activity of some current interest. It tries to make the scene audible, visible, even smellable.

Special-page Materials   Household hints, child care columns, health and hygiene columns, how-to-win-at-bridge, etiquette, gardening, movie gossip columns, comic strips, do-it-yourself material . . . the list is endless. Such materials have no time element. They are often syndicated, prepared by a distant agency and provided on contract in similar forms to many media. They are not to be considered further in this book.

All of these are "features." Many of them are, as news jargon has it, time copy. The remainder of this chapter is devoted to examination of the kinds of features that are strong in human interest and that come within the usual ranges of operation of reporters: human interest stories, news features, color stories.

Human Interest Stories

A story strong in human interest is one that gives the reader or listener a sense of personal relationship as he responds to the event it describes. There are often human-interest elements in hard news, elements that provide the sense of personal involvement to the news consumer. But the true human-interest story establishes emotional contact quickly with its audience, and remains primarily an emotional rather than an informative or intellectual experience. When a story horrifies or amuses a reader, excites or depresses him, stimulates his sympathy or his sexual appetites, saddens or angers him, or appeals to his self-interest in any way, he becomes a vicarious participant instead of an outside observer. Since such a story allows the consumer to respond emotionally rather than intellectually, it requires less concentration and effort than are demanded by hard news.

Should this definition look familiar, it is because it is lifted from chapter 3. Human interest is one of the factors of "good" news, one of the factors that newsmen look for in deciding what news situations are worth space and time. It is the factor that most strongly draws and holds readers or listeners; it is commonly the element that gives them "immediate reward" satisfaction (see page 42), the element that one of Hearst's talented editors implied when he said, "We run our papers so that when the reader opens it he says, 'Gee whiz!'"

In 1949 America was stirred to its bones by the tragedy of a little girl in California, little Kathy Fiscus, who fell into a well shaft and there died. "For two days the great affairs of a nation took second place in the minds and hearts of the people," commented the St. Paul Dispatch *in an editorial. Its concluding paragraph helps to define the place of emotion in the lives of men and women:*

"The tragedy of a little girl in the shaft of a well is one that the human heart comprehends at once, and to which it responds with all the nobility that distinguishes it from the base and the brutal. But the tragedy of a million people in China or India in the grip of a famine, or of a city wiped out at a flash of a bomb, or of an army being cut to

Recognition, understanding, and evaluation of human interest as a constituent in news appeal have to run through any thinking about news. You take it into account when you examine the composition of news audiences, when you talk about effective news style, when you consider functional patterns by which to package news, when you plan and execute a newsgathering assignment. Realization of emotional and sensuous values is basic to every phase of the work of a newsman.

DEVELOPING HUMAN INTEREST NEWS   A city editor does not assign a reporter to a human-interest beat as he does a man to the city hall or the police station. Human interest news does not center in circumscribed areas as does most solid news. It is true that much police news, for example, is strong in human interest qualities. But the police reporter learns to think of these qualities as a kind of bonus—something always to be sought, but not always present. The city editor does not ask his reporters to "go out and get human interest stories"; he talks in spe-

pieces on the steppes of Russia—this kind of mass calamity becomes as something read about abstractly in a book. The fate of the individuals is swallowed up in the vastness of the event. It is only when human suffering is broken down into the terms of one particular human being that it can be directly felt by the heart and comprehended by the mind."

cific terms: "See whether you can get a good yarn about how the family feels about their son's becoming a racing driver"; "Be sure to find out how people are acting, and what they say, when they're flooded out of their homes"; "Don't report just what firms have floats in the parade—get me the comments people are making about them." These examples suggest the principle that human interest is likely to show itself in *human* situations—in situations involving people.

The development of the human interest story, to put it differently, is likely to result from the news imagination reacting to a set of news facts. The reporter observes an event or a situation; he thinks, "If I ask such-and-such questions, I can build a human interest story out of it." Sometimes there is no other way to get a publishable story from it. Sometimes a sidebar or secondary story may develop out of an event's emotive aspects. Sometimes a news situation can be shown in its true light only by building the emotive values integrally into the major story (as, for instance, in the story of the Udall tornado, page 115).

One of the news services reported the development of one such story by Alvin L. Krieg, its reporter covering the Ohio Department of Education. Krieg learned that a little girl had written plaintively to ask whether her school was to be shut down. Krieg recognized in the occasion "a swell news story in itself . . . it had human appeal." He suggested to the Department a sympathetic reply, and got it—but in terms of three-mill levies and tax rates. Krieg redrafted the letter for the Department "so that a 12-year-old could understand it" (he confessed his debt to the New York *Sun's* famous "Yes, Virginia, there is a Santa Claus" letter). And the story he wrote not only had deep meaning for the whole state, but it was told in terms everybody would read. Its opening paragraphs:

The State of Ohio today gave its word that "the schools will stay open."

The promise was given in a letter . . . sent by Joseph W. Fichter, assistant Ohio director of education, to a little Alliance girl, 12-year-old Mary Eileen Kelly.

But it is more than a letter to one little girl—for it is the state's "word of honor" to every last one of the million and a quarter boys and girls in the public schools of the state. Fichter's letter contained this message:

"Yes, Mary, your school will stay open. I cannot tell you at this moment just how long it will be done, but your question will help us to find the answer."

[*The story goes on at length to recite details of the girl's question and official action to answer it.*]

This kind of story depends not alone on its intrinsic material but also on the reporter's recognition of its values. Without the personal contribution the newsman makes to the news situation—not often in direct participation, as in the Krieg case, but always in perceptiveness and sensitive writing—human interest news would be rarer and less meaningful than today's journalism has made it. (How much space would the appendectomy-under-enemy-waters story have earned, for example, if it had been written "straight," without George Weller's sensitive perception?)

THE SUSPENDED-INTEREST FORM   Human interest stories are often presented in a formalized rhetorical package that takes advantage of the emotive nature of the components: the suspended-interest form.

This form employs a particular compositional device, as does the straight-news form. The straight-news form, to repeat what the reader of this book already knows well, opens with a summary of the major facts, an opening that lets the consumer decide instantly whether the subject is for him.

The suspended-interest form, as its name implies, moves in the opposite direction: it forces the reader to stay with the story if he is to learn its major fact. It intentionally holds back one or more of the story's principal points so as to inveigle, trap, or beguile reader or listener to stay with it. It is a self-conscious form, one having kinship with the narrative pattern of the short story; its purpose is to keep its audience in doubt as to the outcome throughout some, if not all, of the story.

Were it not for the effectiveness of this pattern, many trivial events that find space in crowded news columns or air time would die unrecorded. The straight-news pattern is useless with news of this kind. A straight face would make ludicrous the publication of much of it, as the following familiar example illustrates. It concerns the ambulatory fire that goes looking for the firemen. Take these facts (they're real):

Two policemen in Denver stopped auto driver John Marselle on a crowded viaduct, their siren halting traffic. Marselle, puzzled, asked, "Why?" Police explained that his car was on fire. They radioed the police dispatcher, who told them to take the car to a fire station two blocks away. The dispatcher notified the fire station. When the car arrived, firemen put the fire out.

Were this story to be written as straight-news, it would probably be told something like this:

> Firemen at Blank Station this morning extinguished a flame in a car owned and driven by John Marselle, such-and-such an address. Marselle had been halted on Midtown Viaduct, informed that his car was on fire, and sent to the fire station.

In straight form, the story has little interest for anybody but Marselle and his friends. It certainly is not worth putting on press service trunk wires. But the Associated Press sent it, in suspended-interest treatment, throughout the nation:

> DENVER, March 25 (AP)—"What in blazes are you stopping me for?" asked John Marselle when two policemen sirened his car to a stop on a crowded viaduct today. "Your car's on fire," they replied, radioing the police dispatcher for instructions. They were told to take the car to a fire station two blocks away. Firemen were waiting, and quickly extinguished the blaze.

The principal characteristics of the suspended-interest form appear in this brief story. The factual material is marked by one of the common human interest characteristics: amusing oddity. Its lead is of the hold-back type: it gets the story going and, its writer intends, arouses reader curiosity, but it avoids "giving away" the heart of the event. Finally, the reader must go to the end of the story to learn its denouement, the dousing of the fire, which the straight story put first.

This story follows a chronological pattern (as, incidentally, does the statement of basic facts—a common conversational pattern). Many suspended-interest stories are told chronologically, beginning at the start of the event and ending at its close. The following story is notable not only as an example of expert handling of the chronological pattern but also for the economy of its style. By short sentences, lack of adornment, and exclusion of unnecessary detail, its writer has made it move as fast as the event itself.

"My sister's in the hole . . . my sister's in the hole . . ."

This alarm, sounded quick and loud by 5-year-old Suzan Frazier, 8308 17th Av. S., Bloomington, produced a chain reaction about 8 P.M. Monday.

Tony Koval, 45, 8313 17th Av. S., who was fixing his fence, saw the girl running across the street from a storm sewer excavation.

Koval understood. He dropped his hammer and ran toward the excavation, shouting for help.

Raymond C. LeValley, 8301 17th Av. S., dropped his newspaper and raced through his front door. Bruce Swenson, 8337 17th Av. S., was talking to Marvin Goulet, 580 Holly Av., a contractor's man keeping an eye on a pump.

The two men broke into a sprint. By the time they and LeValley reached the spot, Koval had discovered a speck of Jeanmarie Louise Frazier, 8, almost completely buried by an earth cave-in.

"First I saw a hand, then I could see her eyes," Koval said.

The four men got down on their knees and dug with their hands "like gophers," releasing the girl before emergency equipment arrived.

Jeanmarie, flustered and frightened, ran home unhurt.

QUESTION OF TACTICS: *In the AP story Marselle is credited with asking, "What in the blazes are you stopping me for?" One wonders whether this is not a reportorial invention—gratuitous embroidery by a reporter who thinks the play on words makes his story more effective. It can be argued that this kind of "bright"* *writing sharpens a story, and that its false tone is unimportant since it misleads nobody about the major facts.*

But the astute reader is likely to spot the play on words as the reporter's fiction; and he can hardly be blamed if, seeing one piece of fiction, he asks what others the reporter (and *perhaps the paper for which the reporter writes, and perhaps all news media) may have indulged in. It is one thing to hang an invention on a participant in an event, as apparently has been done here. It is another, a defensible variation, to write it so that it is indisputably clear that it's invention, not reporting.*

But there is also a suspended-interest pattern, either chronological or more complex of structure, that holds back the significant fact only partly through the story. The Marselle story, for example, could have been constructed thus:

John Marselle took a fire to the firemen today.

Stopped by policemen on Midtown Viaduct with word that his car was on fire, Marselle drove to the Blank fire station, two blocks away. There the fire was put out.

Firemen at Blank station had been warned by the police dispatcher, whom the police had radioed.

In this version the key fact is revealed at the end of the second paragraph; the third paragraph, secondary material, could be omitted without much loss. This kind of compromise between the straight-news form and the form that holds back until the end typifies what may be the most common usage in suspended-interest stories.

It does not follow that, because the suspended-interest form is used almost exclusively for news of emotional impact, human interest news is always presented in this form. For one thing, some news exceedingly strong in human interest—a riot in New Delhi, an earthquake in Santiago, the death of a Churchill, the crushing of a rebellion—is so evidently important that sober, straight treatment is mandatory. The human-interest elements in the rebellion story—the savagery of conflict, the death of humans and their hopes, open and secret passions—shine through the structure of the conventional story even though they are not emphasized. If you open a story "Angry peasants swinging machetes and ax handles today swarmed over the Chancellery of . . . ," you don't have either to tell the reader there's human interest in it or tease him into reading it.

The reporter who brings imagination to his work sometimes finds in story material itself the inspiration for special story treatment—special adaptation of form to matter. For example: a court reporter who found himself with a little feature about a woman juror whose stocking had been torn on a jury chair. The lady wrote a piece of doggerel to the judge, asking damages. The reporter opened his story in this way:

A letter terse but rhythmic, and framed in phrases gay, arrived upon Judge

> Leary's bench in court the
> other day. The judge saw
> no one bring it and can't
> remember, now, the incident
> described therein, nor when,
> nor why, nor how.
>
> But ever since the letter
> came the judge has tried to
> find a way to solve the is-
> sue and get it off his mind.
> He's thumbed his tomes,
> he's scratched his head, he's
> racked his aching brain to
> reach a just decision the
> high court might sus-
> tain . . .

Some of the examples later in this chapter demonstrate adaptation of pattern to material.

HUMAN INTEREST NEWS ON THE AIR   Of the communication of human interest news on radio, at least insofar as gathering and writing such news is concerned, there is nothing to say that has not already been said in this book. Except that a radio reporter adapts his style to the special needs of a listening instead of a reading audience, he performs no differently from the print reporter. Radio uses less human interest news than most newspapers do, both in sum and in ratio, largely because of its lack of time (though a good many of the more folksy newscasters like to close their newscasts with human interest "kickers" if they can get them). The informality and personalization of radio style, however, often seem to give radio news a more personal impact than the printed page offers.

News on television, in contrast, has given heavy emphasis to human interest. TV's need to take advantage of its distinctive tool, the picture, leads it to put stress on news that can be interestingly illustrated; and interesting illustrations are likely to be those of parades, of dramatic accidents, of sports and fires and policemen's clambakes—pictures involving news of people doing extraordinary things or of spectacles, rather than of ideas or sober governmental procedure. The most responsible TV newscasters are aware of this impulse to overemphasize human interest and many are meeting it with the development of new techniques or with resorting to a greater use of man-on-camera.

The banality and unhumor of many of the short "brights" or "kickers" with which some radio newscasts close, and with which some newspapers fill the holes at the bottoms of columns, have led a number of newsmen to satirical comment. In the Arizona *Republic, Don Dedera burlesqued the wire service "brights" with a number of parodies pointed at their hackneyed character and "predictable punchlines." Here are two:*

BROOKLYN—The customers of Lily Liefgreen, who dressed in rags and sold flowers in the streets, always assumed she was penniless.

Yesterday she died. Officers searched her humble apartment. Sure enough, she was penniless.

APPLECORE, Ore.— Six months ago Mink, a Persian cat, leaped out of the car of the vacationing Harvey Snowdecker family at St. Joseph, Mo.

Yesterday the cat turned up in Jacksonville, Fla., still walking in the wrong direction.

A number of human interest stories, or stories strong in human interest, in the earlier pages of this book illustrate other facets of news handling. Note especially those (see pages 115, 156, 204, 209, 229) that are only secondarily human interest stories, but in which it has seemed appropriate to bring out human interest values.

For additional study, here are a number of stories chosen to illustrate both strengths and weaknesses.

These two short stories hold the punchline to the last:

WASHINGTON (AP)— Alfred C. Peterson takes great pride in saving money. And he puts his money in the bank.

But he made banking history yesterday when he persuaded the Second National Bank to let him see the $163 he had saved over the last year.

He was admitted to the teller's cage, where the money was shown him. Peterson counted it carefully, expressed satisfaction, and then left with his mother.

After all, a 7-year-old boy who has earned $163 in after-school chores has to be careful.

The city editor's telephone rang. "When is Robert Penn Warren scheduled to lecture?" the caller asked.

The city editor got somebody to look it up, and reported.

"Thank you," said the caller. "Where's it to be? And what's the subject?"

The city editor told him. Then he got curious?

"Who is calling?" he asked.

"Robert Penn Warren," was the answer.

The material for the following story is ready made—nobody could miss its general interest. But the writer of the story, by failure to organize his facts and tighten his writing, came close to killing its effect:

BRIGHTON, England (AP)—A 22-year-old student brought a touch of Elizabethan England to the 20th century Friday.

As Queen Elizabeth II walked among the puddles on a visit to the new University of Sussex near Brighton the student, Peter Horne, threw down his black plastic raincoat for her to step on.

The queen smiled at the gallant gesture, as her namesake, Elizabeth I, had done four centuries earlier when Sir Walter Raleigh, so legend has it, threw down his cloak for her.

The queen walked across

one corner of the raincoat and turned a handsome royal smile on Horne.

Crowds had waited in continuous rain for a glimpse of the queen as she drove from Brighton to the university—Britain's newest.

It was as she walked from her car to open a new 400,-000-pound ($1.1 million) library that the modern-day Raleigh act took place.

As she picked her way among the puddles, student Horne dashed forward and threw down his plastic coat —price, when new: 30 shillings ($4.20). Horne is a post-graduate student studying politics.

Once in a while an outright trick adds zest to a story (remember also the two-word story on page 121):

> MUNICH,   Germany
> (UP)—
>
> Could be the first paragraph is there all right, but you just don't see it. Invisible colors, you know, like the whistle that a dog can hear but a man can't.
> A scientist here in Munich says it may be the answer to the atom bomb: invisible factories and invisible men. His name is . . .
> [*and so on*]

Sympathy and understated writing, in the story that follows, turn a neighborhood incident into an appealing story. Note the chronological pattern, following the generalized "mood" opening:

> Most little boys have dreamed at one time or another of building a real fort —complete with stockade and lookout towers.
> Bruce Nauth, 8, and Bruce Barker, 9, did their dreaming one stormy day last month. And they wrote this letter to Mayor Eric Hoyer:
> "Dear, Mr. Mayor Hoyer:
> "We would like to build a fort on a swamp across from E. 58th St in the woods at Minneapolis, Minn.
> "May we please cut down trees for our fort. well you please take this up at one of the meetings. Thankyou
> "My friend and I are 8 an a half. We will build it in the next summer.
>
> "signed
>
> sincerely your
>
> Major Bruce Nauth
> Colonel Bruce Barker"
>
> Today, by official directive of the mayor, the boys will stand inspection by Col. Joseph M. McCarthy, chief of the Minnesota military district.
> City Engineer Hugo Erickson will join a party of city and military officials who will survey the site.
> Hoyer directed the party to be present at a "southern exploratory outpost at the corner of Fifty-eighth Street and Sixteenth Avenue S. at 1600 hours in accordance with the urgent request of Col. Barker and Maj. Nauth."
> Hoyer said a decision on construction of the outpost probably will be made after the survey and inspection.
> What do the boys think about the official reaction to their letter? Col. Barker summed it up in one word: "Gee!"
> He's the son of . . .

The chronological pattern of the story from Germany persists only halfway; then it goes to background. The final four paragraphs return it to the immediate scene:

BAMBERG, Germany (AP)—The little Jew stood sadly in Bamberg's Jewish cemetery and tears came to his eyes.

Before him were gravestones smeared with swastikas and anti-Semitic slogans.

"During Hitler's time there were worse things done," he said sadly. "But now, 20 years after, this . . . it is a real shock."

Venom was smeared in red, brown, gray and white over the Hebrew and German inscriptions on the tombstones. On one, a picture of Hitler had been attached. Under it was written, "Here rests a Jew pig."

Across four stones was "The SS is alive . . . 6,000,-000 are too few." The Nazis murdered 6 million Jews.

The little Jew watched as two young men from Bamberg's YMCA placed a wreath on one of the defiled graves. A ribbon on the wreath said: "Bamberg's Youth Mourns. Forgive Us, Brothers." A representative of the city's workers laid a similar wreath.

Bamberg, a conservative Bavarian city, saw its synagogue burned down by SS (elite guard) men and rowdies in 1938. Willy Lessing, a popular Jewish citizen, was beaten to death when he tried to save the synagogue's holy scriptures.

After the war, city authorities named a street for Willy Lessing. It quietly pursued its Bavarian politics and predominantly Roman Catholic ways—until Sunday, June 12.

That was the day the city fathers had scheduled the unveiling of a monument to the burned synagogue. Two hours before the ceremony, a swastika was discovered smeared on the shrine. On the wall of a building facing the monument were the words "Judas verrecke," a misspelling of the old Nazi cry "Juda verrecke" that incited mobs to kill Jews.

Two days later the wife of the cemetery caretaker found the desecrated gravestones.

Who? Why?

"I think a new organization has sprung up and will get bolder yet," said the sad little man, one of the 71 Jews left in Bamberg. There were 1,200 before Hitler.

Police and religious authorities have received anonymous calls warning that the smearings will continue.

The writer of the Freddy the Robot story succeeds in giving the firm impression of his presence at the event, without naming himself. He has concentrated the attention on Freddy, perhaps at the expense of the surrounding event.

Freddy the Robot is looking for a girl friend.

She doesn't have to love him—robots don't have emotions—just keep him "company" as he goes on tour with Ford Motor Co.'s "Magic World of Ford."

The Magic Talking Robot (or "Freddy Ford" as he's called by his intimates) is a 9-foot, 800-pound robot. He is on display at Southdale Shopping Center through June 26.

Built from automobile parts—with blinking parking light eyes, brake-drum hands, oil pan feet and muffler arms—Freddy gives stock answers to a dozen questions fed by a push-button machine on the Southdale plaza floor.

Occasionally, when the management isn't looking, he ad libs to curious children and roving reporters.

Yesterday, while talking on the sly from his dash panel chest, Freddy disclosed that he could use a girl friend on his job.

"I'm not lonely," he assured his audience. "Robots don't suffer as humans do . . . I'd just like a little company."

Freddy told his audience, mostly of youngsters, that he hadn't voiced his complaint to the company higher-ups. "There aren't enough of us in the country to unionize yet," he said. "When there are, maybe we'll refuse to talk."

He explained that robots like himself would never be able to picket. "We're too cumbersome," he said.

When he told the group of youngsters crowded around him that he was superior to man, not only in his lack of emotions but in height, one little girl popped up with a remark that left Freddy speechless: "I bet you're not as tall as the Green Giant," she said.

Freddy's head and arms move by 120 volts of electric current. His answers are fed by 20 tape recordings located in his interior. A Ford representative ad libs through a concealed microphone hookup on the floor of the plaza.

The artificial holdback until the end of the story can be applied to a longer as well as a shorter story. In the following piece, the writer has made effective use of dialogue:

COLUMBUS, Ohio (UP) —"Dapper Dan," the gun-waving fashion plate currently bothering Columbus merchants, got his comeuppance early Saturday from Korean War veteran Ernest (Ernie) Knight, 38.

At 2:30 A.M. the manager of the Y-Not Cafe, Tom Hanson, was sacking the nights receipts. Barmaid Mae Davis was wiping the bar.

The young thug emerged from a dark corner booth and fished a nickeled .32-caliber revolver from his pocket. The barmaid nudged Ernie and said, "That guy's got a gun pointed at you."

"Freeze. Don't take a step," the gunman ordered.

Ernie, waiting to take Miss Davis home, quietly sipped his beer.

"Get over there or I'll shoot," the bandit cried impatiently. Ernie sipped more beer, then said:

"I've looked down too many barrels to be afraid of a punk like you. If you're planning to use that rod, boy, go ahead and use it. I think you're too yellow to shoot."

Flustered, the bandit pistol-whipped Ernie. "Chicken," Ernie taunted the man.

But young Dapper Dan was busy with the bar's receipts, about $350, he had forced the manager to sack for him.

"Let's see," Ernie said

aloud, "you're about five feet eight, weight about 145, blue overcoat . . ."

"You won't live to see me again," the bandit screamed.

". . . white shirt, blue and white tie."

Dan was shaking with fear and rage. But he had the money, so he started for the door. Only then did Ernie move from his bar stool. Stiffly he started after the bandit. But the thug ran down an alley into darkness.

"Ernie would probably have got him and dragged him back," Hanson said later, "except he couldn't run that fast on his artificial legs. He lost both his legs in combat, you know."

More a socio-historical commentary than a news story, the following story understandably comes from a weekly news review, the *National Observer*.

By tradition, the Mississippi Delta begins in the lobby of the Peabody Hotel here in Memphis and runs south to Catfish Row in Vicksburg.

Between these points lies the richest soil west of the Nile, nurtured through the centuries by the topsoil deposited by the Mississippi River.

Over the years, the planters have grown rich by harvesting three or more bales of cotton to an acre. Much of their cash has been spent in Memphis and, in particular, at the Peabody Hotel.

Not too many years ago, candidates for governor of Mississippi announced their

availability in the Peabody lobby, and more than one Mississippi campaign was charted in a smoky upstairs room.

Memphis is just some 70 miles north of Oxford, Miss., home of the University of Mississippi, one of the nation's great football powers. Over the years, Ole Miss has played many of its home games here in Memphis.

On such weekends, the Peabody has served as alumni house and fraternity row. The story is still told —but not quite vouched for —about the night an old grad, a wealthy Mississippi planter, broke his flask of bourbon on a lobby pillar

after Ole Miss had dropped a close one.

"You can't do that, sir," the manager told him.

Without a word, the old grad pulled a $100 bill from his pocket and dispatched a bellhop to buy a case of bourbon.

When the boy returned with the bourbon, the planter smashed all the bottles, slowly, one at a time. Or so the story goes, in a Delta land that changes slowly.

But if the Delta remains pretty much unchanged, the Peabody hasn't.

With no announcement, the Peabody a few days ago quietly registered its first Negro guest.

Finally, one of Dorothy Kilgallen's syndicated New York columns. Its subject and treatment place it clearly in the human-interest category; and it is of particular interest here because of Miss Kilgallen's caustic scorn for a certain form of journalism:

I suppose in Europe a genuine, 14-karat accredited member of a royal family gets used to saying black is white and having the subjects murmur, "You said it, Prince, that black shoe cer-

tainly is the ghostliest." Just as he can check into a hotel as Mr. Doodad and have everyone pretend not to notice the coronets embroidered on his sleeves.

If they find this fun, and

the subjects agree, I don't mind at all—but I do think some liaison expert ought to tell them when they come over here that the system doesn't work quite the same in the USA, even for so pretty and well-tailored a chap as Prince Christian of Hanover.

Okay, his sister is a queen and he looks like an absolute darling, but this is not going to make me lose my journalistic head to the point where if I see him walk into a plush rhumba joint with a flashy blond on his arm I am going to write that he took an ugly old aunt to high tea at the Tuesday afternoon meeting of the Socrates Society.

In her diverting column the other day Miss Elsa Maxwell noted that "because he is a brother of the queen of Greece, he is always written up as dining tête-à-tête with some charming actress, or dancing cheek-to-cheek with a famous mannequin. Christian said, 'I only wish I knew these lovely girls. Unfortunately, I am not so lucky!' "

I know Elsa did not intend to cast any slur on the newspaper profession with this paragraph, because some of her best friends own newspapers, but of course she did, because it is quite true that chroniclers of the lighter side have been reporting (or "writing up") His Royal Highness as get-ting around with several ladies of notable pulchritude.

Christian was itemed as wining and dining these ladies for just one elementary reason: he wined and dined them.

I'm not talking about what I've heard, I'm talking about what I've seen with my own baby blues.

After the prince arrived in this country, the first two females I glimpsed in his company were, in the order named, Miss Arlene Dahl and Mrs. Ghislaine Alexander, respectively an actress and a BBC television panelist.

If the prince didn't know them, he sure is the type that talks to strangers, because in each instance he was no further away from them (at a desirable table in Le Pavillon) than I am from my typewriter, and he was yakking away as if he had been formally introduced.

I also saw him at El Morocco with Miss Gita Hall, a beauty contest winner, and Miss Evelyn McBride, a model, or mannequin, not to mention a 6-foot showgirl-type dazzler named Monique Van Vooren who is so inconspicuous that on a clear night she can stand in 54th Street and be seen at Kennedy Airport.

In fact, if the prince doesn't know he's met her I recommend he obtain a copy of an evening edition of my favorite newspaper—the same one in which, two days previously, Miss Maxwell quoted him as saying he hadn't met any of the belles with whom those columnists persisted in linking him.

On page 6, the prince will find a picture of himself—worth, as the Chinese say, a thousand words.

It's a nice picture. El Morocco's zebra-striped background, and HRH leaning close enough to a lady to fit into a nice one-column cut.

What lady?

Well, it isn't Edith Sitwell.

Not even Madam Pandit or Grandma Moses.

It's Monique—doe-eyes, Italian haircut, ruby lips, burgeoning decolletage, and all.

Prince, meet Miss Van Vooren. Miss Van Vooren, meet the prince. He hasn't much of a memory for names, but his sister is the queen of Greece.

Color in News Stories

Color [says a statement by one of the wire services] is part of the news. But news must never be colored.

The distinction is sharp and clear, and artificial coloring is usually easy to detect. . . .

One way to avoid false color is to omit human interest and confine each story to a dull, bald recitation of the barest facts minus all atmosphere. That would be safe; but it would be neither adequate nor complete coverage of the news. *The reader should be able to see, feel, sense the complete picture in every news story.* He should be able to capture the atmosphere as well as the basic facts.

Color in the news, to put it differently, is its seasoning if not its meat—its hues, its sounds, its flavors, its looks. It is the *mood* of the crowd that attends the political convention—the *setting* of the regatta on Lake Cayuga's waters . . . the *atmosphere* of the smoke-filled room, rather than what the politicos do there. It is often secondary news, not the heart of the news event nor the who-what-why, but the surrounding human or emotive background that throws the major facts into understandable relief.

Color is not discoloration. Color is fact; color is reporting, just as genuinely as the statement of what the speaker said. The wire service quoted previously continued its remarks:

> To draw color from the imagination rather than from accurate, unbiased observation is an unforgivable sin. It departs from the field of reporting into the realm of fiction, and fiction has no place in news.

To call the audience "enthusiastic" when it was cold or apathetic, to write of an "exciting" game when it was dull and listlessly played is discolor, not color, and can be nothing but dishonest. It not only lies to reader or listener; it also destroys the integrity of the reporter, and to the consumer who knows the facts it becomes evidence of untrustworthiness.

It would be an error to assume that every news story must contain color. In practice, most news is reported flat, without the extra dimensions that color gives it; much news, especially minor news, is not worth the extra space that color requires. But some news is less than fully revealing without it.

COLOR IS DESCRIPTION   Writing a color story is a venture in description, just as clearly as is the "descriptive theme" in an English composition class or the fiction writer's painting of background for action he wishes to develop. The purpose of color in news is to take the reader to the scene, to provide him the sensory stimulants he would have felt had he been in the reporter's place. Its tool is accurate verbalization of the stimuli that would have actuated the reader's five senses had he been present—what he would have heard, seen, smelled, touched, tasted, and perhaps what he would have "sensed" or "felt" without full articulation.

The color story presents both similarities to and differences from descriptive themes and fiction. Like them, it depends on careful selection rather than on photographic detail. It must grow out of the writer's decision as to basic theme—gaiety, confusion, noise, banality, anguish, or whatever—and his astute choice of specifics to support the theme. It must not include nonessentials that would be distracting.

But since it differs in purpose from essay or fiction, it differs also in approach and, to a degree, in method. The essay or theme, though it reports, does so from a single, single-minded point of view: that of its writer. Its purpose is to tell somebody else what the writer sensed and felt about a scene or an event— how it struck him personally, what it meant to him alone. The fiction writer composes a picture, describes an Alpine slope, a Victorian drawing room, a bar or a bawdy house, as a background contrived to throw into relief, or perhaps to swallow up, a contrived life situation. The novelist or short story writer is bound by the limits of his imagination and knowledge and his artistic integrity, the essayist by the necessity to be honestly subjective.

The reporter, on the other hand, must seek what may loosely be called a

universal point of view—universal, at least, for whatever "universe" his audience comprises. He has to see things as he thinks his particular universe would
see them; and like the fiction writer, he has to provide the supporting and revealing backdrop against which the event occurs, one that will develop the
theme of the "net impression" he thinks the event ought to leave.

And—it cannot be said too often—he is rigidly bound by the necessity to observe the facts.

Make this distinction: A color story is one whose purpose is color; a story with color is one whose purpose is reporting a substantive event against enough of its background that the consumer may get an emotional as well as an intellectual message from it. This book, in its discussion of writing speech stories and elsewhere, has pointed out that straight news stories are often strengthened by the judicious use of color.

OBJECTIVITY AND COLOR   A legitimate and of-
ten-asked question: Can the writer of a color story
achieve thorough objectivity? Can he "keep himself
out of" such a story?

Rarely. It is fairly easy for the reporter covering
a political speech to approach objectivity in recording what the man said, who sat on the platform, and
how many attended. But when he attempts to capture
the flavor of the event, there is no such thing as complete detachment. His obligation to see the scene as
most of his audience would likely see it is governed
by his experience, his wisdom, and his devotion to
the principle of excluding his own emotions and ideas
from the story. This exclusion he cannot fully achieve,
and it is not even desirable that he should: Some shading of personality or of
individual attitude, held within controls, is necessary to a vital selection of materials for either a color story or a story with color. This kind of shading may
become a major factor when the writer is a "trained seal," a star performer, a
newswriter known to the audience and of interest to it as a personality. For most
reporters, however, since they are anonymous, the obligation to maintain a high
level of objectivity remains paramount.

WHAT MAKES A COLOR STORY?   Most color stories deal primarily with
people. The horror-stricken crowd on a Dallas street as a murderer shoots a
president—that is a source of a color story. The fans lining up in the rain at a
World Series ticket window, 12 hours before it opens . . . spectators taking
advantage of sidewalk-superintendent knotholes at a Main Street building project . . . hymn-singing sit-in demonstrators demanding Congressional action for
civil rights . . . women storming a department store anniversary sale—all are
subjects for color stories. The circus, the annual parade of ancient gas buggies,
the Christmas party for homeless youngsters—the list reaches from here to
1984. Such events are charged with plenty of men, women, and children, and
crowds of people are warm in many kinds of emotional manifestations.

There are other color settings. The *Saturday Evening Post* once published
a color story about a night on the University of Chicago campus, a story that
took much of its savor from the very lack of people. A solitary exploration
through the maze of heating tunnels under a great industrial installation yields

such a story . . . a reportorial vigil at an isolated forest ranger's station, watching for sign of forest fire . . . a visit to Coney Island in midwinter . . .

Nevertheless, most color stories grow out of circumstances rich in human interplay—crowd situations. Examination of illustrative stories, both in this chapter and elsewhere in the book, will demonstrate this principle.

More words of wisdom from Theodore Bernstein: "Some writers brush words onto their canvases with gentle precision and the utmost feeling for color; others spray them on and leave them to drip." Understatement and restraint mark most effective color writing.

COLOR REPORTING   The key to gathering material for a color story: *See what you see. Hear what you hear. Smell what you smell.*

This means not only keen perception of the facts, but also the ability to winnow, to select, to discard, to pick details that tint the event's description in honest colors. Suppose the subject is the crowd at the Homecoming football game, and suppose a sudden downpour in the second quarter soaks 40 thousand fans. You decide that the rain and its effects give you your theme, your point of emphasis, your springboard, and you concentrate on the sodden hats, the newspaper-sheltered coiffures, the rush for the exits, the dripping blankets. You find out what the rain did to the sale of coffee and hot dogs, you report the effect of sudden slime on the gridiron. You keep your ears open for pungent remarks about the rain. You note in the stands across the field the bare spots that 5 minutes ago were jammed with spectators.

Not only that. You also decide what not to use. The bit about the sharp new band uniforms goes out (or should you keep it to contrast with the soggy look of a well-soaked bass drum player?). The notes you took during the flag raising—throw them out because the story has taken its new tack. As for the welcome speech by the president of the alumni association—well, it was dull anyway.

All of this points up several characteristics of color stories: that they must have central points or themes; that they depend for vividness and credibility on skillful choice of detail; and that the reporter must depend on specifics, on facts so clear and clean that his presentation of them convinces the reader or listener of their reality. There is hardly an occasion when a reporter's fact-gathering has been too careful or too thorough. A reporter on a color story becomes both spy and eavesdropper. He notes the adoration on the face of the little girl cuddled under her father's plastic raincoat. He listens to the good-natured complaints of a plump matron that she's wet to the skin, and as he makes quick notes of her exact words for precise quotation, he asks himself whether he should use the simile that flashed into his mind: "She looks like a drowned rag doll." But as he thinks, he asks—and gets—her name and address.

Of one unfailing aid the experienced reporter is always aware: the reader's or listener's imagination. The news consumer does not have to be told that there are 9247 soaked topcoats in the crowd, for description of one of them suggests the scene. He can generalize readily from the specific; when the reporter gives him a sharp individual picture, he places it in a context created out of his own knowledge and experience.

Structurally, the color story has no characteristic pattern. Because it is an appeal to the senses, it is a little more likely to follow the suspended-interest model than the conventional; but it may use a thousand forms. Often it is what might be called episodic: it states the theme in a lead section, then supports it with evidence in the form of one specific after another. The simple color story is perhaps less difficult to compose, in one way, than the story with color, for in the story with color the emphasis is on a major news event set against the color as a revealing background. The interweaving necessary to combine the two elements in proper proportion and order may be anything but easy.

Fabrication of detail in color stories is hard to conceal. One of America's most competent reporters, Damon Runyon, also a fiction writer, covered the funeral procession of Franklin D. Roosevelt in Washington. His story was widely praised for its warmth and color. But in one respect it came a cropper. Runyon reported a man and his small son as spectators at the Pennsylvania Avenue curb, and quoted them five times in a long story. Each time they speak they become less real. The reason: Runyon gave them no clear personality or physical reality, and he let them speak dialog that "sounds like people in a book." Correctly or not, a reader is impelled to think that Runyon put words into fictional mouths because they were typical words. They may be real; but they carry no truth to the reader who doubts their reality.

The effectiveness of both types appears in examples already presented in this book and by those that follow here. Look first at a "pure" color story from the Chicago *Tribune*—"pure" in the sense that its primary purpose seems to be to paint the sordid scene, to let the reader experience emotionally what the reporter experienced. (It may also have the editorial goal of arousing public concern. This kind of reporting is often a more vigorous catalyst of public opinion than hortatory editorializing.) The bulk of the story goes to detailed description of the squalid task of the police; it opens with specific detail, and devotes its last half to a series of sharp vignettes. Note, however, that, after the interest-catching opening, the story devotes seven paragraphs to general background.

At processing time in the Monroe Street police station the zombies of Skid Row line up before two policemen filling out arrest slips on duplicating machines. Some are complaining and some are cheerful, but most just go through the motions. There are wasted alcoholics and men in their 20s, all drunk, and the thugs who prey on them, also drunk. They are of all descriptions. Most have swollen features and a raw, liverish flush.

Names? They cover all nationalities. Ages? Here is a surprise. Birth years are heavily in the 1918-1923 bracket—the World War II generation. Places of birth? Mississippi, Kansas, North Dakota, Washington, New Jersey—backwash of a nation.

Now and then a drunk raises his voice.

"I'm going back to be a sailor," says a Kansan of 26.

"That's what you've been telling us for years," says the policeman.

"Isn't this terrible?" says another drunk. "Not even drunk and I'm getting pinched. Awful."

It is 9 P.M. Outside, a block north, is another surprise. On Madison Street in the heart of the cheap wine and flophouse section not a bum is sitting or lying in the street.

The drunks are in the lockup—190 of them. There will be 250 before the night is over.

A new policy is in effect on Skid Row. The rule is to pick them up before they are down. Under the direction of Capt. Thomas A. Harrison, patrol wagons cruise caravan style up and down the street and around in the alleys and behind truck loading docks.

In the first half of July there were 3,146 "pinches" by Monroe Street police, more than most of the other police stations make in half a year. For the year to date there have been 25,525, a quarter of all the arrests in Chicago.

It is unpleasant work, loading a staggering drunk in a wagon. The drunks protest. The saloonkeepers are sour about the effect on their trade. Politicians are conscious of the thousands of easily bought votes which may be disturbed.

With a police job done, the sidewalks and curbs are clear of the "downers" who used to sprawl by the dozen. Jostling panhandlers stay away from respectable citizens. The bums themselves are saved from the street cars, autos, and jackrollers periling them.

But a social problem remains. Most of the judges turn virtually all loose again. Judge Harry Beam on week days has been sentencing about a fifth of the approximately 250 a day. But on Sunday, Judge Sigmund J. Stefanowicz had 514 men before him and sentenced just four. On the holiday weekend of July 3, 4, and 5, Judge Stanley Pulaski tried 683 and discharged all but 14.

There are crippled drunks, lunatic drunks, and sick drunks. Hundreds of them die every year, with the toll heaviest when the sun sears them in 90-degree weather.

They must be cleared from the street. Society and their own welfare demand this. It is a job which goes on day and night.

A Tribune reporter and photographer followed one of Harrison's caravans throughout an afternoon and evening. In the lead was the captain's car, with Detectives John Casey and John Clair. Behind was a patrol wagon staffed by Policemen Louis Krotz and Stephen Schumack. Their job eight hours a day is picking up drunks. There are two other wagons subject to radio call and another available when Detectives Larry Doyle and Martin Reidy can man it.

First in the wagon were four walking drunks in front of the McCoy Hotel, 949 Madison. The wagon men greeted them, "How are you today?", and in a few seconds they were in the van.

In front of 602 Madison, the captain's arm pointed again. The detectives said to the stumbling alcoholic, about 25, "Want you to meet a friend." He shook hands with a wagon man as he was helped in.

The first "downer" was on his face in front of a hotel at 551 Madison. Krotz and Schumack turned him over. Eyes glazed, he stared up helplessly. He was carried to the wagon. A dozen other bums looked on without a change of expression.

"How about him?" asked Casey, pointing to a bushy-haired oldster.

"No, he's just an old bum who's always around," said Harrison. "He doesn't do any harm. Doesn't beg or anything. There are a lot of age pensioners around here because living is cheap. They are happy when you chase the jackrollers. One old guy, about 70, had 73 cents and an old-fashioned watch. They asked him what time it was and then smashed him."

Turning north on Union Avenue, the caravan picked up another downer, slumped in praying position in a doorway.

A half block north was a bottle gang, huddled on a loading dock at an alley corner. Four of the six stumbled away but halted at a shout. On the ground below the dock was a litter of jagged glass, mixed with garbage and filth.

"Come on. Get down," the captain ordered.

One of the two remaining was helped down by a detective. The other lurched forward—too far. He teetered like a skinny puppet on the edge and plunged toward the glass, his face expressionless.

Harrison caught him, saving a bed at County Hospital.

In an alley off Des Plaines Street, the wagon got another downer. He was lying face down in trash, dressed in khaki shirt and trousers with a straw hat jammed on his head. He muttered but wouldn't wake. Schumack hoisted him and slid him onto the wagon floor.

At Peoria and Madison one of a party of three thrust a pint of muscatel under his belt. He was fast, but not fast enough.

All afternoon the loads moved in, 90 men and a few women by dusk, when the lights came on and the groups grew larger.

Another sweep through the district. First the caravan checks a large hidden area under the superhighway west of the post office. An estimated 100 bums had made a jungle there until they were routed recently. There was nothing but litter.

A husky character gave the policemen a tussle in front of the Legion Hotel. It turned out he was hanging on to a post because he thought his trousers were falling down. At Monroe and Halsted a young man leaned sickly against a lamppost. Around the corner an Indian leaned stone-drunk against a wall. He collapsed when one of the policemen said, "Hi, Chief."

Back at the station, "the Chief" slid out of the wagon, lying with his head on the bumper. A cripple dragging his crutches skidded on top of him and went to sleep. Krotz and Schumack hauled him off. They asked

"the Chief" what his name was.

"U. S. Marine," he replied. "His name's Thunder," said Schumack. "He's a good fellow. It's just the wine, huh, Chief?"

A woman and a few more men came out, but the wagon was not empty.

"He's sick," said Krotz helplessly.

They eased the drunk out, feet first, and carried him into the lockup. Schumack held his hands away from his uniform and went in to wash them. Krotz looked at his uniform.

"A shirt a day on this job," he said.

Political stories do not often become color stories (perhaps news of politics would be better read if they did). The following story, reporting a minor behind-the-scenes adventure of a political pressure group, is a mild satire on the smoke-filled-room cliché (note the twist the reporter gives the cliché), told with enough bite to give an edge to what would otherwise have been routine news. Note that, as in the preceding story, there are sharp details, abundant dialogue, and short, simple, clear sentences.

SAN FRANCISCO, Calif. (Special)—The scene was a smoke-filled bathroom on the 15th floor of the Mark Hopkins Hotel, battle headquarters of Sen. Barry Goldwater, newly nominated Republican candidate for the presidency of the United States.

It was 3:45 A.M. Thursday, Minneapolis time.

Jammed into the room were seven of Minnesota's top Republican leaders, two of Goldwater's closest advisers and three reporters.

They were there to discuss a matter of high political significance—the selection of Goldwater's vice presidential running mate.

The bathroom provided privacy from the champagne celebration outside.

An unidentified man, apparently intent on using the room for other purposes, opened the door, recoiled in surprise at the imposing assemblage and decided to come back later.

The man the Minnesotans had come to see, Richard Kleindienst, Goldwater's co-director of field activities and a candidate for governor of Arizona, stepped into the bathtub to relieve the congestion.

Arrayed before him were Robert Forsythe, Minne-

sota Republican chairman; George Etzell, national committeeman; . . . [the paragraph names other members of the delegation].

In the back, against the wall, stood F. Clifton White, Goldwater's other field director.

Forsythe flicked the ashes off his cigar, put his foot up on one of the major appurtenances, leaned over and started to talk.

"We are here on behalf of the Minnesota delegation, which has expressed interest in doing something on behalf of Dr. Walter Judd for the vice presidential nomination if there is reason to do anything.

"But the first thing we would have to know, of course, would be whether the choice of a candidate would be left to an open convention or whether Goldwater himself will be picking someone."

Kleindienst, dapper, composed, a drink in his hand and his face creased by the smile of the victor, replied as if speaking from a pulpit.

"It will not be open," he said curtly.

"All right," said Forsythe, "that answers one question. The other thing, of course, is whether as long as Goldwater will make the choice,

the matter is already foreclosed or whether Dr. Judd might still be under consideration."

"It is foreclosed," said Kleindienst.

The Minnesotans blinked. Etzell was the first to speak.

"Thank you," he said. "We appreciate your candor and your brevity."

Kleindienst, starting to unwind slightly now that the pressures of securing the nomination for Goldwater were over, made a little gesture with the glass in his hand.

"I do not," he said, "mean to be abrupt. We all know the high regard in which the senator holds Dr. Judd . . ."

[After reporting Kleindienst's three-minute response, the story reports the breakup of the bathroom huddle. It closes:]

Their mission concluded, the delegation went down the elevator, skirted a crowd cheering and singing "Dixie" in the hotel lobby and walked out into the chill early morning air.

"That," said one, "didn't take long."

The political story, told straight, could almost have been compressed into a sentence: *Sen. Goldwater's decision to select his running mate himself has ruled out Dr. Walter Judd as a vice-presidential candidate.* The graphic portrayal of a briefly dramatic moment at shipside, the story that follows, would never have been published had it been offered as straight news. Its color is what makes it. Two characteristics are worth observing: first, even though it is a color story, it is constructed in standard straight-news form, with a one-paragraph summary lead, a second paragraph of secondary facts, and a third paragraph introducing the body of the story, the chronological recounting of the incident; second, it uses color words and phrases as well as color facts (*calloused mitts, pretty even when drenched, swaying gently, big man with a voice to match* among them).

NEW YORK, N. Y.— One hundred thirty steel-muscled longshoremen flattened their calloused mitts against the side of a 10,000-ton ship Wednesday, pushed it away from a Brooklyn pier, and held it back to save a 4-year-old girl from being crushed to death between the vessel and the pilings.

The feat was performed with a slight assist from three small loading machines and a large assist from a daring stevedore who was lowered by the heels into the narrow space between the ship and dock to help bring the child to safety.

The girl is Diana Svet, a blue-eyed blond, and pretty even when drenched. The villain of the piece was the Yugoslav ship Srbija, hitting 10,000 tons with her cargo. The Srbija docked Wednesday morning. In the afternoon the stevedores began unloading her. In mid-afternoon, Diana came to the pier with her mother, Anna, 25, to visit one of the vessel's officers, a cousin of Mrs. Svet.

They went aboard, learned that the cousin wasn't there, then began descending the stairway leading down the ship's side.

The lowest step of the stairway was one foot above the pier. Mrs. Svet, holding onto Diana's left hand, made it, but Diana, who jumped, didn't.

The jump carried her out of her mother's grasp, and into the 10-inch space between ship and dock outerstructure.

Screaming, she plunged 15 feet into the water, where she managed to grab a slippery piling.

The Srbija was swaying gently. But even the slightest sway, with 10,000 tons behind it, could be fatal.

Pier superintendent Ignatio Scibilia, a big man with a voice to match, bellowed an order, and 130 stevedores scrambled off the ship. The two lines holding the ship to the dock were cut.

Then the men and the three little machines pitted themselves against the ship. Inch by inch, it gave way.

John Balzano, 45, Giuseppe Gambino, 49, and Joseph Zapulla, 25, went into action.

Balzano and Gambino lowered Zapulla, head down. Diana's strength was waning as Zapulla dropped a noosed rope and pulled it taut. Then he and the girl were pulled up to the pier.

Outside of a scare and a thorough wetting, Diana was all right. Mama took her home.

Zapulla, who had taken a banging around against the piling, went home, too.

It's easy to write a dramatic story about a dramatic event, and the process of integration in the American South provided many such occasions. Some of the most effective reporting of the century has resulted. The story that follows, a masterly piece of restraint as well as of skillful selection, was printed as a sidebar: the principal story, much shorter, reported the school-integration process in broad terms. This story employs the magazine writer's device of using one specific case as an example to tell a larger story. Its structural dependence on the clock, continually reporting the minutes as the dramatic event develops, adds to its effectiveness.

NORFOLK, Va. (AP)— It was cold Monday morning at 8:30 at Maury high school—cold, windy, overcoat weather with the temperature hovering near 25 degrees.

Across the street from the high school entrance, an old man leaned against a wire fence and shook his head. "I have lived near this school—right around the corner there—for 40 years," he said. "I've had three children in this school and I love it. I wouldn't want anything to happen now, after all that time . . ."

It was 8:35, and in front of the three massive doors at the top of the 29 marble steps that led into the school, a crowd of about 150 students had gathered. In the teen-age uniform of jackets, jeans and dirty bucks they looked chilly, but they did not go inside.

As kids do, they talked loudly, swapping old acquaintances, telling each other how good it was to be back. For until yesterday morning Maury high school had been closed since September, along with five other Norfolk schools, to avert integration.

Now reopening was only minutes away and if the kids were shaken, as their elders had been, by the fact that a Negro would come among them, they gave no hint. Nonetheless, in the cold air there was an unspoken sense of anticipation.

It was 8:43 A.M., and through a gate in the brick fence that separates the left side of Maury high from the street came a serious-faced Negro boy, accompanied by his mother.

Lewis Cousins looks not at all like a maker of history, as he and 16 other Norfolk Negro children became yesterday, breaching the color barrier in Virginia's white schools for the first time.

He is a small, wiry, studious-looking lad. He wears heavy black-rimmed glasses. He was clad in brown jacket, black trousers, rubber-soled shoes, white shirt —and necktie.

At the moment Lewis and his short, smiling mother rounded the corner of the school and, ignoring two side entrances, started up the marble steps to the front entrance, silence fell upon the crowd of teen-agers congregated at the doors.

In this ghostly quiet Lewis and his mother slowly mounted the 29 steps. Before them the white students fell back to open a narrow aisle. There was no word of greeting, no hostile word. Only curious stares— and silence.

For a fleeting instant tension crackled in the air. There was an indefinable feeling that trouble might be only a word, a hiss, a gesture, a step away. The instant passed, and the feeling was gone.

Lewis Cousins, Negro, entered Maury high school. Behind him the assemblage at the doors quickly broke up. The wait was over. The students went in to get warm. Lewis's mother, a few minutes later, came out the door she had entered.

"People couldn't have been nicer to us," she said.

Inside, at 9 o'clock, new students gathered at an assembly in the auditorium. Lewis was there, and about 300 white children.

He sat alone up front in the second row. Behind him, three rows of seats were empty.

Robert Steckroth, assistant principal, spoke casually to the youngsters. There was no mention of anything unusual about this day.

"Maury high has traditions you will all learn to honor and be proud of," said Steckroth.

Steckroth began reading a list of room assignments for the new students. Nearly all had been assigned when Lewis Cousins was assigned —alone—to room No. 4, in the basement.

Again the silence, the curious stares, as the Negro boy walked slowly up the aisle to the rear of the auditorium, to go to his classroom where he would join older, more mature Maury students.

Now, finally, someone spoke to Lewis. A friendly-looking upperclassman met him at the auditorium door.

"Room No. 4?" he asked cheerfully.

Lewis nodded assent.

"This way—come on with me," said the upperclassman with a quick grin. He and Lewis went out together.

It was 9:38 A.M., still cold, but getting warmer.

Like other effective stories in this book, the account of a dramatic day in a small boy's life takes its strength from astute use of specific detail.

Look, finally, at a tongue-in-cheek story about a routine and, to most reporters who have seen many versions of it, a banal event. The reporter mocks not only the event but also the solemn academic footnote; but he does it with good humor, interesting detail, and the purpose to report the event even though he laughs at it.

Astute observers, after a close look at sensitive precincts Friday, hazarded the cautious guess that sentiment at the University of Minnesota and environs was running strongly in favor of the Golden Gophers.[1]

As a corollary, it was concluded that the Hawks[2] were unlikely to pick up much strength from the undecided segment of the population.[3]

Although motivational research is beset by many statistical imponderables, the analysts gave considerable weight to the circumstance that approximately 3,489 University of Minnesota students assembled at forenoon in front of Northrop Memorial auditorium[4] and gave themselves over to a "pep rally."

Furthermore, for whatever external significance it may have, many of the students (17.3 percent) were carrying totemistic placards which, while often of crude construction, were of unquestioned sincerity and enthusiasm.

The placards carried such legends as the following: "Muray for President"[5]

---

[1] Popular nickname for the University of Minnesota's football team.
[2] Nickname for the similar, but not identical, athletic aggregation maintained by the University of Iowa.
[3] This assumption gains substance from the fact that no undecided element was discerned yesterday.
[4] Inside this building at the time, the Minneapolis Symphony was holding a rehearsal, but it is believed this was coincidental and that the students were not cheering Stanislaw Skrowaczewski—unless, perhaps, under the delusion that he was a Gopher halfback.
[5] Presumably a misspelling of "Murray," first name of Mr. Warmath, Minnesota football coach. It is not believed Mr. Warmath has any presidential ambitions.

"Who the Hell Likes Corn?"[6]
"Poison Evy"[7]
"Fight Fiercely, Rah, Rah"[8]
"We Got the Jug, We Want the Pig"[9]

The Minnesota band enlivened the proceedings with several numbers, following which Leonard Levine, assistant sports editor of the Daily and master of ceremonies for the occasion, told the throng:

"This is the first time in 150 years we have had something to cheer about.[10] We've been waiting for this for a long time." The students cheered lustily.

Shortly thereafter, the football team and coaches filed to the steps of the auditorium through a corridor of humanity, which uttered tumultuous cries of affection and encouragement.

Mr. Stanley Wenberg, a vice president of the university, then addressed the students. He observed that there is biblical justification for college football and quoted the verse: "Many shall run to and fro and knowledge shall increase."[11]

Mr. Warmath appeared on the rostrum and was greeted by a thunderous ovation, the stormiest to be heard up to that point. Mr. Warmath, after his manner, was succinct:

---

[6] Corn is the principal agricultural product of Iowa.
[7] "Evy" is the sobriquet of Forrest Evashevski, Iowa coach. Evidently a pun is intended upon poison ivy (Toxicodendron radicans).
[8] A facetious parody of more aggressive slogans.
[9] An obscure reference to which we have been unable to attach any meaning.
[10] This may be dismissed as a pardonable exaggeration on the part of Mr. Levine.
[11] Mr. Wenberg did not further identify this scriptural authority, but precise scholarship in this area is not essential to our present purpose.

"We are very awed, extremely pleased and a little touched at this display you are giving our football team," he said. "We are very proud to be on your team and are happy to know that you are on our team.

"Iowa is the first team in the nation," Mr. Warmath continued, amid a chorus of boos. "It is undefeated" (still louder boos). "We wouldn't have it any other way!" (prolonged cheering).

Mr. Warmath then was boosted upon the shoulders of several students at the rostrum. The sounds of approbation became quite unrestrained.

A chanting then broke out. "We want Sandy!"[12] We want Sandy!" the crowd iterated.

The individual so denominated appeared and, with becoming modesty, commented:

"I really have nothing to say. All I know is that I'm really in for a rough day."

Mr. Warmath again was hoisted on shoulders and joint cheers for him and Mr. Stephens were heard.

By popular insistence, a Mr. Tom Brown[13] took the microphone.

"We shall provide you with the utmost in sports entertainment tomorrow," Mr. Brown pledged humorously.

Greg Larson[14] then was presented with an immense ear of corn, mounted tastefully as a trophy. He smiled appreciatively, but made no comment. The crowd was less taciturn.

---

[12] Sanford E. Stephens, Gopher quarterback and folk hero.
[13] Guard and oft-mentioned candidate for All-American. Not to be confused with the English youth whose school days at Rugby and Oxford were described in novels (1857 and 1861) by Thomas Hughes.
[14] Gregory K. Larson, captain of the team and minor deity.

In conclusion, it is worth noting that, although the many speakers represented a wide diversity of ethnographic and religious backgrounds as well as varying age groups and vocational interests, not a single favorable sentiment was expressed toward the Iowans.

Praise of Minnesota's virtues and prospects, on the other hand, was unreserved.

Predictions in such matters have proven in the past to be a rash undertaking, but experts said certain inferences are inescapable and they uniformly expressed a belief that Iowa's corn will be creamed in today's contest.

PROJECTS

1. Rewrite the little-girl-in-the-water story in the suspended-interest manner, condensing it to no more than two thirds of its original length.
2. From a newspaper, select a color sidebar accompanying a parent story—for example, a color story about the shivering crowd at a football game (the "parent" in this case is the game story)—and see whether you can combine the two in a condensed story. Evaluate the effectiveness of the new story in contrast to the two that it replaces.
3. Attend and cover an event such as a major address, the dedication of a new public edifice, or any occurrence that draws public interest and public attendance. Write two stories: one the major story reporting the important facts, the second a color sidebar.
4. Examine a week's issues of a metropolitan newspaper to discover the extent to which it uses feature material (using the description of features at the beginning of this chapter as a guide). Write a commentary of 500 words or more on what you find—whether the paper uses features well or badly, widely or sparingly, and so on.
5. Develop several topics on which you think you could write human interest stories (see suggestions on page 242) and write the appropriate stories.

CHAPTER 16

Developing News

Warnings against the emptiness of covering the mere surface of the news come from every side. Both print and air editors talk solemnly about the need for reporting in depth at every one of their conventions. Lay critics of the news media ask an unattainable goal that every newspaper report the news as thoroughly as does the New York *Times*. This book has more than once censured photographic reproduction of the veneer of events, without penetration to find what lies beneath. Reporter Finnegan told you that a beat man is "doing only 51 percent of the job" if he is satisfied with mere routine coverage.

A writer on the changing problems of reporting today, Walter A. Steigleman of the University of Iowa School of Journalism, plays a variation on the same theme in a report on an empirical examination of superficial news. Steigleman says that time pressures in newsrooms have developed a "hit and run reporter." This is the man who "partly through production pressures and partly because of inadequate skill . . . appears content to grab a few facts, bang them out on paper, and turn to something new." Steigleman points to many stories in which reporters have not asked enough questions, stories that report adequately the *who*, *what*, *when*, and *where*, but fail to develop the all-important *why* and *how* (as Elmer Davis put it, *merely* objective reporting isn't good enough):

A story reports that a policeman stopped a car with a kidnaped man in it, then let it proceed. But the story fails to say why the car was stopped, and why it was not held.

A story says that postal inspectors "swooped down" on the Boston post-office to check on suspected fraud by workers, but does not say what led to the suspicion.

A story reports that a university faculty member with spurious credentials was exposed after a student became "curious," but does not show what led to the curiosity.

In these cases and hundreds of others, Steigleman was able to get answers, usually by letter, to the *how* or *why* questions the reporters seem not to have asked.

These cases illustrate a debilitating departure from the thoroughness that must be a component of reporting if it is to be revealing. Such reporting, seeking to state only the facts that are already uncovered, has no more depth than the copy paper on which the stories are typed. It lacks entirely the resourcefulness, inventiveness, and patiently energetic curiosity with which competent newsmen, newsmen whose future is bright, look behind the obvious.

Reporting that gives news events meaning and perspective, that does not leave the consumer asking "Why?" and "How?", must pierce the crust. Its driving power grows from news imagination, energy, perception, and a passion to find causes and explanations. It is, in a sense, a luxury, for the newspaper or the broadcaster *could* cover the surface of the news without it. It is expensive in dollars, time, manpower, and gray matter. But without it the customers of the news media are likely to find their news, however glossy its surface, opaque rather than revealing.

Look at the problem through specific examples:

1) Congress passes an appropriation bill that provides 100 million dollars for damming the river that flows through your town. The dam will create a flood-control reservoir; it may also provide cheap electric power to a whole corner of your state. Routinely your paper or radio-TV station, with assists from the wire services, covers the parts of the news that can be seen with the naked eye: how much, when, where, who voted *aye* and *nay,* and the like. This is elementary coverage—minimum reporting of the flow of events.

"Elementary" coverage like this is obviously the essential basis for anything that might follow; without it there can be no follow-up. But note that the wire service could, and often does, do most of it for you, without a lick of local effort. You are either dull or very tired if you stop here.

The energetic and imaginative newsman, at this point, starts asking himself questions: When will construction begin? When will it end? How much of the money will flow into the local community? Will the big artificial lake dispossess farmers or villagers in the area above the dam? How will those who lose property be compensated? Is there a chance that power rates will decrease? Or tax rates rise? How will agriculture benefit or suffer?

From questions like these grow more and more news stories—stories that give future meaning to past news, that provide perspective as well as breadth . . . stories that tell the individual citizen what effects the palpable events will have on his own, his family's, his neighbors' lives. They are largely stories that could be ignored by the newsman who is satisfied with reporting, as one shallow definition of news has it, "what God lets happen." But to the newsman for whom making news meaningful is a passion and a religion, they are the blood and the marrow of revealing news work.

Newsmen today recognize this kind of under-the-surface digging as the most exciting as well as the most significant reporting they can do. Further examples show why:

2) A major nation sends troops into a small country next to it and takes over the government. Primary coverage reports the event. Vigorous follow-up coverage calls for speedy and thorough evaluation of the event by expertly qualified sources (diplomatic officials, experts on international politics and law): Does this presage widespread war? Will other powers intervene? Do international law and the United Nations sanction the action? Note that many such stories will emerge from Washington and other centers of national and international affairs; but that local angles also may be—and should be—developed.

3) The city council refuses to increase police wages, and policemen declare a strike. Do they have the legal right to strike? What is their responsibility for civic protection if they are on strike? What has been the experience of other cities in like situations? How will citizens take the situation? Are they upset? concerned? apathetic? Any vigilante committees in process of formation? Will your own state governor follow the precedent set by a governor named Calvin Coolidge and intervene?

4) Two local grade schools burn down in the same week. Do the police and the fire marshal think arson is involved? What will be done with the children these schools ought to serve? Does the city carry covering insurance? When can new buildings be ready? In what ways will new buildings be improvements?

5) The Federal Communications Commission grants a TV license to an applicant in a city 30 miles distant from yours. How well will this TV signal be received in your community? What kinds of programming does the new licensee propose? Do local broadcasters expect appreciable effect on local listening habits?

6) The governor signs a bill outlawing fireworks in your state. How will this affect the 50-year tradition of July 4 fireworks in the city park? Do neighboring states have similar laws? Are there likely to be difficulties in enforcing or interpreting the law?

7) The Citizens Protective Association has started a campaign demanding that a higher proportion of local tax money go into paving city streets. What is the impulse behind this campaign? Who are the moving spirits in the CPA? Do any of them own stock in concrete, paving machinery, or other interested businesses? What is expert opinion about the need for a stepped-up paving program? What streets would the CPA pave? Why? How does the percentage of paved streets in your city compare with that in others of like population and area?

8) The biggest local manufacturing concern, always locally owned, announces the election of an unknown nonlocal man as president. Does this mean a change in the ownership pattern? Who is the man? What are his background and experience?

Enterprisers

In some newsrooms, newspaper or broadcasting, you hear the term "enterpriser," or its parallel, "made news," applied to stories of the kind just described, the "developed" story. In this book these terms are reserved for a different, though in some ways similar, type of story. Developed stories like those suggested in the eight examples take their initial impulse from overt news events. Though the development of related follow-up news requires enterprise, it cannot be considered outside the "normal" orbit of news coverage. It is basic in every newsroom's routine practice.

Another kind of developed news, one to which the terms *enterpriser* and *made news* seem more aptly applied, is that with no immediate relation to current spot news. This is the story that grows from a reporter's or an editor's observation and his news imagination, from his realization that a certain set of questions asked in the right places, or a certain effort of observation or digging in a library, will yield a story worth publishing or broadcasting. Such a story—note the lack of spot-news peg—might be produced by any of these efforts:

An investigation of city council records to develop a story showing just how every councilman has voted on major issues in the last two years

Interviews with real estate dealers, supplemented by material from appropriate public records, to show the trends and quantity of real estate transfers in the last one, two, five, or 10 years

Interviews with school officials, public health officials, doctors, and police to find whether use of pep pills, tranquilizers, and other drugs is a problem among high school students

Interviews with individuals having unusual occupations, hobbies, or vacation plans

Interviews with a number of the residents of the city's newest public housing project to ascertain their attitudes toward its facilities

What is "creative writing"?

It is not merely putting words on paper effectively, though that is part of it.

It is not limited to belles lettres—to fiction, poetry, and the essay—though they are likely to prove sterile without it.

It is the kind of writing that grows from creative imagination . . . writing that evokes lucid and accurate images, writing that brings ideas and concepts to life (and that has underlying it the kind of

Such stories, going beyond the coverage of the flow of events, add depth and meaning to the news consumer's understanding or appreciation of the life of which he is a part. Competently used, they may offer more illumination, and often more entertainment, than most of a news medium's routine content.

Nothing need be added about the journalistic forms of made stories for the clear reason that they are of all forms. When you develop a story beyond the minimum call of duty, it is imagination and energy that you add, not new form. Though most enterprisers are what were defined in chapter 15 as features—stories in which the spot news or time element is secondary to the *how* and *why* factors—they can take every form

substantive and emotive base that only lively and perceptive vision can provide). It involves the creative generation of ideas, ideas for dramas or news interviews, novels or newspaper color stories, poems or journalistic personality stories, as well as the rhetorical or "literary" sensitivity to use language creatively.

For the journalist, creative imagination means the story idea, the base on which he composes his story, as a first step. It means the curiosity and the inventiveness with which he envisions what materials he will need, and the deftness with which he elicits materials. And it means the art and the craft, knit into effective composition, with which he writes.

Creative writing is a totality. It is the goal of any worker with words, not of one or another category of writers.

news craft has developed. They are often treated effectively in the suspended-interest form.

The wide range of stories of the two types, follow-up stories and enterprisers, is suggested by examples in this chapter. The first (its lead sentence unfortunately clumsy) takes its cue from a national magazine story that suggests a local angle. Note that its form is that of the news interview.

Minneapolis parks are safe "but I would not advise using these areas after midnight," according to Park police Capt. James T. Curran, head of the department.

Curran was referring yesterday to a recent story in McCall's magazine, which cited Minneapolis parks as being among the safest in the country.

"I would hesitate to walk through our parks at night," Curran said, "but I would especially recommend against their use in the early morning hours."

The parks close officially at midnight.

"Some of these parks have dark, wooded areas," Curran explained. "People shouldn't use such areas at night—and our experience shows that most people don't."

Park police statistical records show that there have been only three molestings and five robberies reported in city parks during the first eight months of this year.

There are 152 parks in the police jurisdiction of Hennepin county. Twenty-four patrolmen work the 600,119 acres of park property lying within and outside the city.

"Lighting is a deterrent to crime," Curran said. "The lighting is good now, especially at Powderhorn, Armatage, Kennedy, and Longfellow Parks."

Since the lighting was improved at Powderhorn early last year, Curran said, there have been only three reports of crime. During the same period of the preceding four years, there were 30, he said.

A story growing from a current crime is of a type that American newspapers, to their credit, have developed with increasing frequency in recent years, the story that attempts to show both what led a man to a crime of violence and what efforts society had made, or failed to make, toward his social adjustment. Whereas the park-safety story depends entirely on one interview, the next one goes to several official reports for its material; it closes with the news peg and with a brief quotation from a police officer, the only specific personal source the story names. (For no apparent reason, the story moves back and forth between the man's first and last names—a puzzling practice and one that many newsmen consider objectionable because it suggests disrespect.)

Psychological evaluations made on Emmett Ripton (*name fictitious*) last July and again this month emphasized his aggressive nature and warned of his sudden impulses, it was learned Friday.

Ripton, 20, who confessed yesterday to the hammer slaying of Walter and Mabel Messina (*names fictitious*),

was adjudged "of low borderline intelligence," with an IQ range between 50 and 80.

He was enrolled in a state school for the retarded between the ages of 12 and 17.

In reports made by county welfare and probation offices, phrases such as these were used to describe him: "He has more energy than he can handle. He acts out impulses with little planning, forethought or regard to consequences."

"It is likely he will continue to have problems with authority because of his lack of self-restraint."

"Because of his low inertia, poor motivation and low frustration tolerance, he will need close supervision for a long time."

According to the reports, the youth could not read and could write only his name. He could speak well, but his speech belied his capabilities. He had apparently suffered brain damage of undetermined cause.

According to welfare sources, Emmett was the youngest of four children. Shortly after his birth, his mother, who still lives in this city, suffered a polio attack which left her seriously crippled. While Emmett was a baby, the parents were divorced.

By the time the boy was 12, his mother determined that she could no longer

care for him and committed him to the State School for the Mentally Retarded.

He was released in 1960 when an uncle promised him a job. He couldn't get along with coworkers, however.

During a psychological interview last July, the youth said he hated the State School so much that he had nightmares every night for a year after he left, fearing someone might make him return.

"I would rather go to prison than go back there," he was quoted.

He said he didn't get along too well with his mother, but "she is the best mother I have . . . We fight a lot and she tells me I better get a job or she will sic the Welfare Board on me and I'll have to go back. But I don't think she means it."

Last September Emmett got involved with a nurse during a drinking party. The nurse said they were both intoxicated. She said he struck her and raped her. Ripton said he didn't remember the attack.

After Ripton pleaded guilty to the attack, an investigation was ordered. In a probation office report,

Emmett was judged capable of working only at menial, repetitious jobs, such as light janitor work.

But the report added, "However, he thinks and talks in terms of becoming a truck driver so his income would warrant owning a new car and other material things that are coveted as marks of the successful in our society."

Although describing him as "a dull, dependent person who needs considerable guidance," the report said a lengthy sentence for the complaint of indecent assault would not be necessary.

"The assault was the result of a combination of the situation, poor judgment and being intoxicated. . . . A short period of supervision may help to serve as a further deterrent to acting out in this manner."

In District Court, Ripton was given a 90-day sentence, suspended to a year's probation.

Last night Ripton was remorseful. He told a detective, "When I realized what I had done, it was terrible. I wanted to tell someone, but I couldn't. I wanted to cry, but I couldn't."

The following long story is a "pure" enterpriser, without a current news peg (though it doubtless relates to many news stories of the fairly recent past). The story is distinguished by its use of color, the large number of information sources, and the technical and legal information it weaves in with anecdotal and specific case material.

In a dimly-lighted neighborhood tavern a 17-year-old high school girl sits drinking beer with "older" friends.

On the table is a plastic card case containing her driver's license. The red imprinted date of birth on the card gives her age as 22.

Across town a youth "proves" to a bartender that he is old enough to drink by first showing an

altered driver's license, and then displaying a doctored selective service registration card.

False identification that serves teen-agers as "beer permits" is causing authorities increasing concern.

A rash of fake and altered drivers' licenses in the state recently brought a warning directed at the youthful offenders by A. L. Murton (names changed), director

of the state drivers license division.

Murton said that his office will cancel or suspend valid licenses of any person producing or possessing a false driver's license.

Col. J. C. Sorensen, state director of selective service, also warned minors that severe federal penalties can result from the forgery or alteration of registration cards.

Driver's licenses are the most popular official forms that are faked or "revised" by teen-agers. Some of the forgeries are virtually miniature works of art, police said.

One such license recently was taken from a 16-year-old local girl. She gave police this account of the phony license.

The blank application card was obtained from the office of the county district clerk under the pretense of applying for a legitimate license. She then filled in her name, address and physical description with pen and ink, as is customary.

She then took a needle point pen and red ink and faked the date of birth imprint. The imprint is made by a machine similar to a check-writing machine at the license division.

With the same pen and blue ink, she almost perfectly forged a postmark, indicating that the license had been mailed to her by the drivers license bureau.

One youth, with less artistic skill, used a check-writing machine to simulate the state's date of birth stamp. He then mailed the card to himself from the state capital.

A close comparison of the two date of birth imprints revealed the variation.

In the first instance the girl violated city, state and federal laws:

City ordinances prohibit the possession or display of false identification for the purpose of obtaining intoxicants. Penalty upon conviction is $100 fine or 90 days in jail.

State statutes prohibit the forgery or alteration of a state driver's license. Suspension and cancellation invariably result. Such offense is recorded by the state and is considered in future administrative actions.

It is a federal violation to forge a United States postmark. The violation can bring a fine of $1,000 or imprisonment for five years, or both.

Both the boy and the girl in the two cases received disciplinary action and probation because they had no previous records. Others, police said, may not be so fortunate.

Bar and tavern keepers are constantly on guard and extremely cautious of youthful-appearing customers. Their alertness and close cooperation with police is their best insurance.

Operators are put under heavy pressure by city liquor ordinances. For the first sale to minors, a tavern or bar owner is subject to a $100 fine or 90 days in the workhouse.

After the first conviction his license is reviewed by the city license committee. Invariably he is ordered to close for 10 days as penalty.

On proof of second offense, his license is revoked permanently.

Because of the need to show positive identification, some teen-agers want better evidence. The state legislature several years ago authorized clerks of district courts to issue official identification cards, but failed to provide the means.

Applicants to the clerk here are referred to Fingerprinters, Inc., 7149 Buedell Ave. This firm, and others like it in the state, produce for a small fee an identification card enclosed in plastic that bears thumb prints, a photograph and physical description.

Fingerprinters, Inc., is licensed and bonded by the city to provide such services. It conducts its own investigations and demands authentic proof of information necessary to produce the card.

One teen-ager tried to use an altered birth certificate to get a card from the firm.

When confronted with the fault, the girl walked out in a huff, saying, "I know where I can get it done for less."

Examples abound. Note a few that seem to grow not from specific news but from the enterprise and invention of newsmen who look behind the obvious:

A reporter for the Eugene, Oregon, *Register-Guard* visits a nudist camp and comes up with a story that is distinguished because it avoids the temptation to jibe or snigger (as most reporters in this kind of assignment have done), and instead offers a temperate account of the rationale offered for nudism.

A Racine, Wisconsin, paper tells its readers about the annual costs to the county of caring for families abandoned by their husbands and fathers.

A Chicago paper builds an entertaining detective story from information about the sleuthing of the Pullman Company in its efforts to return to customers the baggage and valuables left in sleeping cars.

Many reporters develop stories about archaic local ordinances—stories that not only entertain but also illuminate.

A Knoxville reporter, by interviewing a University of Tennessee graduate student, works up a novel story about the "singin' families" of the hill country that keep folk music alive.

Made stories can be short, like the one that follows. But sometimes, like this one, the short story seems no more than a synopsis of a report that ought to be much longer and more detailed if it is to be truly revealing.

Homeless unemployed men in the seventeen relief shelters maintained by the Illinois emergency relief commission last month drew from the Chicago public library 3,500 books, 4,000 magazines, and 4,500 daily newspapers. They worked an aggregate of 11,269 days in the handicraft shops of the shelters.

Some 18,000 unattached men receive aid in some form through the shelters. About 13,000 live in them. Three thousand get meals and 2,000 receive grocery orders there. Medical care and clothing also are dispensed.

Recent enumerations revealed that the men are 16 to 96 years old; the average age is 45 years and 3 months. They are descended from 27 nationalities and are said to represent almost as many living religions as there are.

Last year 11,453,773 meals were served in the shelters. Average cost of maintenance was slightly over 14 cents daily per man.

Radio and television use enterprisers, too. Following a sensational catastrophe when a jet plane crashed into a group of homes, a St. Paul radio-TV station developed more than 50 stories about the growth of sentiment to move military flying to an airport farther from the residential section. Some were enterprisers in the strict sense; others grew from overt news events that arose out of currents stirred into motion by the enterprisers. A Miami TV newsroom investigated and reported, with sound film, the operation of a local gambling ring. A radio newsman in a Great Lakes city broadcast a series of stories about the shabby reception facilities for visitors reaching the city by ship and aroused the city to meet the problem.

OTHER USES OF MADE STORIES   Made stories, clearly, can be turned to many news purposes. For instance:

The Campaign or "Crusade"   Newspapers, radio, and TV often develop stories to reveal corruption, to present community needs, or to promote "causes." The radio newsman's campaign to make his city more hospitable was one of these.

The Series   An Albany newspaper assigned a reporter to write a series of stories about the city's amusement and recreation facilities. The New York *Times* put 20 experienced reporters to work doing 20 stories on contemporary changes in New York City and its suburbs, showing the impact of the move to suburbia. The themes that have been used are countless: a city's educational needs, what other cities are doing to meet local crime problems, local attitudes toward everything from teen-age drink to mental health, the effects of automation on industry and employment, the needs of minority groups, the problems of literary and theatrical censorship, rowdyism, why Johnny can (or can't) read. Such series are built largely of made stories.

Historical features are made stories. So are many features on subjects in the fields of science, medicine, industry, sports, and education. The front page of the business section of one Sunday paper showed these made stories:

The increasingly sober and businesslike conduct of men attending conventions

The prospects for a profitable shipping season in the local port

The development of a serious and purposeful approach to their work among secretaries and stenographers in local offices

The importance of good weather to retailers as the Easter sales season approached

The changes in laws relating to agriculture probably to be proposed in the current state legislative session

The rousing success of a new pizza emporium in the city.

Most such stories are built around facts or ideas that would yield similar features in any good-sized city. City editors and reporters who are on their toes read papers from other communities regularly.

The stories on pages 221, 222, 228, 229, 233, 234, and 259, in whole or in part, are made stories.

STORIES FOR SPECIAL OCCASIONS   Newsmen have learned to smile sadly when they are asked to do "special occasion" stories, the usually brief stories that have become conventions in holiday coverage. These are the pieces that tell you how Labor Day came about, what really happened to Washington's father's cherry tree, and the way April Fool's Day is celebrated in Scotland. The sad smiles arise from reportorial suspicion that every approach known to man for such stories has been exploited. Yet the stories appear year after year, and though many look more than a little familiar (the whimsical interview with a groundhog on February 2 is a favorite), fresh approaches can always be found.

The genuine special occasion story is not, in most cases, spot news. It is, rather, timely general information, timely in the sense that it must be published on a given day or not at all. But it is timeless, too, for it usually would be as well-used in 1980 as in 1960. It is the story that gives the reader something new or entertaining to add to the flavor of a familiar holiday or season. Reportorial ennui with it comes more from the fact that it is a stereotype than from any inherent or inevitable dullness. Imagination and digging continually produce new "angles."

Essentially a sidebar, this story is distinguished from the straight holiday news story. On July 4 there are always the stories about community celebrations, speeches, fireworks; at Christmas, stories about church observations, caroling, and other seasonal events. These are spot news stories. But the special occasion story is time copy, related to the occasion but not to the news about it.

Materials for special occasion stories often derive from reference books:

histories, encyclopedias, almanacs, specialized volumes. A Lincoln's birthday story telling the world that Lincoln was the first president to wear a beard came from an old biography. One on the origin of Memorial Day came from the *World Almanac*. A long story reporting that only two men actually signed the Declaration of Independence on July 4, 1775, came from histories.

The Paris correspondent of the New York *Times*, Drew Middleton, used historical material that came largely from his personal experience to develop a special occasion story for the twentieth anniversary of V-E Day. But he added other sources. Before reading the striking story he developed, note his explanation of its sources in a letter to the writer of this book:

> A good deal of the story originated in my memory; it was not easily forgotten. The description of the school room and its surroundings on the day was reporting on the spot. I spent the day in Rheims talking to people in the city. By luck, I had come through the city earlier in the month on my return from Strasbourg and had met five couples, two American and three British, who had stopped to see the place "where it ended." These provided me the material about the middle-aged men from Oklahoma and Yorkshire.
>
> I also looked through *Times* files in Paris to check some of the facts about the surrender and to get some of the atmosphere of the time.
>
> The genesis of the story was this: I thought we should have a piece from Rheims rather than Paris, told the foreign news desk in New York, and went up to Rheims to write it.

The story that followed these efforts, you will note, combines the material from the background sources Middleton names with spot news. In this sense, it is not the conventional special occasion story.

RHEIMS, France, May 7 —Up the street the boys were waiting for the girls to come out of school. When they walked off arm in arm in the soft May air, none gave a thought to the dusty room in the school where it all ended.

The room nowadays has that unreal air that haunts all shrines. The battle maps still hang on the walls. But the armies marked on it, and even the place names, seem irrelevant to the busy life that flows around the school.

A long plain table stands at one end of the room. There are seven chairs on one side, three on the other. Twenty years ago the three were occupied by Adm. Hans Georg von Friedeburg, Col. Gen. Alfred Jodl and Major Wilhelm Oxenius.

At 2:41 in the morning Jodl and Friedeburg signed the instrument that signified the unconditional surrender of the Third Reich. It was over, in Europe at least.

History chooses strange sites for her great acts of surrender.

Someone knew that the McLean house at Appomattox was undamaged and Lee rode up in his best uniform. There was a convenient railroad siding at Compiègne and to it came the Germans of 1918 and the French of 1940.

In May, 1945, Rheims was the advance command post of the Supreme Headquarters Allied Expeditionary Force Europe. Millions of men over half a continent answered the orders that came from the big red brick school.

Great men came and went: Eisenhower, Montgomery, Bradley, Tedder, Spaatz. Here were planned the last blows that felled Hitler's Germany.

But today the people of Rheims couldn't care less. The schoolroom, once General Eisenhower's "war room," is closed to the public until Sunday because it is being used by a television company for a program.

No one is going to miss it. The kids waiting outside the school know there was a war but they are a little vague about what actually happened there. And in the good cafes in the arcades of Rheims the surrender is good for perhaps two minutes of personal reminiscence and then on to today's business: the next vintage, the new car, the trip to the Riviera.

They may be callous to the touch of Clio, the Muse of History. Or perhaps Rheims knows the lady too well. What is the date May 7, 1945, to such a city?

Not far from the school, the great Mars Gate built

by the Romans in the third century still stands. The archbishops of Rheims consecrated kings of France from the time of Philip Augustus to that of Charles X. Outside the medieval walls Joan of Arc dispersed an English army.

So, 20 years after, this is a shrine for one generation among many. They come, of course. Middle-aged men from Oklahoma or Yorkshire with rather impatient wives who can't understand why their husbands are interested.

The men, however, won't be hurried.

They look at the maps and point. "There's where we were, Edna," or, "The map must have been bloody well out of date. We were well east of Hamburg."

The room, the school, the city amount to a punctuation point for a whole generation. This was the end of the belly-tightening, desperate years.

It is not dramatic now and it was not dramatic then. A friend once asked Lieut.-Gen. Walter Bedell Smith, General Eisenhower's chief of staff, who signed the document for the Allies, what he had thought of when it was all over.

"To tell you the truth," he said, "I thought of all the damned paper work this was going to mean in the morning."

The only touch of drama was provided by Jodl, the schoolbook soldier with the face from a medieval painting and the mind of a computer.

When he had signed, he stood at attention and said to General Smith:

"General! With this signature the German people and the German armed forces are, for better or worse, delivered into the victor's hands. In this war, which has lasted more than five years, both have achieved and suffered more than perhaps any other people in the world. In this hour I can only express the hope that the victor will treat them generously."

Outside, the street is almost deserted. The few passers by don't even glance at the door with its brass plaque. After all, it was a long time ago.

Sources range all the way from learned interviewees to unadulterated fantasy. A Friday the 13th story offers mock-serious interviews with community leaders about how to avoid bad luck. Few April firsts have passed without stories that open with some such lead as "Federal income taxes have been abolished" or "Importing green cheese from the moon would wreck the Wisconsin dairy industry, according to . . ." The Lockport, N.Y., *Union-Sun & Journal* one year published a doctored photograph showing the huge liner *United States* entering Lockport's little harbor. Oslo newspapers urged readers to pour boiling water down their drains to set up a warm current to melt ice masses in Oslo Fjord. The Galveston *News* is still wondering why so many of its readers, in 1954, spent hours looking for the nonexistent grocery named in the story it thought it had so clearly labeled a spoof:

The Monument Food Store at 25th and Broadway is doing something about the price of coffee. For one day only, L. Irpaloof, proprietor, is offering assorted brands at 33 cents per pound. "I won't make any money on this deal," says Irpaloof, "but I expect to have a lot of fun and I can't think of any better way to throw away money."

Incidentally, the sale has been set for April Fool's Day, if that means anything to you—and it should!

PROJECTS

1. Suppose that in your city or town the police announce that the number of juvenile arrests in the last three months has been only half that of the preceding three. Suggest at least five enterprisers—showing both the nature of each story and the sources of its material—that might be developed from this news peg.
2. Watch the wire news in your local paper until you find a story originating elsewhere that suggests a local angle. Follow up the angle and write a local story.
3. Write for your local paper a time-copy special-occasion story to be published on the next holiday on your calendar.

CHAPTER 17

Investigative Reporting

Joseph Pulitzer, at his death in 1911, left behind not only two distinguished newspapers, the New York *World* and the St. Louis *Post-Dispatch*, but also two significant bequests which, he hoped, would perpetuate his devotion to public service through enlightened and tough-minded, sometimes fighting reporting. One was a fund to establish the Columbia University School of Journalism. The other was the endowment of the Pulitzer prizes, awards for "distinguished and meritorious public service" in journalism and related fields. Every year since World War I these awards have been made; the two that have come to be thought of as *the* Pulitzer prizes, the ones that newsmen cherish most, are those that go annually to newsmen for outstanding reportorial achievement and to newspapers in recognition of extraordinary service to the communities they represent.

This is certainly what Pulitzer wished. His *World* and his *Post-Dispatch* stood for the sturdiest kind of reportorial zeal, skill, courage, and imagination. "Never be satisfied with merely printing the news," he commanded. He might well have said "merely printing the news you can see," for he believed in digging deep and aggressively—and, when necessary, dangerously—for hidden facts. He urged especially the search for hidden corruption, for concealed or private misbehavior. Though he insisted on the development of a vigorous editorial page, he believed that hard-hitting, thorough reporting was the heart of newspaper service to the public. It had to be reporting that was unafraid, that dared probe the deeds of a President as readily as those of a town constable (Theodore Roosevelt brought about a criminal libel indictment again the *World* in 1908—an indictment that did not come to trial).

Though few newspapers have excelled the *World* and the *Post-Dispatch* in devotion to "crusading" or "investigative" journalism, achievement of high order in this field neither began with Pulitzer nor ended with him. James Franklin is given credit for America's first newspaper crusade in his *New England Courant* fight of 1721 on the issue of smallpox inoculation. John Wentworth of the pre-Civil War Chicago *Democrat* was an example, with his booming campaigns for improved schools, fire protection and parks. The great cartoonist Thomas Nast devastated New York's corrupt Tweed Ring in the 1870s through *Harper's Weekly*, which worked with the New York *Times* to drive Tweed from power. The period in which Pulitzer himself directed his newspapers, the turn-of-the-century years, was in a sense the heyday of journalistic crusading—the period of the "muckrakers," of the exposure of crime and antisocial behavior in government and business, by such magazines as *Collier's* and *McClure's* and such writers as Lincoln Steffens, Ida M. Tarbell, and David Graham Phillips (a *World* editorial writer). Pulitzer's greatest campaign, that against the towering life insurance companies and their misuse of policyholders' investments, started in 1905.

When the editor of the San Diego Union, *Richard F. Pourade, spoke before an annual California Editors Conference at Stanford University on the state of investigative reporting, he distinguished between two types:*

"1) The cases of exposure of corruption in public office. These are the more dramatic cases of investigative reporting.

2) The cases of solid community-interest investigative reporting that lead to progressive action. These justify the existence of the newspaper and its championing of the public's right to know so that it can act informedly."

Not all "meritorious public service" by newsmen, that is to say, is of the crime-exposure type. Many newspapers and some broadcasters have undertaken and carried through campaigns or crusades with the purpose of persuading their publics to new points of view, of supporting such projects as

The pattern has continued. A campaign by the Canton, Ohio, *Daily News* in 1926 against lawlessness in its city cost its editor, Don Mellett, his life and won the paper a Pulitzer prize. The Sacramento *Bee* fought for public power in California and against corruption in Nevada (another Pulitzer prize campaign). The Indianapolis *Times* in the mid-50s spent three years driving at what it believed to be dishonesty in state government. Two Portland *Oregonian* reporters won Pulitzer, Sigma Delta Chi, and Heywood Broun awards (the Broun award given annually by the American Newspaper Guild) for their dogged and sometimes dangerous revelation of "scandal" in management of the teamsters' union on the West Coast and of its tie-in with rackets.

In brief, investigative reporting, reporting in depth to present to the public important information that has significant bearing on affairs of public concern, has always been a favorite tool of responsible newsmen. Though some critics, among them the acid-tongued H. L. Mencken, have described what they believe to be the apathy and "the decline of crusading" in twentieth-century journalism, the man who has taken the longest look at the record—Silas Bent (himself a sharp critic of the press), whose book *Newspaper Crusaders* recounts many notable campaigns—finds the charge unsound. One of the judges of an annual Heywood Broun competition, Dr. Ralph D. Casey, then director of the Minnesota School of Journalism, commented that reading the nearly 100 entries gave him

improved community sani-
tation or police protection,
or of bolstering aspects
of community economy,
morale, or social well-being.
A Pulitzer prize went to the
Bismarck, N.D., Tribune
for a carefully-wrought series
of reportorial articles that
aided a drought-stricken
community to develop its
own resources for irrigation,
diversification of agriculture,
and other methods of pulling
itself up by its own boot-
straps.

The extraordinary variety
of such enterprises is well
illustrated in John Hohen-
berg's excellent book about
Pulitzer awards—The Pu-
litzer Prize Story (New
York: Columbia University
Press, 1959).

"renewed confidence in the performance of the working journalist on the newspaper firing line."

That this kind of news enterprise is not limited to the giant newspapers or, indeed, to the printed press is evidenced by performances of community weeklies and of broadcasters (lack of space denies a catalog of them), and by the awards established by the Radio-TV News Directors Association, other broadcasting agencies, and many other state and regional associations to honor worthy public service. The Case of the Wooden Doors, detailed later in this chapter, is an example of this kind of work by a small-city daily that is committed to aggressive reportorial attack on attempts to throttle voices that the public ought to hear.

Finally, it hardly needs to be said that the reportorial weapon is not the only one in a newspaper or broadcasting campaign to achieve a public purpose. The editorial columns, which bring interpretation and opinion to the support and supplement of factual reporting, are as much a part of journalistic crusading as the news columns. But editorials without the undergirding that thorough investigation provides have not won many battles.

No "new" techniques of reporting have to be invented for this kind of news work. Investigative reporting differs from day-by-day leg work not in methods but rather in the circumstances that surround it—in the fact that the tip or idea on which it is based is more commonly obscure than sharply visible, that the reporting itself takes longer, demands more patience and perseverance and often imagination than everyday fact-gathering, that the reporter is likely to meet resistance, roadblocks, and often threats or genuine danger, and that the deadline may be not today's or tomorrow's, but that of a date months in the future.

If the reportorial techniques of the investigative reporter are not new, however, they must be intensified and searching, sharpened not alone by experience but also by the honing that analysis of experience gives. One of America's most gifted and effective investigative reporters, Clark Mollenhoff of the Washington bureau of the Cowles newspapers and magazines (more about him later in this chapter), illustrates the depth of knowledge of news sources needed for needle-point reporting in a "Check List for Investigative Reporters" he developed for use at the American Press Institute of Columbia University. The check list is prepared as a guide for local news investigations—reporting at the city and county levels—but it suggests the character of similar sources that a reporter working at state or national topics would probe. In giving permission for the following digest of the check list, Mollenhoff gives credit for some of the material in it to John Seigenthaler, editor of the Nashville *Tennesseean*. The digest, less complete than the full list, indicates both the kinds of sources an investigative reporter working on a local topic would need to develop and the special kinds of hidden material he might need to ferret out.

CHECK LIST FOR INVESTIGATIVE REPORTERS
(Local Level)

A   SOME COMMON EVILS FOUND IN LOCAL GOVERNMENT

1) *Payroll padding.* Check budget requests and payrolls to find whether they are loaded with relatives, friends, or political hacks. Who approves hiring? Are there deadheads or moonlighters on the payroll? How is a substantial increase in a payroll to be explained?

2) *Personnel: Hiring and qualifications.* Are there adequate civil service requirements and pension fund protections? Is the promotion system sound? Is there nepotism?

3) *Vacations, sick leave, work time.* Is supervision adequate? Could "dummy" employes be on the payroll, with higher-ups pocketing their pay?

4) *Property management and inventory control.* What special services (such as automobiles) are furnished to employes? How are they bought and paid for? Who gets the business and why? Where is control lodged? How does it work?

5) *False billing.* This practice is easy to conceal. A reporter can unearth it only by a direct check of all questionable items.

6) *Expenses: Travel per diem, etc.* Are expense accounts padded? Is the mileage claimed and paid for actually traveled?

B   PRINCIPAL COUNTY OR CITY OFFICES TO CHECK

1) *Board of Supervisors, Commissioners, or Councilmen*
   Check: *Budget-making process.* Use of appropriated money. Are all claimed payments actually made?
   Conflicts of interest. What businesses are the officials engaged in? How do they make contracts? Who gets county or city contracts? Are bids properly examined? Are specifications on bids honest, and are they observed? Are bills checked? Is the payment system water-tight?
   Licenses. Are liquor and beer licenses properly issued? Who controls their issue? Are public hearings held? Are pinball machines and juke boxes properly controlled? Who furnishes them? How much does he get?

2) *City or County Auditor*
   Check: The *"common evils"* suggested above.
   Cash fees for various licenses—any chance they are being concealed?
   Beer bonds and cigaret bonds—any conflict of interest?
   Election machinery—is there opportunity for fraud?

3) *Sheriff's Office or Police Department*

Check: Is the sheriff on *salary,* or is there a *fee system?* Are fees appropriate? Could they be misused?

Liquor seizures. Are seizures legally made? Does seized liquor get back into circulation? How is seized property identified?

Gambling equipment seizures—same questions.

Jail practices. Is there a trusty system? Does it work? Does anybody in jail get "special treatment"? Why?

4) *Clerk of Court*

Check: *Records* of all kinds—probate, divorce, marriage.

Criminal indictments, grand jury reports. Are indictments properly disposed of? Are "old" reports or indictments being ignored?

Warrant handling. Are all warrants served? Are they properly issued? Are John Doe warrants used to conceal names of figures with "pull"?

Bail bonds. Is property offered for bonds properly assessed? Are professional bondsmen held rigidly to forfeitures? Are any bondsmen favored?

Witness fees. Are any such fees being collected improperly? If so, is there any kick-back to higher-ups? Are "dummy" witnesses being paid?

Jury selection. Are jury lists up to date? Is there danger of stacked panels? Do handpicked jurymen get selected—a strong union man, for instance, on a labor case?

Civil suits. Look for conflict of interest. Watch for financial details of damage suits.

5) *Recorder*

Check: *Filing fees*—is the recording system adequate?

Service fees for copies of records, etc. Who gets the business?

Corporate records. Are they properly kept?

Personal property mortgage records. Do these records—such as automobile mortgage records—show any "unusual" financial transactions by public officials?

Real estate mortgage records. These can be used in manner similar to that suggested for personal property mortgage records.

6) *The School System*

Check: *Building contracts.* How awarded? Who gets them? Are low bids often disregarded? How are architects selected?

Purchasing. How is school equipment bought? Sealed bids? Is information about purchasing operations open to inspection? If not, why not?

Selection of teachers. Are the standards adequate? Are they observed? Who makes the choices? Any "outside" influences?

7) *The Highway Department*

Check: Questions like those under Section 6 on contracts and purchasing.

8) *Tax Assessor*

Check: Property owned by officials and influential political or business figures. Does anybody get "special consideration"?

9) *City or County Health Department*
   Check: *Hospital standards.* Are they adequate? Are they enforced?
   Food establishment standards. Are restaurants and hotel dining rooms required to maintain adequate standards of sanitation? If they aren't, who is at fault? Should U.S. Public Health officials be brought in?

C   SOURCES FOR A COMPLETE PERSONAL INVESTIGATION

1) Birth records, Bureau of Vital Statistics. Parents' names may be used to run mortgage records on their economic status, and for examination of probate records if they are dead.
2) Clerk of court: marriage and divorce records
3) Municipal or state courts: criminal records, civil disputes
4) Recorder: military service discharge, mortgages, tax liens, corporation records
5) Federal court: bankruptcy actions, federal tax disputes
6) Treasurer: automobile and driver's licenses, property assessements
7) Assessor: property assessments
8) Miscellaneous: Kefauver Committee reports; immigration records; election records; credit ratings; passport records; McClellan Committee reports in some areas

(Note that differences in state laws and local practices may mean that some types of information may be found in offices other than those named above in particular situations.)

The Mollenhoff suggestions, you will note, are directed toward the discovery of public misbehavior: bribery, graft, error, deceit in public places. Investigative reporting is heavily of this nature. And the seed from which such reporting grows may be hard to recognize, since one of its prime characteristics is that it is secret. The initial hunch that gives a reporter or his editor the start toward a campaign or investigation may be pink and blue on its surface; it becomes significant only when a newsman finds that its combined color is mud or a murky purple. It is not news that a member of the city council has bought a car; but the fact that the three county commissioners who voted in favor of building a glossy new sports stadium blossom out with Cadillacs just as glossy bears looking into.

If the insight, curiosity, and awareness that help a newsman to see a promising news lead rather than overlook it are sometimes difficult to bring into play, the thoroughness that investigative reporting demands is more so. In some cases a reporter, or a team of reporters, may be released from other duties to give full time to an investigation. It is more common, however, that the reporter carries his search for hidden answers, at least in its early stages, along with his regular work. "You just have to keep everlastingly at it," explains the reporter in the Wooden Doors case. "You do a little now, and a little tomorrow. Sometimes you think you're getting nowhere. Sometimes you *are* getting nowhere—you run up lots of blind alleys. But you keep plugging, working plenty of nights and weekends that don't show on your overtime card, and eventually, if you don't give up and if you juggle the pieces often enough, you find that they'll start fitting together."

(The Tampa *Tribune* kept a man on an investigation full-time for 12 months before he wrote a line of copy. Six weeks of preliminary and unpublished work went into the Chicago *Daily News's* exposure of a state auditor's irregularities.)

By its very nature, investigative reporting runs head on into resistance. Its purpose is to bring to light deeds and facts that principal information sources would prefer curtailed. Here is where the skills of reportorial experience become vital (as was shown in the Mollenhoff outline): the knowledge that any news fact can be gained in more than one way, the ingenuity to find roads that are not blocked, and the determination never to let false starts end in discouragement. Though real personal danger is more common in Hollywood reporting than life, it is by no means unknown. Don Mellett was murdered by a gunman who rang his doorbell one evening. Jake Lingle of the Chicago *Tribune* was shot to death because he knew too much. William N. Oatis of the Associated Press was imprisoned behind the Iron Curtain for many months on the allegation that he was a spy. The editor who kept a sixshooter handy disappeared with the frontier, but the reporter who undertakes an investigation of underworld crime may now and again wish he had one.

Sixshooter or no, he is not likely to lack for support. Though many reportorial investigations start as one-man jobs, they tend to grow into matters of teamwork. The Chicago *Daily News* and the St. Louis *Post-Dispatch* combined two teams of reporters on the notable investigation that disclosed that half a hundred Illinois newspapermen were illegally on the payroll of the state government. A Seattle *Times* reporter gave significant aid to Wallace Turner and William Lambert, Portland *Oregonian* reporters, in their teamsters' union investigations.

The approach taken by one metropolitan newspaper, the Detroit *Free Press*, appears in a list of "general observations" on investigative reporting prepared by Fred Olmstead as its city editor. The observations, aimed at news executives, say just as much to reporters:

1) Don't overlook a tip from any source. Some of the best leads may come from unpromising tips. Many, perhaps most, won't pan out. But don't overlook any possibilities.

2) Give those doing the investigating the full support of your staff. If men are needed to help check records or for other assistance, provide them.

3) Keep your own interest and enthusiasm alive and focused on the problem. You can't expect your men to show the pursuing spirit unless you do.

4) Stay within the law. Don't attempt to open safes or burglarize offices for evidence.

5) Don't be a policeman. Remember, you represent a newspaper, and you have a better weapon than a nightstick or a gun. If a policeman isn't doing his job, you don't take it over. You go to someone higher.

6) Don't scatter your shots. Select your best lead and pursue it. You can get bogged down in diversionary actions.

7) Don't be afraid to abandon a lead—or an investigation. But don't do it until you're convinced you're on the wrong track.

8) Don't be afraid to tell what you know. If you print it, more leads will come your way.

9) Think what you *can* do to get the story out, not what you *can't* do because of libel or other obstacles. A positive-thinking attorney will help you say more, not less—and still keep clear of libel.

10) Take time out and appraise your situation once in a while. Take a good look at what you have done as a guide to where you should go. Adding things up from time to time may give you a new answer.

11) Make plans before you start. Don't leap into it. Check the evidence and keep checking it as you go along. Keep up your lines of communication with those working in the field. See that they maintain communication with each other.

12) Keep going. The investigative way is hard, but don't stop if you think you have something. If your curiosity is burning you as it should, you won't.

How Gene Goltz Got His Nose Broken   Gene Goltz became a suburban reporter for the Houston *Post* in November, 1962. At 32, Goltz was an experienced newsman; he was also an accountant. Perhaps his knowledge of accounting procedures helped him to smell out what appeared to be irregularities in the municipal finances of Pasadena, one of the Houston suburbs whose city hall he covered. After six months on the beat he started investigation of rumors that there was a "real story" in the manner in which 6 million dollars from a city bond issue had been spent. For six months he got nothing but a run-around, refusals to let him see records that were supposed to be public, denials of irregularities, finally threats and secret meetings of municipal officials. But he garnered enough information to assure him that irregularities existed, and to convince his city editor that the "real story" might be found.

By November 1963, he was able to write a series of stories about irregular procedures in city government. These stories told of no illegality; but they triggered responses from many sources—some of them anonymous, some by midnight telephone call—that opened new avenues of investigation. One led to a major investment firm which, Goltz was able to prove, had received a 2 percent commission for handling city bond sales (four times the usual fee) and had "kicked back" half of it to city officials. Others developed information that city officials, mayors, councilmen and others, had made a practice of paying themselves illegal fees.

And one avenue led Goltz to an encounter with the Pasadena police commissioner, whose furious punch broke his nose.

Eventually, though Goltz was warned that he better stay away from Pasadena, though his wife's safety was repeatedly threatened, though the citizenry of the suburb was reluctant to believe the stories the *Post* printed, the crusade won out. A grand jury indicted a handful of city officials. The electorate, finally convinced, cleaned house by voting in new officers. Many communities in the area re-examined their own financial procedures, some of them adopting resolutions requiring open public records.

And the *Post* and Goltz were awarded an armful of prizes including the Heywood Broun Award from the Newspaper Guild, a National Headliners Award, and the Pulitzer prize for local reporting.

The classical tools of investigative reporting won these prizes: keen observation; patient, tireless digging; persistence over weeks and months (grand jury indictments came a full year after Goltz's first story appeared); courage (and, Goltz has added, a wife who can take punishment). One of the truisms the campaign demonstrated was that many sources knew the facts that Goltz worked so hard to find; but that to open mouths it took the public knowledge that a newsman and his paper were fighting to right a wrong.

THE CASE OF THE WOODEN DOORS   As an example of aggressive investigative reporting by a small-city daily firmly committed to this kind of journalism, the East St. Louis, Ill., *Journal*, listen to its story from the reporter who carried most of the load. He is Bruce Kipp, whose work on another case, a series of stories that led to conviction of a school principal for forgery, won the sweepstakes award in an Illinois Associated Press reporting contest.

> I was fresh on the school beat, knew no one, and found school officials close-mouthed and distrustful. The district was building a new senior high school under contracts adding up to nearly 4 million dollars. Suspicious of a number of "change orders" on the job, my editor, Thomas Duffy, asked me to work up a complete tabulation of the costs. We found that these change orders altered original specifications so as to boost the cost to the school district by more than $150,000. Among them was a change order calling for substitution of hollow wooden doors for the hollow steel doors originally specified, at an added cost of $68,455. This looked odd to me. I called the structural engineer on the job to ask about it. He defended the change and the added cost mightily (and 10 minutes later appeared in the newsroom for no apparent reason other than to see what I looked like).
>
> We printed our compilation of construction costs and sat tight, but there was no immediate reaction other than the momentary interest in the breast of the structural engineer.
>
> About six months passed. We thought of using our own money to get an outside audit of the school district's construction program, but the plan fell through. I kept those doors in mind, however, and checked their costs with a lumber dealer, an outside architect, and others. This information was enough for Duffy to give me the go-ahead on the investigation.
>
> It took two weeks of cost checking to make sure we were not wasting our time. The powers-that-be always have enemies. One of these who was most helpful was an architect hired by the prime architect on the job and later replaced. We located him by long-distance telephone in Lincoln, Nebraska.
>
> When we felt we were well grounded in information about the costs and

quality of wooden, steel, and aluminum doors, as well as door frames and hardware, it was time to approach the principals.

The first approach was made to the prime architect. I considered him evasive, but truthful. He said the general contractor was the man to see.

The general contractor furnished explanations, but no concrete figures. He did supply the name of a kind of middle man who had dealt in one capacity or another with all the change-order items.

After checking into facts about this middle man, I went to the general contractor again, this time with a witness. He repeated essentially the information he had supplied before.

Then I went to the middle man, his former employer, and the head of the local lumber company which supplied the change-order items to the contractor; from them I obtained the names of several distributors. Included among those I approached was a school board member whose name came up repeatedly.

We now wrote our story, letting all the conflicting statements about door costs and the change orders speak for themselves, without attempting to evaluate any of them. We wrote a separate story about the middle man, who was dealing in the wooden doors shortly after quitting a supplier who had used him to try to sell competitive steel doors to the high school.

We roughed out a door cost sheet to show that the taxpayer was paying $240 for each of the replacement doors, installed. The manufacturer of the very wooden doors used regarded a price anything like that as "crazy."

We didn't stop with the initial stories, which we published in December. Duffy, who was more than cooperative all along and contributed a great deal of the thinking, worked up a separate door cost story from a supplier's catalog. Later, to add strength to the investigation and show we weren't the only ones interested, we induced the St. Clair County Taxpayers Association, an independent private agency, to come up with something approaching an exact cost analysis.

Two investigations were launched by official agencies. One was by the office of the state superintendent of public instruction. The school board made an investigation of sorts. Both resulted in whitewashes.

We kept after statements from the contractor, the school board, and others mixed up in it. We twice published mug shots of the board and other figures in the case with lines to the effect that "these men refuse to tell the public the public's business."

Finally the state's attorney, who had meanwhile received an anonymous letter with a copy to us about alleged fee-splitting, put the door issue before a grand jury. We were instrumental in getting a key witness into the hands of the state's attorney. Through our assortment of school administration "enemies," we were able to locate this witness, who lived beyond Illinois subpoena power in Missouri, when he came to Illinois one Sunday.

The grand jury handed down two indictments, one for perjury against the general contractor and one for malfeasance in public office against a school board member whose name had scarcely crept into mention during our investigation.

OTHER CASES IN BRIEF   Clark Mollenhoff, whom you met earlier in this chapter, was given both a Sigma Delta Chi award and the Heywood Broun award in 1955 for his work involving no illegality but rather what Mollenhoff believed to be both a personal injustice and an offense against public policy—

the so-called Ladejinsky ouster case (Mollenhoff later won a Pulitzer prize for investigative reporting of labor union corruption).

Mollenhoff started digging into the story upon learning that Wolf Ladejinsky, a Russian-born land reform specialist in the Department of Agriculture, had been fired "for security reasons," even though the State Department had earlier given him security clearance. Smelling something he didn't like, Mollenhoff went after the facts; among many steps in developing them were these:

Persuading a Congressman to go on record in Ladejinsky's defense, thus giving the case official standing.

Breaking the story over protests and requests that it be kept secret. (A sidelight: the news broke first in Cowles Sunday papers, the Des Moines *Register* and the Minneapolis *Tribune*—familiar newspaper timing of "exclusive" news to take advantage of a jump on newspaper competition.)

Asking the chief security office of the Department of Agriculture for information about his own background when the officer refused to discuss the case. To the officer's second refusal, Mollenhoff responded, "I can sit right here and write a story on a security officer completely secured." Within 10 minutes he had full biographical information on the man, and later an interview with him.

Finding and gaining an hour-long interview with the Secretary of Agriculture at his home, after Department offices had asserted that he was on vacation and would be unavailable for two weeks.

Investigating a letter from a White Russian editor of a trade magazine which supported Ladejinsky's firing; discovering strong anti-Semitism in the letter; writing an "explosive" story to describe it.

Following dozens of leads and angles, and developing them until at length the Department of Agriculture withdrew the charges.

Award judges' comment on Mollenhoff's work suggests the qualities that mark able investigative reporting at any level:

> It was a case in which a newspaper reporter smelled out a story, investigated it, found that an injustice existed, and pursued a course to rectify it. Literally, he pursued it into the White House. In terms of results, he not only gained redress for the individual who was the central figure, but brought changes in federal security program procedures which of themselves ought to protect against repetition. Beyond all that, it was a topflight job of searching, objective writing.

William Jones, a reporter for the *Independent* and *Press-Telegram* of Long Beach, Cal., took 10 weeks, during part of which he posed as a salesman seeking to add to his income, to investigate eight "ordination mills" in and out of California. He bought himself a $50 ordination as a minister and a $30 qualification as a "faith healer" (he could have become a bishop for $200). As a result of his investigations, which he carried out in cooperation with the state attorney general's office, the operator of one of the "ordination mills" was charged with a felony and attention was drawn to California's inadequate laws in this area (the felony charge, incidentally, was brought under a law passed following a similar investigation by another *Independent-Press-Telegram* reporter several years earlier).

"Race Relations in Riverside—a Study in Subtlety" was the title under which the Riverside (California) *Press* and *Enterprise* ran seven articles on every phase of its topic in the city. Fifteen reporters had worked over a five-month period to gather the material. The series showed that serious problems of discrimination and segregation existed in Riverside, and that they had grave effects on all segments of the community, not merely on those discriminated against.

A stunt that had investigative reporting overtones was carried out by two members of the staff of the Washington *Daily News*. A woman reporter, Clare Crawford, attended a meeting of a Maryland White Citizens Council chapter (whose views she rejected) because she had learned that a member of an opposing group had joined it secretly "to keep tabs on it." She scented a story. But she was promptly elected recording secretary of the group; and her lawyer husband, attending with her because he did not want her to attend alone, was made its legal adviser. Before long another *News* reporter, Tom Kelly, joined, and soon their friends came along and gained control. They persuaded the national office of White Citizens to bar the genuine segregationists from the chapter, and ended up by affiliating it with the Congress of Racial Equality—CORE—as the last act in the comedy.

It need hardly be added that the story was first told to the world, and to the discomfited White Citizens, through Crawford-Kelly stories in the *Daily News*.

PROJECTS

1. This chapter makes the assertion that "no 'new' techniques of reporting have to be invented for this kind of news work" (investigative reporting). Write a 200-word definition of investigative reporting, showing what its distinctive features are if they are not " 'new' techniques."
2. Talk with reporters or other newsmen working with local media about possibilities for investigative reporting in your community. If there are potential areas for this kind of reporting, why are they not explored?
3. If you identify an area in which investigative reporting might be profitable, write out a tentative assignment sheet to direct a reporter toward appropriate fields of inquiry.

CHAPTER 18

Interpretive Reporting

The publisher of *Time* magazine, James A. Linen, was talking to a group of Chicago businessmen about news:

> Just what is news? Well, it's not what it used to be. It's not simply something that happens on a well-trod beat, or on a platform, or to a particular person in a particular place—although all of these are indeed part of it. And curiosity is still of root importance. The journalist goes on asking: What's going on here? Where are we heading?—very proper questions for the eternally curious journalist. But the important new dimension in journalism's own redefinition of news is the context in which the questions are posed —and the answers probed.

How has the context changed? What is the "new dimension"?

In many places in this book you find these "questions . . . posed" and their "answers probed." The dynamic, volatile nature of news in an unstable world is a theme of the early chapters; the use of interviews and "developed" stories to give depth and perspective to the day's reporting is emphasized in the four chapters preceding this one. The danger of an objectivity that substitutes superficiality for penetration has been more than once red-flagged.

Like Linen's comments, these themes and emphases grow from the revolution in communications that has accompanied the swell of social complexity in the modern world. To recall some of the familiar facts: The world suddenly contracted in the first half of this century. Air transportation and broadcasting reduced distance and time. The headlong race into space of the postwar years means that man can more knowledgeably and realistically speak of his universe than ever before. Meanwhile, every phase of his life has grown more involved. The sciences, the interplay of social organizations, frantically-expanding knowledge in a thousand areas of human thought and activity, all have grown and changed at such speed that no man, however learned . . . much less the man in the street, the nonexistent "average" news consumer . . . can nurture the sophistication to be at home with more than a few of them.

If it is impossible for a man to understand all the complicated threads of medicine, religion, business, politics, the modern arts and philosophies and social and natural sciences, it is equally beyond his capacity to keep abreast of the bewildering flow of current events that grow out of them.

It was soon after World War I that newsmen, examining their product and the needs of their audiences, began to develop sharp awareness that something was missing. Their perception was stimulated in 1923 when two young men of brief news experience but broad vision invented *Time* magazine, founded in the hope of reporting the sweep of the news, its background, its subsurface meanings—its "new dimension." One of the first newspaper efforts to meet the challenge was the "interpretive" column, a daily news analysis or commentary by an experienced and competent journalist (usually in Washington) who sought to bring authoritative opinion and relevant background fact to aid his reader's understanding of current national and international affairs. By the early 1930s commentary of this type was well established in the press, and the late 1930s brought radio commentators onto the scene. With World War II the need for this kind of aid to news comprehension was widely recognized; newspapers offered Walter Lippmann, Marquis Childs, Howard W. Blakeslee, Hanson Baldwin among many, as radio was bringing Edward R. Murrow, Elmer Davis, Eric Sevareid, and others to its listeners.

The newsmagazine view of the problem discussed in this chapter was described by Andrew Heiskell when he was publisher of Life *(reprinted by permission):*

"The journalistic tradition has wrongly been interpreted to mean that the editor's duty is just to tell what he sees happening as events occur. It seems to me that good journalism, except where acts of God are concerned, is a continuous story. The good editor does not simply pick up an event as it goes by the window. The good editor foresees what will happen, prepares for it, and often prepares his public for it. He relates it to other happenings, and finally carries it through to its conclusion. Most importantly, he decides how to make it the most interesting, the most dramatic tale."

These men's "commentaries" were often just that, comments and opinions about the rush of the news, rather than its factual reporting. Men like Raymond Gram Swing and Lippmann were essentially editorialists, men who brought factually fortified interpretation and opinion to the explanation of news events. Others such as Davis, Childs, and Sevareid combined factual reporting with personal analysis and explanation. Some, especially the best-known radio figures, were essentially reporters who presented personalized versions of news events. Some, such as Fulton Lewis, Upton Close, and George E. Sokolsky, were men whose strongly-felt opinions about the meaning of the events they reported led to a distorting failure of objectivity.

Newsmen came at this time to emphasize a distinction that was not new but that needed recognition with the expanding efforts at news explanation: the distinction between commentary and "background." The first was taken to mean what the word denotes: comment, criticism, and illumination of the news in the light of whatever knowledge *and opinion* the com-

CBS, under its distinguished news director, Paul White, insisted that news interpretation and news analysis are two different processes. Interpretation, it said, means subjective and personal explanation of what a man believes the news means. Analysis is the presentation of relevant background and tangential material that permit the listener or reader to form his own conclusions in full possession of the necessary facts.

"Nonsense!" scoffed critics. "An 'analyst' is only a commentator by a different name. Nobody can illuminate the news without letting personal attitudes and views creep in."

CBS "analysts" and White himself agreed that total impersonality is a goal that can't be achieved. But they also agreed that this fact is no reason for not striving toward it (see page 24).

•   •

"What," demands the perplexed student of journalism, "is the difference between news interpretation and editorializing?"

A fair question, and one not easy to answer because sometimes there is no difference. The purpose of either may be only to clarify complexity. But some distinguishing features can be discerned:

1) The prime purpose of interpretive reporting, honestly used, is just what the term implies: clarification and illumination (if it is used to lead or shape opinion, it departs from its defined purpose, and may be deceitful). The purposes of editorials may legitimately be many: clarification and illumination, opinion-shaping, incitement to action, even entertainment.

mentator could bring to it. Thus a departure from the principle of objectivity was reintroduced to news presentation. It was not strictly new, for editorials often were, and are, of this nature. But it was recognized that responsible journalism called for the presentation of responsible subjective analysis, always clearly identified for what it was.

Background, in contrast, became the term for factual material underlying or surrounding or affecting a news event, presented on its own merits and solely with the purpose of helping the news consumer to place the event in appropriate context. This was no more new than the presentation of "editorial" matter. But it received, and today receives even more, emphasis as an essential to the understanding of the news. The radio listener, if he is to understand the acts of something called "the Viet Cong," has to know what the Viet Cong is. The newspaper reader learning from a column before him that "radioactive fallout has doubled in the last two weeks" must be informed whether the increase is meaningful to him, where the increase came from, perhaps even what radioactive fallout means. The presentation of this kind of relevant contextual "background" does not evaluate its meaning for the consumer, but asks him to provide the evaluation himself.

The awareness of the need to supply materials of these kinds to the public led to the development of many weapons—beyond the labeled commentary or explanation of the recognized expert—in the war against complexity and obscurity in the news. Among them:

The insertion of "background paragraphs," passages providing relevant information against which a news development may be laid. Such material may be used as a "background precede," a passage at the head of a story, or as material inserted into its body, usually within parentheses or in italic type, or both.

The regular use, on the editorial page or elsewhere in the paper, of material in a department designed for the purpose. A Columbus paper, for example, developed a staff-written column under the title "Reviewing the News." The London *News-Chronicle* provided explanatory information in a column called "The World This Morning."

2) The editorial is commonly institutional—the acknowledged voice of the newspaper or the broadcasting station as an institution. The interpretive news story is the voice only of its writer.

3) The editorial is anonymous (except for its institutional nature). The writer of the interpretive story is identified, and if his story presents opinion it is known to be his.

It is true that any kind of news presentation may be colored by editorial purpose. As the earlier chapters of this book have made clear, permitting this to happen is considered improper practice. It occurs infrequently.

The use of supplementary stories—sidebars—to elaborate or explain complex news developments (the news interview is commonly so used).

The development of "news review" departments, such as the New York *Times* Sunday "News Review of the Week," or similar features in the Washington *Star* and other papers.

The development by radio and TV newsrooms of periodical broadcasts aimed at explaining rather than reporting the news.

Special departments or features—both in print and on the air—bringing together opinions from many sources on current news topics.

But the most fruitful approach of any has been the development of a form that, though not new, has become one of the most significant efforts of modern American journalism (as it is of European journalism): what has come to be called "interpretive reporting." This is reporting in context, with the purpose either to develop news of a current event in such a way as to present the revealing background along with the spot news, or to dig out information and present it as supplementary to the spot news story. It may be reporting with background woven around the account of the event itself; it may be reporting presented in the light of the writer's personal opinions and explanations. It is generally accepted that such reporting, especially that involving the writer's opinion and evaluation, must be under a byline, so that the consumer may know whom to credit (and, in some cases, whether to credit him). It yields the kind of story to which the New York *Times's* Bernstein once referred as "the long-look piece in which the writer backs away from a complicated subject in the news to get a clarifying view of it." It is what another man, Director Harold L. Nelson of the Wisconsin School of Journalism, calls "the journalism of cause-and-effect relationship." As Nelson suggests, it may be the kind of reporting that says, "The causes that led to the news event were such-and-such . . ." or that speculates, "The results of this news event may be expected to be such-and-such . . ."

"News interpretation" is at best a fuzzy term, one that means something particular in each man's mouth. But in general it connotes adding meaning to the news, helping the puzzled "average man" to understand his puzzling world. It is the outstanding development of twentieth-century news journalism—as great a contribution to professional news practice as were the principle of objectivity and the unadorned news story form in the nineteenth century, and as important an advance over "simple objectivity" as was the noneditorialized spot news story over the partisan "reporting" of pre-Civil War years.

Nobody should deceive himself with the hope that the millennium has arrived. Since World War II and the advent of television, newspapermen's conferences have been dotted with warnings from their own corps that newspapers have only begun to exploit this new tool adequately, and that if they don't develop it they may forever forfeit a major function to news magazines and even to broadcasting. These warnings have been given point by the growing audiences of such weeklies as *Time, Newsweek, U.S. News and World Report,* and the *National Observer,* by the penetrating news analyses in "serious" magazines like *Harper's,* the *Atlantic,* and the *Reporter,* and by such superb news backgrounding as radio and TV have accomplished through documentaries and panel examinations of current news developments—the kind of thing done by "Meet the Press," "CBS Reports," the Huntley-Brinkley specials, and many local-station productions. Developments like these constitute long strides in the direction the news media must take toward the goal of full responsibility. Yet, as a whole, the media are far from arrival at the goal.

All the news media, in short, are painfully aware of the need for making the news clear and understandable. The addition of specialists to many news staffs —writers on everything from social service to space science, conservation to education—is a recognition of the need. One of the clearest statements of the awareness (as well as the introduction of a new term) comes from the much-quoted T. M. Bernstein of the New York *Times:*

> Journalism of the future is almost surely going to have to encompass a new dimension to make increasingly complex stories understandable. The new dimension is a phase of interpretive writing that might be called motivational reporting: explaining the reasons—the real reasons, so far as they can be discovered—for the actions of groups and individuals. Some of this is being done now. For example: "Some powerful Democrats in the city are either opposed to charter reform or want to delay action on it beyond this election. Those who oppose it generally fear that it will reduce powers they now have. Those who seek delay generally fear that a fight over charter reform during the election would further split the already badly divided Democratic party." There are plenty of stories that cry out for this kind of treatment. Think, for instance, how greatly the Congo complexities could have been clarified had it been possible to report the motivations of Kasavubu and Ileo, of Tshombe, and of Lumumba and Gizenga. Admittedly this is a difficult and perhaps dangerous area of reporting, but it often can be accomplished by a reporter who is knowledgeable and digs in the right places. There are, of course, various levels of motivation. There is the ostensible motivation—the reasons Gizenga assigns publicly for his actions. This level is adequately reported, but it does not disclose much. Then there is often a submerged general motivation—Gizenga's ties to a nation or bloc. Finally, there is a personal, perhaps selfish, motivation—what Gizenga hopes to gain for himself. It is these submerged levels that are the fruitful ones for explaining what the news is all about. In getting at them the reporter must be wary as well as diligent. But the rewards can be great.

Bernstein is talking here about only one kind of interpretive reporting. But what he says has broad application. The "submerged levels" are often the levels that tell the story—and they are the ones that the reporter must reach because his readers or listeners can't.

The Interpretive Story

News stories that help the news consumer with his own analysis of the meaning of the news he reads or hears are of many kinds. You can no more delimit "the interpretive story type" than you can define specific and exclusive patterns for color stories, speech stories, or made stories. On the contrary, stories of all these varieties, and others, may be interpretive. Indeed, a number of the stories presented earlier in this book because of other characteristics are examples of interpretive, or background, journalism (see pages 117, 221, 222, 228).

Interpretive news stories are usually marked by these characteristics (as well as others): first, the purpose; second, the depth of reporting that serves the purpose; third, the occasional absence of the spot news element (a background story about the "deliberate speed" with which American schools have been integrated, for example, might contain no reference to the most recent relevant occurrence). Examples of interpretive stories of various kinds, on pages 298 to 302, make these and other patterns evident.

Before going to them, however, note four different treatments of one event —a news story, an editorial, and two interpretive stories with different approaches. The event is described in the news story (a somewhat shortened version of a Washington *Post* story that appeared in the St. Paul Pioneer-Press, a subscriber to *Post* service):

AUSTIN, Texas—President Johnson has asked Pakistan's President Mohammed Ayub Khan and India's Prime Minister Lal Bahadur Shastri to postpone until fall visits to Washington that had been scheduled for the next few weeks.

The President also has decided definitely against any foreign travel for the time being.

White House Press Secretary George E. Reedy read this statement to newsmen Friday:

"In light of the Congressional workload for the next two or three months and the situation in Vietnam, the President is not planning any trips abroad and is keeping his schedule to a minimum.

"We have already had several visits this year and the President has agreed with other governments that some anticipated visits will be scheduled for the fall instead of late spring.

"The governments of Pakistan and India have graciously agreed to the postponement of the prospective visits of President Ayub and Prime Minister Shastri."

Ayub was scheduled to visit the President April 25 and Shastri's visit was scheduled for June 2 and 3.

There was no further explanation for the President's decision affecting the Indian and Pakistani visits, both of which had been considered important for political and economic reasons.

Reedy said that Italian Prime Minister Aldo Moro, as scheduled, would confer with the President Tuesday and Wednesday.

When asked if that is the last visit scheduled, Reedy said that it is and added that any other visits under discussion "we have deferred."

When it was pointed out that Korean President Chung Hee Park is scheduled to visit the President May 17 and 18, Reedy confirmed that Park would make the trip as planned.

A spokesman later said that direct involvement of the Koreans with the Vietnam situation is one of the factors in the President's decision to meet with Park.

In New Delhi, India reacted icily to the abrupt postponement of the visit of Shastri to the United States and viewed the move as a calculated display of White House displeasure with freewheeling Indian policy statements on Vietnam.

The editorial, from the *Christian Science Monitor*, clearly has as its purpose the persuasion of readers that the President had blundered:

UNDIPLOMACY

India and Pakistan are two of the most important lands in the world. Their combined populations come to nearly 600,000,000. They lie within the extremely sensitive geographic belt of Communist China's ambitions. India is a leader among the earth's non-aligned Afro-Asian countries. Pakistan has close ties with the vast Moslem world. Both India and Pakistan, much influenced by their British past, have many ties to the English-speaking world.

For all these reasons and many more, India and Pakistan would seem to merit special consideration and careful handling from Washington. Unhappily, neither feels that of late it has had such consideration and handling, and the evidence indicates that they are right.

Last week the White House, with great abruptness, called off a visit to Washington by Pakistani President Ayub Khan on less than ten days' notice, while also canceling a visit by Indian Prime Minister Lal Bahadur Shastri for June.

In both countries the reaction has been bitter displeasure and acute embarrassment. President Johnson's action was all the more galling in that he did not simultaneously cancel visits by Italian Premier Aldo Moro and South Korean President Park.

The State Department is believed to have told the Indian Ambassador that the cancellation was due to the present use by both India and Pakistan of American arms in their exchange of fire in the Great Rann of Kutch borderland. If this is true, we find it hard to follow the reasoning behind it. We should have supposed that the border trouble between India and Pakistan would have made visits to Washington doubly desirable.

As things now stand, New Delhi is left with several sharp diplomatic problems on its hands. Not suspecting that the Washington bid would be called back, Prime Minister Shastri had arranged a visit to Ottawa while in North America. He also has before him a luncheon invitation from United Nations Secretary-General U Thant for the same period. Should New Delhi imitate Washington's abruptness and cancel these?

The Soviet Union has used the cancellation of diplomatic invitations as a means of expressing displeasure—as when it withdrew the bid to President Eisenhower after the U-2 incident —and Washington has not liked this Moscow tactic. It is therefore sad to see Washington adopting it. And the harm is particularly great when it is used against two such sensitive key lands as India and Pakistan.

The chief Washington correspondent of the New York *Times,* James Reston, waited a week before he wrote the following interpretation of the event and some of its results. Careful reading of the story will show that it is almost entirely reporting. Reston injects a number of opinions or evaluations; but he is careful to support them with evidence. The opinion statements in the following story are italicized; note how they fit into factual material surrounding them.

WASHINGTON—In the last few days, President Johnson has asked the leaders of India and Pakistan to postpone their state visits to Washington, and informed the press that he has changed his mind about traveling soon to Latin America and Europe.

This has irritated the Asian leaders, and encouraged the view in Europe and Latin America that Johnson is more interested in domestic than in foreign affairs. *But there is a good reason for his decisions.*

He is preoccupied not with home-front problems but with the devilish dilemmas of Vietnam—and the ceremonial aspects of the Presidency, while important, are proving for the time being to be a burden.

The fact is that every American President since the war has felt the same way —*Johnson is merely more blunt about it*—for the procedures of modern diplomacy are at least 100 years out of date, and everyone knows it.

State visits are going on today as in the leisurely days of the early 19th century. The procedure is the same: the greeting and the gun salutes when the visitor arrives; the state banquet at the White House; the Secretary of State's elabo-

rate luncheon in the John Quincy Adams Room at the State Department; the return dinner and reception at the visitor's embassy; and two or three working sessions of an hour or two each with the Secretary of State and his principal aides.

All of this made sense after the Congress of Vienna, where diplomatic protocol was established. The pace of diplomatic intercourse was slow. It took a long time for a king or president to travel half way across the world, and he expected to be treated with elaborate and leisurely courtesy when he arrived. Also, after the official lunches and dinners in those days, the principal characters could retire to rest for the next elegant blowout on the schedule. But it is different now.

In Washington, there is no time for siestas. Officials here are involved in running a world-wide policy. The cables come in while the dancing goes on. Decisions have to be made. The Congress is in session, and Vietnam has to be watched every minute.

This is not a casual question of diplomatic manners. It is a serious problem of how busy and harassed men in Washington are to keep their ceremonial duties from overwhelming their executive responsibilities.

Since the first of the year, President Johnson has received Eisaku Sato, the Premier of Japan; Maurice Yameogo, the President of Upper Volta; Lester Pearson, the Prime Minister of Canada (twice); Prince Bernhard of the Netherlands; Harold Wilson, the Prime Minister of Britain; and this week Aldo Moro, the Premier of Italy.

There was nothing urgent to be discussed with the Premier of Italy. He had just taken office. *He wanted to get acquainted in Washington. It was all part of the modern political ritual: everybody campaigns for office in somebody else's coun-*

try, thereby proving that he is part of the larger world. It is useful, but it is exhausting.

Sensible efforts to modernize diplomatic protocol have made little progress. Every courtesy extended to one country is expected by the others. Johnson originally wanted to go to Rio de Janeiro, and there meet with all the heads of the South American states, but this was frowned on as elevating Brazil at the expense of the other countries. So the Latin American trip has had to be put off.

Many polite reasons have been given for postponing the visits of the Indian Prime Minister, Lal Bahadur Shastri, and the Pakistani President, Ayub Khan. They would be here, it was said, during the Congressional debates on the foreign-aid bill, and since both have recently been opposing U.S. policy in Vietnam, this might lead to embarrassing questions and to a hostile reception for aid to India and Pakistan on Capitol Hill.

The main reason, however, *is the simplest,* namely that the press of executive work on the President and his principal aides is more urgent than ceremonial meetings, no matter how pleasant or useful.

President Johnson has been taking the same atti-

tude toward other ceremonial occasions. In the past, he has taken time out, for example, to attend newspaper conferences and dinners in the capital. This year he skipped the Gridiron Dinner, the meeting of the American Society of Newspaper Editors, and the publishers' convention in New York.

Also it is known that, in addition to postponing his trips to Europe and Latin America and his meetings with the Indian and Pakistani leaders, he has instructed his aides to hold up on negotiations for at least five other state visits to the capital.

This is not standard operating procedure for Johnson. More than any other President since Roosevelt, he has been a great believer in personal diplomacy. In fact, he has tried to adapt to the international field the techniques of personal politics he has used to such great advantage on Capitol Hill.

The combination of the jet airplane and the diplomacy of the clipper-ship days, however, is proving too much for him. He has not been very adroit in making his point, but he does have a point, and as long as the Vietnamese crisis lasts he will probably stick to it.

When the *National Observer* reported on the same event (two weeks after the initial news broke), it took a different tack. The Reston story was devoted to explaining why the President had found it necessary to cancel the two visits. The *Observer*, with more time and additional evidence, chose to analyze the results. Both are interpretive stories, both depending heavily on facts—but both injecting writers' comments growing from the facts.

If Aldo Moro wasn't impressed by the reception he got in Washington last week, it wasn't Lyndon B. Johnson's fault. The President met twice with the Italian Premier, treated him to a stroll through the White

House grounds, and invited him to a 30-minute Cabinet session. At a formal dinner, the President thanked Mr. Moro for his "unwavering support of our effort" in Vietnam.

The lavish welcome ac-

corded Mr. Moro came at a time when India and Pakistan were fuming over the President's postponement of springtime visits by Indian Prime Minister Lal Bahadur Shastri and Pakistani President Mohammed Ayub

Khan. Washington's official reason for the postponements was that the President was busy with his "Congressional workload" and with the situation in Vietnam.

Hardly anybody in Pakistan or India accepted this explanation. For one thing, Mr. Johnson has been having an easy time getting legislation through Congress, and his "workload" doesn't seem too heavy. Besides, the President has found time within the past three weeks to see President Maurice Yameogo of Upper Volta, British Prime Minister Harold Wilson, Mayor Willy Brandt of West Berlin, and Mr. Moro. In mid-May, Mr. Johnson will play host to President Park Chung Hee of South Korea.

Why, then, did the President call off the visits?

White House aides came up with several explanations last week, some of them even less convincing than the "workload" excuse. Mr. Johnson, said one Presidential assistant, believes that too much of his time is being taken up by meeting with foreign visitors—meetings that "don't accomplish anything." The White House said, too, that the President was worried that President Ayub or Prime Minister Shastri might say something critical about Vietnam during their stays in Washington, thereby hurting chances for the Administration's foreign-aid bill now pending on Capitol Hill.

The most plausible explanation was that the Administration wanted to exhibit its displeasure at Pakistan, a member of two Western military alliances, for cuddling up to Russia and, particularly, Red China. Washington also has been irritated at President Ayub for his attacks on American policy in Vietnam. Furthermore, U.S. intelligence officials believe Pakistan started the most recent flare-up of fighting between Indian and Pakistani border patrols, hoping to pry more military aid out of Washington.

So the Administration postponed President Ayub's visit just 10 days before the Pakistani leader was to arrive in Washington. But the Administration, in an apparent effort to stay aloof from the Indian-Pakistani battling, chose to balance off the snub of President Ayub by also postponing the visit of Mr. Shastri. That way, the reasoning seemed to be, Mr. Ayub would be properly snubbed but some of the sting would be taken out of the Administration's action by giving equal treatment to India.

It didn't quite work out that way. The Pakistani government had no formal response to the postponement. One Pakistani official did say he believed Washington had acted "in ill grace."

But India reacted vehemently. Mr. Shastri was furious when he heard of Washington's action. Indian officials announced in Parliament that Mr. Shastri "has canceled" plans to visit Washington and that any trip to the United States "will be at his convenience."

The Indian prime minister chose a meeting of the Indian-Soviet Cultural Association in New Delhi to renew his criticism of American policy in Vietnam. Russian diplomats applauded when Mr. Shastri took the Soviet line that stopping the U.S. bombing raids on North Vietnam was a "necessary prerequisite" for any talks on Vietnam. And he said he was "eagerly" looking forward to a visit to Moscow. Indian officials were particularly displeased by Washington's linking of India and Pakistan in calling off the trips. "I would not like India to be equated with Pakistan," said Swaran Singh, India's minister for external affairs.

U.S. officials realized last week that they had committed a diplomatic gaffe, particularly toward India. Washington said it hoped that the continuation of heavy American aid to India would help dispel some of the anger. The United States last week pledged $435,000,000 as its share of a 10-nation, $1-billion aid program for India. But the big American outlay hardly seems destined to cool Indian tempers. Indian officials remarked that U.S. aid to Pakistan, amounting to $225,000,000 last year, was twice as much per capita as U.S. aid to India.

You have observed one interpretive story in the field of science earlier in this book, the story on page 117 about the wandering cancer cells. The following story takes another abstruse subject and presents it in lay language. Unlike the cancer-cell story, this one brings together facts from many sources; its writer, Victor Cohn, Minneapolis *Tribune* science writer, has searched news files for relevant material. Its highly specific facts and its simple language, speckled here and there with incident or color words, make it easy for the lay reader to take, and helpful to him in understanding a puzzling phenomenon.

Clear air turbulence, an invisible, unpredictable peril that helped bring down a Northwest Airlines Electra over Indiana in 1960, is a greater air menace than ever.

With faster-flying jet airliners, it has become apparent, the problem is far more serious.

The chances are even greater of occasional jarring contacts between high-speed, high-altitude planes and turbulent air, resulting sometimes in crashes and other times in long, uncontrolled dives that suddenly toss unbelted passengers helter-skelter.

As one result, the Federal Aviation Agency (FAA) recently asked airlines—as "voluntary" acts—to urge passengers to keep their seat belts fastened all the time.

So far there has been no such general move by the airlines. Many fliers nonetheless recommend it.

As another result, several airlines, firms and agencies are working on devices to try to detect unseen turbulence.

A local firm, it was learned Saturday, is working on what could become a kind of laser—that is, light beam —radar for such detection. Tests of its equipment are starting this month from Colorado mountain tops.

Northwest Airlines, with headquarters here, has been a leader in studying the problem. This is only in part because of its 1960 crash— structural defects of the early Lockheed Electra were that accident's main cause, with sudden clear air turbulence called a "contributing factor."

On Feb. 12, 1963, Northwest was given further reason for concern, when one of its Boeing 720B jets crashed 13 minutes after takeoff from Miami, Fla., killing 43. Here, too, sudden turbulence is strongly suspected, though the Civil Aeronautics Board report has not yet been made.

Paul Soderlind, North-west's director of flight standards, has spent hundreds of hours since the Florida crash studying turbulence and possible answers. His technical reports and recommendations, distributed throughout the world, have become the basis for new FAA recommendations to pilots.

Northwest has been flight-testing two possible turbulence detectors—standard, radio-wave radar (of one special variety) and a temperature-change sensor.

"Both offer some promise," Soderlind summed up last week. "But neither is the final answer."

Flying, it should be emphasized, is safer than ever. Domestic fatalities are now only one per 300 million passenger miles; worldwide fatalities, one per 100 million passenger miles.

You are safer per air mile than you are per mile in your car on the highway.

The big jets have improved safety, carrying more people at a time more reliably. Most kinds of air failures have been reduced in number. U.S. lines last year carried 71 million passengers 50 billion miles with 121 deaths.

Ironically, however, the fast, swiftly reacting jets plus swift turbulence have created a whole new problem. Thorough reports have appeared in three aviation publications—Aviation Week, Space-Aeronautics and American Aviation—and in the current issue of Life.

They report that:

The February, 1963, Florida crash occurred after the plane (by evidence of its flight recorder) was first shoved upward by a vertical current at a rate of 8,800 feet a minute, then seized in a violent downdraft.

In July, 1963, a United Boeing 720 over Nebraska, with 50 aboard, fell completely out of control for five miles before control was recovered. No one was hurt.

In August, 1963, an Eastern DC8 took off from Dul-les Airport outside Washington and, still not a mile up, hit what the pilot called "the most violent jolt I have ever experienced." The plane was flipped over sideways, almost upside down. A mother lost hold of her baby, who lay on the ceiling crying. Control was recovered 1,325 feet from the ground.

In November, 1963, an Eastern DC8 over Texas, climbing between thunderstorm cells, swooped into an uncontrollable high-speed dive. Several passengers were thrown to the ceiling—26 needed medical attention. One engine was torn away. The pilot landed his ship safely.

In November, 1963, a Trans-Canadian Air Lines DC8 crashed four minutes after take-off from stormy Montreal, killing 118. Again turbulence is suspected.

Turbulence is under suspicion in the crash of an Eastern DC8, killing 58, near New Orleans last February. In 25 lesser cases since 1960, at least 18 stewardesses and passengers were thrown around and seriously hurt. The Air Force assigns loss of three B52 bombers, plus other accidents, to "CAT."

"CAT" has become aviation's familiar term for the clear air turbulence that caused most of these accidents.

The name is in some ways misleading. Sometimes the trouble indeed occurs in clear, storm-free areas. But other times pilots have steered—or been directed by ground controllers—toward areas between storm cells, mistakenly considered turbulence-free.

Both CAT and other turbulence are poorly understood. CAT does often involve wind shear—two air currents meeting to pull an aircraft structure in two directions. It is common in association with the high-altitude jet stream.

It can be found, it is painfully apparent, between

thunderstorms several miles apart.

But it can be encountered in clear air where other pilots enjoyed sweet, smooth air 15 minutes earlier.

The Weather Bureau and Air Force are trying to study and forecast it. The forecasting is still highly imperfect.

Several possibly promising detection devices are about to be tested by the FAA on airliners.

But, Space Aeronautics concludes, all the efforts to solve CAT are "under-founded and uncoordinated," and it is an "unsolved and increasingly grave threat."

There is "no solution in sight," says American Aviation, and the FAA has had its research funds cut "at a time when a number of projects should have priority."

Life says the National Aeronautics and Space Administration is converting a small executive-type jet to turbulence study, but its studies and the Air Force's may not help commercial aviation for years. It says "a really serious effort" would require converting a full-sized jetliner to turbulence research (at a cost of about $3 million, less than half its original cost) "but so far such a program has found little official support."

The Weather Bureau has at most $100,000 a year for turbulence studies.

"It seems strange," Life quotes one specialist, "that it's so much easier to get money to study the atmosphere on the moon than to hunt down the unknowns of turbulence here on earth."

How background and explanatory material may be skillfully interwoven with the spot news in a story is shown in the following example. It is also noteworthy that the story is constructed in suspended-interest form, although it reports spot news and could be handled, less interestingly, "straight":

A frustrating question of how a neighborhood is supposed to go about getting a place for its children to play came to light Wednesday at a meeting of the Board of Park Commissioners.

A proposed formula, as it was revealed by an apparent majority of the commissioners and Superintendent Howard Moore, consists of the formation of a neighborhood lobby group that is willing and able to get the consent of more than half of the property owners who would be benefitted by a new park or a major improvement to an existing park.

It is unwritten board policy, said Moore, to require petitions signed by at least 51 percent of the benefitted property owners. Otherwise, he said, the board may be subjected to forceful majority opposition when the public hearing on the project takes place.

As it turned out yesterday, the Pearl Park neighborhood in the 11th Ward has the lobby group—the Pearl Improvement and Recreation Council (PIRC) —but lacks the signatures that the board wants for consent for a proposed $615,-000 improvement.

The reason PIRC lacks the signatures has little, if anything, to do with any neighborhood opposition to the improvement. The problem is, rather, that it is difficult—perhaps impossible— for PIRC to survey the neighborhood.

The area served by the park and in which property owners would be assessed for half of the cost of the improvement (the other half being paid by the entire city) is the largest in the city. Bounded roughly by Mortensen Pkwy. on the north, Rosen Av. on the west and Maple Av. on the east, the park's assessment and service district contains some 8,000 homes.

Said PIRC to the Park Board: It lacks enough volunteers to canvass that many homes.

What it has done, however, is survey the area closest to the park and near Leafe Elementary School. That area overwhelmingly (two to one) approves the proposed improvement, said PIRC.

Said the Park Board, informally, to PIRC: It hesitates to proceed until the rest of the assessment district is surveyed.

With that, the leaders of PIRC went home, feeling that their two years' effort has led into a blind alley.

The next story was the result of an assignment to find out the answers to questions that were being widely asked in a community: How much did it cost to send a university football team to the Rose Bowl extravaganza, and was it justified? The reporter, Miriam Alburn, provides no answers of her own. Rather, she presents the facts as she found them, along with the questions, and permits her reader to arrive at his own conclusion.

Three big questions were involved in University of Minnesota participation in the Rose Bowl festivities.

The athletic question was answered by the football game itself, and the score of 17 to 7 in favor of the University of Washington.

The issue that might be labeled "propriety"—the concern of administrative and academic leaders over whether, as an institution of learning, the university might properly involve itself in a time-consuming, perhaps over-publicized post-season sports event—also has simmered down.

At least, many of the officials and faculty members who went to Pasadena were impressed by the smooth and relatively dignified way in which the whole festival was conducted.

But the third issue—the financing of the operation—still has people both within and without the university asking questions.

They ask about the cost of the project, and whether the university will end with a profit or loss.

They wonder about the expensive float representing Minnesota in the Tournament of Roses parade.

They question whether it was right for the university to pay expenses of so many people attending the game.

Some have a nagging feeling that the Rose Bowl budget might make things a bit uncomfortable for the people who must present the basic university budget to the legislature.

And inevitably, faculty members who feel that a general financial pinch restricts them on staff and equipment purchases in their teaching work are resentful about the apparent free spending for the Pasadena excursion.

From university officials comes this information about the financial aspects of the project:

Reports are not yet final, but receipts to the university are expected to be about $120,000, and officials expect to "just about break even."

An allotment of $6,000 for a float was made to each of the two participating universities.

Money was raised from private contributors to send the university band to the game. At last report this fund, needing a total of nearly $40,000, was still about $12,000 short.

The university did pay expenses (transportation, meals, hotel, buses) of about 70 persons besides the athletic department contingent, which included football coaches, wives of coaches, children of coaches, players and wives of married players.

The university-sponsored group included:

The university president, his wife and two children; three vice presidents and their wives; six other university officials and their wives; eight regents, seven wives of regents, one regent's grandson, one regent emeritus and his wife.

Seven faculty members of the university senate committee on intercollegiate athletics and their wives; two alumni members and their wives; two student members of the committee; two deans; director of the news bureau and two photographers.

The governor-elect and his wife.

In addition, a few other faculty members, who did not make the whole trip with an official group, had part of their expenses paid.

With the band group were university staff people and wives of some of them, about 18 in all, who served as chaperones to the students (nearly 150). Some of the staff people had working assignments in Pasadena.

Why did the University of Minnesota make the Rose Bowl such a big-scale project, with so many persons besides the players and the coaches going to the event?

Stanley Wenberg, vice president and chairman of the university's Rose Bowl committee, explains it this way:

Public funds are not involved. The game itself was bringing in special income that would pay expenses. . . . The Rose Bowl promoters expect a "high level of participation," with top officials and representatives of both administrative staff and faculty there to meet similar groups from the university of the competing team. The event is expected to involve much more of each institution than just its athletic department.

The university follows a policy of including regents' wives in as many events as possible, Wenberg said. Coaches' families and wives of married team members were included largely for team morale, in an effort to keep the families together over the holidays.

As to the question of whether a surplus in the Rose Bowl account might not benefit the university, Wenberg pointed out that the game receipts would be kept in the athletic department fund, used only for athletic program and equipment.

One question still in doubt, however, is whether the deficit in the privately-raised fund for band members' expenses will be made up by late contributors. Any final gap here would have to be made up by dipping into some other university fund.

A university staff member familiar with the arrangements made this observation on the Rose Bowl Philosophy: "It was a special event, apart from all the normal routine. It brought in extra money, and so it just seemed like an easy-come, easy-go affair."

The writer of the story about river pollution makes no attempt at the detachment with which Miss Alburn approached her findings. Jean M. White of the Washington *Post*, attacking a national problem, shows her point of view clearly, and seeks to bring the reader to the same opinion. She is outraged, and she thinks the facts she presents justify it.

This is the first of four articles on the growing pollution of America's rivers and the prospects of doing anything about it.

Long stretches of many of the nation's rivers and streams are shamefully and perilously dirty.

The Merrimack, one of the rivers polluted earliest in the United States—from the days of the Massachusetts Bay Colony and the first textile mills—has turned filthy brown and bubbles like soda pop with nauseating gases. Thoreau complained about it in 1839, and since then it has only become progressively worse.

Along the lower reaches of the Mississippi, queen of the nation's rivers, millions of fish turn belly up and die. Near St. Louis, chicken feathers and viscera collect in patches almost thick enough to stop a motorboat.

A stream in the Southwest may be so crystal-clear that you can read the inscription on a coin on the shallow bottom. But it is a biological desert, left deceptively clear after oil grime settles in a black precipitate.

On the Hudson, near Troy, N. Y., scavenger eels —about the only thing that can live in waters befouled by raw sewage—cling to wastes and attack New York State Health Department engineers taking water sanitary samples.

The Missouri sometimes flows red with blood from slaughterhouses and carries grease balls almost as big as footballs. The Mahoning, a workhorse river for industrial areas of Pennsylvania and Ohio, is rust-colored from the "pickle" liquor of steel mills and topped off with debris-strewn scum.

A housewife on Long Island draws a glass of water and gets a head of detergent foam.

On the Presumpscot River near Portland, Maine, mists of rotten-egg hydrogen sulfide gas rise from flats of paper-pulp sludge piled up over more than a century. White houses turn gray and silver tarnishes.

Some of our waterways are in such bad shape that they are dangerously close to a point of no return technologically and economically. It will take an enormous, expensive effort to clean up waters muddied by man's use and abuse.

Water pollution is nothing new. It has been going on for decades, and that's part of the reason for the rising tide of trouble today.

Over many years, cities and industries have been flushing their wastes into the waterways and letting nature do the disposal job. Water has a tremendous capacity for self-purification, but there is a limit.

"The blithe assumption was that the water would purify itself in seven miles of flow," explains a water management expert. "That was OK for the Indians, but there are too many Indians today."

Today more and more people are living closer and closer together. More and more industries line the water courses, producing thousands of new exotic chemical compounds each year.

The refuse of this industrial and urban growth is pouring into streams and rivers already overloaded beyond their natural capacity to assimilate wastes.

As someone has put it, we are in danger of becoming the "effluent society."

Each day a typical city of 100,000 produces 17 tons of organic suspended solids, 17 tons of organic dissolved solids (including a ton of detergents), 8 tons of inorganic dissolved solids, and 69 cubic feet of grime.

The amount of waste being dumped into our rivers —treated and untreated— is the equivalent of the untreated sewage of 75 million people. Of the 11,420 communities that have sewer systems, nearly 19 percent still discharge untreated waste into the nation's waterways. To this are added the enormous wastes of industry.

The cost of past neglect is going to come high, into billions of dollars. Despite some clean-up progress in recent years, more rivers and streams are going bad.

The backlog of municipal waste treatment needs alone is placed at $1.9 billion. The Public Health Service estimates that it will take about $800 million a year through this decade just to catch up on the backlog—new plants, replacements for aging facilities, and expansion for population growth.

But a remedy for one of the biggest problems of pollution control could prove far more costly than treatment facilities.

The sewer systems of many of the older cities were laid in the 19th century and designed to handle both sanitary waste and storm water. After a heavy rain, these systems now overflow and dump untreated sewage into rivers even if the city has a treatment plant.

The cost of providing separate systems could be tremendous—estimates run as high as $20 to $30 billion. This is the ultimate answer, but other less costly solutions are being sought.

Chicago has applied to the PHS for a grant to study a plan to store storm overflow in huge underground caverns. Then it could be run through treatment at "off-peak" hours.

A   special   committee headed by Gardner Ackley, chairman of the President's Council of Economic Advisers, has just begun a study of the economics of pollution control.

One suggestion has been an "effluent charge"—a tax on polluters, both industries and cities. Such a tax has been levied in Germany's heavily industrialized Ruhr region. Other proposals are for tax write-offs and tax credits for pollution-control devices.

Legislation is now before Congress to . . .

[*The story concludes with a description of proposed legislative and other control plans. It promises next a story about the rivers that are turned into "open sewers" by unchecked pollution.*]

PROJECTS

1. Write a brief essay defining the similarities and differences among follow-up reporting, enterprise reporting, investigative reporting, and interpretive reporting.
2. Examine a week's issues of a leading American daily to discover the extent to which it uses the interpretive reporting technique. List all the examples of interpretive reporting you find, and write a commentary on the effectiveness or ineffectiveness with which the paper employs the technique.
3. Select a local subject-field of particular interest to you—growth of "radical" movements (right or left) on campuses, free speech for college students, problems raised by federal aid to education, the highway safety problem, problems of teen-age behavior. Plan and execute an interpretive story, or several of them, to illuminate the problem for the "average reader."

CHAPTER 19

Today's Newsman: Professional and Citizen

Is journalism a profession? Is a newsman a professional, or merely an artisan? These questions are argued vigorously, both inside newsrooms and out.

A profession, by common definition, is an occupation with a number of well-defined characteristics. It has a set of operational principles and practices that can be handed from one worker to another; it operates with a precise and growing body of knowledge; it has its base in general culture; it possesses a code, or at least a formulated concept, of ethical conduct; its practitioners are motivated by a concern for the public welfare.

At its best, the news journalism of today demonstrates these characteristics to a degree satisfactory even to its warmest critics. Newsmen themselves, however, are not always ready to describe their field of activity as "professional." A paradoxical disagreement followed the rise of labor legislation in the 1930s: Some publishers, with eyes on their ledgers, sought formal definition of news work as professional because professional workers are exempt from some of the protections of labor laws; surprisingly, on the contrary, newsmen's organizations such as some units of the American Newspaper Guild denied that reporters, deskmen, and other news handlers are professional for the same reason, but in reverse —that they might lose such protection.

There are debates among newsmen, indeed, on less formalized or pragmatic questions:

"How can you say that a newspaper office that puts untrained high school kids on as reporters has any professional standards?"

"Yes . . . but the reputable news operations today—the truly strong ones, both print and air—hire their employes from among college graduates, often insisting on school of journalism training. And how about the American Society of Newspaper Editors' 'Canons of Journalism,' and the Radio-TV News Editors' standards of practice statement? Aren't these codes of ethics?"

"Certainly—on paper. But do all reporters and editors live up to them?"

"Well . . . do all lawyers live up to the principles of the American Bar Association? Isn't there ever a doctor who violated his Oath of Hippocrates?"

Two thorough and scholarly studies of the ethics and performance standards of American news media have been published recently:
The Social Responsibility of the Press, *by J. Edward Gerald* (Minneapolis: University of Minnesota Press, 1963); and Responsibility in Mass Communication, *by Wilbur Schramm* (New York: Harper & Row, 1957).

Whatever the outcome of such debates, there is rarely disagreement that many—I dare to say most—newsmen conduct themselves according to widely accepted professional standards, that the need for the cultured background on which professional practice must be based is more fully recognized each year, and that journalism of the mid-twentieth century deserves the term "profession" more fully than did that of any earlier period.

• •

One of the superficial generalizations about American newsmen, often thoughtlessly supported by newsmen themselves, is that they belong to a "cynical" brotherhood. Read the comment of a Toronto newsman, Frank Tumpane:
"Part of a reporter's professional equipment is the ability to avoid being deceived by the frauds and hypocrites who attempt to mislead him. . . .
"This gives rise to a healthy skepticism—but there's a difference between skepticism and cynicism. . . .
"I've never known a truly first class newspaperman who was a cynic, for cynicism can stifle a man's sense of compassion and his ability to see and feel things. . . .
"Newsmen often deal with tragedy or human weakness, but don't get the notion their avocation is heartlessness. A newspaperman often does things he hates to have to do—but so does a doctor or a policeman. . . .
"The public's right to know often takes a news-

What Are "Professional Standards"?

The standards of behavior that guide self-respecting newsmen have their roots in the implied responsibility of the news media to recognize service to the public as their first concern. The First Amendment to the Constitution is not the sole source of this right and responsibility, but it is an important one; the constitutional principle implies that, since a democratic society must have a selfless source of information as the wellspring of its thinking and action, society is willing to forego organized or statutory power (which might become self-seeking) to direct it. Turned around, this means that freedom from governmental restriction—a privilege—imposes on the news media the obligation to forward and protect the public interest—a responsibility.

The responsibility is all-embracing: it covers both the conduct of a newspaper or broadcasting owner with respect to the editorial content and functioning of his enterprise and the conduct of his news employes as well. In daily practice the two levels of responsibility show themselves in different ways (though sometimes, as in the case of the publisher of a small weekly, they are borne by one individual): the owner's responsibility may show in his decision as to what political party to support, the reporter's in his efforts to get a piece of news somebody is trying to conceal. But the source of the two is the same: the

paperman into situations that are uncomfortable for him and from which he would escape if he could. But his duty to the public and his paper often makes escape impossible."

expectation of a democratic society that its news media will perform in the interests of all of society—a community or a complex of communities, a single human or a mass of humans.

Let it be said again, for good measure, that failure to live up to the principle in every particular is no denial of the principle. The fact that one lawyer lends his talents to gaining acquittal for a murderer he knows to be guilty may tarnish a high profession, but it does not blacken every member of it.

In this book the focus is narrowed to the man on the news front—the reporter. He is the primary contact between his medium and the public; for many laymen he is the essence and the prototype of the entire news-dissemination process. The question here posed is this: How define the ground on which principles for "good" news conduct by reporters is based?

It is ground that is described in such terms as these:

The newsman's responsibility is to govern his behavior so as to serve the best interests of society—to bring to the members of his public, in the most compelling way possible, the information that is useful to them. He puts broad social interest at the head of his list of masters. But he recognizes that there are individual interests, too; he respects individual dignity and a man's personal and private rights as foremost *except* when the broader community interest overrides them. He guides his conduct not only by the needs and concerns of society, mass and individual, but by his own self-respect; he knows that he can serve best if he has the regard of others and that the regard of others follows from, rather than precedes, his regard for himself.

All these criteria are generalizations. Let us put them into more specific form by examining some—though by no means all—of the problem areas in which newsmen operate.

Let us begin by saying that many of a newsman's problems of behavior may be classified under two broad headings: problems in the gathering of news information, and problems in its handling, writing, and treatment.

Problems in News Gathering

NEWS BY SUBTERFUGE   Fiction about newsmen is full of reporters who disguise themselves as gardeners, grease monkeys, or bespectacled schoolmarms in order to get the news (Hollywood prefers to put it "to crack the case"). Like most creation of fiction, they have their prototypes in reality. A reporter borrows a white jacket and a tray to get into a senator's hotel room. Or he puts on a khaki shirt, bags the knees of his trousers, and lets his beard grow for days before going incognito to an underworld hangout. Can this deceit be defended?

No two cases are alike; the two suggested here may be as far apart in values as they are in circumstance. Presumably the "waiter" gains entree to the senator's room by his deception; but does he maintain the disguise after he's in? Should he do so, can he hope to conduct a successful interview to ask acceptable questions, to get respectful answers? And what is his moral position if he uses material thus elicited? Is this a form of theft? Is he not invading privacy? Is the fact that the senator is a public servant an excuse or a mitigating circumstance? What if the reporter gains information the public has a right to, information the senator has no right to cover up? Does this justify the method of gaining access to it? What effect would it have on the ethical problem if the senator planned to make the information public 12 hours later in a broadcast talk? What if the reporter asked only personal questions?

As for the seedy reporter in gangland: What if he gets information about criminal activities that the police and the public have been unable to get? Does the fact that he is bringing crime to light justify his method of unveiling it? Is the acknowledged interest of the public in gaining the information an acceptable defense?

These are difficult problems. Each has to be evaluated individually, in full knowledge of its circumstances. But they are problems met frequently by reporters and their editors. Some newspapers express an unequivocal attitude by telling their men never to seek, take, or accept information without the knowledge and consent of the source; others ask no questions. Some newsmen, either because they believe that getting information at all cost is their job or because they think of outwitting news sources as a game, do not hesitate at subterfuge; others refuse to countenance it.

The news world is well aware, however, that the once fairly common art of "picture stealing" and the like has gone into decline. Time was when a young reporter for the Hearst Chicago *American* said soberly that he feared he could not have held his job through the first tough weeks if he had not been so skilled at getting into apartments through their coal chutes. That this kind of confession —it is not today a boast—is rare may be explained in part by the lessening of newspaper competition. It is consistent with what a Midwestern newspaper editor referred to in 1955 as the growth of "the newspaper game" into "the profession of journalism." The fact that newsmen more and more decry coal-chute news gathering is a symptom of maturation.

A tired and hackneyed practice in news journalism is to write that information comes from "a source who preferred not to be named." In the first place, this term does not give the source's reason; in the second, it suggests that the source rather than the newsman made the decision; and in the third, the verb is in the wrong tense.

● ●

Careful newsmen have learned to use cautiously such anonymous and occa-

A similar, though more subtle, problem has arisen often since news gathering became a systematic craft and those engaged in newsworthy activities knew they were being reported: the problem of attendance at "closed" meetings. Examine the following case:

A reporter on a big-city paper was assigned to cover a Central Labor Council meeting at which a decision on a proposed general strike was to be made. The chance that a strike might occur had been painstakingly covered by his paper and by others in the city. The reporter entered the Labor Temple auditorium where delegates were gathering and seated himself among them; he believed himself unrecognized. The chairman opened the meeting by announcement that

sionally shabby attributions as "informed sources," "a spokesman high in the Administration," or "authoritative circles." The reason for the ill repute of such attributions is evident: They can be used by careless or irresponsible writers to veil lack of source, and in any case they do not give the news consumer full information.

Sometimes there is no avoiding them, just as a reporter must sometimes protect his "underworld character." But many newsmen consider them unacceptable. When the first news codes were being drawn up for radio just after World War II, by the news committee of the National Association of Broadcasters and by the Radio-TV News Directors Association, these practices were labeled improper. One reason for broadcasting's singling them out for particular mention was that radio and TV news, with their limited time, found especially alluring the temptation to use loose attributions instead of longer and more definite phrases.

Perhaps the best counsel in print on this vexing problem is that by Alfred Friendly of the Washington Post, in the July 1958 issue of Neiman Reports, which was noted earlier.

• •

The comment of the reporter at the CLC meeting on his problem and his solution for it:

"I sat tight and thought, for about five long seconds. I kept feeling that every eye in the place was on me, though I'm sure nobody identified me.

"Then I got up, in a shattering silence, and left the room.

no "outsiders" were admissible; he asked, though without apparent recognition that any were present, that reporters leave the hall.

The meeting was large. The reporter believed himself unidentified. Should he leave? Should he deprive himself of the opportunity to get information that would be of profound importance to his community? Had the CLC the right, moral or legal, to ask him, as a representative of the public, to leave?

The reporter's solution is to be found below.

"CONFIDENTIAL" INFORMATION   Highly respected and conscientiously observed among the newsman's ethical concepts is the principle governing information given him "in confidence."

When a news source tells a reporter, "I'm revealing such-and-such to you for your own information, but not for publication," he can be sure that only once in a thousand times will his confidence be misplaced. The eminently practical reason is that a betrayed news source becomes a news source no longer. The more impelling reason is that newsmen have professional pride in the sanctity of a promise so made.

The very insistence of newsmen that a confidence is inviolate, however, raises problems. The two most troublesome problems are manipulation by crafty news sources to dam up information that ought to become public, and the "protection" of the identity of informers even though the information they provide may be published.

The first problem, familiar under the term "off the record," is discussed on pages **98** and **99**. It is enough here to say that the promise "not to use it" should never be given lightly; sometimes a reporter is wiser to refuse information than to allow his lips to be sealed.

The question of concealing the identity of news sources is one of the most trying that newsmen face. "Sure—go ahead and use the story," says the news source. "But don't let on that I told you." It is not difficult to understand how this tactic may be used by the irresponsible informant to escape responsibility for carelessness with fact, or by the cunning informant to plant lies, libel, or selfishly calculated information. It takes no reporter long to realize that the danger is always present and to learn to guard against it.

"I believed that my paper's readers had a right to the news; but it seemed to me wrong for the paper to get it by theft. And that's what my staying there would have amounted to—nonstatutory larceny.

"Besides, I was pretty sure I could get the news anyway. You can almost always find ways nobody can criticize.

"I stayed in the foyer of the building until the meeting ended; as I waited, I tried to figure what actions might come out of it. When the doors opened and the delegates started out, I collared the first man I could get and asked him the important question: 'Did they decide to strike?' 'Hell, no!' he shot back . . . and I had the key to my story.

"With this lead, I asked more questions. Within a few minutes, though some of the men refused to answer and some swore at me, I had it wrapped up. Then I went to the chairman—the man who had asked reporters to get out.

" 'What was the final vote not to strike?' I asked him. My leading question surprised him, and I thought at first that he might tell me off. But finally he grinned, and talked freely.

"I think I handled it right. I got the story; I didn't have to cheat or feel like a thief; I kept the good will of the CLC for myself and my paper. Handled the other way, we might not have been able to get a foot in a labor door for five years."

Often it is quite appropriate to conceal a news source. When you have assurance of the accuracy and reliability of the source, when revealing his identity would put him into embarrassing, compromising, or even dangerous position, and *when you can make the news just as meaningful without his name as with it,* you may choose to refer to him as "a broker who asked not to be named" or "a responsible spokesman for the party," or even "a dope pusher who said he would be rubbed out if he were fingered." But complete confidence in the dependability of the source (or, when appropriate, clear warning that it is not dependable) is a minimum necessity of this usage; a second necessity is that the news so revealed is important enough to warrant this less-than-thorough method of reporting it.

The problem of unnamed sources and refusal to reveal them has more than once sent a newsman to jail or forced him to pay a fine for contempt of court. Courts have sometimes held that, though the newsman is personally admirable in unwillingness to reveal a name he has promised to shield, the welfare of society may demand that he break his promise when a court orders it. The principle is that public interest in such cases takes precedence over personal or professional codes of behavior. Nevertheless, a number of American newsmen have defied such court orders and have paid penalties.

Since the 1930s about a fourth of the American states have enacted so-called shield laws which outlaw the charge of contempt of court in cases in which a newsman's protection of a confidence is involved. Sharp conflict of opinion exists, and will continue to exist, as to whether the reporter's fidelity to his promise of keeping information confidential should be regarded in the same light as that of the clergyman, the doctor, the lawyer, or the social worker. A commonly held principle is that, highly as the reporter's integrity is to be esteemed and deserving as it is of protection, the court is the instrument of society vested with the right as well as the wisdom to decide whether private promise or public weal carries the greater weight. Some courts have criticized the wisdom or judgment in reporters' refusals to name sources, but have honored them nevertheless.

The Supreme Court of the United States, in late 1958, approved (by refusing to review) what may turn out to be the definitive rule in such cases. A New

York *Herald Tribune* reporter-columnist refused to tell a court a source for damaging statements she had quoted about an actress, Judy Garland. Miss Garland's suit for damages rested on the authenticity of the quotations; when the reporter remained silent in spite of court order, the damage suit failed. The court declared it respected the reporter's "high motives," but sentenced her to ten days in jail for contempt. The decision said in part:

> Compulsory disclosure of a journalist's confidential sources of information may entail an abridgment of press freedom by imposing some limitation upon the availability of news. But freedom of the press, precious and vital though it is to a free society, is not an absolute. What must be determined is whether the interest to be served by compelling the testimony of the witness in the present case justifies some impairment of this First Amendment freedom.

The Court added that its ruling did not attack the whole journalistic system of confidential news sources, but stated only that the right of a citizen to compel testimony in his defense might seem more central to democratic values than the journalistic right.

Under this view, it is the court's responsibility to decide where the fundamental social values reside. To hold otherwise would seem to deny a basic American right of individual protection.

"GET IT OUT OF HIM"   There are scores of reportorial tools for inducing reluctant news sources to talk. Some of them are as necessary and proper in the reporter's kit as the no. 5 iron in a champion golfer's bag; others may be as questionable as nudging the ball out of a hollow with your toe.

The "good" tools have been suggested or described in earlier chapters: tact, courtesy, and consideration; knowledge and sound preparation; convincing a news source that giving information will serve a useful purpose, showing him that it will redress or avert an injury; convincing him that, if he doesn't talk, only the other fellow's case will see the light . . . and so on.

The questionable ones are harder to catalog. Let actual examples suggest a few:

As a reporter, you are asked to get a story "with art" from a young woman whose husband has blacked her eye because she refused to cut her long hair. She is reluctant to talk or permit photography—"He'd do it to the other eye," she says. But you find that you can appeal to her vanity: "You'd sure look good on our front page." She assents. Is the merit of the story, or its importance to readers, such that the trick is justifiable?

You are permitted to go with police on a raid on a gambling joint. The proprietor clearly thinks you are a member of the police party, and answers your questions under the assumption that he's talking to a plain-clothes man. Defensible procedure?

A woman has not yet been informed of her husband's arrest on a burglary charge. You question her without informing her, and she gives you information that destroys the alibi you know he has offered police. Is it "moral" to report it?

A businessman gives you information about his plans for local business expansion, and promises to hold it "exclusive" for you in return for your agreement to try to persuade the news editor to give the story front page emphasis. You feel sure there is no chance the editor will do so. Honest?

You hint to the builder who didn't get the contract that the successful bidder charged him with using inferior materials in his last job. You have no basis for the hint. This so infuriates your interviewee that he readily answers questions on which he had theretofore been cagy, questions that dig into his suspicions of irregularities in his competitor's relationships with the city purchasing department. You have developed an important story-lead. Is your method defensible?

You are "morally certain" that the local college's football coach is making the payments on his quarterback's convertible, but you can't prove it. You tell the quarterback falsely that the coach has admitted the payments; the player delivers the whole story. Glad you got it?

You take the bright blonde seen often lately with a prominent local minister to a night spot and help her to half a dozen highballs; her loosened tongue spills her plans to elope next month. Do you use the story?

Such methods of eliciting information raise a related question: Is it proper for a news medium to pay, in cash, for news? The answer is frequently *yes*. It is just as proper to compensate the holder of private information for releasing it as it is for a magazine to buy an article from a free-lance writer, or for *Life* to pay the man who just happened to be there with his camera for his photography. Private information is a form of private property; it may be honorably bought and sold. The fact that in practice it is almost always released without compensation has no ethical bearing. A public official, however, should not consider knowledge or news material related to his public duties as personal property, and a newsman would be wrong himself if he contributed to such an official's private gain for its release.

"FAVORS"   When is a newsman justified in accepting "considerations," actual or potential, from news sources? Or from those whose businesses or welfare may be affected by the handling of news related to them or their affairs?

It is clear that any such acceptance is questionable. It may be dishonest and dishonorable, and it is almost always debasing.

The truth is that practice has accepted the tradition of special favors for newsmen—favors all the way from free movie tickets to free trips to Europe. A small percentage of newspapers, and a smaller proportion of broadcasting stations, have held that refusal to accept such "gifts" leaves a reporter and his

employer entirely free of any impulse to return the favor. The number of newspaper and broadcasting editorial directors and business managements that outlaw the practice is slowly growing. But very slowly.

The forms taken by such frank attempts to gain newsmen's good will and
"good treatment" are many, and they are widely known. Madison Square Gar-
den in New York one Christmas presented to each of a number of sports writers
sterling silver dinner services; to their credit, some writers refused the gift.
Sports writers and broadcasters, incidentally, are special targets for this kind of
persuasion; their Christmas stockings bulge with expensive gifts, bottled or
packaged, and they are given travel opportunities, vacations at resorts, fishing
junkets, and the like. Theaters have traditionally provided free tickets for dramatic writers, and sometimes for anybody else on news staffs who would accept
them. One state legislature made it a custom to give correspondents covering
it Christmas packages including costly brief cases, pen-and-pencil sets, and
stationery ("acceptance of this gift, purchased by public funds, to my way of
thinking is highly improper," commented the editor of a daily newspaper in
the state). Transocean junkets by airlines are arranged "for reporters to observe
foreign politics for themselves" (apparently on the principle that a newsman
can learn all about the Common Market by two-hour stays in three or four
Common Market capitals). The Radio-TV News Directors Association, Sigma
Delta Chi, and like groups are elaborately entertained by public utilities and
private corporations, in the name of good will and hospitality—but the surface
purpose is clouded by understandable questions as to the hosts' intent.

More direct attempts to affect news treatment, less common, come to light
from time to time. The St. Louis *Post-Dispatch* and the Chicago *Daily News*
in the 1940s exposed the fact that a number of Illinois newsmen had been receiving regular income from the state's treasury. Now and again an individual
reporter is asked to accept a "reward" for what somebody thinks a praiseworthy
story, sometimes with the open suggestion that similar future treatment would
be welcome.

One reason the practice is firmly rooted is that most newsmen are loud—
and no doubt genuine—in their avowals that attempts of this kind to curry
favor do not commonly fall in productive soil. They point out correctly that the
reporter covering the Rotary meeting does not often say to himself—consciously,
at least—"That was a good free meal. I'll give the talk a good story." He is
more likely to take the complimentary ticket as a routine aid to coverage—he
says and believes—and can evaluate the news on its merits rather than on a
free-ride basis.

But newsmen are human, and they don't always read their subconscious impulses accurately. The newsman who values his independence and the integrity
of the news would do well to remember that there is no such thing as keeping
his hands too clean. The problem is to keep them clean enough. Each time he
accepts a favor, suspicion falls not alone on him but on everybody working in
news.

Affiliations   A distant cousin of the favors problem is that of affiliation of newsmen with newsmaking groups. There is no agreement among newspapers and broadcasters on this problem. The Pros and the Cons may be briefly reviewed:

> *Pro:* We want our reporters to be associated with all kinds of public enterprises and community activities. How can they keep abreast not only of the specific events but also of the movements in public thinking unless they hold many memberships among business organizations, clubs, churches, civic associations, and the rest of the newsmakers? Moreover, this kind of community activity is good for us as an institution. If the citizens of our city know that our staff men are active in civic affairs, everybody will think more of us.
>
> *Con:* But the instant you have a man in any kind of activity your attitude toward it is under suspicion. How can you either praise or criticize the school board if your reporter, or your editor, is a member? How can a reporter cover labor news if he's a union member, or business news if he's a wheel in the Chamber of Commerce? Newsmen should sit on a hill and look at all these activities from outside. They have no perspective if they're inside.

THE COMPETITION   Competition among reporters was keen to bloody in the days when every city had two or more newspapers. That was the day of the scoop and the constant fight by newsmen to outwit or out-distance their rivals. Competitive news gathering of this kind, except in about 50 cities, seemed well on the way to extinction when radio and television gave it new life. Today in some one-newspaper cities there are news-on-the-air competitors who keep rivalry as sharp as any the newsmen of ink and paper ever enjoyed.

It has always been true, even when competition has been bitter, that reporters from rival media have developed labor-saving ways of working together. In the police station or the city hall of a good-sized city, where complete coverage of every news source may be more than the one man assigned to a beat could manage in 36 hours a day, it is the familiar practice to "syndicate." This means that the reporter for the *Graphic* covers the first and second floors of the police station, the man from Station WWWW the third and fourth; they "protect" each other by sharing routine news—news each knows the other would get were he covering the same ground. Thus each gains fuller coverage than he could alone.

But each reserves the right to his own "exclusives," and each has well-guarded private alleys to news information. Each is continually on the watch to try to divine what the other may be up to in the hours not given to routine. There have always been tales of bottling up news sources—for example, that of the reporter who, having developed an "exclusive" about plans for a new guided-missile installation in his city, took the Army official who was the only source of the news on a full-day picnic and sight-seeing tour so that rival newsmen could not get at him. An ancient newsroom legend tells of the correspondent who, having got to the only telegraph operator ahead of other reporters, sent his dispatch and then put the operator to sending the New Testament, with instructions not to stop for twelve hours, thus keeping his rivals off the wire.

Some news directors lay down firm rules against "syndication" or any other kind of cooperation with competitors. Initiative is dulled by it, they say; reporters get lazy; the result will be routine coverage. In such cautions there is merit. But the syndication practice is firmly rooted, and in many situations fully accepted. It will die hard.

Competition brings up problems of news ethics now and again. An example: The police reporter for paper A "lifted" the carbons of his paper B rival from B's desk in the police pressroom. Legally, the A reporter was liable to prosecution for theft of physical property, the carbon copies, and for theft of news as property (the law usually holds that the gatherer of news materials owns and controls them so long as they have commercial value, which means so long as they are "newsy"). But reporter B handled it differently. He planted a sensational but phony story among the carbons. Paper A put an eight-column banner on it in its first edition . . . and shamefacedly reduced the story through the day until its final edition denied the "rumor" that the event had occurred.

Question: Was B's ruse not in itself unethical?

Problems in News Presentation

Distinctions between problems of ethical behavior in news gathering and in news presentation—the writing, editing, and display of news—are not always sharp. Often the handling of a news story is conditioned notably by the manner of its gathering or its occurrence. If, for example, a reporter gets material for a story by persuading a doddering physical culture enthusiast to stand on his hands on a night club table, the writing of the story is not likely to attain more dignity than the event itself.

A number of areas of news treatment, however, develop in particular ways what newsmen call "policy problems"—a phrase that often means ethical problems. They cannot all be pondered here. As in the consideration of news gathering problems, a sampling must suffice.

NAMES AND IDENTIFICATIONS   The reporting of a newsworthy event is not considered complete unless principal participants are fully identified. Yet the news media are in general agreement that certain circumstances call for the modification of this news maxim. Examine, for example, the reporting of juvenile misbehavior.

In this area the media have for years agreed that omission of names is often desirable. The boy or girl of 18 or younger, runs the argument, is not likely to be a hardened evildoer. Especially when he is a first offender, society appears to believe it should be concerned more with rehabilitation than with punishment. Juvenile courts, child psychologists, and social workers usually hold that omission of the child's name from the public record of newsprint or broadcast will decrease the probability of his "going bad" again.

Many media, in sympathy with this view, operate habitually on rule of thumb forbidding use of names of such offenders. But the national concern about the rising curve of juvenile arrests in the 1950s and 1960s led to a number of re-examinations and a number of rejudgments.

One of the spokesmen of the "new" view, Executive Editor J. Russell Wiggins of the Washington *Post*, told officials of the District of Columbia juvenile court that "secrecy has not brought about any diminution in the amount of juvenile crime." The position taken by Wiggins and his paper was that, since withholding juvenile names involved in crime news had kept from the public information of an important nature without achieving the purpose of the withholding, the whole practice demanded review. He added:

> By the secrecy with which we have surrounded the administration of our juvenile courts and our care of youth in crime, I think we have shielded youngsters from public notice of their offenses. We have also shielded them from public interest, understanding, compassion, and support. . . . This kind of secrecy has deprived the citizens of this community . . . of that ready knowledge of conditions that is the forerunner of community action.

A number of paper and broadcasting stations, sharing the Washington *Post* view, modified their no-juvenile-crime-names policy in cases of extreme offense. The publisher of the St. Louis *Globe-Democrat*, Richard H. Amberg, thus described a changed policy:

> We no longer withhold from publication the names of juveniles involved in atrocious crimes. We believe that if a person is old enough to attack and rape a 14-year-old girl, for example, he is old enough to get his name in the paper.

The *Globe-Democrat* at the same time adopted a policy of throwing sharp emphasis on names, addresses, and economic status of parents of teen-age misbehavers. The paper asserted its belief that "parents should share in the public opprobrium" of their children's misdeeds, and that wide public knowledge .of crime serves as a deterrent.

Some juvenile court officials have expressed similar sentiments. County judges in New York state approved the position taken by the Buffalo *Evening News* in sharp criticism of secrecy provisions of the New York "Youth Court Act," with the declaration that the provisions were not achieving their purpose. A juvenile judge in Minnesota opened criminal cases to the press, announcing that he believed full news coverage would help young offenders more than would privacy.

Many newspapers and newscasters have decided that a youth who beats another with brass knuckles, or drives through a city street at 80 miles an hour, or pushes marijuana among schoolmates, has made himself a social menace beyond the protection of anonymity. T. R. Sunde of the New York *Daily News*, speaking as president of the New York State Society of Newspaper Editors, said: "Why not continue to leave such decisions . . . to the good sense and responsibility of the press?"

Assurance as to whether it is best to print or omit will await years of experience and careful study, not by journalists alone but by sociologists and psychologists. The weight of opinion continues to support the policy of omission of names except in "atrocious" crimes. But nobody thinks the final answer is in hand.

Another kind of name-and-identification problem is that of use of racial, religious, or national labels with names in the news. The most familiar is the propriety of identification of news figures by the word "Negro."

It is increasingly common today for newspapers and news broadcasters to follow a policy thus described for his paper by an editor of the New York *Post*: "When a man's color doesn't matter we don't print it." Elaborated, this policy says that a news figure is to be identified as "Negro" only when full understanding of the news cannot be reached without knowledge of the man's race.

By no means universal in American news handling, this policy has developed only since about the time of World War II. Especially in the South, it had been routine to show a Negro's race in news stories even though it added nothing to the news. Objection to the practice grew largely out of recognition that identification of even a few criminals, real or alleged, as Negroes tends to prejudice hasty readers and listeners (or loose thinkers) against an entire social group. One defense—offered, for example, by the New York *World-Telegram and Sun* —for use of the racial tag is that "we make such designations in the case of good deeds as well as in the case of law violations." But such organizations as the National Association for the Advancement of Colored People argue against any identification except that that is genuinely relevant. "You don't say 'John Smith, white,'" they point out, "unless perhaps you are reporting that a white singer is playing the part of a Negro in an otherwise all-Negro opera. Why not give Negroes the same treatment?"

Chicago radio and TV stations, at a time when gang violence in the city was widespread, agreed to eliminate racial and national tags in news of such outbreaks "to minimize the danger of attracting additional participants to the scene. . . ." A study of racial-tag practices in Southern newspapers made by the Southern Regional Council, producing evidence that matter-ofcourse labeling was almost universal, is given credit for leading a number of newspapers to alter the practice.

The problem of this kind of identification arises not alone in the use of the word "Negro": in Texas and Southern California the term may be "Mexican," in New York "Puerto Rican," in several Northern and Southwestern states "Indian." It is always the same problem.

IS MISFORTUNE FUNNY?   A confirmed alcoholic is brought before a police judge for the 94th time for drunkenness. A reporter—perhaps bored by monotony and aware that such a case makes no story unless a human interest angle is developed—makes a comic piece of it:

> Andy Silkes, 49, no address, chalked up Appearance No. 94 in police court yesterday and went back to the workhouse to sober up for No. 95.

Reported in some such fashion as this, the news becomes what has been defined earlier in this book as a "bright." Its writer presumably hopes that it will produce chuckles (or snickers) in its reader.

The question it raises is this: Is alcoholism, a disease (or the poverty and despair that might have contributed to it), a fit subject for comedy? Is not the reporter entertaining his customers by ridiculing illness and misfortune? Many newsmen think so, and try to avoid this kind of "humor."

The temptation to indulge in light writing with inappropriate subjects is common. A well-known radio commentator, annoyed at and objecting angrily to somebody's label of Gypsy Rose Lee as a "security risk" on the flimsiest of grounds, could not help adding the wisecrack that it "was a patent absurdity to think that Miss Lee had ever had anything she wished to conceal." This mildly satiric reference to Miss Lee's reputation as a stripteaser had nothing to do with her acknowledged gifts as a writer and a civic figure, and less with the dispute which the commentator was otherwise treating with appropriate sobriety.

Note other more or less typical examples:

Paul D. Matovich, erstwhile University of Idaho journalism student, began his freshman year in one state-supported institution, but the finish of it finds him in another one.

[*He had been sentenced to a penitentiary for murder.*]

VERSAILLES, France— Mrs. Leopoldine Schmitt, 54, was convicted Saturday of burning up her husband because she was burned up by his attentions to another woman.

[*She had set fire to and murdered her husband.*]

In the following story the reporter's skepticism about the merits of the case may have been humanly justified. His lick-lipping satire, however, does not belong in a newsman's bag of tricks.

NEW YORK, N. Y.— Those three rude Hotel Taft detectives who burst in on Mario DelMonte and his pretty wife Josephine on their wedding night bruised them $10,000 worth. This was disclosed in a sealed jury verdict opened Monday by Supreme Court Justice Edgar Nathan.

Injuries to Mario, owner of a beauty shop, were physical, he testified during trial of the suit last week. Josephine had the marriage annulled two years after that humiliating night in the hotel. She said her wounds were spiritual.

She had so wanted a beautiful evening, she said, but it wasn't beautiful because of "those awful men."

Jurors scorned defense testimony that the trio burst in on the DelMontes because they'd been creating a disturbance.

EXPLOITING HUMAN INTEREST   Emotional impact is fundamental to the reporting of the news of the day, as every newspaper or newscast makes clear. Chapter 3 and other sections of this book have suggested that this component of news, the human interest component, may rank lower on news editors' scales than the quality of significance.

But it often draws the audience with far more compelling magnetism than the significant. It is a commodity that every news medium seeks as spice for its less alluring offerings; in some newspapers and some newscasts it tends to dominate. And it provides the kind of reporting, or reportorial writing, that is often the most fun both for writer and reader.

For all these reasons newsmen seek out human interest news. Sometimes, in their desire to develop "good" stories, they give more thought to the readability of their yarns than to the effect they'll have on the men and women reported—more emphasis on readership than on human values. It is easy to step into this kind of water, and it is always muddy in spite of its shallowness. Several examples show the kinds of problems it raises.

A young man, learning that his fiancee is soon to die from leukemia, marries her without letting her know of her condition. A wire service story about his decision ends with this paragraph:

"The girl, now hospitalized, still hasn't been told. All radios and newspapers have been banned from her room for fear she will discover the truth."

A moving story—but an essentially private circumstance. Are the loyalty and courage of the man fit subject for exploitation, for circulation building? Is any reader enriched by the news? And, if these questions are answered "yes," is not the story's wide publication questionable in view of the desire to keep it secret?

Two young women, held up in their all-night restaurant, are forced by the bandit to undress as an aid to his escape. A photographer next day finds them willing to pose behind a tablecloth as though they are naked, and a reporter gets a clinical description of the event. The story and picture make front page. Are newsmen justified in letting the women show themselves in so undignified a light, even when they are willing to do so? Is the newspaper within bounds in its sly suggestion that the photograph is "real"? Hasn't it lost the respect of readers who recognize its phoniness?

A young couple, unable to find a home in the city where the husband has taken a job, spends nights for a week in the city bus station. With their permission, they are photographed asleep on a bench, their baby in the mother's arms. The story is "good human interest." But what about the couple's loss of dignity as they are made the object of public pity? Is this story better as a means of aiding them than a story that does not identify them? What if the paper pointed out, first to the couple and then to its readers, that there are better ways of meeting this kind of emergency?

A mother is caught by a camera at the moment she learns her child has drowned . . . a policeman writhing in agony from gunshot wounds is pictured on a stretcher . . . a husband bends in misery over the body of his wife after an auto accident . . .

These are familiar newspaper and television photographs. They are moving and sometimes tragically beautiful. But newsmen are more and more often asking whether they make legitimate news. That they tell stories powerfully and that they have high reader interest nobody denies. But, ask the questioners, what is more personal and essentially private than a mother's grief, a man's torture? Is it decent to make capital out of the intimacy of human suffering? Do reader interest and audience attraction justify the invasion of privacy that such pictures represent?

The Newsman and the Public

The problems that face newsmen—those just described, those illustrated throughout this book—are at once old and eternally new. They all relate to the journalistic ideal of service, the principle that the reporting and illumination of the daily triumphs and tragedies of mankind justify themselves only insofar as they enable mankind to know, to understand, and to decide. The reporter must meet, and sometimes fight to fulfill, frightening obligations. He must face up to the men and the organizations and the social and governmental institutions that seek to bar him from getting and transmitting the news. He must equip himself so that he can observe events accurately, record them truthfully and understandingly, and present them in meaningful terms to his particular audience. These are the minimum requirements for newsmen as the world races through the second half of the twentieth century.

But the audiences and the news sources themselves bear obligations—toward the newspapers, the magazines, the newscasters . . . toward themselves. These are obligations too often ignored. The public has an inclination to take the services of the news media for granted, to accept them as a providential gift or an inherent right, without need to offer either thought or thanks. Simultaneously, most news consumers are critical of news performance; it is commonplace for newsmen to say caustically that "every subscriber can run the paper better than the editor." One reason for this consumer attitude, perhaps the dominant one, is that the printed news media expose themselves mercilessly, issue after issue, to public scrutiny and appraisal; there are not many activities in which the product of the professionals' effort is so glaringly open to its users' inspection and analysis. Nevertheless, newsmen are convinced that lay criticism is more likely than not to be ill-informed, hasty, thoughtless, and unfair.

The responsibility of the reader of the press and of the listener or viewer of broadcast news, involves several express undertakings:

If he wants the news to come to him uninfluenced by special interest, he should himself scrupulously avoid making demands that might hamper responsible news-handling. If he expects news of local law enforcement to come to him fairly and fully, he can hardly justify a request for special consideration from the press if his son or his neighbor's son gets into a scrape with the police.

If he wants all the news, he must accept the condition that news channels on which he has influence must be kept open. He cannot expect everybody else to tell all if he himself bottles up information at its source.

He must work both to be informed about the news media and to make logical rather than sentimental or prejudiced judgments about them. His criticisms— the more the better if they meet these criteria—must be based on some knowledge of journalistic problems and procedures, and it must be directed at fundamentals, at causes, not at symptoms.

He must recognize that he is not the sole consumer at whom a piece of news is aimed. Even though he's a world affairs expert, he shouldn't demand that the paper or the newscaster throw out all except world news. His criticisms will make no sense if he fails to recognize the "mass" character of the major news media; and he will be forever dissatisfied if he decides to make unrealistic demands.

He should heed the warning of the news media that powerful influences seek to close some channels of information; he should lend whatever support he can muster to the journalists' efforts to keep the channels open.

The Reporter as Specialist

What should a reporter know?

The simple answer to this sweeping question was once a sardonic "Everything." In today's labyrinthine world this answer is both more and less appropriate: more because there are today more areas of knowledge, deeper funds of information, wider sweeps of newsworthy activity than ever before; less for almost the same reasons; it is increasingly difficult for any man to know even a little about everything going on about him. The result: the newsman today is more and more often asked to know "everything" in a limited area. All kinds of news media are seeking specialists—the business editor, the science writer, the religious writer, the welfare reporter. Though broadcasting does not yet challenge the newspapers and magazines in the depth with which they explore specialized news fields, there are signs that it will some day rival them.

The all-purpose reporter was the rule in yesterday's journalism. Life was not then so departmentalized nor society so complex; man's horizons were narrower insofar as specific fields of knowledge were involved, and a reporter was a man who could bring judgment, character, energy, imagination, and a fairly good fund of general knowledge to his work.

But scores of new fields of study and knowledge have opened in the last century, and the pace of the advance of knowledge has increased in fields old and new. The horseless carriage came on the scene as the century opened, and its impact on American life gave birth to the automobile editor. Broadcasting appeared in the century's third decade, and with television in the sixth it profoundly changed American life; it not only created a new kind of journalist but led to a new label on newspaper and newsmagazine office doors—Radio-TV Editor. Medical discoveries and the development of nuclear physics, the headlong progress in many fields of technology, these have demanded men and women qualified as journalists in many technical areas.

The developments in all these areas have underlined the need for more education, and better education, in other older fields as well as in the new. The political writer today is likely to be a man with a solid background in political science and history, but with a knowledge of psychology, sociology, and literature as well. The education reporter must know a lot about education, but he may also be a master of arts in a special subject matter field.

To many newsmen this trend means that they ought to find for themselves particular fields of interest of activity in which to become "experts." It is possible for a prospective newsman to choose such a field, within broad if not narrow limits, while he is in college (college training itself, with emphasis on sound general education, is widely considered a minimum foundation for journalistic work). But he may choose it later, as his interests and capacities mature through professional work. Victor Cohn, the writer of the story on page 298, spent several years on a newspaper copy desk before he entered science writing; as his interest in the new field of atomic energy developed into wide knowledge, he increased his competence in other fields of science.

The time is not here when every newsman must channel his interests and his hopes into one field. But there is no denying that the need for specialists is greater now than it was yesterday, and that it will expand again tomorrow. Specialist or not, every newsman needs increasing breadth of knowledge, not alone to deal with the grand opera story today and the radioactive fallout story tomorrow, but also to arrive at sound judgments as to interrelationships among news developments in a dozen fields and to approach widely differing topics with informed emphasis and understanding. To do his job well a reporter must be a truly educated man, and true education means not alone what the classroom offers but also what the man himself provides. A specialist the reporter *may* be. A well-informed generalist he *must* be.

PROJECTS

1. The Supreme Court of the United States, in the case described on page 308 declared that "freedom of the press . . . is not an absolute." It was saying that in some cases the reportorial privilege of concealing news sources must be subject to limitation in

the broader interests of society. Write a 500-word statement of your views of the Court position.

2. Examine in depth one of the four examples of "exploiting human interest" and write a statement of your views of the questions it raises—perhaps suggesting what you believe would be the most appropriate method of handling its news problem.

3. Write for the bulletin board of the newsroom of a local newspaper or broadcasting station what you think would be an appropriate statement of policy with regard to the acceptance of "comps"—free tickets—by the news staff.

4. From thorough study of several issues of a metropolitan daily, write a description and evaluation of its policy with regard to national, racial, and religious identification in news stories.

APPENDIX A

Communication as a Science

A new kind of behavioral scientist has established himself, in the period since World War II, as a full-fledged member of the corps of students of human activities: the communication scientist or research specialist. He is the man whose task is reducing the practices and knowledge of organized human communication to a meaningful set of theorems, a set of valid principles that will stand the tests of practice, that will remain substantially reliable under any circumstance. This is the essence of scientific theory.

This new specialist draws from, and adds to, other bodies of theoretical knowledge: those of the sociologist, the psychologist, the semanticist, the mathematician and statistician, the electronics communication expert, and others. He does not pretend to know all the answers. His formulas have not become fixed and immutable, and he does not expect them to do so. It has been said of him that he is sure of only one thing: that though his science is young, it is vast. The horizon beyond his frontier is not a limit, but rather an invitation to explore far beyond his line of vision.

Communication, *without the s? Or* communications, *with it?*

Communication *means the process of moving a "message" from one place to another. This is, in simple language, telling somebody something. But note that however simply described, it dictates four elements: a source, a message, a carrier, and a recipient. With-*

He has been interested in two kinds of research: broad general rules and the applications of the rules. Much of the applied research of such a man has been woven into this book: studies of readership and readability, of content and emphasis in news communication, of audience attitude, and of many other phenomena of journalistic practice. But the research specialist has also made significant advances in scientific description of the mass communication process, and thus in description of the journalistic, or news communication, process. What he has reported should be

out any one of the four, there is no communication. Mass communication is assumed arbitrarily to mean that the message goes to a mass or group of recipients —an audience of some size. It virtually never means "communication between masses."

Communications *is a term commonly applied to a formalized system for communicating. A newspaper, a wire service, a broadcasting organization, a magazine is a communications system; so is a publishing house or a film company. The term is taken, too, to refer to a complex of individual communications apparatuses— the newspaper system, including newspapers, wire services, and auxiliary agencies, is an example. And it is used in broader sense: "American mass communications," "the international communications system." All these systems, by the meaning of the term, are available for mass communication.*

familiar to every worker in the communications industries, if he is to have more than surface understanding of what he is doing.

One qualification, before passing to a brief examination of some aspects of modern mass communication theory:

The scientific approach to news in no way denies that journalism partakes importantly of the characteristics of art. Its practice involves subjective personal contributions that can never be prescribed in theorems. Will Irwin sat at his desk on an April day in 1906 with a passion for San Francisco as he knew it, and his artistry produced a newspaper classic, "The City That Was." George Weller's story about an appendectomy performed by a pharmacist's mate in a submarine under enemy waters (pages 113-114) might have been routine or hack in other hands. Describing news communication on a plane as nearly scientific as we can achieve does not deny that individuals can and do contribute individual gifts. Journalism would be a sorry craft, and nothing but a craft, if it did not prize and court the talents that so many of its devotees bring to it.

Charting the Communication Process

Communication researchers have developed a series of diagrams to simplify description of the theory they are developing. The simplest (Figure A-1) shows a *source,* the origin of the message that is to be delivered; the *message;* and the

Figure A-1   *Communication in its simplest form.*

destination. This is communication theory in its rudimentary form (it does not even show the carrier or channel by which the message is delivered). The source may be a news event, the commercial purpose of an advertiser, the imagination of a novelist, or a single man—any event, action, activator, or other impulse that provides material for the construction of a message. The message may be the news story, the advertisement, the novel, or the piece of gossip that one neighbor whispers across a back fence to a listener. The destination is the mind of a "consumer," reached usually through eye or ear.

But note that two intermediary agents are shown in the diagram—an *encoder* and a *decoder*. The encoder is the agent who puts the materials from the source into message symbols—words, pictures, music, or other meaningful forms: the reporter who writes a news story, the advertising copy writer who describes his wares, the novelist, or the lady at the fence. The decoder is usually the human brain at the destination, the reader or listener whom the message reaches. "Decoding" is the process of translating the symbols into a meaningful pattern.

Note, now, in the second diagram (Figure A-2) how the bare bones of the first are expanded to describe the specific problems of news communication. The *source* becomes either the event or some other kind of phenomenon from which

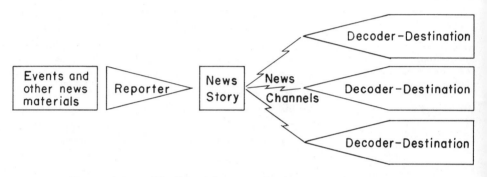

FIGURE A-2   *The "simple" communication process in news terms.*

a news story is drawn; the *encoder* is the reporter who writes it; the *message* is the news story itself. By one or more of the news channels, newspaper, broadcasting, magazine, the story is carried to the decoder-destination, the reader or listener or viewer himself.

The diagram shows news communication at its simplest; but even here it is apparent that one piece of news has a number of carriers and destinations. And the message, the news story, may go untranslated at some destinations, either because they can't understand it or aren't interested; and at others it may be translated into something quite different from the reporter's intent. It will mean nothing whatsoever if the reporter has put into English a message that reaches ears that understand only Arabic, or if it is encoded in language suitable for students at the London School of Economics but delivered only to seven-year-olds. And its intended meaning may disappear if the decoding is done by somebody to whom the message-symbols carry denotations different from those intended by the encoder.

The scientists, therefore, have added another factor to the diagram by showing that both ends of the process, the source and the destination, must share a field of experience. The diagram (Figure A-3) now becomes more complex.

The encoder and the decoder must use the same language, the same jargon; they must have shared, or similar, experiences that will enable the second to take from the message the meaning the first intended.

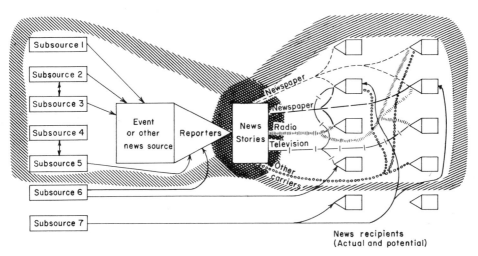

FIGURE A-3   *Some—though by no means all—of the complications of news communication are suggested in this diagram. First, it is clear that a "major" source is acted on by, or draws material from, a number of subsources, and that reporters, too, draw from many sources. Second, some relevant sources (Subsource 7) may reach the news consumers without going through the organized process. Third, different consumers get news from different sources, in differing combinations; and some may miss the news entirely. Fourth, the news has impact on those whose experience fields overlap with regard to particular news. But what the diagram does not show is that no two of the consumers offer identical total-experience fields—the news stories represented in the diagram are in fields common to both sides of the process, sending and receiving, but each consumer's field, conditioned by a thousand other experience-fields, is a little different from his neighbor's.*

And it goes without saying that the encoder, the news communicator, the reporter, ought to have enough skill, perception, and knowledge both of his subject and of his audience to make it reasonably sure that the decoder will get from his message symbols precisely what he put into them—and that what he put into them is precisely what his source materials mean.

Communication Has Many Paths

The three simple diagrams suggest that communication is a passably straightforward, uncomplicated process. Occasionally, even in the maze of the modern world, this is true. But much more commonly, and especially in news communication, it is a vastly complex set of interactions, moving in several directions at once and affected by dozens of secondary influences. Let us examine some of them.

INFLUENCES ON THE REPORTER (ENCODER)   The task of a reporter is to get information about an event, or a condition, or an opinion, and to verbalize a selection from among all the facts he has gathered (to encode it) in such a way that his audience can extract correct meaning from his message. It would be impossible to name all the influences affecting him in even a simple news situation, let alone an involved one. But note a sampling of them:

The skill and accuracy with which he observes an event or conducts and records an interview, the skill with which he writes his "message"

The influence of "purposeful communicators" such as publicity agents, voluntary informers, and the like, many of whom may seek to persuade him to accept their views (sometimes biased) of the event

The extent of his knowledge and experience in the field in which he is reporting

The degree to which he controls his prejudices and biases as he reports

The influence of editors and others who may affect the manner in which he writes his story

INFLUENCES ON THE CARRIER   The extent and breadth of the facilities the newspaper, broadcaster, or publisher of a magazine provides.

The purposes and attitudes of those who control the carrier

The "natural" limitations of the medium (that is, the differences characteristic of different media in reporting the same events)

INFLUENCES ON THE RECIPIENT (DECODER)   In news communication, the decoder is typically the consumer, the destination; for though the communication of news is a mass process, the message is aimed at individuals who do their own deciphering and usually their own interpretation. What each individual does with the message is conditioned by variables:

The extent of his knowledge of the subject: He may have seen the game or heard the speech the news story reported. He may have studied widely in the field of the news event. He may have been told about it by others, getting either the information the reporter offered or differing information. He may have received messages about it from other news media.

He may have biases about the subject that color his acceptance of the message.

He may have no knowledge whatsoever to prepare him for the message.

FEEDBACK   In simple person-to-person communication, the process called "feedback" is fundamental. Feedback is the return message from original receiver to original sender, both of whom, at this stage of the process, reverse roles. In mass communication there is ordinarily little feedback. The newspaper reader may write a letter, cancel his subscription, or order 100 extra copies. Broadcast listeners may call the station, scold or praise the sponsor, or write postcards.

But the mass-communications systems make little provision for audience response, and they get little.

INTERFERENCE   If the housewife is minding the baby at the same time she is trying to read the paper, the meaning of its messages may be impaired. If a radio is reporting a ball game in the room to which the TV screen is bringing a news show, messages from both sides are clouded. Communication scientists apply the convenient term "noise" to interferences such as these (they are legion.) The effectiveness of the message is likely to be inversely proportional to the height of the "noise" with which it competes.

REPETITION   The communication scientists say that about half of ordinary English prose is in entirely familiar patterns—adjectives preceding nouns, articles preceding both, verbs preceded by subjects and followed by objects, particular words in familiar combinations, such as "face-to-face," "lying down," "conscientious objector," and thousands more. This fact is an aid to communication. It makes the arrangement of word symbols so as to carry immediate meaning to their recipients immeasurably easier than would be possible if every structure or word arrangement were strange.

Writers of all kinds not only make use of this kind of repetition of the familiar, but also employ conscious repetition to enhance meaning or gain emphasis. One fact may be repeated, in varying forms and contexts, several times in a news story. Writing for the ear—radio writing, in particular—constantly uses repetition: "To get the free sample, just write to Box Seven Four Seven, Cleveland, Ohio—that's Box Seven Four Seven, Cleveland, Ohio."

This kind of use of the familiar, and of making sure particular words or phrases become familiar, is called *redundancy* by the communication scientists.

Preparation of Copy

Nothing is more practical than the "rules" for getting copy ready for the printer or the announcer. Their purpose is to insure speed and ease of handling, along with accuracy of presentation. The word "rules" is in quotation marks because it represents a body of customs rather than formalized dicta; the "rules" are, indeed, the outcome of time- and practice-tested newsman habits, and they are not absolute (except in any one office). There is no one way to mark a paragraph opening or delete a phrase that is universally practiced or indubitably preferable to any other way.

In general, however, professionals have agreed on fairly standardized copy-handling procedures. The "rules" below are those on which there is broad consensus.

Newspaper Copy

1) Always typewrite copy. Ordinarily you double-space it (*never* single-space), though some newsrooms—both print and broadcast—ask for triple spacing. The ribbon should be black, and not over-antique—clear typing is essential. Keys should be clean.

2) Write copy on one side only of soft-finish "copy paper"—often, in newspaper offices, copy paper is blank newsprint cut to the standard 8½″ × 11″ size. Some newsrooms use half sheets, 8½″ × 5½″; some provide yellow copy paper. Never use onionskin; avoid hard-finish paper.

3) Keep your copy decently "clean." This means that, though it need not be stenographically perfect, it should be legible and always clear. If typing errors or editing has made it hard to read or hard to understand, retype it.

4) Always put your name and a short slugline at the upper left corner of page 1. Thus:

Cooper
Valley basketball

If you need to give other information to the city or copy desk, type it either under name and slugline or opposite them in the upper right corner: "For release March 16" or "Hold for check on name" or "Use on basketball page."

5) Leave the upper third of page 1 blank, except as described in the "rule" above. This leaves space for the copy desk to write headlines, a new slugline, or typographical instructions. Leave margins of about an inch on each side.

6) Indent paragraph about ten spaces from the left margin.

7) At the upper left of pages following page 1, write your name (or the slugline) and the page number. Thus:

Cooper – 2
Valley basketball – 2

Some newsrooms prefer to have page 2 numbered "Add 1" or "1st add," and succeeding pages marked correspondingly. In this system, the third page would be headed:

Cooper – add 2

8) Best practice is to avoid splitting words at the ends of typewritten lines, and to avoid breaking sentences (or, indeed, paragraphs) from one page to the next. Some newsrooms ask that the word "more" be written at the bottom of each page of a story that continues to another page.

9) Write an endmark, either in typewriter or pencil, at the end of the story; circle it in pencil to make it unmistakable. The most common end marks (use one or the other, not both, placed *below* the last line of copy) are these:

– 30 –
###

Some newswriters use their own initials, lower case—a practice borrowed from the wire services, whose writers so "sign" their copy.

10) Edit all copy completely and carefully with a black pencil, using the accepted copyreading symbols employed in your office (see traditional symbols on page 330). *Do not use proofreading symbols.* Mark all paragraph openings, make final factual checks, clarify anything that might be questioned or subject to misunderstanding.

11) If your office asks it, paste the sheets of the story together to make one continuous piece of copy. Never put more than one story on one copy sheet.

Copy Editing and Proofreading

On page 330 is an example of a reporter's copy marked for the printer, with the editing symbols explained at the left. On the following page you will find the proof for the story as it has come from the composing room. It contains, as you'll

Italics *Center in column*	Other basketball news on Page 11
Paragraph *Insert letter*	Mitford remaind the only undefeated team
Insert word or phrase *Overline longhand o, m, n*	in the Valley school basketball race Thursday
Substitute phrase *Delete word and letter, draw together*	by beating Perkins on the big Perkins floor
New paragraph	in a tight game, 59 to 54. The victory, fourth
Delete fault *Clarify bad typing*	straight from for the ponies, kept them
Spell out figure *Spell out abbreviated word*	1 game ahead of Pt. Arthur, which has won
Use figure instead of word *Abbreviate word*	fourteen games since December 1.
Insert comma *Remove space*	Perkins always troublesome for Mitford
Insert space *Capitalize*	athome, carried the ponies right down to
Use small letter	the wire, but the closest game of the night
Transpose words *Transpose letters*	Alhambra found edging Littledale 52 to 51.
Continue without paragraph break *No new paragraph*	No ¶ Dave Larson scored 15 points in the
Period (or ⊙)	last period, when Alhambra rallied to win
Overline longhand o, m, n, underline a, w, u *Insert quotation mark*	"We felt lucky to win that one, Peter
Ignore change; "let it stand"	Edmond, Alhambra coach, said.
Boldface	Other results last night:
Correct spelling—do not change	Port Arthur 62, Shantietown (CORRECT) 41
Correct spelling—do not change	FOLO COPY Washburn 70, Retreet 67
Endmark (or # # #)	-30-

note, an altogether unlikely number of errors, all properly marked by the proof-reader for correction. Notice the differences between copyreading and proofreading symbols.

Finally, the story as it would appear on the printed page, with all copy and proof corrections made.

Other basketball news on
page 11

Mitford remained the only undefeated team in the Valley conference high school basketball race Thursday when it beat Perkins on the Perkins floor 59 to 54.

The victory, fourth straight for the Ponies, kept them one game ahead of Port Arthur, which has won 14 games since Dec. 1.

Perkins, always troublesome for Mitford at home, carried the Ponies right down to the wire, but the closest game of the night found Alhambra edging Littledale 52 to 51. Dave Larson scored 15 points in the last period, when Alhambra rallied to win.

"We felt lucky to win that one," Peter Edmond, Alhambra coach, said.

Other results last night:

Port Arthur 62, Shantie-town 41
Washburn 70, Retreet 67

Proof from the composing room, with the proofreader's marks.

The story as it appears on the printed page.

Copy for Broadcasting

Some of the copy editing practices of air newsmen are identical with those of the editor-for-print; some differ widely. The differences stem largely from two dominant facts: one, copy for print can be read only as fast as a linotype operator's fingers can trip keys, but copy for the air can be read at the greater speed of speech; two, errors made in transcribing copy into type can be corrected at any of several later stages, but errors made in reading copy into a microphone are instantly and irrevocably "published." Copy for radio and TV, therefore, must be totally accurate, legible and understandable. When it isn't, its mistakes or its muddiness may become part of a broadcast that can't be called back.

Editing copy for broadcast employs fewer standard symbols than does newspaper or magazine editing. Its purpose is to express every change or correction in indubitably clear and "pronounceable" form. For this reason, editors tend to write out corrections rather than to use symbols, and often to retype copy that might be made unclear by pencil editing.

Radio and TV copy are written and edited in the same manner. TV copy carries two columns on a page, the left for video and the right for audio.

Practices in editing air copy may be summarized as follows:

1) Copy is always typewritten, with ribbon fresh and keys clean. It is more commonly double- than triple-spaced, though triple spacing is demanded in some newsrooms and by some newscasters. Because wire service copy comes from the teleprinter in capital letters, some newsrooms type local copy in caps too.

2) Copy is written on *one* side of copy paper. The paper must be soft finish so that it won't crackle into the microphone as its reader handles it.

3) Each page of copy is identified by slugline and page number at the upper left of the page.

4) Paragraph openings are indented 10 to 15 spaces.

5) Splitting words at the ends of lines or sentences from one page to the next is taboo. It is best not to split paragraphs from one page to the next. An endmark (usually the typewritten or longhand symbol ######) or a "continued" line (usually the penciled MORE) should be the last symbol on every page.

6) Copy should be meticulously edited and corrected, with editing marks that a tyro (some news announcers are just that) could read at a glance. Copy made confusing by poor typing or involved editing must be retyped.

The writing as well as the editing of air copy differs from writing for the printer. Among the special precautions observed by radio and TV newsmen:

1) Never merely strike over a typing error. Black it out, with pencil or the typewriter's xxxxx, and rewrite. This is especially important in correcting errors in initials, other capital letters, and figures.

2) Provide phonetic spellings where they're needed. Thus: ". . . *spent the next few days at Plock (PLOTSK)*"; ". . . *the Hungarian statesman Szilagyi (SHE-LAHG'-YEE)*."

3) Make generous use of punctuation—especially commas and dashes—to indicate voice pauses and the like. Use capital initial letters freely—they help to identify important words. Underline words that ought to be called to the announcer's special attention—names, difficult words, words that ought to get vocal emphasis.

4) Use few abbreviations, or none. Write out titles such as Mister, Doctor, and President. Write figures precisely as you want them spoken: *sixteen hundred*, not *1600; a thousand*, not *1000*. Use round numbers when precise figures aren't necessary: forty million families instead of 40,007,214 families.

5) Put on the copy paper *only* what the announcer is to read (excepting such necessities as sluglines, page numbers, and clearly identified instructions).

6) Use copyreading symbols stingily.

A typical sample of broadcast news copy, edited, as it appears:

There's only one ~~undrefreated~~d
undefeated team left in the Valley Conference. That's
Mitford High School. Mitford beat Perkins at Perkins
last night, 59 to ~~58~~ 54.

The victory was the fourth straight for
~~the Ponies~~ Mitford . . . and ~~it~~ *it* left them one game ahead of
Port Arthur. Port Arthur, by the way, won last night
too --- 62 to 41 over Shantietown. Port Arthur has won
fourteen games since the first of December.

Mitford had to go right down to the
wire to beat Perkins. Perkins has always been tough
for the Ponies ~~at home~~ on ~~their~~ *its* own floor, and the game
was close until the end.

But the closest game of the night was
that between Alhambra and Littledale. Alhambra pulled
it out by one point --- 52 to 51 --- largely through the
15 points Dave Larson made in the last period. The ~~Alham.~~
Alhambra coach, Peter Edmond, said his team "felt lucky
to win."

Washburn won the fourth game in the
conference last night. It beat Retreet by three
points, 70 to 67.

######

APPENDIX C

The Language of Newsmen

Newsmen, like specialists in every field, have developed a private language—a jargon made largely of common words and terms with special meanings. Because its characteristics are simplicity, informality, and practicality, it is not a difficult language. Familiarity with it is a necessity for every news worker.

The glossary here presented is limited to terms and usages that newsmen are likely to employ in their daily gathering and writing of news, or to hear in the newsroom. The technical language of printing and broadcast engineering is excluded, except for terms in common newsroom use.

ad   Short for "advertisement"

add   Addition to a story already written, or in process of being written

advance   Story announcing a coming news event. See "prelim"

angle   The approach or perspective from which a news fact or event is viewed, or the emphasis chosen for a story. See "slant"

AP   The Associated Press

art   Pictures or other illustrative material for print media

assignment   An assigned news task—a single story, or a continuing responsibility such as a beat

audio   The aural, or sound, portion of a telecast

background   Informative factual material related to current news, presented to aid audience understanding

bank   A section of a newspaper headline. Same as "deck"

banner   A headline across, and near the top of, all or most of a newspaper page. Same as "line," "ribbon," "streamer"

beat   (1) A group of news sources assigned to a reporter for regular coverage. Same as "run." (2) A story published by one medium ahead of others. Same as "exclusive," "scoop"

bf Boldface (also blackface)—heavy black typeface

body type The small type in which a news story (excluding heads and display lines) is printed

boil or *boil down* To shorten or condense a piece of copy

boldface See "bf"

break (1) The point in time at which a news development becomes known and available. (2) The point of interruption in a story continued from one page to another (noun and verb usage in both meanings)

bridge The transition or movement from one element or story in a newscast to another (noun and verb)

bulldog An early, usually the first, of a day's editions of a newspaper

bulletin A promptly issued first announcement of an important news event

by-line The writer's name at the head of a news story

cap Capital letter. Same as "upper case"

caption Title or legend above a printed picture (sometimes used loosely to refer to any descriptive text with a picture)

'cast Short for "newscast"

clc or *c & lc* Capital initials followed by small letters. See "lower case."

clip A news story clipped from a newspaper, usually for future reference

clip sheet A printed sheet of news stories—usually publicity—from which an editor may clip for his own use

copy The written (usually typewritten) form in which a news story or other material is presented to the printer or the newscaster

correspondent A reporter who transmits his copy by wire, radio, or mail

credit or *credit line* (1) The printed or spoken acknowledgment of the source or ownership of a picture or other news material. (2) The phrase showing the source of quoted material ("he said")

cut (1) The metal or plastic plate from which a picture is printed. (2) The printed picture. (3) To shorten or condense copy

cutline Descriptive text accompanying a picture

dateline Words opening the first paragraph of a news story to identify its place and date of origin

deadline Stated hour by which all copy for an edition or a newcast must be ready

deck See "bank"

delete Take out (primarily a proofreading term)

dog watch Latest shift on a morning paper, or earliest on an afternoon. Same as "lobster trick"

dope story A story of speculation, prediction, comment, or background. Much used in sports and political reporting

down style An editing pattern calling for a minimum of capital letters

dummy A chart or pattern showing how a page is to be made up. See "makeup"

dupe or *duplicate* A carbon copy

ear Upper corner of page one

edition One version of a newspaper. Some papers have one edition a day, some many. Not to be confused with "issue," which usually refers to all editions under a single date

effects   Sound or music used to back or support voices in a broadcast

exclusive   See "beat (2)"

feature   (1) A news story or other material differentiated from straight news. See page 241. (2) To emphasize or play up

file   To send a story to the home office, usually by wire; or to put news service stories on the wire

filler   Material used to fill space or time

flag   The printed title of a newspaper on page 1. See "logo"

flash   Brief news service bulletin on news of utmost importance, taking precedence over all other materials

fluff   An announcer's error on the air—analogous to a "typo" in print. Similar terms are "beard" and "booboo"

folio   Page number

folo   Short for "follow"—a story about an event after its occurrence

format   The pattern or structural outline of a newscast

galley   A metal tray for carrying type

graf   Paragraph

guide or *guideline*   Identifying word or words written at the top of pages of copy to facilitate handling and editing. Same as "slugline"

halftone   Metal or plastic plate from which a photograph is printed

handout   Prepared material given to newsmen in the hope that it will be printed or broadcast without change, or that it will be helpful in preparing news stories. Applied commonly to "free publicity" material

head or *headline*   The display type over a printed news story; also the concise summary of a news story sometimes used in radio and TV news

hold   Do not release without permission

HTK   Copyreader's shorthand for "hed to kum," used on copy that goes to the printer before its head is written

insert   Words, phrases, sentences, or paragraphs inserted in previously prepared copy

issue   The editions of a newspaper or other periodical under one date. See "edition"

italics   Type designed so as to slope to the right

jump   To continue a story from one page to another; or, as a noun, the continued material. See "break (2)"

kicker   (1) A short story, usually humorous, used to close a newscast. (2) A small-type phrase preceding or following the main deck of a headline

kill   To throw away type matter or to eliminate portions or all of a story

lc   Lower case (small letters as contrasted to capitals)

lead (pronounced and sometimes spelled lede)   Opening section of a news story

lead (pronounced led)   A thin metal space used between lines of type

lean against   To be contiguous to. A local newscast "leans against" a network newscast if it immediately precedes or follows

lede   See "lead"

leg man   A reporter—especially one who does not write his own stories

line   See "banner"

live   A radio or TV program using "live" rather than recorded talent or sound

lobster trick   See "dog watch"

lower case   Small letters, in contrast to capitals

logo   Short for "logotype." The printed title design of a periodical

make over   To change the design of and re-form a newspaper page already in type

makeup   The arrangement of body matter, headlines, and illustrations on a page

masthead   The formal statement of a paper's name, officers, point of publication, and other descriptive information. Usually on the editorial page

morgue   The newspaper or broadcasting station library

move   To send a story by wire

must   A story whose publication or broadcast is imperative

net   Short for "network"

obit   Short for "obituary." See page 214

off the record   Information provided without permission for its use. See page 98

one-shot   A single broadcast, not part of a series or continuing pattern

overhead   A story sent by commercial telegraph rather than on leased wire or by news service

overset   Stories set in type but unpublished because of lack of space

pad   To fill out, extend, "stretch" a story

paste-up   A newscast made of wire service copy pasted into the desired order

pix   Short for "picture" or "pictures"

play   The emphasis given a piece of news. A story may be "played down" or "played up." The most-emphasized story in a paper or a newscast is the "play story"

precede   A descriptive or explanatory passage preceding the lead of a story

prelim   Story announcing a coming event. See "folo"

printer   A teletype receiver used in wire service transmission

proof   A print-off of newly-set type on which corrections are to be marked

publicity   Promotional material in news form

punch   To emphasize a word, a story, or an idea in a newscast

put to bed   To take the final steps necessary to get the press rolling

query   A correspondent's inquiry as to whether an editor wants him to cover a story

release   A story provided to news media for use at a stated time

remote   A broadcast originating outside the studio

replate   To make over a page and restereotype it

revise   A revised or rewritten version of a story

rewrite   (1) Same as "revise." (2) The newsroom operation in which writers take stories by telephone from leg men and write them

ribbon   See "banner"

rim   The edge of the copy desk around which copyreaders work

roman   Vertical (in contrast to italic) type

roundup A newscast that summarizes the principal up-to-the-minute news

run See "beat (1)"

running story A continuing news development whose stories encompass a period of two or more days

runover Same as "jump"

scoop See "beat (2)"

script The copy written for a broadcast

shoot To take photographs

show A radio or TV program. A "news show" is a newscast

sidebar A secondary news story, supporting or amplifying a major story. See page 160

slant (1) Same as "angle." (2) To write a story so as to lead the consumer's thinking; to editorialize in news, to color or misrepresent

slot The space between the arms of a U-shaped copy desk, or the particular position occupied by the head of the desk

slug or *slugline* See "guide"

sob sister A reporter who specializes in tear-jerker stories

sob story A human interest story strong in pathos

spike To hold a story in reserve—to place it on a "spike" or spindle for possible future use

spot news News printed or broadcast as soon as possible after it becomes available

stet Copyreader's or proofreader's term meaning "let it stand"—ignore editing changes or corrections

still A single-exposure photograph, as distinguished from motion pictures

straight news News presented in straightforward manner for informative purpose, as distinguished from human interest or feature news

streamer See "banner"

stringer A correspondent paid by the piece—according to the number of stories he provides, or their length

tack-up A newscast made by assembling wire stories and pasting or stapling them in order, with little editing. Much the same as "paste-up"

take A section of a story taken from the typewriter before the story is completed (usually one or two paragraphs), to hasten its movement to the copy desk

text The verbatim report of a speech or public statement

30 Symbol widely used in newscopy to indicate "the end"

time copy Copy which has no immediacy. See page 45

top head A major headline at or near the top of a page

transition The verbal device used to move from one part of a newscast to another. Same as "bridge"

trim To cut or condense copy. See "boil" and "cut (3)"

typo A typographical error

underlines Descriptive matter under illustrations. See "cutline"

UPI   United Press International
upper case   Capital letters
up style   Editing pattern calling for liberal use of capital letters
video   The visual portion of a telecast

A Newsman's Style Sheet

Why a "Style Sheet"?

A "style sheet" or "style book" is like a set of traffic regulations. It does not describe the *only* rules of usage in writing, any more than traffic laws describe the *only* way to turn corners or park at meters. What it does describe is the pattern of usage in writing for a specific publication.

(The term *style* as used here refers to the mechanics of grammar, punctuation, and usage, not to "literary" characteristics or the impact of individual art and craft on writing. *Style* in this broader and usual sense is the subject of chapter 9 in this book.)

Every well-edited periodical has its own style guide, simple or elaborate. Whatever its nature, its purposes are three: to make writing and editing its parent publication as simple, precise, and rapid as is reasonably practicable, to make sure that consistent patterns of usage appear throughout the publication, and to make reading and understanding easy. Specifically, a style sheet tells you when to capitalize, when to abbreviate, how to write numbers, how to punctuate. It is arbitrary; some of its rules you will find in conflict with others you know. But conflict with other sets of rules suggests no departure from its own purposes.

The Style Sheet provided here is a typical newspaper style guide. If follows what newsmen call a "modified up-style"; that is, it leans toward liberal use of capital letters. For years newspapers favored "down-style," eliminating many capitals and thereby saving space and a little time. The increasing use of the teletypesetter by the press services during the 1950s led to standardization on up-style by Associated Press and United Press International (since many papers were receiving "TTS" service from both), and a resulting trend away from down-style.

Nobody is expected to memorize every rule in a style sheet. Every user, however, must be able to apply or interpret its rules accurately and quickly. This means that he must familiarize himself with its general patterns and principles, as well as its organization. Familiarity will aid him to use it efficiently. As he uses it, he will find that he learns many of its rules without conscious memorization.

No style sheet is unalterable; none is ever quite finished. Changes must be made as new demands arise or better patterns are devised. Nevertheless, a style sheet is to be followed unswervingly unless proper authority directs changes or departures. The Style Sheet here is offered for whatever use news workers, students, or publications choose to make of it. Particular publications using it may find expansion of some sections desirable, omission or modification of others helpful. Though it is similar to most newspaper guides, it differs in some details from others a newsman may use later. Learning to use this, however, ought to help in using others.

(The differences among style sheets are illustrated by the fact that this book, following the Holt, Rinehart and Winston style, does not always accord with this Style Sheet. For example, rule VI, 1, a tells you to omit the comma in a series when a conjunction appears: *simple, precise and rapid.* But in the body of this book you find conjunction plus comma: *simple, precise, and rapid.* The Style Sheet tells you to write it *per cent;* this book uses *percent.* You'll find other variances.)

Note that a style sheet applies only to copy that is to be printed. Copy for broadcast does not require the same mechanical precision.

STYLE SHEET

Section I—CAPITALIZATION

General rule: This Style Sheet prescribes a modified up-style. Usually this is similar to common grammar or composition-manual prescriptions.

1) Organizations and Institutions

Capitalize all principal words in names of schools, clubs, buildings, churches, industries, associations, institutions, firms, etc.: *Independence Hall, Parker School, Ford Motor Co., American Civil Liberties Union, Daughters of the American Revolution, First Congregational Church, Olympic Club, Ohio State University, College of St. Thomas, Bach Society*

2) Titles of Individuals (see also Section II, Names and Titles)

   a. Titles before names are capitalized. Titles following names use small initials: *Drum Major* Harry Shotwell; Harry Shotwell, *drum major.* Long titles (such as *city superintendent of schools*) should usually follow names.

   b. Descriptive or occupational words used in titular manner are not capitalized: *quarterback* Fran Tarkenton, *actress* Claudia Cardinale.

   c. Title modifiers such as *former, the late* are not capitalized: *the late* Adlai Stevenson, *former* President Eisenhower.

   d. When the title *president* refers to a specific president of the United States, it is capitalized and unabbreviated: *President* Kennedy, *President* Taft, *the President* said. When it is used generally, it is not capitalized: *All American presidents . . .* (see II, 5).

3) *Governmental Names and Titles*

   a. Capitalize the names of formally established governmental bodies: *Senate, House, Supreme Court, District Court, Legislature, Cook County, Department of Agriculture, Parliament, Federal Trade Commission, City Council, Senate Judiciary Committee, Arkansas* (or *State*) *Highway Department.* But do not capitalize subordinate or *ad hoc* governmental divisions: *licenses committee* of the Council, *arson squad, homicide division.*

   b. Capitalize political or governmental subdivisions: *Second Ward, Fifth Congressional District.*

   c. Capitalize military names and titles when they make specific reference: *Army, Navy, Air Force, Marine Corps, Women's Army Corps, Veterans Administration, Joint Chiefs of Staff, War College, Naval Academy, Oklahoma National Guard.*

DO NOT CAPITALIZE such terms when they are generic: The law applies to *all district courts; seven state legislatures; the armies of NATO countries.*

   d. Capitalize the generic words in specific titles when they are used without particularizing words: Marine Corps, *the Corps;* Federal Communications Commission, *the Commission.*

4) *Geographic Terms*

   a. Capitalize the principal words in geographic terms: *Great Lakes, Orinoco River, Gulf of Mexico, Lac Qui Parle County, Ural Mountains, Lake of the Isles.*

   b. Capitalize generally accepted descriptive or fanciful terms applied to specific areas: *Middle East, North Pole, South, Midwest, Orient, Barbary Coast, East Side, Hell's Kitchen.*

   c. DO NOT CAPITALIZE words indicating direction only: going *west, west* of Nebraska, *western* Nebraska, *northeasterly, south.*

5) *Nations and Nationalities*

   a. Capitalize names of all countries and nationalities.

   b. Capitalize formal names of races: *Negro, Caucasian, Indian.*

6) *Publications, Theater, Music*

   a. Capitalize the main words in, and write without quotation marks, the titles of newspapers, magazines and other periodicals such as yearbooks, reference books, university bulletins and the like: *The New York Times, Winona Daily News, Christian Science Monitor, Time, Reporter, Ladies' Home Journal, Who's Who, Coe College Bulletin, Charleston City Directory, Citizens League News.* DO NOT use italics for periodical or other titles.

   b. Capitalize the main words (including opening words and prepositions of four or more letters) in, and write with quotation marks, the titles of books, plays, motion pictures, poems, paintings, and the like: *"Moby Dick," "Who's Afraid of Virginia Woolf?" "La Dolce Vita," "The Ballad of Reading Gaol," "Mona Lisa," "The Killers."*

c. Capitalize the main words in, and write with quotation marks, the titles of musical compositions when they are "created" titles: *"Alexander's Ragtime Band," "Peer Gynt Suite," "Emperor Concerto," "Symphonie Fantastique."* But omit quotation marks around generic words or technically descriptive titles, even though they are capitalized: *Concerto No. 4, Symphony No. 9, Etudes for Piano* (note that this is a departure from the general rule in Section IV, Numerals).

7) *Religious Terms* (see also Section II, Names and Titles)

   a. Capitalize all words denoting the Deity (including pronouns) in all religions.

   b. Capitalize, but omit quotation marks around, names of sacred writings: *Bible, Koran, Book of Genesis, Gospel of St. John, Veda.* (But note that the adjective *biblical* carries no capital.)

   c. Capitalize the names of recognized denominations and creeds and of their adherents: *Protestant, Catholic, Methodist, Confucian, Hindu, Muslim, Jewish.*

   d. Capitalize the names of recognized religious events and observances: *Yom Kippur, Passover, Easter, Christmas, Ash Wednesday, Hanukah, Lent.*

8) *Miscellaneous*

   Capitalize the principal words in:

   Names of wars and battles: *World War II, Civil War, Battle of the Bulge.*

   Names of ages and eras: *Middle Ages, Twenties, Victorian, Dark Ages.*

   Names of holidays and special days: *Christmas Eve, Mothers Day, Fourth of July.*

   Names of flags: *Old Glory, Stars and Bars, Union Jack, Tricolor, Rising Sun.*

   Names of most astronomical bodies: *Venus, Mars, Saturn, Big Dipper, North Star, Milky Way.* But make it *earth, sun* and *moon* unless these terms are used in series with comparable capitalized terms: *Venus, the Sun and Saturn.*

   Names of breeds and varieties: *Brown Swiss, Great Dane, Palomino, Buff Orpington.* But use lower case for names of types or kinds, and for descriptive terms: *terrier, bantam, whiteface, hairless.*

   Fanciful names and recognized nicknames: *Evergreen State, Galloping Ghost, Sultan of Swat, Brown Bomber.*

   DO NOT CAPITALIZE derivatives of proper names which are no longer identified with the meaning of the original terms: *dutch treat, plaster of paris, french fries, brussels sprouts, hollandaise sauce*

Section II—NAMES AND TITLES

General rule: Names should be presented as their owners prefer. Titles preceding names should usually be abbreviated. Accepted directories and reference books —city, village and university directories, state manuals, *Who's Who* and the like —should be consulted frequently as guides to correct usage.

1) *Full Names*

   a. In its first appearance in a news story, a name should be given in full, in the manner its owner prefers: *Robert Penn Warren, Billy Graham, Judy Garland, J. Edward Gerald, Hubert H. Humphrey.* In later uses of men's names in a story, only last names should appear (but see II, 2). For use of women's names, see II, 3.

   b. Do not use first or familiar names (except in first appearance) unless they refer to children or characters for whom first-name use is reasonable and appropriate to the nature and purpose of the story.

   c. Do not separate *Jr., Sr.* or *III* from the name it follows: *George B. Brown Jr.; Winthrop Rockefeller III.*

2) Use of Mr.

   a. Mr. is primarily a designation of respect or of formal courtesy. It is never used with a full name; it is proper to use it in certain clerical titles (see II, 4). It is correct, but not mandatory, to use it with the last name of a national president currently or recently in office: *Mr. Eisenhower.* It is proper in naming a married couple: *Mr. and Mrs. Joseph A. Johnson, Mr. and Mrs. Johnson.*

   b. Mr. should be used in second and succeeding mentions of Protestant clergymen (see II, 4, a).

3) Women's Names

   a. A married woman's name is preceded by *Mrs.* when the last name alone is used: *Mrs. Stanton;* and usually when the full name is used: *Mrs. Frank Stanton, Mrs. Margaret Sanger.* The *Mrs.* may be omitted when the name is widely known and used without the title: *Margaret Mead.* The name should follow its owner's preference: *Mrs. George B. Palmer, Mrs. Geri Joseph.*

   b. An unmarried woman's name, used in full, needs no title: *Mary Brown, Jane Addams.* This rule applies to maiden names used by married women: *Elizabeth Taylor, Miss Taylor* (though her legal name is that of her husband).

4) Clergy

   a. Use a clergyman's full name, with proper title, in first mention. "Proper title" is likely to be *the Rev.,* or *Rabbi,* or *Father.* In later mentions, use *Rabbi* or *Father* when appropriate; never use *Rev.* or *the Rev.* Replacing these may be *Mr.* or *the Rev. Mr.* (which is often cumbersome), or *Dr.* if the clergyman holds a doctoral degree. In some denominations *Pastor* may be used in the same manner as *Father.*

   b. Such titles as *bishop, monsignor, archbishop, cardinal* and *dean* may ordinarily be used throughout a story. In all cases, follow the approved usage of the church or denomination concerned.

   c. Among clerical titles, abbreviate only *reverend* and *monsignor: Rev., Msgr.*

5) Style of Titles (see also Section III, Abbreviations)

   a. Short titles should ordinarily precede names, usually abbreviated according to style (see III, 1): *Prof.* John P. Bilker; *Asst. Prof.* Emmett Salisbury; *Gov.* Nelson Rockefeller; *Lt. Col.* Arthur M. Swinton. Longer titles should follow names (see I, 2): John P. Bilker, *professor of Romance languages;* Emmett Salisbury, *director of human relations;* Arthur M.

Swinton, *director of civilian evacuation.* (Note exception in I, 2, d: *President* Kennedy; John F. Kennedy, *President* of the United States.)
  b. After first use, many titles need not be repeated: *Prof.* John P. Bilker when the name first appears, *Bilker* in later uses. But note that II, 4 requires titles with clergymen's names. Note also that it is accepted practice to refer to physicians by title: *Dr.* Foster B. Enwright, *Dr. Enwright.*
6)   *Nicknames*
  Use nicknames only when their use is clearly appropriate. In a personality or a human interest story calling a character "Butch" may evoke understanding or feeling that more formal usage would not produce. To refer to a child by nickname is often appropriate; and nicknames (and first names) are often well used in sports stories. When a nickname is used with the full name, it should appear in parentheses: Leo (*Lippy*) Durocher. Used alone, it should appear without quotation marks: *Lippy.*
7)   *Foreign Names*
  a. Spell a foreign name the way its owner spells it: *Sukarno,* not Soekarno; *Gustaf* of Sweden, not Gustav.
  b. Chinese and some other Oriental names are usually written (unless anglicized) with surname first: *Chiang* Kai-shek becomes, in later mention, *Chiang.*
  c. Prefixes such as *de* and *von* should be written with capital letters only when they open sentences: *DeQuincey* was an English author; Thomas *deQuincey* was an English author.

Section III—ABBREVIATIONS

General rule: When common abbreviations are unquestionably clear, they should be used. When they might confuse, they should be avoided.
1)   *Titles* (see also Section II, Names and Titles)
  a. Abbreviate (and capitalize) commonly used titles before full names or surnames: *Prof., Dr., Sen., Rep., Maj., Gen., Gov.*
  b. Longer titles should usually follow names, spelled out and uncapitalized (see II, 5, a).
  c. Less common titles should ordinarily be spelled out: *Commissioner* Lee Loevinger, *Attorney General* Simpson, *Coroner* Adam Brackett.
2)   *Geographical Terms*
  a. Abbreviate state names of six or more letters (to their simplest forms: *Pa.* rather than Penn., *N.D.* rather than No. Dak.) when used with names of cities: Rockford, *Ill.;* Santa Fe, *N.M.;* Ames, *Iowa.* Spell out state names used independently: *Illinois, New Mexico.* Omit state names after names of cities in the same state in which the paper is published, unless confusion might result. Omit state names after names of widely known cities such as *Chicago, Houston, Reno, Memphis.*
  b. Abbreviate *United States* in adjectival uses: The *U.S.* Supreme Court. Write it out in noun uses, except in headlines.

3) Streets and Addresses

Such words as *street, avenue* and *boulevard* should be abbreviated and capitalized in addresses; directional indications should be abbreviated, with periods; numerical designations should follow the general rule for numbers (Section IV): *1234 Fifth Ave. S.; 129 38th Ave. N.; 6781 N. Pelham Blvd.; 86 Park St. S.E.; 7769 Golden Valley Rd.* Directional indications (*N., S.*) should be placed as local usage dictates. The same rules apply when street numbers are omitted: *Fourth Ave., N. Bark St., Washington and University Aves. S.E.*

4) Organization Names

   a. Names of widely known organizations may be shortened to initials without periods: *YMCA, AFL-CIO, UN, NATO.*

   b. Names of less well-known organizations should be written in full at first mention, and followed by initials without periods in parentheses; in later mention in the same story, initials only may be used: The National Association for the Advancement of Colored People (*NAACP*) went to court today. The *NAACP* is . . . NOTE: Do NOT insert such initials, as in the example above, unless they are to be used again in the story.

   c. Common generic or group words in titles of businesses and most associations should be abbreviated and capitalized when they end the title: General Motors *Corp.*, Ford Motor *Co.*, Newspaper Enterprise *Assn.*, Time *Inc.*, Women's Physical Education *Assn.* When the generic word is not the final word in the title, or when it is not one commonly abbreviated, write it in full: National *Association* for Mental Health, American *Institute* of Chemical Engineers, Columbia Broadcasting *System*, University Band Social *Organization*, Core Curriculum *Foundation*, Modern Technological *Institute.*

5) Degrees

Names of degrees may be abbreviated with capitals and periods: *M.A., B.S., Ph.D.* degree, *M.P.H.* candidate. Also correct: *bachelor's* degree, *doctor's* degree.

6) Military Terms

In titles before names, commonly understood service terms should be abbreviated in accordance with service usage: *Gen., Lt. Gen., Rear Adm., M. Sgt., Sfc., Sgt., Cpl., Pfc., Pvt., Sp. 1/c, Lt., Ens., Lt. jg, Capt., Maj., CPO.* Noncommissioned Navy grades below CPO should ordinarily be spelled out. See II, 5, and III, 1.

7) Months

Abbreviate names of months when used with dates, except *March, April, May, June, July: Dec.* 21, 1965. Spell out names of months when they appear without dates.

Section IV—NUMERALS

General rule: Spell out numbers from *one* through *nine,* both cardinal (indicating quantity) and ordinal (indicating order): *one, three, eight; first, third, ninth.* Use figures for all numbers, cardinal and ordinal, of *10* or larger: *12, 253; 12th, 253rd.*

NOTE: Most of the rules following in this section have to do with variations from or exceptions to the general rule.

1) *Round Numbers*

When an exact figure is not required, a round number may be used. Instead of *$1,010,327*, you may write *a million dollars;* instead of *4,897 head of cattle,* you may say *about 5,000 head of cattle.*

2) *Ages*

a. Always express ages in figures: *1 year, 5-year-old* horse, *8 days old*

b. Ages under *2* years may be given in months or days: *1 month, 19 months, 8 days*

3) *Money*

a. Exact sums of money should always be expressed in figures: *6 cents, 45 cents, $1.29, $6,034,119, $3, $25* (no zeros with even-dollar sums)

b. Do not use the awkward form *$1 billion, $250 thousand.* Write *1 billion dollars, 250 thousand dollars* (or *$250,000*). In series or groups of numbers it may be desirable to use figures only. It is permissible to write *8.7 billion dollars.*

4) *Terms of Measurement*

All numbers indicating precise measurement are written in figures, unless otherwise specified in this Style Shet: *6 feet 4 inches, 7 1/2 yards, 4 pounds, 2 degrees below zero, 8-hour day, 7 years old,* and the like. But follow the general rule in nonprecise uses: *about two weeks, six or eight pieces.*

5) *Fractions*

Simple fractions may be expressed either in figures or in words: *1/2, one-half; 2/3, two-thirds.* It is sometimes desirable to replace fractions with decimals: *.5* for *1/2, .4* for *2/5.*

6) *Miscellaneous*

a. In a series of related numerical expressions, treat all alike even though you violate the general rule for numerals: The farmer had *14 hogs, 6 cows, 64 chickens* and *2 dogs.*

b. In special circumstances, it may be clearest to combine words and figures: There are *two 6-room* houses, *twelve 5-room* and *one 10-room.*

c. Never open a sentence with a figure. Spell it out, or rephrase the sentence.

d. Use figures for:

Time: *2 p.m., 7:32 a.m.* But use *noon* instead of *12 a.m., midnight* for *12 p.m.*

Percentages: *14 per cent, 7 per cent, 1.4 per cent*

Votes: *Yes 54, no 9*

Scores: Los Angeles *10*, San Francisco *5; St. Louis won, 15 to 6.*

Odds: a *14-to-1* shot

Numbered highways: *County Road 36, U.S. Highway 8, U.S. 8*

e. Use the abbreviation *No.* when it appears in titles or other formalized use such as *Symphony No. 9.* Do not use it in such phrases as *number nine on the list. . . .*

f. Do NOT use a hyphen to replace the preposition *to* between figures:

The score was *5 to 3* (not *5-3*); Dancing will last from *3 to 5 p.m.* (not *3-5 p.m.*).

Section V—SPELLING AND USAGE

General rule: The first form in *Webster's New International Dictionary* will be considered correct, unless this Style Sheet makes specific exceptions. (Useful rules and aids in spelling appear in Chapter 19, "Grammar for Journalists.")

1)   Plurals

Anglicized plurals are preferred to Latin forms in cases in which Webster gives both: *Radiuses* instead of *radii, indexes* instead of *indices.*

2)   Short Forms

In general use the short forms of such words as *cigaret, glamor, employe, dialog, whisky.* DO NOT use such abbreviated forms as *thru, thoro, nite.*

3)   Feminine Forms

Use "feminine" forms of such commonly accepted words as *actress, saleswoman.* DO NOT use rare or labored forms such as *aviatrix, sculptress;* no coinages such as *Jewess, Negress.*

4)   Combined Words

Common, well-understood two-word combinations should appear as one word: *Postoffice, citywide, prewar, baseball, airport, semifinal, newsman.* Combine without hyphens such words as *cooperate, nonspecific* unless confusion results.

5)   Trademarked Words

Some words that have achieved common or generic usage should be used in specific meanings only. The word *Coke* is one; it is copyrighted by the Coca-Cola Co., and should be capitalized and used to refer to Coca-Cola only. Other such terms are *Vaseline, Ping Pong, Formica, Frigidaire, Seeing-Eye Dog.*

Section VI—PUNCTUATION

General rule: The purpose of punctuation is to make reading easy and meaning clear. Skillful use of punctuation marks, in journalistic writing, usually means sparing use. (Chapter 18, "Grammar for Journalists," offers useful guides to punctuation.)

1)   Commas

  a. Use commas to separate words, figures or phrases in series, but omit them when conjunctions appear: He visited *Paris, Berlin and Rome.*

  b. A comma may be used before a coordinating conjunction in a compound sentence: He lived in *Redland, and* his family was born there. (But in some instances meaning is clear without the comma.)

  c. A comma may be used after a subordinate clause or phrase introducing a main clause: After Kindall *singled, Pascual* tripled him home. Aware of the *danger, Smith* pulled his gun.

  d. Use commas in pairs to set off appositives: Bing *Crosby, the popular singer, is* also a sports fan.

  e. Use commas in pairs to set off parenthetical words and phrases: The *work, he said, was* exciting. The *collapse, after all, was* inevitable.

f. Commas should usually be used to set off nonrestrictive clauses: The *speaker, who belongs to the Lambs Club, was* not well received. BUT commas usually are not necessary, and even may be misleading, with restrictive clauses: The *speaker who advocates segregation will* not be welcome.

g. Commas should always be placed within quotation marks: "The water's *cold*," he said. In spite of the *"handicap*," the book was a winner. (This rule does not follow grammatical logic. Sometimes it requires placing a comma within quotation marks enclosing an expression to which the comma does not belong. But it is a common journalistic style rule, adopted in the interest of uniformity and ease of aplication.)

h. Use commas to set off the state in a place name and the year in a date: The event took place in *Ten Sleep, Wyo.,* between *Sept. 12, 1947,* and *Jan. 1, 1948.*

i. Use commas in all numbers larger than **999** (*1,495; 6,213,444*) except years (*4000 B.C.; 1939*) and street numbers (*1214* Second Ave. S.; *21634* Richfield Blvd.).

j. Remember that a series of clauses in a long sentence broken up by commas may often be reshaped into shorter sentences to improve clarity and readability.

2) Dashes

Dashes may be used to set off parenthetical or other material within a sentence when it presents an abrupt break: He *claimed—and no one denied—owner-ship* of the boat. But dashes should be used sparingly. (In typewriting, make a dash with two or three hyphens, preceded and followed by spaces, thus: `claimed --- and . . .`)

A hyphen is NOT a dash.

3) Parentheses

Parentheses may properly be used to show political designation or a nickname: Sen. Wayne Morse (*D., Ore.*) ; Leo (*Lippy*) Durocher. See also III, 4, b. Parentheses are used sparingly in news writing.

4) Colons

a. The colon introduces formal statements, usually in separate paragraphs:

The secretary's statement said:
We shall never again have so excellent
an opportunity to conserve our water
resources. . . .

b. The colon may be used to introduce lists or series (see V, 5). But it should NOT appear after a verb introducing a list: Among those present were Bellow, Warren and Cozzens.

c. The frequent use of the colon in this Style Sheet shows that it may take the place of an implied *for instance:* See how it's used here?

5) Semicolons

a. Semicolons are used to punctuate lists of three or more names followed by identifications, or similarly complex phrases: Four sons are survivors: *John,*

St. Louis; George L., Detroit; Albert, Springfield, Mass.; Thomas, New Orleans. The drug will be used in Korea, where the disease is *widespread;* in the Hong Kong area, where traces have been *found;* and in infected areas in southern Peru.

DO NOT open a sentence with a list thus punctuated: Mary Smith, *president;* Jean James, vice *president;* and Lora Lee Allison, secretary, are the new officers. Instead, turn the sentence around.

    b. A semicolon may be used to separate clauses between which a conjunction is implied but unwritten: She went to *Paris;* I returned to Florence.

6) *Hyphens*

In general, dashes separate but hyphens connect. Use the dictionary as a guide for hyphenation, if the rules here given do not cover.

    a. A hyphen is common between a prefix ending with a vowel and a root word opening with the same vowel: *Re-employ, co-officer.* But some such words have become so common that they do not need hyphens: *cooperate, reelect.* When the two vowels differ, hyphens are unnecessary: *Coed, reassure.*

    b. Hyphens are used between prefixes and proper adjectives or nouns: *pro-English, trans-Atlantic, anti-Communist, un-American.*

    c. Fractions are written with hyphens: *One-third, two-fifths.* But it is permissible to write *a third* if the meaning is clear.

    d. Use hyphens in modifying or adjectival constructions: *Green-eyed* monster, *1-acre* plot, *15-year-old* boy, *24-to-7* vote (but the vote was *24 to 7*).

7) *Apostrophes*

In general, apostrophes indicate contractions (*we'll, it's, I'm*) and make possessive forms. A modern tendency is to limit rather than extend their use.

    a. Restrict the use of the possessive apostrophe to purely possessive cases: The *boy's bicycle,* but *Boys Town; veterans' benefits,* but *Veterans Administration.* Omit apostrophes in organization titles: *Rangers Club, Parent-Teachers Association.*

    b. The apostrophe may be used in date abbreviations where usage approves: *Class of '65, the gold rush of '49, Days of '76.* Usually, however, dates should be written in full. The war ended in *1945* (NOT in *'45*).

    c. Words ending in *s* may form the possessive by adding only the apostrophe: *Jones'.* Words ending in *z* must add *'s: Natchez's.*

    d. Apostrophes are NOT used in forming plurals: *Joneses,* not *Jones'* or *Jones's; 1920s,* not *1920's; POWSs, B29s, Alpha Delts, Chi Omegas.*

    e. The possessive of *it* is *its. It's* is a contraction for *it is.*

8) *Quotation Marks*

    a. Quotation marks are used with all direct quotations except those in which verbatim texts appear. In such cases the statement usually follows a colon (see VI, 4, a) and often opens a new paragraph.

    b. Quotation marks are normally used in pairs, one before and one after quoted material. When a continuous direct quotation runs for more than one paragraph, quotation marks open each paragraph, but close only the last.

    c. Use quotation marks around titles of books, plays, songs, speeches, lectures, magazine articles and the like. Do not use them with names of characters in books or plays, names of ships or trains, newspapers, magazines, or well-known publications such as the *Bible,* the *Koran,* the *Social Register, Who's Who* and the like (see I, 6).

d. Quotation marks may be used to indicate figurative or fanciful usage and at times to distinguish slang or jargon; but they should not be used apologetically. DO NOT write: Each *"hoofer"* did a *"soft-shoe"* number. Instead, make it: Each *hoofer* did a *soft-shoe* number. This kind of faulty use of quotation marks is a way of saying, "Reader, I really know better . . ." If the usage is questionable, find another way of saying so.

e. Use single quotation marks (' ') ONLY in quotations within quotations ("The play is *'Pygmalion,'* " he said) and in headlines.

9) *Punctuation Marks*

a. Place all commas and periods within quotation marks (see VI, 1, g).

b. Place other punctuation marks according to the meaning. If the punctuation mark accompanies quoted material place it inside the quotation marks. If it does not, place it outside. Examples:

> "The best road," Jones said, "is thataway;" he pointed to his left.
> The play is "Pygmalion"; the author, Shaw.
> "Is the road thataway?" he asked.
> Is the play "Pygmalion"?

Section VII—SPORTS-WRITING STYLE

Effective sports writing is guided by the principles of style, grammar, clarity and simplicity laid down for other newswriting. A sports story can be made bright, lively and colorful without overuse of slang, without bromides and without gutter diction.

a. Names of sports are written as one word: *Basketball, football.*

b. Names of formal sport organizations and major sports events should be capitalized: *Big Ten, Pacific Coast Conference, Ivy League, National League, World Series, Rose Bowl, Olympic Games.*

c. Write scores thus: *Harvard 20, Yale 13.* Harvard beat Yale, *20 to 13.*

d. In general, sports stories follow the rules in Section IV for use of numerals. Examples:

> Jones weighs 210 pounds. Jones is a 210-pound tackle.
> Johnson is 6 feet, 8 inches tall. Johnson is the 6-foot, 8-inch center.
> As a sophomore, he ran the mile in 3 minutes, 58.4 seconds (or 3:58.4).
> Willie Mays hit three for four, including two doubles. He raised his average to .345.
> Baylor scored eight field goals and four free throws for 20 points.
> In the tennis finals, Jones beat Smith 6–4, 3–6, 6–0, 10–8.
> In track and swimming: 440-yard dash—Jones (Cornell), first; Smith (Mich.), Taylor (Baylor), Yates (Bates). Time 46.5 seconds.

INDEX